UNIVERSALS of LANGUAGE

UNIVERSALS of LANGUAGE

SECOND EDITION

EDITED BY JOSEPH H. GREENBERG
PROFESSOR OF ANTHROPOLOGY
STANFORD UNIVERSITY

REPORT OF A CONFERENCE HELD AT
DOBBS FERRY, NEW YORK
APRIL 13-15, 1961

THE M.I.T. PRESS
MASSACHUSETTS INSTITUTE OF TECHNOLOGY
CAMBRIDGE, MASSACHUSETTS, AND LONDON, ENGLAND

Second Edition

Second printing, first paperback edition, March 1966
Third printing, August 1968
Fourth printing, January 1973

ISBN 0 262 57008 4 (paper)
ISBN 0 262 07020 0 (hard)

Library of Congress Catalog Card Number: 62-22020
Printed in the United States of America

PREFACE

The Conference on Language Universals was held at Gould House, Dobbs Ferry, New York, April 13-15, 1961, under the sponsorship of the Linguistics and Psychology Committee of the Social Science Research Council with a grant from the National Science Foundation. Although the topic of universals of language was one of the first to receive interdisciplinary interest from linguists and psychologists in the course of collaboration under the aegis of the S.S.R.C. Committee, the immediate stimulus for the Conference came during the academic year 1958–1959 from Joseph B. Casagrande, at that time a staff member of the Council. He suggested that the three members of the Committee who were resident Fellows that year at the Ford Center for Advanced Studies at Stanford, California — Joseph H. Greenberg, James J. Jenkins, and Charles E. Osgood — prepare a memorandum on the subject of universals in language which might serve as a basis for theoretical investigation in this area, and for the planning of a Conference. This document, "Memorandum Concerning Language Universals," was subsequently distributed in slightly revised form to those invited to the Conference and was itself one of the subjects of discussion at the meeting. It is printed on page xv of this book.

The original plan for papers for the Conference was based on a cross-cutting division of the field of universals into those of phonology, grammar, and semantics on the one hand, and synchronic and diachronic on the other. While it was realized that such a scheme might cause neglect of topics which did not readily fit into such a pattern of organization, it was felt that in view of the exploratory nature of the meeting no great harm would result. Moreover, no viable alternative had presented itself. As it turned out, various modifications in individual instances largely obscured this ground plan, and this was perhaps just as well. In addition to these invited papers, prepared and circulated in advance, final oral summaries from the viewpoints of linguistics, cultural anthropology, and psychology were presented by Roman Jakobson, Joseph B. Casagrande, and Charles E. Osgood, respectively. These summaries, as subsequently edited by the authors, appear as the three final chapters of this book.

The results of the Conference as reported in this book do not contain either verbatim or edited reports of the highly stimulating and productive discussions which took place. However, the recordings of these discussions and subsequent written comments and criticisms were circulated and have been incorporated in essential ways.

In addition to individual bibliographies, a general bibliography of language universals has been compiled as the final section of this work. This bibliography is obviously not exhaustive. It necessarily overlaps to some extent with bibliographies of the individual chapters but contains many items not cited elsewhere in the present work. I have sought to include specific proposals regarding universals, discussions of the nature of universals, typological analyses from which universals might be derived through empirical investigation, and, in a few cases, analytical discussions which seem suggestive from this point of view. I am aware of the looseness of these criteria. The present brief compilation is intended merely as a general orientation for the nonprofessional to the problems discussed in the book. I am grateful to Uriel Weinreich for advice and assistance in its preparation.

I wish to thank all those who participated so enthusiastically and effectively in the work of the Conference. A complete list of participants is included on page ix of this book. In particular, I wish to thank Dr. Francis H. Palmer of the S.S.R.C. staff, to whom fell the task of final preparation of the meeting and the further responsibilities arising from it including aid and advice in the editing of this volume.

JOSEPH H. GREENBERG

CONTENTS

LIST OF PARTICIPANTS

The participants in the Conference, in addition to Dr. Francis H. Palmer as S.S.R.C. staff member, were the following:

Dr. John B. Carroll
Graduate School of Education
Harvard University

Dr. Joseph B. Casagrande
Department of Anthropology
University of Illinois

Dr. Harold C. Conklin
Department of Anthropology
Yale University

Dr. Franklin S. Cooper
Haskins Laboratories
New York 17, New York

Dr. Warren C. Cowgill
Linguistics Department
Yale University

Dr. Charles A. Ferguson
Center for Applied Linguistics
Washington 6, D.C.

Dr. William J. Gedney
Department of English Language and Literature
University of Michigan

Dr. Joseph H. Greenberg
Department of Anthropology
Stanford University

Dr. Einar Haugen
Department of Scandinavian Languages
University of Wisconsin

***Dr. Charles F. Hockett**
Department of Linguistics
Cornell University

Dr. Henry M. Hoenigswald
Department of Linguistics
University of Pennsylvania

Dr. Fred W. Householder, Jr.
Department of Linguistics
Indiana University

Dr. Dell H. Hymes
Department of Anthropology
University of California

*Professor Charles F. Hockett of Cornell University could not attend the meeting, but in addition to submitting a paper, he cooperated fully in the activities growing out of the Conference.

Dr. Roman Jakobson
Department of Slavic Languages
Harvard University and
Department of Linguistics
Massachusetts Institute of Technology

Dr. James J. Jenkins
Department of Psychology
University of Minnesota

Dr. Sydney M. Lamb
Computer Center
University of California

Dr. Wallace E. Lambert
Department of Psychology
McGill University

Dr. Eric H. Lenneberg
Speech Research Laboratory
The Children's Hospital Medical Center
Boston 15, Massachusetts

Dr. Leigh Lisker
Department of Linguistics
University of Pennsylvania

Dr. John Lotz
Department of Uralic and Altaic Languages
Columbia University

Dr. Floyd G. Lounsbury
Department of Anthropology
Yale University

Dr. George P. Murdock
Department of Anthropology
University of Pittsburgh

Dr. Charles E. Osgood
Institute of Communications Research
University of Illinois

Dr. Herbert H. Paper
Department of Near Eastern Languages
University of Michigan

Dr. Sol Saporta
Department of Spanish and Portuguese
University of Washington

Dr. Thomas A. Sebeok
Center for Anthropology, Folklore and Linguistics
Indiana University

Dr. Stephen Ullmann
Department of French
University of Leeds

Dr. Charles F. Voegelin
Department of Anthropology
Indiana University

Dr. Uriel Weinreich
Department of Linguistics
Columbia University

Dr. Rulon S. Wells
Department of Philosophy
Yale University

INTRODUCTION

Since a number of the papers in the present volume, including the three final statements and the Memorandum, are largely concerned with the basic theoretic and methodological issues involved in the investigation of language universals, a brief statement here seems sufficient to orient the reader to the papers. These remarks are intended to summarize some of the salient points which emerged from the papers and the discussion. It should be understood that while all, or almost all, of the participants in the Conference might concur in what is said here, this introduction represents the personal reactions of the editor to issues discussed at the meeting.

In view of the present level of methodological sophistication of both synchronic and diachronic linguistics and the truly enormous mass of empirical data on languages of the world now at our disposal, the time appears ripe for generalizing efforts on a wide scale. Indeed, this is imperative for linguistics both to fulfill its own promise as a science and to make the contributions to the formulation of a general science of human behavior which its sister disciplines may legitimately expect.

Such attempts should not be identified with earlier approaches based on categories formulated a priori from supposed necessary categories of thought derived from normative logic. One of the recurrent themes of the meeting was, indeed, reference to Bloomfield's well-known dictum in his classic work *Language* that "the only useful generalizations about language are inductive generalizations." However, it seemed also to be generally agreed that the method of science is both inductive and deductive. The formulation of generalizations attained by inductive examination leads to higher-level hypotheses from which, in turn, further generalizations may be deduced. The latter must then be put to the test of empirical validation.

Such principles derived from generalizations concerning linguistic change and linguistic structure reflect important and fundamental aspects of human behavior. They cannot be fully understood without to some extent abandoning the traditional self-sufficiency of linguistics in favor of fundamental collaboration with psychology and the social sciences. Such a statement should not be construed as a criticism of the great and continuing value of the standard synchronic and diachronic procedures. Indeed, as will be evident in much of what follows, they form the indispensable bases for arriving at generalizations about language.

There was general agreement that it was necessary and completely legitimate to include as universals in addition to statements of the simple type "all languages have a given feature *x*," likewise implicational relations, universal frequency distributions, statistically better than chance correlations, and other logic types as set forth in greater detail in the Memorandum. From a purely logical point of view this might be summarized as follows. All statements of the form $(x)\ x \in L \supset \ldots$, that is, "for all *x*, if *x* is a language, then . . . ," are permitted.

Finally, two matters of particular concern to linguists may be mentioned: the question of typology and the question of universals in relation to the two major divisions of scientific linguistics (synchronic and diachronic studies). The usefulness of typologies in the present connection may be illustrated from my own paper on which a typology based on the order of elements in certain major constructions appears as a virtually indispensable tool in the search for cross-linguistic regularities in this aspect of language. It is perhaps not overstating the case to say that one of the values of this Conference was the realization that typological classification finds its sought-for justification in the investigation of universals. This also means that the proposed research on universals finds a very real and useful foundation in earlier linguistic work on typologies; for example, in the grammatical typologies of the nineteenth-century pioneers, in those of Sapir and Bally, and in the phonological endeavors of Trubetskoy, Jakobson, Hockett, Menzerath, and Voegelin, to mention but a few.

Another motif of this Conference was the interrelationship of synchronic and diachronic approaches both of which are seen to complement each other in that neither can be fully understood without the other. There is perhaps a lesson here for cultural anthropology where there has been a tendency to identify the search for laws with an ahistorical functionalist orientation and to oppose to it a historical particularistic approach. In fact, generalizations may apply equally to diachronic processes and synchronic states. The possibility of universals of change, moreover, would seem to be of particular relevance to psycholinguistics since change of habits over time is the very stuff of learning, which is such a central concern of contemporary psychology.

Perhaps enough has been said to indicate some of the more significant aspects of the study of language universals exemplified in the papers and discussions of the Conference. It is hoped that the report of the Conference will serve to amplify and elucidate these brief introductory remarks.

JOSEPH H. GREENBERG

New York, New York
October 1962

MEMORANDUM CONCERNING LANGUAGE UNIVERSALS

presented to the Conference on Language Universals, Gould House, Dobbs Ferry, N. Y., April 13–15, 1961

1. Introduction

Underlying the endless and fascinating idiosyncrasies of the world's languages there are uniformities of universal scope. Amid infinite diversity, all languages are, as it were, cut from the same pattern. Some interlinguistic similarities and identities have been formalized, others not, but working linguists are in many cases aware of them in some sense and use them as guides in their analyses of new languages. This is an important but limited and incomplete use of these consistencies. Language universals are by their very nature summary statements about characteristics or tendencies shared by all human speakers. As such they constitute the most general laws of a science of linguistics (as contrasted with a method and a set of specific descriptive results). Further, since language is at once both an aspect of individual behavior and an aspect of human culture, its universals provide both the major point of contact with underlying psychological principles (psycholinguistics) and the major source of implications for human culture in general (ethnolinguistics).

It is our belief that coordinated efforts beyond the scope of individual researchers will be necessary to establish on firm grounds the actual facts concerning universals in language. Thus, the illustrations cited later in this Memorandum must be taken *cum grano salis* as based on the specific knowledge of the writers which, however wide it might be, could not in the nature of things be exhaustive. Organization of some central source of data, something like a cross-cultural file for a large and representative sample of world languages would vastly facilitate the establishment of well-grounded universals and their continued study by scholars. As a first step, it is proposed that the Committee on Linguistics and Psychology of the Social Science Research Council arrange for a Work Conference on Language Universals. This Memorandum, which has grown out of discussions held at the Center for Advanced Study in the Behavioral Sciences during 1958–1959, is offered to stimulate activity leading to such a conference and to suggest the kinds of topics which might appropriately be discussed.

2. Examples of Universals

Before going further, it is perhaps wise to describe a few examples of language universals which will illustrate some of the scope and diversity involved in the types of similarities seen between language systems.

First, we may take an example from phonology. The phonemes, or individual sound units, may be looked upon as consisting of the simultaneous occurrence of several elements called *features*. For example, in English the phoneme /b/ is characterized by voicing, stop articulation (that is, it involves a complete closure as contrasted with various types of fricatives), and it is oral, that is, nonnasal. There is another phoneme /p/ in English which shares all of these characteristics except voicing. In general, the features of a particular phoneme are not unique, and the entire set consists, of varying combinations of the same small inventory of features. More often than not, there is a parallelism or symmetry in the combinations observed. This leads to certain expectations on the part of the investigator. For example, in the investigation of a hitherto unstudied language in Nigeria, a phonemic contrast was found between the two velar stop consonants /k/ and /k'/, the former unglottalized and the latter glottalized, as well as a pair of dentals /t/ and /t'/. Since the third unvoiced stop consonant /p/ was also found, the linguist at this point formed the hypothesis that a glottalized counterpart /p'/ was also likely to occur even though it had not yet appeared in a fairly considerable body of linguistic material. Ultimately it was found to occur in a very small number of words. This expectation might, of course, have been disappointed, but investigators do form such hypotheses and find that the alertness engendered pays off in a majority of cases.

The tendency toward symmetry in the sound system of languages described here has, of course, psycholinguistic implications. The articulatory habits of speakers involved in the production of the phonemes consist of varied combinations of certain basic habits, those employed in the production of the features. This appears, for example, in language acquisition by the child. At the point in the development of the English-speaking child that he acquires the distinction between *b* and *p* based on voicing versus nonvoicing, he simultaneously makes the distinctions between *d* and *t*, *g* and *k*, and other similar pairs. In other words, he has acquired the *feature*, voicing versus nonvoicing, as a unit habit of motor differentiation. Such facts have an obvious importance for learning theory in psychology.

A quite different sort of universal may also be illustrated within the domain of phonology. As stated earlier, distinctive features are combined to generate the phonemes employed in any given language. It is of some linguistic interest and great psycholinguistic interest to examine the relation between the number of distinctive features required to generate the number of different phonemes employed by the language and the number of distinctive features actually in use. A maximally efficient code, in the information theory sense, would employ just the number of features necessary to distinguish its phonemes; for example, the 32 phonemes of English would require only five distinctive binary features (that is, the features could be combined in two to the fifth power different combinations, or 32 combinations). However, in English nine binary features are actually employed. The efficiency of English in respect to phonology is therefore about five ninths, or 56%. Investigation of several languages suggests the generalization that the phonetic efficiency of languages is distributed roughly around the 50% point. A study of one language (Spanish) as it has changed over time reinforced this generalization by revealing that the efficiency of that language oscillates around the 50% value over time.

It appears that there are sets of pressures bearing on any phonetic system which cause it to maintain some optimal efficiency value. If the language becomes too inefficient, that is, has too many features overdetermining the phonemes, it becomes possible to neglect some of them and still be understood. We presume that such lapses become more frequent and the sound system begins to change toward simplicity. On the other hand, if the system is too efficient, mishearing and misperceptions should become frequent, and we assume that the speakers are led (or driven) to make additional distinctions to maintain clarity. It is obvious that this "explanation" generates a complex statistical function, but one that presumably reflects universal processes in the total dynamics of communication between speakers and listeners.

3. The Nature of Universals

The examples just cited illustrate that the term "universal" is used here in a somewhat extended sense. We have not limited ourselves to statements of the type that all languages have vowels; all languages have phonemes; all language sound systems may be resolved into distinctive features, etc. We feel that it is important to include generalizations which tend to hold true in more than a chance number of comparisons (such as symmetry of sound systems) or which state tendencies to approach statistical limits across languages or in one language over time. We are convinced that the wider use of this concept will prove to be most fruitful from the psycholinguistic viewpoint. All phenomena which occur with significantly more than chance frequency in languages in general are of potential psychological interest.

With this expanded view of universals, confusion may be most easily avoided by pointing out that types of universals may be differentiated both with respect to logical structure and with respect to substantive content.

4. Logical Structure of Universals

From a stictly logical point of view, it is possible to define universals as any statements about language which include all languages in their scope, technically all statements of the form "$(x)\ x \in L \supset \ldots$," that is, "For all x, if x is a language, then ...". These statements fall into various logical subtypes. Such an analysis is useful since in addition to specifying clearly what is to be considered a universal, the distinct subtypes do to some extent present distinguishably different problems from other points of view. We have considered and will present here six types of universals. The first three may be considered as universals which concern existence (that is, "X does or does not exist") and the last three as universals which concern probabilities (that is, "X (or some value of X) is more probable than Y (or some other value of X)").

4.1. *Unrestricted universals*

These are characteristics possessed by all languages which are not merely definitional; that is, they are such that if a symbolic system did not possess them, we would still call it a language. Under this heading would be included not only such obvious universals as, for example, that all languages have vowels, but also those involving numerical limits, for example, that for all languages the number of phonemes is not fewer than 10 or more than 70, or that every language has at least two vowels. Also included are universally valid statements about the relative text or lexicon frequency of linguistic elements.

4.2. *Universal implications*

These always involve the relationship between two characteristics. It is asserted universally that if a language has a certain characteristic, (φ), it also has some other particular characteristic (ψ), but not vice versa. That is, the presence of the second (ψ) does not imply the presence of the first (φ). For example, if a language has a category of dual, it also has a category of plural but not necessarily vice versa. Hereafter we express such relationships between predicates by an arrow, for example, dual → plural.

Such implications are fairly numerous, particularly in the phonologic aspect of languages.

4.3. *Restricted equivalence*

This is the case of mutual implication between characteristics which are not universal. That is, if any language has a particular nonuniversal characteristic, φ, it also has ψ and vice versa. For example, if a language has a lateral click, it always has a dental click and vice versa. In this example, unfortunately, all the languages are from a restricted area in South Africa, and the equivalence is really a single case. Equivalences of more frequently appearing logically independent characteristics are difficult to find. They would be of great interest as indicating important necessary connections between empirically diverse properties of language.

4.4. *Statistical universals*

These are defined as follows: For any language a certain characteristic (φ) has a greater probability than some other (frequently its own negative). This includes "near universals" in extreme cases. Only Quileute and a few neighboring Salishan languages among all the languages of the world lack nasal consonants. Hence we may say that, universally, the probability of a language having at least one nasal consonant (φ) is greater (in this instance far greater) than that it will lack nasal consonants (not φ). We may extend this type to include cases of more than one alternative. For example, of the three devices of suffixing, prefixing, and infixing, the probabilities are not random and in fact are here stated in decreasing order. In this case the alternatives are not mutually exclusive, for example, a language can have both prefixes and suffixes.

4.5. *Statistical correlations*

This differs from the preceding in a manner parallel to that in which universal implications differ from unrestricted universals. In this instance also we are interested in the *relation* of several characteristics. By a statistical correlation we mean, then, that universally, if a language has a particular characteristic (φ) it has a significantly greater probability of possessing some other characteristic (ψ) than if it does not possess (φ).

The following is a probable example. Languages with gender distinctions in the second person singular are rarer than in the third person. Usually a language with gender distinction in the second person singular also has this distinction in the third person singular but not vice versa. If this were without exception, we would have the implication: Second person singular pronominal gender $\rightarrow$ third person singular pronominal gender. There are apparently, however, a few languages in central Nigeria which have the distinction in the second person, but not in the third. The proviso here is that these languages have not been well studied. If the exceptions are genuine, then we have the following statistical correlation: If a language has pronominal gender in the second person singular, it has a greater probability (much greater in this case) of having this distinction in the third person singular than of not having it.

4.6. *Universal frequency distributions*

Finally we have instances where a certain measurement, for example, redundancy in information theory, as mentioned earlier, may be applied to any language. When this is so, it is possible that the results of each measurement over an adequate sample of languages will show a characteristic mean and standard deviation. Means, standard deviations, or other statistical measures derived from such distibutions may be considered as universal facts about languages.

5. Substantive Classes of Universals

A second basis of classification which obviously crosscuts the division by logical type is that which operates with the aspect of language involved. While a variety of alternative categories is possible, in general, this principle of division will give us four types: phonological, grammatical, semantic, and symbolic. In this classification, the first three involve either form without meaning or meaning without form, whereas the last, which is concerned with sound symbolism, involves the connection between the two. For example, the near universality of nasals is a phonologic universal in whose statement we are not concerned with the meanings of the linguistic forms in which the nasals do or do not figure. The grammatical statement that suffixing is more frequent than infixing is not concerned, on the other hand, with the particular sounds utilized in suffixing. Again, the semantic universal that all languages have some metaphorically transferred meanings is not concerned with the particular sounds of the forms in which they occur. On the other hand, a statistical symbolic universal such as "there is a high probability that a word designating the female parent will have a nasal consonant" involves both sound and meaning.

6. Domain of the Universals

All the examples thus far cited in this Memorandum have been synchronic; that is, the statements refer to universally discoverable regularities arrived at by observing the characteristics of language states rather than of language changes. The definition of universals, moreover, and the further classifications of their occurrence into phonologic, grammatical, semantic, and symbolic have all been framed with a view to synchronic universals. However, we feel it is essential to extend the consideration of universals to diachronic facts of language. From the present point of view, it would be unwise to exclude these from consideration, in spite of the important differences to be noted, since universals of change have important psycholinguistic implications. From the general linguistic point of view, some universals are most easily understood as the outcome of dynamic processes, for example, *semantic metaphor as the result of metaphorical semantic change*, or again the universal, or almost universal, existence of variant forms of meaningful units (that is, morphophonemic alterations) as the result of the diachronic process of regular conditioned sound change. From the psychological point of view, such universals may serve to focus attention on phenomena, which may be brought under experimental control in the laboratory for study (e.g., the historical instability of liquids and nasals suggests both articulatory and auditory studies of interest in motor skills and perception).

Diachronic universals do differ in several fundamental ways in regard to bases of classification mentioned earlier. To begin with, although there are important universal hypotheses concerning change such as "all languages change" or "the rate of replacement of fundamental vocabulary is constant over time," the particular substantive diachronic universals are probabilistic. We can never say with certainty that a particular class of changes will always occur. The varied development for distinct but related languages from the same basis is enough to show this. Further, the logical form for universals presented earlier requires significant modification. Whereas for synchronic universals we always start with "For all *x* if *x* is a language (i.e., a single synchronic state), then ... ," in the case of diachronic rules the reference to two synchronic states is essentially with the further proviso that one be the historical continuation of the other. It is common usage to say that these are the same language unless the chronological distance is great, that is, Latin and French. Logically, then, diachronic universals are of the form "For all (*x*) and all (*y*) where (*x*) is an earlier and (*y*) a later stage of the same language...". Further, for diachronic change, the division into phonologic, semantic, and grammatical processes holds, but symbolism is not a type of change, although changes can result in forms which are more or less similar to universal sound symbolic norms.

Synchronic and diachronic regularities are obviously interrelated. The most general statement of this interrelationship is in the form of limitations, namely, that no synchronic state can exist which is not the outcome of possible diachronic processes (except perhaps *de novo* for artificial and pidgin languages) and no diachronic process can be posited which could lead to a synchronic state which violates a universally valid synchronic norm. It is important to note that, just as was indicated earlier that some synchronic universals are most easily understood as the outcomes of certain widespread processes, so specific diachronic changes cannot be understood without reference to the network of synchronic relations within the language at the time of the change. This is the basic contribution of structural linguistics to the study of linguistic change. Diachronic universals are probabilistic precisely because simultaneously with the universal tendencies toward changes of one kind as against other possibilities there are significant variables in the language structure itself, and every language structure is unique in some way.

An example of a diachronic process with important psychological implications is the tendency found in the most diverse languages for unvoiced consonants between vowels to become voiced. The psychologist has a background of experimental data dealing with the processes of *anticipation* (performing an act or portion of an act before it is wholly appropriate) and *perseveration* (continuing a behavioral element beyond the time it is wholly appropriate). He expects adjacent phonemes to influence one another — the commonly observed phenomenon of conditioned allophonic variation. Given a sequence of vowel, consonant, vowel he must predict on the grounds of both anticipation and perseveration that there will be a strong tendency for the consonant to be voiced rather than unvoiced since both the preceding and following elements are voiced. The psychologist would select the vowel–unvoiced consonant–vowel sequence as a "weak" spot in the language and one where change is more likely than either consonant-vowel or vowel-consonant alone. This prediction, of course, has two aspects: first, that diachronically unvoiced consonants between vowels will tend to become voiced and, second (all other things being equal), in a language at any given time there will tend to be more vowel–voiced consonant–vowel combinations than vowel–unvoiced consonant–vowel combinations. The verification of these findings also suggests to the psycholinguist methods for working with the phenomena of anticipation and perseveration of sound pattern in the laboratory setting.

7. Interrelations of Language Universals

In addition to its importance for the interdisciplinary field of psycholinguistics and psychology proper, this study of language universals is intimately connected with the establishment of scientific laws in the linguistic aspects of human behavior. It is thus of general significance for the development of the behavioral sciences. The study of universals leads to a whole series of empirical generalizations about language behavior, some as yet tentative, some well established. These are the potential material for a deductive structure or scientific laws. Some, indeed, probably most, of these have the status of empirical generalizations which cannot at our present state of knowledge be related to other generalizations or deduced from laws of more general import. For example, it seems well established that every language has syllables of the form CV (consonant followed by vowel) in addition to whatever other type it may possess. We cannot say why this should be so, on the basis of general laws of wider scope. For this reason it has a certain fragility. We would be quite astonished if someone discovered a language which did not have this kind of syllable, but we cannot give any reason why this should not be found.

It is clear, however, that some universals having to do with the same aspect of language are interconnected. For example, we have chains of implications in this very area of syllabic structure.

Thus, CCCV → CCV → CV, where V may in any case be preceded by sequences of C, and VCCC → VCC → VC → V, where V may be followed by sequences of C. In this instance we can deduce all of these from the general statement that if syllables containing sequences of n consonants in a language are to be found as syllabic types, then sequences of $n - 1$ consonants are also to be found in the corresponding position (prevocalic or postvocalic) except that CV → V does not hold. The possibility of deducing these five universal implications (and it probably holds for still larger consonantal sequences) gives a degree of certitude to the individual statements that they would not otherwise possess.

General statements of this kind may be called internal since they contain predicates of the same kind as the individual universals that they explain. In other cases, we have external deductions, as in some of the examples discussed earlier, where psychological principles are adduced which do not specifically involve linguistic predicates and which serve as explanatory principles for a much wider variety of phenomena, for example, the behavior of rats in mazes. These wider principles need not always be psychological in the narrower sense. For example, they may be cultural with a social-psychological aspect as when we consider the prestige and power relations of two linguistic communities as a variable in accounting for tendencies of universal scope involving the effects of one language on another.

8. Present Needs

The importance of the study of languange universals to both the burgeoning field of psycholinguistics and the development of linguistics as a behavioral science has, we believe, been sufficiently indicated. It has been further suggested that important consequences for several others of the behavioral sciences may be involved. It remains to be considered whether coordinated efforts outside the scope of the individual researchers can be useful for the development of this area of study. The first step methodologically is obviously to establish on firm grounds the actual facts concerning the universals of language. For some of the more elaborate hypotheses concerning, for example, semantic universals, it is clear that there is no substitute for special individual research projects aimed at particular problems and involving fieldwork (so, for example, the Southwest Project in Comparative Psycholinguistics). For many types of universals, however, particularly synchronic phonologic and grammatical universals, the organization of something of the order of cross-cultural files for a large sample of languages would vastly facilitate the establishment of factually well-grounded universals concerning language. The area of sound symbolism might be selectively indexed since an exhaustive body of data would obviously include all the morphemes of all the languages of the world.

Such a project would obviously require careful planning. The categories to be selected, the manner of selecting, recording, and indexing the data, the question as to how the results could be made available generally to interested scholars, problems of organization and financial support would all have to be considered. It is, therefore, suggested that a work conference on the subject of language universals be organized to include linguists, psychologists, and anthropologists interested in this area under the sponsorship of the Council in order to consider both the theoretical problems of universals and the possible organization of such a project as that mentioned earlier. In addition to the specific problems of such a project, such a meeting might well stimulate individual scholars in carrying on their research in this area.

JOSEPH H. GREENBERG
CHARLES E. OSGOOD
JAMES J. JENKINS

CHAPTER 1

THE PROBLEM OF UNIVERSALS IN LANGUAGE*

CHARLES F. HOCKETT
Cornell University

1. Introduction

A language universal is a feature or property shared by all languages, or by all language. The assertion of a (putative) language universal is a generalization about language.

"The only useful generalizations about language are inductive generalizations" (Bloomfield, 1933, p. 20). This admonition is clearly important, in the sense that we do not want to invent language universals, but to discover them. How to discover them is not so obvious. It would be fair to claim that the search is coterminous with the whole enterprise of linguistics in at least two ways. The first way in which this claim is true is heuristic: we can never be sure, in any sort of linguistic study, that it will not reveal something of importance for the search. The second way in which the claim is plausible, if not automatically true, appears when we entertain one of the various possible definitions of linguistics as a branch of science: that branch devoted to the discovery of the place of human language in the universe. This definition leaves the field vague to the extent that the problem of linguistics remains unsolved. Only if, as is highly improbable, the problem were completely answered should we know exactly what linguistics is—and

* In preparing this article (originally written early in 1961) for the second printing of the volume, I have confined myself to the correction of misprints and of a few infelicities of expression. I would now (1965) state many of the points differently, and withdraw several of them altogether.

at that same millennial moment there would cease to be any justification for the field. It is hard to discern any clear difference between "the search for language universals" and "the discovery of the place of human language in the universe." They seem rather to be, respectively, a new-fangled and old-fashioned way of describing the same thing.

But, however described, the problem is important; and it is fitting that from time to time we set aside our sundry narrower professional concerns and take stock. What are we really sure of for all languages? What are the outstanding gaps? Can we point to specific investigations of probably crucial importance? What are the most important differences of expert opinion, and how are they to be resolved?

In the present paper the writer will touch on five matters. The balance of the Introduction sets forth a number of assumptions, warnings, and pitfalls; these might be regarded as an expansion, perhaps even as a clarification, of Bloomfield's terse remark quoted earlier. Section 2 summarizes some features found (if the writer is right) in all human languages but lacking in one or another system of nonhuman animal communication. Section 3 proposes a set of features as criterial for language; that is, if a communicative system has all the features of the set, it is proposed that we call it a language. Sections 4 and 5 list a very few properties, respectively phonological and grammatical, that seem to be shared by all human languages but that are not obviously necessitated by the presence of the features of the criterial set.

1.1. *The assertion of a language universal must be founded on extrapolation as well as on empirical evidence.*

Of course this is true in the trivial sense that we do not want to delay generalizing until we have full information on all the languages of the world. We should rather formulate generalizations as hypotheses, to be tested as new empirical information becomes available. But there is a deeper implication. If we had full information on all languages now spoken, there would remain languages recently extinct on which the information was inadequate. There is no point in imagining that we have adequate information also on these extinct languages, because that would be imagining the impossible. The universe seems to be so constructed that complete factual information is unattainable, at least in the sense that there are past events that have left only incomplete records. Surely we seek constantly to widen the empirical base for our generalizations; equally surely, we always want our generalizations to subsume some of the unobserved, and even some of the unobservable, along with all of the observed.

1.2. *The assertion of language universals is a matter of definition as well as of empirical evidence and of extrapolation.*

If the next "language" on which information becomes available were to lack some feature we have believed universal, we could deny that it was a language and thus save the generalization (cf. Kemeny, 1959, pp. 97–98). Triviality from this source can be avoided by various procedures, but they all involve making decisions in advance—and such decisions are definitions. We can decide that any system manifesting a certain explicitly listed set of features (the *defining set*) is to be called a language. The universality of the particular features we have chosen is then tautologous. Of course, the list itself can be revised, for each successive round of the search for universals.

1.3. *A feature can be widespread or even universal without being important.*

This is most easily shown by a trick. Suppose that all the languages of the world except English were to become extinct. Thereafter, any assertion true of English would also assert a (synchronic) language universal. Since languages no longer spoken may have lacked features we believe universal or widespread among those now spoken, mere frequency can hardly be a measure of importance.

1.4. *The distinction between the universal and the merely widespread is not necessarily relevant.*

The reasoning is as for 1.3. Probably we all feel that the universality of certain features might be characterized as "accidental"

—they might just as well have turned out to be merely widespread. This does not tell us how to distinguish between the "accidentally" and the "essentially" universal. On the other hand, that which is empirically known to be merely widespread is thereby disqualified as an "essential" universal—though careful study may show that it is symptomatic of one.

1.5. *The search for universals cannot be usefully separated from the search for a meaningful taxonomy of languages.*

(Here "taxonomy" refers to what might also be called "typology," not to genetic classification.) Suppose that some feature, believed to be important and universal, turns out to be lacking in a newly discovered language. The feature may still be important. To the extent that it is, its absence in the new language is a typological fact of importance about the language.

Conversely, if some feature is indeed universal, then it is taxonomically irrelevant.

Here is an example that illustrates both 1.4 and 1.5. It was at one time assumed that all languages distinguish between nouns and verbs—by some suitable and sufficiently formal definition of those terms. One form of this assumption is that all languages have two distinct types of stems (in addition, possibly, to various other types), which by virtue of their behavior in inflection (if any) and in syntax can appropriately be labeled nouns and verbs. In this form, the generalization is rendered invalid by Nootka, where all inflectable stems have the same set of inflectional possibilities. The distinction between noun and verb at the level of stems is sufficiently widespread that its absence in Nootka is certainly worthy of typological note (1.5). But it turns out that even in Nootka something very much like the noun-verb contrast appears at the level of whole inflected words. Therefore, although Nootka forces the abandonment of the generalization in one form, it may still be that a modified form can be retained (1.4).

The Port Royal Grammar constituted both a putative description of language universals and the basis of a taxonomy. The underlying assumption was that every language must provide, by one means or another, for all points in the grammatico-logical scheme described in the Grammar. Latin, of course, stood at the origin in this particular coordinate system. Any other language could be characterized typologically by listing the ways in which its machinery for satisfying the universal scheme deviated from that of Latin. This classical view in general grammar and in taxonomy has been set aside not because it is false in some logical sense but because it has proved clumsy for many languages: it tends to conceal differences that we have come to believe are important, and to reveal some that we now think are trivial.

1.6. *Widespread* (or universal) *features are most apt to be important if they recur against a background of diversity.*

1.7. *Widespread* (or universal) *features are the more apt to be important the less readily they diffuse from one language to another.*

Given a taxonomy, if we find that languages of the most diverse types nonetheless manifest some feature in common, that feature may be important. It is not apt to be, however, if it is an easily diffusible item. Thus the fact that many languages all over the world have phonetically similar words for 'mama' is more significant than a similarly widespread general phonetic shape for 'tea'. (On the former, see now Jakobson, 1961.)

In allowing for diffusion, we must also take into consideration that even features that do not diffuse readily may spread from one language to others when the speakers of the languages go through a long period of intimate contact. This fact, if no other, would seem to render suspect any generalizations based solely on the languages of Western Europe. And it is true that some such generalizations are refuted by the merest glance at an appropriate non-European language. But contrastive study based exclusively on European languages also has a merit: our knowledge of those languages is currently deeper and more detailed than our knowledge of languages elsewhere, so that generalizing hypotheses can also be deeper. They may be due for a longer wait before an appropriately broad survey can confirm or confute them, but they are valuable nonetheless.

1.8. *Universal features are important if their presence in a system can be shown not to be entailed by the presence of features of the "defining set"; or if they are entailed thereby but not obviously so.*

The notion of a "defining set" was introduced in 1.2. For examples illustrating the present point, see 5.7 and 5.6.

The second part of the point may need some justification. Mapmakers have found empirically that they never need more than four colors in order to guarantee that any two continuous regions that share a boundary (not merely a point) shall be assigned different colors. This is presumably a topological property of planes and of spherical surfaces, yet it follows so unobviously from the mathematical definitions of those surfaces that no mathematician has yet succeeded in proving the implication formally. If a proof—or, indeed, a demonstration that five colors are needed rather than four—is attained, the glory of the achievement will not be diminished in the slightest by the fact that the conclusion is implied by the premises.

1.9. *A universal feature is more apt to be important if there are communicative systems, especially nonhuman ones, that do not share it.*

It may seem peculiar at first to propose that we can learn more about human language by studying the communicative systems of other animals; but a moment's reflection is enough to show that we can only know what a thing is by also knowing what it is not. As long as we confine our investigations to human language, we constantly run the risk of mistaking an "accidental" universal for an "essential" one—and we bypass the task of clearly defining the universe within which our generalizations are intended to apply. Suppose, on the other hand, that after discovering that a particular feature recurs in every language on which we have information, we find it lacking in some animal communicative system. In some cases, this might lead us to add the feature to our defining set for language. In any case, this seems to be one way of trying to avoid triviality in the assembling of our defining set.

The point just proposed threatens a very lengthy program of investigation of the communicative behavior of other animals, since zoologists recognize approximately one million living species and one can never be sure just where in this vast collection some relevant property (or its notable absence) may appear. Who would have thought, fifteen years ago, that we would learn something crucial in linguistics from bees!

It might be suggested that we bypass the whole task by an appropriate definition. We could simply assert that a communicative system is not a language unless it is manifested by human beings. Good enough; but we must now ask our confreres in anthropology and biology to identify for us the class of human beings. A serious reply is apt to include the remark "human beings are hominoids that talk"—and the circle has been closed and nothing achieved. We had better define language without reference to human beings. Then, if it appears that—on our planet—only human beings talk, this becomes a significant empirical generalization.

The comparison with nonhuman communication can be revealing in another way. We have already noted that many languages have a nursery word like *mama*. If we ask whether the gibbon-call system has this feature, we find it embarrassing merely to give the technically correct negative answer. The question has been put badly. One hesitates to speak of "words" in discussing gibbon calls. Thus we are led to examine more closely what we mean in speaking of "words" in various languages, and just why we are uncomfortable using the word "word" for gibbon calls; and such lines of inquiry may yield a more meaningful comparative question and a significant generalization about language.

1.10. *The problem of language universals is not independent of our choice of assumptions and methodology in analyzing single languages.*

This is a terribly unstartling proposal, yet important. We must generalize from our information about specific languages; we must collect information about a specific language in terms of some general frame of reference. The latter includes notions as to what language must be as well as points of methodology. The study of individual languages and the search for universals thus stand in a dialectic complementation that can equally well propagate error or truth.

To force such a system of investigation toward truth, the point of entry is our way of manipulating data on specific languages; and the procedure is the familiar one of contrapositive assumption. Whatever one's favorite notion about language design, one asks "if I assume that this particular language does *not* conform to my pet scheme, can I describe it satisfactorily?" A single success refutes or requires the revision of one's pet hypothesis. A failure, on the other hand, merely means that the hypothesis is still *tentatively* usable. Hypotheses, about language universals or anything else, are by definition proposals to be knocked down, not beliefs to be defended.

2. The Search for Universals through Comparison with Animal Systems

The design features listed here are found in every language on which we have reliable information, and each seems to be lacking in at least one known animal communicative system (cf. 1.9). They are not all logically independent, and do not necessarily all belong to our defining list for language—a point to be taken up separately, in Section 3.

All but the last three of these features have been presented in detail elsewhere (Hockett, 1960). Exact repetition would be inappropriate here, and the writer shrinks from the task of replacing the earlier treatment by a newly formulated one of comparable detail. Therefore the reader is requested to accept the present listing as the briefest sort of synopsis, and to turn to the reference just given for fuller information.

2.1. *Vocal-Auditory Channel. The channel for all linguistic communication is vocal-auditory.*

Some animals have communication that is auditory but not vocal (e.g., crickets); some have systems with totally different channels (bee-dancing is kinetic-tactile-chemical).

The phrasing of this first design-feature excludes written languages from the category "human language" just as it excludes African drum signals. The exclusion is intentional; the grounds for it will be discussed later (Section 3).

2.2. *Broadcast Transmission and Directional Reception. All linguistic signals are transmitted broadcast and are received directionally.*

These properties are the consequences of the nature of sound, of binaural hearing, and of motility, and are thus implied by 2.1. "Tight-beam" transmission is rare in the animal world, but occurs in the nerve-nets of coelenterate colonies. Directional reception is the general rule, barring occasional masking. An example of the latter is that in a field full of crickets locating any one cricket from its call is difficult, even for another cricket.

2.3. *Rapid Fading. All linguistic signals are evanescent.*

To hear what someone says, one must be within earshot at the right time. Spoors and trails fade more slowly. The property of fading is also a consequence of 2.1.

2.4. *Interchangeability. Adult members of any speech community are interchangeably transmitters and receivers of linguistic signals.*

Among some species of crickets, only the males chirp, though both males and females respond to the chirping of others.

2.5. *Complete Feedback. The transmitter of a linguistic signal himself receives the message.*

There are pathological exceptions (as, also, to 2.4). In certain varieties of kinetic-visual communication, as in the courtship dance of sticklebacks, the transmitter cannot always perceive some of the crucial features of the signal being emitted.

2.6. *Specialization. The direct-energetic consequences of linguistic signals are usually biologically trivial; only the triggering effects are important.*

Even the sound of a heated conversation does not raise the temperature of a room enough to benefit those in it. A male stickleback will not court a female unless her abdomen is distended with roe; the distension is thus an essential part of her signal to the male; the direct consequences of the distension are of obvious biological relevance.

2.7. *Semanticity. Linguistic signals function in correlating and organizing the life of a community because there are associative ties between signal elements and features in the world; in short, some linguistic forms have denotations.*

The distension by roe of the belly of the female stickleback is part of an effective signal, but does not "stand for" something else.

2.8. *Arbitrariness. The relation between a meaningful element in language and its denotation is independent of any physical or geometrical resemblance between the two.*

Or, as we say, the semantic relation is *arbitrary* rather than *iconic*. There are marginal exceptions, including traces of onomatopoeia. In bee-dancing, the way in which the direction toward the target site is mapped into a direction of dancing is iconic. The relation between a landscape painting and a landscape is iconic; the relation between the word *landscape* and a landscape is arbitrary.

2.9. *Discreteness. The possible messages in any language constitute a discrete repertory rather than a continuous one.*

Any utterance in a language must differ from any other utterance of the same length by at least a whole phonological feature. Utterances cannot be indefinitely similar to one another. Bee dances can be: the repertory of possible dances constitutes a twofold continuum.

In a continuous semantic system (one with property 2.7 but with the converse of 2.9), the semantics must be iconic rather than arbitrary. But in a discrete semantic system there is no necessary implication as to iconicity or arbitrariness; therefore, for language, 2.8 is independent of 2.7 and 2.9.

2.10. *Displacement. Linguistic messages may refer to things remote in time or space, or both, from the site of the communication.*

"Remote" means out of the perceptual field of the communicators. Gibbon calls are never displaced. Bee dances always are. Utterances in a language are freely displaced or not.

2.11. *Openness. New linguistic messages are coined freely and easily.*

We can transmit messages (produce sentences) that have never been transmitted before, and be understood. Bees do this; gibbons do not.

Actually, this property reflects two partially separate facts about language that deserve individual mention:

2.11.1. *In a language, new messages are freely coined by blending, analogizing from, or transforming old ones.*

This says that every language has *grammatical patterning*.

2.11.2. *In a language, either new or old elements are freely assigned new semantic loads by circumstances and context.*

This says that in every language *new idioms* constantly come into existence.

The openness of bee-dancing might be described as due to a very special sort of "grammatical patterning"; surely there is no evidence that bees create new idioms.

2.12. *Tradition. The conventions of a language are passed down by teaching and learning, not through the germ plasm.*

Genes supply potentiality and probably a generalized drive, since nonhuman animals cannot learn a (human) language and humans can hardly be prevented from acquiring one. Bee-dancing is probably genetic.

2.13. *Duality (of Patterning). Every language has both a cenematic subsystem and a plerematic subsystem.*

More commonly, we speak rather of the phonological and grammatical (or grammatico-lexical) subsystems of a language. The unusual terms, borrowed from Hjelmslev, are more appropriate for the discussion of communication in general, since they circumvent the unwanted connotation that the physical channel of a system with duality must necessarily be sound waves.

By virtue of duality of patterning, an enormous number of minimum semantically functional elements (pleremes, morphemes) can be and are mapped into arrangements of a conveniently small number of minimum meaningless but message-differentiating elements (cenemes, phonological components). No animal system known to the writer shows a significant duality.

Some contemporary investigators strongly suspect that a human language involves not just two, but at least three, major subsystems: for example, "phonemic," "morphemic," and "sememic."* For our present purposes this possibility can be set aside with the remark that a system with "triality" of patterning would a fortiori have our property of "duality." The essential contrast is between one and more than one subsystem.

2.14. *Prevarication. Linguistic messages can be false, and they can be meaningless in the logician's sense.*

I can assert that it is ten miles from the earth to the moon, or that the interior of all opaque solids is green until exposed to light. Lying seems extremely rare among animals.

This feature is not independent. It would seem to rest on semanticity (2.7), displacement (2.10), and openness (2.11). Without semanticity, a message cannot be tested for meaningfulness and validity. Without displacement, the situation referred to by a message must always be the immediate context, so that a lie is instantly given away. Without openness, meaningless messages

* George L. Trager and Sydney M. Lamb have been exploring the "triality" notion (or even more complex proposals), as yet without published accounts to which reference can be made. The present writer's most thoroughgoing discussion of duality is Hockett, 1961.

can hardly be generated, though false ones can: a gibbon could, in theory, emit the food call when no food had been discovered. Perhaps, however, one can imagine a system with these three underlying properties used by a species (or a collection of machines) that never lied.

It ought to be noted that without the property here labeled "prevarication" the formulation of hypotheses is impossible.

2.15. *Reflexiveness. In a language, one can communicate about communication.*

Bees dance about sites, but they cannot dance about dancing. This property, also, is presumably derivative, resting largely on 2.11.2.

A tempting alternative to this property is "universality": in a language one can communicate about anything. Reflexiveness would obviously follow from universality. The difficulty is an empirical one: if there are indeed things that we cannot communicate about, the fact that we cannot communicate about them may prevent us from recognizing that they exist. Anyway, the idiom-forming mechanism of openness (2.11.2) guarantees that we can come to communicate via language about anything that we are capable of experiencing.

2.16. *Learnability. A speaker of a language can learn another language.*

In a science-fiction story (wisely rejected by all editors), the writer once invented a nonterrestrial species that had a communicative system like human language in all respects except that its conventions were transmitted entirely through the germ plasm. The members of this species could learn a new language, but only with terrible effort. On earth, at least, it seems likely that the relative ease with which humans can learn other languages rests on design feature 2.12.

There is probably more of this sort of flexibility of readaptation among animals than we give them credit for; but some systems, at least, lack the feature altogether (bee-dancing, stickleback courtship).

3. Definition and Basic Hypotheses

The design features just presented are admittedly diverse. The list was originally assembled not in a search for language universals, but rather through a series of comparisons of human speech with the communicative behavior of certain other animals. It includes any point that such a comparison suggested. Thus it comes about that some of the points apply directly to a language as an "abstract" system (though "abstract" means different things to different investigators); others rather to the organisms that use the system; still others to how the organisms use or acquire the system. This is also why some of the points mention physics or biology (a most un-"abstract" policy), while others do not.

In reweighing the sixteen design features for our present purposes, the first decision we must make concerns writing. Shall we attempt a defining set of properties that subsumes writing systems, or some of them, as well as "spoken languages"? Or shall we class writing systems with drum signals and other clearly secondary and derivative phenomena, as something apart from "language"?

Either choice can be justified. In the long run we should probably do both. But in this paper I shall exclude writing. The reasons are as follows:

1. Spoken language is part of the "common denominator of cultures," and its antiquity is undisputed. Any generalization about spoken language is also a hypothesis about human cultural universals (Murdock, 1945). Writing is a recent invention, and has not yet spread to all human communities. Although this in itself does not preclude an attempt to determine what all spoken and all written languages have in common, it seems reasonable to break the total task up in a way that correlates with cultural universality and its absence.

2. One crucial design feature of writing systems is relative permanence, the exact opposite of the rapid fading (2.3) characteristic of spoken language. If we try to characterize spoken and written language at the same time, we have to omit both rapid fading and relative permanence. But the relative permanence of

writing is an important source of its enormous power; and the rapid fading of speech (and of its prehuman precursors) was a crucial factor conditioning the evolution of human communication of all varieties. The joint consideration of spoken and written language can thus best follow the detailed consideration of the two taken separately.

3. Writing systems are quite varied in their designs, so that it is difficult to be sure just what features are common to all. Do writing systems have duality (2.13)? In one view, only a few do. The Ogam script, for example, had cenemes consisting of certain elementary strokes, and pleremes represented by certain arrangements of those strokes; the denotations of the pleremes were the phonemes of Old Irish. In this view, English writing does not have duality of patterning, because our pleremes (letters) are not built out of a small stock of simpler cenemes. If we shift ground and say that a writing system has duality in that it shares (essentially) a plerematic subsystem with the correlated spoken language, manifested cenematically in "phonic substance" in speech but in "graphic substance" in writing, then how do we distinguish between the Ogam script and contemporary English writing, or between the latter and Chinese?

Clearly, these questions can all be answered. The writer claims the privilege of not attempting the answers here.

Having made this decision, we can consider the following defining set for language: openness (2.11), displacement (2.10), duality (2.13), arbitrariness (2.8), discreteness (2.9), interchangeability (2.4), complete feedback (2.5), specialization (2.6), rapid fading (2.3), and broadcast transmission with directional reception (2.2). Any system that has these ten properties will here be called a language; any language manifested by our own species will be called a human language. Every language also has semanticity (2.7), since the contrast between arbitrariness (2.8, included in the defining set) and iconicity is meaningless without it. Presumably, but not so clearly, every language has prevarication (2.14) and reflexiveness (2.15); at least, every human language does.

To show the importance of the features of the defining set, we can think of human language as we know it and consider the consequences of suppressing, in turn, each feature.

A language deprived of openness would generate only a finite number of whole messages. Lying might be possible, but hypothesis-formation would not.

A language deprived of displacement would not allow its users to communicate about the past or the future. Planning would be impossible. Fictions—hence speculation, literature, science—would be precluded.

A language deprived of duality would be extremely cumbersome, since each plereme would have to differ holistically from each other. It is hard to imagine any species remotely like our own being able to handle—or, at least, to evolve—such a system. However, perhaps duality is simply the mammalian way of achieving a system with all other relevant properties. Some extraterrestrial species might do differently.

A system without arbitrariness either lacks semanticity altogether or else has iconic semantics. The former possibility is most unlike language. A system with iconic semantics is constrained to use about things and situations that can be imitated, pictured, or diagrammed. Swift's account of Gulliver's encounter with the Laputans should be enough to show the crucial importance of arbitrariness.

The alternative to discreteness is continuous repertories of signals, as among the bees. But a continuous semantic system necessarily has iconic semantics (Hockett, 1960, p. 413).

It is interchangeability that enables a human to "internalize" the roles of others and to carry on conversations with himself, thus carrying over to the situations in which he is temporarily alone the problem-solving powers of language.

Complete feedback also seems essential to the use of language just described.

Specialization is such a general property of communicative systems (human and animal) that some investigators hesitate to use either the term "system" or the term "communication" of types of behavior from which it is absent. In any case, specialization renders possible communication at a power-level (in the literal physical sense) that is convenient for the species involved. One does not have to increase the power-level to communicate about large-scale matters, or to reduce it when concerned with minutiae.

Rapid fading means, positively, that messages already transmitted do not clutter up the channel and impede the transmission of new ones (as happens sometimes when one has a blackboard but no eraser). Thus, emergency signals can get through. On the other hand, it implies that the import of a message has to be stored internally in the receiver if it is to be stored anywhere at all. The "attention span" required of human hearers to take in a long and involved sentence is considerable, when measured on the general animal scale. The evolution of the capacity for such an attention span has surely been conditioned by the rapid fading property of vocal-auditory communication, and is related to the development of displacement, as well as to such nonlinguistic matters as tool-carrying and tool-making. Rapid fading is not an "incidental" property of human language. When its undesirable implications were overcome, by the development of writing, a major revolution had occurred.

Broadcast transmission and directional reception also carry both advantages and disadvantages. A warning cry may tell all one's fellows something of the location of the danger, but also, if the danger is a predator, it tells the predator where one is.

If we think only of the modern "civilized" world, in times of peace, rapid fading, broadcast transmission, and directional reception may seem relatively unimportant. But if we think of the living conditions prevalent during the bulk of human history, we see that these properties are not lightly to be regarded as secondary. They are part of our heritage from prehuman times; they have conditioned our own evolution and that of language; and they are still with us, their potentially deleterious effects canceled out only under special technological circumstances.

There is, nonetheless, a sense in which openness, displacement, and duality (together with traditional transmission, which does not appear on the defining list) can be regarded as the crucial or nuclear or central properties of human language. From an examination of what is known of the vocal-auditory communicative systems of contemporary nonhuman Hominoids, it seems that the vocal-auditory system of the proto-Hominoids must, at least, have lacked these three or four features. These three or four, then, are human or Hominid innovations. Otherwise, human language is not truly distinguishable from Hominoid communication in general.

Now we are ready for some generalizations that go beyond the defining set.

3.1. *Every human community has a language.*

Surely no one will counter with the instance of a Trappist monastery: there would be no need for a rule against talking if talking were not a possibility.

3.2. *No species except our own has a language.*

This may be disproved at any time by new zoological discoveries. No guess either way is implied about extinct species and genera of the Hominids (*Homo neanderthalensis*, *Pithecanthropus*, *Australopithecus*).

3.3. *Every human communicative system usually called a (spoken) language is a language in our sense.*

The writer is disturbed by the possibility that a few human systems not ordinarily called "spoken language," and that we do not wish to include, may also fit the definition; for example, Mazateco whistle-talk (Cowan, 1948). The derivative status of such a system is obvious, but it is not clear just how to provide formally for its exclusion.

3.4. *Every human language has the vocal-auditory channel* (2.1).

This feature was excluded from the defining list because it seems that its implications (broadcast transmission, directional reception, rapid fading) are structurally more important, and one can imagine other channels—say light, or heat-waves—that would yield the same implications. Therefore this assertion is not trivial.

3.5. *Every human language has tradition* (2.12).

If we design and build a collection of machines that communicate among themselves with a language, this property will be lacking.

3.6. *Every human language has learnability* (2.16).

Probably this is a corollary of the preceding.

3.7. *Every human language has both an intonational system and a nonintonational system; this dichotomy cuts across that into cenematics and plerematics.*

English, for example, has segmental (nonintonational) morphemes that are mapped into segmental phonological features, and intonational morphemes that are mapped into intonational phonological features. A speaker transmits, simultaneously, a nonintonational and an intonational message. The hypothesis is a guess that this basic organization is true in all human languages. It does not imply that the phonic "raw material" for intonation is invariably the pitch of the glottal tone, as it is, in large part, for English.

If true, this generalization is striking, since there seems (at the moment) absolutely no reason why an otherwise languagelike system should have this property. Most writing systems do not carry it over.

Another generalization about intonation is tempting, on the basis of very limited observation, but the evidence is scarcely strong enough to present it as a numbered point: Many highly diverse languages (English, other languages of Europe, Chinese, Japanese, Samoan, Fijian) share a "most colorless" intonation for flat statements, in the face of (1) different phonemic structures for the intonation (which is *phonetically* similar from one language to another) and (2) wide disparity in the remainder of the intonational system.

3.8. *In every human language, plerematic patterning and cenematic patterning are both (independently) hierarchical.*

Grammatically, an utterance consists (let us say) of clauses, a clause of phrases, a phrase of words, a word of morphemes. Phonologically, an utterance consists of macrosegments, a macrosegment of microsegments, a microsegment of syllables, a syllable of phonemes, and a phoneme of phonological components. (Except for morpheme, phonological component, and perhaps utterance, the terms used for this explanation are not part of the generalization.)

3.9. *Human languages differ more widely in cenematics than in plerematics.*

3.10. *Human languages differ more widely, at least in their plerematic subsystems, at small size-levels than at large.*

These two assertions are not of universals, but perhaps point toward some. For example, 3.10 suggests that all languages share certain large-scale syntactical patterns, however varied may be the smaller-scale patterns by which the constituents for the larger patterns are built up. Point 3.9 can be challenged on the grounds that we have no reliable way of measuring and comparing the differences referred to. At present this is doubtless true; but the assertion seems impressionistically valid to the writer, and formal ways to confirm the impression (or to disprove it) may be found.

4. Grammatical Universals

The generalizations of the preceding section mention grammar (or plerematic design), but do not belong in a set of generalizations about grammar proper because they involve the relationship of grammar to other aspects of language design. From what has already been said, we know (or assume) that every language has a grammatical system, and that grammatical patterning is hierarchical. In addition, we can with reasonable confidence propose the following points:

4.1. *Every human language has a stock of elements that shift their denotations depending on elementary features of the speech situation.*

That is, every language has deictic elements ("substitutes," in Bloomfield's terminology): in English, the personal pronouns, demonstrative pronouns and proadverbs, and so on.

4.2. *Among the deictic elements of every human language is one that denotes the speaker and one that denotes the addressee.*

The first and second person singular pronouns are universal. There seems to be no reason internal to our definition of language why this should be so; yet, if we try to imagine a system that lacks them, the results seem quite alien.

4.3. *Every human language has some elements that denote nothing but that make a difference in the denotation of the composite forms in which they occur.*

Such elements are *markers*, for example English *and. Match and book* denotes something different from *match or book* or *match book*, but *and* denotes nothing. The assumption that such elements must denote something just as do *man*, *sky*, *honor*, or *unicorn* has generated much bad mentalistic philosophizing, populating the universe with abstract entities or the human mind with concepts, both of which are as useless as the luminiferous ether.

There are also *impure markers*, for example English *in*, *on*, that have some denotation as well as a marking function. It may be that we should go only so far as to assert the universal presence of markers (pure or impure).

4.4. *Every human language has proper names.*

A proper name is a form that denotes just what it denotes. If it denotes more than one thing in different occurrences, the class of things that it can denote has no criterial property in common other than the (extrinsic) property of being denoted by the proper name. All Americans named *Richard* are probably males, but many males are not called *Richard*, and when one meets someone for the first time, it is in no way possible to examine his properties and infer that his name must be *Richard*.

A form may be a proper name and also something else: *Robin/robin*, *John/john*, *Brown/brown*. The generalization does not deny this.

4.5. *Every language has grammatical elements that belong to none of the three special categories just itemized.*

Comparatively, it is worthy of note that all signals in bee dancing are deictic elements, and that no gibbon calls are of any of the three special types.

4.6. *In every human language there are at least two basic orders of magnitude in grammatical patterning.*

Where there are just two, the traditional terms "morphology" and "syntax" do very well. When the morphology-syntax boundary appears fuzzy, closer scrutiny often reveals a separate order of magnitude of grammatical patterning sandwiched between. As familiar a language as Spanish offers an example. The internal organization of *dando*, *me*, and *lo* is morphology; the participation of *dándomelo* in larger forms is syntax; the patterns by which *dando*, *me*, and *lo* are conjoined to yield *dándomelo* are not conveniently classed as either.

However, 4.6 is shaky in another direction: a deeper understanding of languages of the Chinese type may yet show that they are best described without either the two-way morphology-syntax dichotomy or a more complex three-way layering.

In many languages in which the morphology-syntax dichotomy is clear-cut, phonological patterning correlates: that is, grammatical words are also, for the most part, phonological units of a distinctive sort. But there are many exceptions, so that this points toward morphophonemic taxonomy rather than toward universals.

4.7. *Apart from the three special categories of elements already mentioned (deictic elements, markers, and proper names), no human language has a grammatically homogeneous vocabulary.*

There are always forms with different ranges of privileges of occurrence, so that one can always validly speak of form classes.

4.8. *A major form-class distinction reminiscent of "noun" versus "verb" is universal, though not always at the same size-level.*

This was discussed in connection with 1.5.

4.9. *Every human language has a common clause type with bipartite structure in which the constituents can reasonably be termed "topic" and "comment."*

The order of the constituents varies. Typically in Chinese, Japanese, Korean, English, and many other languages, one first mentions something that one is going to talk about, and then says something about it. In other languages, the most typical arrangement is for the comment, or part of it, to precede the topic. Of course, the generalization refers only to a "common clause type." Every language seems to have clauses of other types as well.

4.10. *Every language has a distinction between one-referent and two-referent predicators.*

In *Mary is singing*, the predicator *is singing* is of the one-referent sort (and *Mary* is the referent); in *John struck Bill*, the predicator is of the two-referent sort.

Both 4.9 and 4.10 are shaky in a special way. Although we tend to find these patterns in language after language, it is entirely possible that we find them because we expect them, and that we expect them because of some deep-seated properties of the languages most familiar to us. For some languages, some scheme that is far less obvious to us might actually fit the facts better. Although this is true of all proposed generalizations, it nevertheless seems especially true of these two.

5. Phonological Universals

From what has already been said, we know (or assume) that every human language has a phonological system, and that phonological patterning is always hierarchical. Purely phonological generalizations are then to be considered within that tentatively established framework.

5.1. *In every human language, redundancy, measured in phonological terms, hovers near 50%.*

The notion is that if redundancy tends to increase much above this figure, communication becomes inefficient, and people speak faster or more sloppily, while decrease much below the figure leads to misunderstanding, and people slow down or articulate more clearly.

It may be that the redundancy figure would be about the same were it measured in grammatico-lexical terms; and it may be that this approximate figure is the rule for a wide variety of communicative systems, at least among human beings. Printed English yields the same figure (Shannon, 1951), in terms of letters.

5.2. *Phonemes are not fruitful universals.*

We can, indeed, speak quite validly of phonemes in the discussion of any language, but their status in the hierarchy of phonological units varies from one language to another, and also, to some extent, through varying preference or prejudice of analysts. The status of phonological components, on the other hand, is fixed once and for all by definition—phonological components are the minimum (not further divisible) units of a phonological system. Given that all phonological patterning is hierarchical, the exact organization of the hierarchy, varying from one language to another, becomes a taxonomic consideration of importance, but not the basis of a generalization in the present context.

There are certain languages of the Caucasus (Kuipers, 1960) where one can, if one wishes, describe the phonological system in terms of perhaps a dozen phonological features organized into some seventy or eighty phonemes, which in turn occur in about twice that many syllables. Each syllable consists of one of the seventy-odd consonant phonemes, followed by one of the two vowel phonemes. It seems clear in such a case that the vowel "phonemes" are better regarded simply as two additional phonological features, so that a unit such as /ka/ is just a phoneme—or, alternatively, that the term "phoneme" be discarded and one discuss the participation of features directly in syllables. Either way, one does not need both the term "phoneme" and the term "syllable." The case may be extreme, but it is real, and underscores the importance of the "anti-universal" given as 5.2.

5.3. *Every language makes use of distinctions of vowel color.*

Vowel color is defined as combination of formants. Acoustically, it is known that for languages like English differences of vowel color do much of the work of keeping consonants apart, as well as distinguishing vowel phonemes.

5.4. *A historical tendency toward phonological symmetry is universal.*

Jakobson has offered a number of synchronic generalizations about phonological systems, to some of which there seem to be a few marginal exceptions. One, for example, is the assertion that a language does not have a spirant of the type [θ] unless it has both a [t] and an [s], nor an affricate like [č] unless it has both a [t] and an [š]. However, Kickapoo has [t] and [θ] but no [s]. Another is that a language does not have nasal continuants at more contrasting positions of articulation than it has stops of some one manner of articulation. It is possible to analyze certain varieties of Brazilian Portuguese so as to violate this generalization. A third is that a language does not contrast unaspirated and aspirated stops unless it has a separate phoneme /h/. Mandarin Chinese is almost an exception, in that the nearest thing to an /h/ is normally a dorso-velar spirant.

Yet these generalizations seem far too widely borne out to merely be thrown into the scrap heap by virtue of a handful of exceptions. When facts invalidate a hypothesis, one tries modifying the hypothesis before one discards it altogether. In each of the cases given, we seem to have an indication of a historical tendency toward some sort of symmetry. The tendency can be disrupted, so that not every system viewed in synchronic cross-section will conform to the rule; but diachronically the tendency is real.

5.5. *There are gaps, asymmetries, or "configurational pressures" in every phonological system, no matter when examined.*

Most systems, by virtue of a sort of semimagical logistics of maneuvering on the part of analysts, can be forced to appear neat and symmetrical. The maneuvering is always worth undertaking, not in order to force symmetry where there is lack of it, but because it is heuristically valuable—it helps to show relationships within a system that might otherwise be missed. But the asymmetries, however pushed about, remain in the system.

5.6. *Sound change is a universal. It is entailed by the basic design features of language, particularly by duality of patterning.*

By "sound change" is meant a mechanism of linguistic change that is not reducible to other mechanisms (see, e.g., Hockett, 1958, chs. 52–54). When a system has duality of patterning, the basic role of its cenematic system is to identify messages and keep them apart. Usually an utterance produced in given circumstances is far more than minimally different from any other utterance that might be produced in the same language in the same circumstances. Thus there is room for much nondistinctive variation in details of articulation and even more in the shape of the speech signal by the time it reaches the ears of the hearer. Therefore there will be sound change. The implications of sound change for the phonological and grammatical systems of a language are another matter. (See the reference given earlier.)

5.7. *Every phonological system contrasts phonemes that are typically stops with phonemes that are never stops.*

Stops are sounds produced with complete oral closure and complete velic closure. By "phonemes that are typically stops" we mean phonemes that are stops in slow careful speech or in key environments, though they may be weakened or spirantized in some environments or in faster speech. The contrasting nonstops vary widely from one language to another. In a few languages of New Guinea, the nearest nonstops are nasal continuants. More commonly, they are spirants.

5.8. *No phonological system has fewer than two contrasting positions of articulation for stops.*

The only attested cases with two are Hawaiian and a slightly archaic Samoan, with labial versus lingual. (In contemporary Samoan a new apical-versus-dorsal contrast has developed.)

5.9. *If a language has a vowel system, it has contrasts of tongue height in that system.*

5.10. *If we define a "vowel system" to include all the segmental phonemes that occur as syllable peaks, then every language has a vowel system.*

For 5.10, clearly some adjustment is required in order to subsume the languages of the Caucasus referred to earlier. If we define a "vowel system" to include all the segmental phonemes that occur *only* as syllable peaks, then at least one language, Wishram, apparently has a vowel system of one element, which is only trivially a "system." With these adjustments, 5.9 becomes a true universal, applying to all human languages.

Another way to express 5.9 is to say that if a language has vowel contrasts other than those of tongue height, it also has those of tongue height, but not necessarily vice versa.

Further generalizations along the line of the last three mentioned can probably be formulated, although all of them are subject to modification at any time by empirical information on some as-yet-unanalyzed language. As a set, however, they point toward something rather puzzling. It would seem easy enough to devise a phonemic system that would have no stops at all, or no vowels at all, or the like. The phonological systems of the world, despite their great variety, all seem to have more in common than is strictly "necessary." That is, the degree of resemblance strikes one as greater than is required merely by the defining features of language and the known cultural and biological properties of our species. Granting that the variety may actually be somewhat greater than we currently realize, there is still a problem in this degree of similarity. Are there constraints imposed by as-yet-unrealized properties of the organs of speech and of human hearing? Is the resemblance due to a common origin, in relatively recent times—say forty or fifty thousand years ago—of all human languages on which we have any direct evidence or can obtain any? (The latter hypothesis does not, of course, propose that human language is only that old, merely that all other older strains have died out.) These questions are open; the answers may actually lie in some totally different direction.

ACKNOWLEDGMENTS

The author is indebted to Sidney Lamb for detailed criticisms and suggestions. He also wishes to thank Fred Householder and Joseph H. Greenberg for comments on certain aspects of the present paper.

REFERENCES

Bloomfield, L. (1933). *Language*. New York.

Cowan, G. M. (1948). "Mazateco Whistle Speech." *Language* 24. 280–286.

Hockett, C. F. (1958). *A Course in Modern Linguistics*. New York.

——— (1960). "Logical Considerations in the Study of Animal Communication." W. E. Lanyon and W. N. Tavolga, eds., *Animal Sounds and Communication*, Publication No. 7 of The American Institute of Biological Sciences, 392–430. Washington, D. C.

——— (1961). "Linguistic Elements and Their Relations." *Language* 37. 29–53.

Jakobson, R. (1961). "Why 'Mama' and 'Papa'?" *Perspectives in Psychological Theory*, 124–134.

Kemeny, J. G. (1959). *A Philosopher Looks at Science*. Princeton, N. J.

Kuipers, A. H. (1960). *Phoneme and Morpheme in Kabardian*. The Hague.

Murdock, G. P. (1945). "The Common Denominator of Cultures." R. Linton, ed., *The Science of Man in the World Crisis*, 123–142. New York.

Shannon, C. (1951). "Prediction and Entropy of Printed English." *Bell System Technical Journal* 30. 50–65.

CHAPTER 2

ARE THERE UNIVERSALS OF LINGUISTIC CHANGE?

HENRY M. HOENIGSWALD

University of Pennsylvania

1. Introduction

On the subject of synchronic universals (see Casagrande, 10.2), linguistic thinking may be said to have gone through three stages. In the first stage—that period with which contemporary linguistics has found so much fault because it was its direct heir—a glossocentric attitude was likely to prevail. Features recognized in a handful of familiar languages, and recognized, more often than not, under the guise of spelling or rhetoric or logic rather than on their own terms, were easily taken to be necessary properties of language per se. Insofar as this is a fair description, the question of universals did not arise, since everything was, in a sense, a universal.

The relativism of the stage which followed was extreme. Nothing in the languages of the world was to be taken for granted. The investigator took care to keep his concepts unspecific. They had to be as formal and as empty as possible so as not to prejudge the case, and to permit the objective discovery of specific properties in each instance. Perhaps it was safe to believe that all languages "have" phonemes, morphemes, and constructions; but it was especially safe if it meant no more than that any language may be analyzed as made up of utterances that partly do, and partly do not, mutually contrast. Our findings may then tell us that all languages observed agree in some respects, and may thus give us universals by induction.

It seems to me that the third stage in the handling of synchronic universals takes off from here. Universals may have to be discovered inductively, from a neutral, formalistic foundation. But, thus discovered, what are they like? There is an ineradicable conviction that all of them are not mere random coincidences; that their identification as universals is not necessarily so precarious as to be thrown out by tomorrow's addition to our store of data; in other words, that universals may form some sort of system in their own right.

This, of course, is not news to our conference. But in turning from the synchronic point of view to the diachronic, we must first of all realize that diachronic studies have developed at a different pace. To be sure, the same three levels or stages are recognizable. But, as has often been said, even the prerelativistic first stage of nineteenth-century historical linguistics, so far from merely being the old rehash of Stoic logic, Latin school grammar, and *grammaire raisonnée*, was a new and aggressive discipline with productive, if somewhat improvised, working concepts. The neogrammarians' ideas on the general (that is, universal) attributes of change processes are elaborate and substantive. They are therefore on the surface much less vulnerable to the charge of glossocentricity; and they are still very much with us. Any text on historical linguistics contains detailed generalizations concerning change processes. If proof were needed regarding the claims made for them, it would be sufficient to point to a dichotomy in the presentation of sound change which has almost become traditional. Schwyzer's *Historical Greek Grammar*,[1] for instance, discusses sound change under two headings: "general language phenomena" and, presumably, others less general. Grammont's *Traité de phonétique*, a great classic (which, incidentally, one hesitates to label prestructural), deals precisely with the universals of sound change. Universalistic beliefs have also long been held in the area of semantic change. The existence, in all languages and at all times, of such happenings as narrowing, widening, elevation, pejoration, metaphor, and metonymy is a venerable tenet.

The elaborateness and substantiality of older historical linguistic results and methods of which these notions are a fair reflection have made a thorough reexamination seem less necessary. They have thus retarded the emergence of the second stage in diachronic studies, let alone the third. We are only beginning to construct a framework of minimal formal concepts—not a table of universals at all; but simply a skeleton of irreducibles which will keep to a minimum any preconceived ideas about processes of change that may be specific characteristics of some languages but not of others. These thereby enable us, conversely, to discover truly universal change processes, if there are any. This is not to say that speculation, and frequently valuable speculation, has not gone beyond that stage, too. As always in the history of a discipline, one must avoid giving too narrow a chronological meaning to its successive manifestations. Yet it seems fair to say that the powers of diachronic linguistics to generalize are at present circumscribed by the factors and in the fashion here indicated.

Even in establishing the very simplest generalizations one soon encounters difficulties which betray weak spots in the foundations. For instance, it seems reasonable to assert that all languages change. But this cannot simply mean that, given a certain idiolect, *i*, it is impossible, after a lapse of time, to find another idiolect *i′* such that the description and analysis of *i* will fit it as well, since the same is true of contemporary idiolects. Perhaps it means that after a lapse of time defined as considerable no idiolects can be found that, under some such criterion as mutual intelligibility, "resemble" *i*, while during the intervening period idiolects can be found which provide a chain of "similar" forms of speech linking *i* with *i′*. For greater concreteness some means is needed to recognize two forms of speech (one, as it happens, more recent than the other) as having the relationship of ancestor and descendant—or, in the case of less serious chronological differences, what are called successive "stages" of the "same" language. Only where this identity is established can we acknowledge "change" as such. Many a controversy of the past shows that this is not mere abstract quibbling over self-evident propositions. Much ink and bile was spilled to prove that Italian is not a later stage of Ciceronian Latin, or that Old Persian is indeed the true ancestor of Middle Persian. It is interesting to reflect that these decisions depend on the so-called comparative method of reconstruction. Language descent, somewhat paradoxically, is a special case of language relationship. Some pairs of related languages, when subjected to the comparative method, yield a reconstruction essentially identical with one member of the pair. It is thereby that this member language is defined as the ancestor (or older stage) of the other member language. A comparison between the two is then known as a statement of *change*.

2. Change

Change is a general phenomenon in the sense that every language (perhaps with the exception of *ex-novo* creations like standard Norwegian or modern Hebrew, but apparently not excluding the pidgins) has an infinite ancestry of earlier and earlier stages. The converse is of course not valid, since languages do become extinct. These are truisms. But a more specific question has been raised within the last decade or two which has to do with the rate of change. It is obvious that the extremes are excluded. After considerable time there is always a noticeable degree of change, however measured; on the other hand, language will not change overnight. It is reasonable to suspect the interplay of two forces at work: one which holds back change in the interest of mutual intelligibility at any given time; and another force, much more obscure in its working, which makes for change, even intense change. That this picture should not be oversimplified is suggested by the famous Charmey experiment and its follow-up by Hermann, who showed that what had been the younger generation did not persist in all of its initial innovations but, in growing older, moved into the subsociety of the middle-aged and in doing so also adopted the subsocietal dialect much as it had existed before. More such studies should be made now that some of the difficulties in the way of making them have become less forbidding. However that may be, Swadesh and his associates have asked whether the long-term results of that balance of forces may not be a significantly constant rate of change and thus a true, specific universal.[2]

It is worth observing that this glottochronology is, in particular, lexicostatistics. What is measured is the replacement of items in the so-called basic vocabulary—a factor which some would regard relatively minor as change processes go. This is not adverse criticism; quite the contrary. It is necessary to understand the surface in order to reach greater depths. It may also be that the clear-cut and sometimes (not always!) enumerable sudden switches in vocabulary are at the same time the events interfering most dramatically with that mutual intelligibility which acts as the governor on the engine of change—if indeed it does. In other words, a clear-cut near-constant rate of change may apply more reasonably to vocabulary replacement than to other varieties of change. A suggestion has been made also that the rate of vocabulary loss, while not an absolute universal, may yet be constant in a given language family or language area. Finally, we note that lexicostatistics casts a new light, obliquely, on the old motif that literacy holds back linguistic change. There is of course no reason to think that this is really so; but in the special case where a language borrows, in the "learned" fashion, from its own literarily preserved ancestor, vocabulary change (though not other change processes) may appear retarded, since at least some such borrowings will not be distinguishable from material that is simply retained. Thus it would not be literacy in general, but Italian or Hindi literacy rather than English or Japanese literacy which can be expected to show that minor effect.

Swadesh's work has the even greater merit of throwing into relief the distinction between replacement processes and others. For the moment we are back at that second level in the search for universals, which we need so badly if we want to keep our bearings. For this purpose, we may picture the analysis of linguistic change as being performed upon a "translation"—a translation, ideally, of the texts of the earlier stage into texts of the later stage.[3] (I need not emphasize that by "texts" I am not referring to anything literary or recorded; I mean "self-sufficient portions of utterances as they can be elicited," or "discourses.") Now we cannot expect *all* the texts or discourses of the earlier stage to have such a "translation." Nor can we expect the reverse:

the later stage includes texts which are lacking in the earlier. This is so because the opportunity for the utterances of a given text may disappear, or, on the other hand, it may not yet exist. The missing text is potentially there in predictable shape but for the lack of a stimulus. The change, as the saying goes, is in the world at large, but not in the language. In fact, the circumstance that a change in stimuli should produce the obsolescence or fresh emergence of utterances is precisely a measure of the constancy of the language. And what holds for entire texts may also be asserted for their component elements. Words limited to obsolete texts disappear, as the terms of medieval crafts and trades disappeared from English. Words limited to newly emergent texts are new: loanwords like *giraffe* or *coffee* were once new. Other elements are adequately described as partly (or, rather, conditionally) dropped, or as conditionally added. *Whelm* has survived after *over-*, but it has dropped out elsewhere, along with the texts in which it figured. *Rail* in *railsplitter* is relatively old, but *railroad* or *rails held firm at closing* are recent additions.

3. Replacement Pattern

True linguistic change, however, involves *replacement.* It is pointless to ask what word was replaced by *coffee*, or what word in active usage has replaced *fuller.* But, clearly, in our hypothetical quasi-translation or matching procedure, the earlier English *inwit* has gone to *conscience* just as, merely in comparing yesterday's English with today's English, yesterday's *coffee* and *conscience* are trivially replaced by today's *coffee* and *conscience.* There are very good reasons why the distinction between plain amorphous addition and deletion, on the one hand, and replacement, on the other, must remain somewhat blurred at certain points; but the distinction is nevertheless of central importance for any unified view of linguistic change. To the extent that there *is* replacement—that, wherever *inwit* drops out, *conscience* takes its place—and to the extent that the replacement is neat, there is change in the proper sense. The replacement process par excellence is of course sound change. After 100 years of practice we are thoroughly familiar with such formulations as that Germanic /d/ "becomes"—that is, is replaced by—/t/ in standard German, or that proto-Algonquian /θ/ and /t/ both "go to" the /t/ of Cree. Mere amorphous addition to and deletion from the language cannot be among the typical effects of sound change.

It does make a difference whether we make our statements, as we have just done, for the morphemes, phonemes, distinctive features, constructions, etc., of our two languages; or else for the morphs, phones, order arrangements, zeros, and what not, all of which may be said to occupy or fill the distinctive units comprised in the first list. In the former instance the emphasis is on the pattern of replacement itself. Insofar as all Germanic /d/'s are replaced only by German /t/'s, and insofar as the only source for a German /t/ is a Germanic /d/, the replacement pattern is one-to-one; and in one important respect [4] no structural change has occurred. Just so, to the extent that *conscience* moves in only where *inwit* has moved out, the vocabulary structure is, in a sense, unaltered. [5] We might say that the phoneme and the morpheme (or morphemic construct—the words are compounds) have remained what they were in a table of mutually defined, Saussurian elements, and that only their phonetic or their morphic content has shifted: a phone, [t], has changed its location; a morph, *conscience*, has done likewise, even more radically. But then, all replacements are not one-to-one; there is merger, and there is split. The plural morpheme of the modern Indo-European languages has replaced both the dual morpheme and the plural morpheme of the ancestor stages. Spanish *tio* as well as French *oncle* replace two different, contrasting morphemes designating the paternal and the maternal uncle in Latin. In Cree, as we have said, both /θ/ and /t/ are replaced by /t/. On the other hand, a Latin expression like *hominem* "translates" into Spanish in some contexts (that is, in some environments) as *un hombre*, in other contexts as *el hombre*, and in still others as *hombre*. Or, an older /u/ goes to Old English /y/ in some environments, but to /u/ in others.

These are examples of various replacement patterns, both in morphemics and in phonemics. For phonemics this is indeed the customary style of statement. Nor is it entirely unfamiliar in dealing with morphemes. For instance, it is not unusual to say that the "concept expressed by the word *inwit* is later expressed by the word *conscience*," or that "the name for a certain part of the body changes from (Old English) *wonge* to *cheek*." But much more commonly talk about such changes is couched in exactly opposite terms. It is the morphs—that is, the stretches as defined by their phonemic shape rather than their own contrastive status—that are followed as they move through the framework of the table of morphemic contrasts, a framework which in itself may remain rigid or undergo its peculiar splits and mergers, as the case may be. From this more usual point of vantage *conscience* is classified as a "borrowing." *Tio* is a borrowing also, although its role in the replacement pattern is quite different from that of *conscience*. *Oncle*, although its replacment function neatly duplicates that of *tio*, is a case of semantic widening inasmuch as the morph is the "same" (under sound change, disregarded on this level) as the Latin morph which used to fill one of the two morphemes ('maternal uncle') that were later merged (into 'uncle'). So is *cheek*, as a morph, an example of semantic change; it used to mean 'jaw' and was replaced by *jaw*.

With this in mind, what may we expect to be the nature of any diachronic universals? Conceivably, such universals might be of three kinds. First, the replacement process itself may turn out to have certain generally valid properties.[6] Second, there may be universals of the sort that make the nature of the resulting language structure predictable—either quite generally (in the sense that all languages work toward certain identical goals) or specifically (in the sense that the resulting structure can in some degree be predicted from the initial structure). Third, there may be something predictable about the movements of the stretches of lower-level linguistic material—phones and morphs[7]—as they take up their positions in the interests either of structure preservation or of structural innovation.

First, then, consider the replacement process itself. We have argued all along on the assumption that the concept of replacement is generally valid. To be sure, this is only a "second stage" concept, so markedly formal that perhaps it deserves the name "universal" no more than does the principle of the synchronic amenability of all language to phonemic analysis, or the like. But there are certain corollaries. Above all, there is the much-labored "regularity" of change. Sound change (certain raw effects of borrowing and of "allophonic analogy" are not considered here), for example, is known to be primarily merger, and only secondarily split. Two phonemes may be replaced by one without producing split, but two phonemes will not replace one without a merger somewhere. Perhaps the machinery involved here is truly still something of a puzzle. But it is far more than likely that a great many mergers, at least, must go forward as the result of contact among subphonemically differing varieties within the speech community.[8] The minimal extent of the difference may be expected to favor something like "total borrowing," complete with the "misinterpretation" of diaphones so commonly observed in the cruder forms of borrowing from language to language. To a very large extent the so-called regularity of sound change flows rather directly from a universally present condition: namely from the subdistinctive heterogeneity of speech communities. Recent comparative work from all over suggests that sound change "is" indeed regular everywhere on earth. This means, incidentally, that the comparative method of reconstruction based on that regularity is universally applicable. Disdainful opinion to the contrary effect, even if held by serious scholars, is hardly more than a bit of naïveté.

It would be wrong to think, and it would hamper us if we did think, that the regular, "law"-like character which impressed earlier generations of scholars so much is a mysterious prerogative of phonemic change. Its exact morphemic counterpart is plain for all to see, and indeed is so much on the surface that it has been remarkable only to those interested in this very analogy. After all, just as all Algonquian instances of /θ/ go to Cree /t/, so all instances of *inwit* go to *conscience*. Likewise with conditioned change (split): Just as those particular instances of /u/ which were followed in the next syllable by an /i/ went to /y/, so also those particular instances of early modern English *flesh* which occurred in certain constructions (say, in *fleshwound* or *mortify the flesh*) went to a later morpheme occupied by a homonymous morph *flesh*, whereas the other instances of *flesh* were replaced by a morph-and-morpheme *meat*. I have treated certain disparities in this confrontation elsewhere—I believe there is a satisfactory theory for them which strengthens rather than weakens the parallel.[9] According to Leumann, the mechanics of semantic change parallels very closely what we have been able to suggest for sound changes:[10] Semantic changes are essentially dialect borrowings, reinterpreted in the receiving dialect, through the agency of a "misunderstanding"—the word sometimes to be taken in its weakest possible meaning. Martinet has made fun of the notion that a homogeneous language, if left alone, would remain immutable. But since no language community is homogeneous and none isolated, it is not so unreasonable to link the universal incidence of change with the observed universality of synchronic differentiation and of outside contacts.

Perhaps the doctrine of the gradualness of linguistic change should be touched on here. It is a commonplace view that changes begin on an infinitesimal scale, as nonrandom deviations from some norm, and then grow in extent ("imperceptibly" is the favorite adverb), until, somehow, the threshold is crossed. It is just possible that this view is simply a carryover from prestructural days. We would now prefer a picture in which changes are made up of discrete steps, some very small, some (physically) zero (namely, where a structural reinterpretation of the "same" physical entity is the decisive event: allophones coming to stand in contrast; allomorphs like *shade* and *shadow* taking on contrasting meanings, etc.). Since, if we are right on this, these discrete steps depend on the amount of nondistinctive variation which exists in the speech community in the first place, they are bound to remain small. Perhaps they are even bound to affect only one distinctive component at a time, as William Austin[11] acutely observed in the special area of sound change. If we have a diachronic universal here, it is one that flows from one of the synchronic universals governing the typology of dialect areas.

4. Target Structure

This brings us to the consideration of diachronic universals in the sense that certain structures may or may not be favorite targets of change processes. Here, too, the typology of change is subordinate to the typology of existing states; and our findings can be no stronger than the findings on descriptive universals. We first select two subjects for discussion: the alleged regularizing action of "analogic change"; and the principle of widening conditioning.

In classical historical linguistics sound change and so-called analogic change (which must not be confused with the factor of analogical creation present in all change processes and somehow connected with the intimate machinery of those processes as adumbrated here) are often regarded, and sometimes even explicitly defined, as opposing principles. It is said that (conditioned) sound change creates "irregular paradigms," that is, morphophonemes, whereas analogic change serves to eliminate morphophonemic alternation. This is a tribute to one admittedly typical role assumed by those two forms of linguistic change; but it is also an exceedingly oblique approach to analogic change. Analogic change is essentially a replacement of one allomorph by another within the morpheme; and it is that quite regardless of possible morphophonemic consequences. As *shoon*, etc., has changed to *shoes*, for instance, the allomorph *-en* has evidently receded one step to the point where it is limited to *oxen*, and perhaps a few other plurals; the allomorph *-z* has been extended to one new class of environments, namely into all texts where the plural morpheme occurs after *shoe*. And it is not true that this dovetailing reciprocal distributional movement within the morphemic unit, will inevitably and exclusively favor one allomorph, or a selection of allomorphs, over all the others, thereby minimizing irregular alternation and "leveling" the paradigm. Analogic change has been known to create new allomorphs (although perhaps not new morphophonemes) and to extend irregular (grammatically conditioned) allomorphs at the expense of their regular, phonemically conditioned competitors. English plurals in *-s -z -iz* may generally have the advantage over their competitors; but newly imported names of fish, like *muskellunge*, are likely to receive the zero alternant seen in *trout*, *bass*, and *fish* itself. Nor, on the other hand, does sound change always increase alternation. Suppose that a given sound change merges two phonemes which alternate. This will reduce, and not increase, morphophonemic complexity. The history of well-known language families is shot through with examples of this sort. In other words, both the processes (sound change and analogic fluctuation of allomorphs) serve the same structural purposes—to use a teleological turn of phrase which is almost inevitable at the present state of our theoretical penetration. It is as though the structural goal were somehow given, subordinating to itself all manners of available machinery. And the goals, alas, impress us again and again as very specific goals, characteristic perhaps of given areas and given broad periods—they do not appear to be universals at all. I would suspect that the older Indo-European languages, which represent one of the best-studied areas and periods in the world, happened to work toward a structural type characterized, among many other features, by comparatively little allomorphic variety, and that both analogic change and a goodly fraction of phonemic merger were merely pressed into that particular service, as it were. There may be more to it, but we would be rash to be as sure of it as Paul and Sturtevant had a right to be.

Greenberg and others feel that sound change has a typical mechanism of successively widening scope.[12] Sound change, they say, may begin as "sporadic," then become phonologically conditioned, and finally unconditional. Before commenting on this notion, let me strengthen it somewhat by what seems to me to be an essential parallel. Once again the parallel comes from the morphemic level (and once again, regrettably, from Indo-European!). One of the most sweeping trends in the history of Indo-European languages, or possibly of the area to which the Indo-European languages belong, is the merging of the two non-singular numbers, the dual and the plural, into one. The various morphs which a componential analysis reveals to contain components for the dual morpheme or for the plural morpheme become complementary in various ways and take on the combined meaning of both (the category is customarily labeled "plural," as though it were synonymous with the old, nondualic plural). But not all such morphs are affected at once. In some conditions the two components contrast far longer than in others. In analogy to the parallel, if much simpler, process observed in phonemic change, we should say that the conditioning of the merger widens until it it becomes complete. In some forms of Greek the dual in the noun outlived the verbal dual. In classical Latin where the same trend was obeyed earlier, both inflectional duals are gone, but contrasting forms still exist for "which (of two)" versus "which of more than two)" (*uter* versus *qui*). The modern English comparatives, as well as the words *either* and *neither*, still contain a contrastive dualic component (vis-à-vis the superlatives, and *any*, *none*).[13] Some Indo-European languages have no remnant left. There is no doubt that here we have an important principle. To be sure, it operates in one direction only. It is not possible to predict that all conditioned change will become unconditional, or even (as we should really expect) go on to engender parallel changes, that is, acquire a wider and wider conditioning for the distinctive feature contained in the phoneme (or morpheme) in question. But it is certainly appropriate to suspect that what is in the end effect an unconditional or nearly unconditional merger has gone through intermediate periods of such characteristics.

So long as we concentrate on sound changes, we have relatively little difficulty with the so-called first step from alleged lexical "sporadicity" to phonemic, but still narrow, conditioning. Instances of so-called sporadic sound change can also be labeled instances of dialect borrowing, and under favorable conditions this is not necessarily inferential but demonstrable from a knowledge of the dialect picture at the time of change. The step from "sporadic" to regular change, where the changing unit is a "phoneme in a given environment," that is, an allophone—that step is, as we have tried to show, merely the step from ordinary selective borrowing to the kind of total borrowing for which there seem to exist typical favorable settings in history. The remainder of the story is more difficult. Why should an allophone, once it has left the fold, continue to attract its erstwhile fellows?[14] There is no simple answer, but a few associations come to mind. It may be argued that in addition to total dialect borrowing, some apparent sound changes are in fact extreme manifestations of analogic leveling. There are perfectly good theoretical criteria to distinguish the two effects, but the evidence available does not in all actual cases permit their application so that ambiguous instances occur. Once a genuine conditioned sound change has phonemically separated an allophone, or block of allophones, from the rest, this may produce a morphophoneme. Further analogic generalizing is now possible, and, under conditions which I will not here stop to define, such generalizing may place the "new" component of the morphophoneme into positions which make the resulting morphs appear as though more sound change had taken place. A second association is more in the nature of a priori speculation. It is possible that the initial amount of phonemic split which is triggered by a bit of dialect borrowing (involving, say, a restricted and particularly vulnerable diaphone) results in a structurally weak, unsymmetrical, poorly integrated phonemic system, one in which the soft spots call for remedy. Reversal of the initial process (which would not be recoverable under most ordinary circumstances anyway) is a less likely possibility since the particular area of distribution in which the small amount of merger had occurred is now presumably the more stable portion of the unbalanced subsystem—and just for that reason, we may expect the pressure to continue in the same direction with somewhat increased vigor. Note that now we are again at the mercy of synchronic typologies—possibly of their universals, but more likely of their individual complexion. The very instances in which the widening becomes arrested halfway are cases in point. In several Algonquian languages vowels are lost in word-final position, but not much in other positions. The result is a powerfully restricted canonical shape for words.[15] Just for this reason, this is not the kind of sound change that we would expect to go on widening until it engulfs nonfinal vowels, and most certainly not to the point where these languages become vowelless—reportedly a rare, even precarious structural type.

At this point the old question arises whether or not the synchronically observable structures (here regarded in their function as targets of change) have themselves significantly changed in the course of history. Of course, our information covers a very small fraction of the history of the species, and within that fraction is monstrously uneven. There is little in it to prove that earlier ideas of "progress in language" (to quote a famous phrase) are more than ethnocentric circularities, matters of fact mistaken for matters of course. Those who point out that advances in material culture are consistently "reflected" in all the languages of the world—earlier or later, as the case may be—have had to base their argument almost entirely on nonreplacement changes, that is, on the amorphous additions and deletions which are a delight to students of general history but do not really alter the language. The more far-reaching claims are also more doubtful. The trend from so-called synthetic to so-called analytic structure may be observable in certain areas, but so is the opposite trend, sometimes even in the same language family or area. It is probably only because the Indo-European idea of progress (or degeneration) from inflection to construction, from morphology to syntax, from bound to free had become such a cliché, that the equally typical notion of "grammaticalization"—the emptying of lexically meaningful morphs (compound members, etc.) and their transformation into "function" elements—was not presented as a counteraction, although at least in a minor way it has served to build up forms that look like new inflections (e.g., the Romance adverbs in *-mente*, from *mente* 'with (such and such) a mind'; the Osco-Umbrian locatives, with former enclitic adverbs intruding into the case system; and so on). This is not saying that such a presentation would have been particularly justifiable—only that it would have been no worse than other popular attempts at interpreting the linguistic history of the species.

Greenberg, Osgood, and Saporta believe that, other things being equal, "the more uncommon a phoneme is in human speech in general, the more likely it is to be merged with another phoneme."[16] What do they mean? Aside from the question of factual support, one would like to know whether it is implied that there are only processes which eliminate "uncommon phonemes," or also others, not named, which give rise to new uncommon phonemes. (The other generalizations offered in the same list do not exclude the latter possibility.) If the former is meant, this would attribute to the human race a consistent history of uniformization, at least in point of sound structure. Would we not then have to extrapolate back to a phylogenetic babbling stage, and extrapolate forward to a radical reduction in the number of existing areal types? P. Friedrich reminds me that such strikingly aberrant traits as are revealed to the present-day typologist (say, the southern African clicks?) could then *ipso facto* be recognized as survivals—not in terms of ordinary microhistory with its mutually compensatory, *plus-ça-change-plus-c'est-la-même-chose* reshuffling, but as true fossils against a background of serious mutation.

5. Morph Histories, etc.

We must now turn to this microhistory. Of course it is made up of the same processes considered thus far: the replacements with their various patterns. (See Casagrande, 10.3.) As far as we can observe, these processes lead very rarely, if ever, to alterations of fundamental importance for the species. They do somewhat more frequently lead to structural changes which are typically either episodes in an areal trend (as are many of the more systematic transformations during the last two millennia in Indo-European or Semitic history), or, more flamboyantly, episodes in the transfer of a language from one area to another, or from a given position in one area (central, marginal) to another position (marginal, central). As we have said, the typology of such structural changes is thus constrained by the typology of possible or probable structures. The exchange which took place between Jakobson and Allen at the Eighth International Congress of Linguists furnishes two interesting viewpoints on these aspects, one sanguine and one carping.

In much ordinary language history the replacement processes function as devices for the preservation rather than for the alteration of the basic plan. They "fill gaps" left by other replacement processes or "restore a balance" which had been upset temporarily—or even only potentially, since the separate formulation of illness and cure is not infrequently only a matter of statement. Where these dramatic interpretations do not simply depend on one out of many possible phonemicizations or morphemicizations of the data, the "shifts," the "drag-chain," and "push-chain" displacements in phonemic systems, the "moves" attributed to vocabulary items on the chessboards of semantic fields, can often be shown to be concretely definable chronological realities which elucidate the dynamics of linguistic history. In dealing with them it is natural not to fix one's attention on the "emic" structure points, but on the "etic" lower-level utterance stretches that occur first at one and then at the next structure point. We have said at the start that it is in this realm that the early persistent and persuasive claims were made. We possess "general" classifications of sound change (like Grammont's) where the criteria are phonetic rather than concerned either with the replacement pattern or with the resulting structure. We possess similar classifications for semantic change by meaning content (or by grammatical "function") where the morphs, as identified according to their phonemic shape (and not the morphemes defined by their pattern of contrast!) are the heroes. These classifications may sometimes be intended as mere conveniences. More often, however, they will lay claim to some systematic or even predictive power. This is quite clear in such works as Havers' manual of "explicatory syntax" with its catalog of "conditions" and "motive forces"; or Kurylowicz' theory of analogic change; or the structuralist theories of change by Martinet and others in which a great deal is said not only about preserved structures and altered structures, but also about the movements of the particular phones (and, where attention is given to grammar and lexicon, morphs) whose shifting privileges of occurrence constitute in the aggregate the systemic reality that matters in the end.

There is wide agreement, for example, to the effect that sound changes are largely assimilatory changes. A given sequence of sound segments is often replaced by an articulation which is in some way less taxing. The same is true, as must be added, and as Martinet has in fact added, of given combinations of distinctive features occurring simultaneously. The assimilatory principle is for that reason not as neatly tied to the superficial category of "conditioned" (as against "spontaneous," that is, unconditional) sound change as some take it to be. With more and more componential analysis brought to bear, more and more presumably unconditional changes turn into conditioned ones. The difference is, of course, more important to those who advocate uniqueness for phonemic solutions. Frequently the articulatory simplifications produce "long components": sequences of consonants between vowels acquire the voicing of the vowels; sequences of back vowel syllables and front vowel syllables acquire an over-all front vowel quality; there is loss and unvoicing at the end of utterance, thereby assimilating, totally or partially, to the adjacent stretch of silence, and so on ad infinitum. I am not implying, by bringing this well-known point into the discussion so late, that assimilatory changes are not "utilized" for purposes of lasting transformations as well as for microhistorical change; but I do not think that anyone would seriously champion the idea that constant assimilatory activity leads to more and more articulatory simplicity in the languages of the world. Somehow, it seems, new "difficulties" are always created. We also encounter the notion that the assimilations constitute the speakers' (erosive) contribution to the flow of history; the hearer, striving for more redundancy and indifferent to the speakers' tendency to ease of articulation, keeps the extent of assimilation within bounds. It is clear that without quantitative controls such a pair of governing factors, located at the two extremes of a scale, has little to commend it: any sound change, by dint of its having occurred, will be shown to have carried just the right amount of erosion and of preservation. But it is possible that the numerical sophistication at which information theory aims will help make these concepts less trivial.

Kent and other scholars have observed that among the known instances there is probably more anticipatory than progressive (progressive = moving with, rather than against, the flow of speech in time) or mutual (e.g., [sk] > [š]) assimilation.[17] But attempts at finding special offsetting features in the still numerous cases of progressive assimilation have been disappointing, and there is a grave possibility that the preponderance of anticipation over "lag" is a specific areal feature characteristic of the more thoroughly studied languages. In any case, not much joy can be derived from a potential universal that presents itself in terms of a rather modest statistical lopsidedness. To be sure, a further effort was made, by Greenberg, to correlate the predilection for regressive assimilation with the reported (Sapir) synchronic predilection for suffixing: prefixes tend to be swallowed up by the regressive assimilations which originate in the core of the word.[18] It would have to be shown, however, that suffixes are not equally threatened by what is a notorious variety of regressive sound change, the anticipation of postutterance silence through merger or loss of the final portion of the word. It is quite true that lapses are also more often anticipatory than otherwise in character; but the observation of lapses is pretty much limited to language structures of one and the same type. Typologies in which word-initials rather than word-finals are morphophonemically variable or otherwise weak have not, to my knowledge, been included; and, in any event, the relationship between individual lapsing and sound change is tenuous.

It has been proposed, as a structural refinement of the doctrine of the assimilatory character of most sound changes, that the distinctive status of an articulatory quality must be taken into account when judging the probability of its functioning as a conditioning factor. Martinet has thought that "a voiced environment in which voice has no distinctive value does not under... ordinary conditions have the effect of voicing a voiceless sound and thereby neutralizing the opposition of voice";[19] but the very ordinary appearance of many a contrary case (e.g., *nt* > *nd* in Late Greek) puts a heavy burden on the term "ordinary condition." One may well feel that more evidence is needed. But in the absence of a satisfactory theory, more evidence—which can at best have statistical characteristics—is not going to create overmuch confidence. In this context we ought also to remember that there is room for nonassimilatory processes in linguistic history, too. I am not so much thinking of dissimilations which although, they are much more part of "regular sound changes" than is often asserted, may yet have special distinctive traits that make them different in kind rather than opposite in degree from the more usual processes.[20] But *hyperforms* are very much part and parcel of ordinary language history, and it is the essence of hyperforms to produce effects which run counter to phonetic plausibility. Thus, Italian *dimestico* from Latin *domesticum* presupposes an assimilatory change from *im* to *om*, with lip rounding as a "long component"—the apparent dissimilation from *o* to *i* is probably the result of dialect borrowing after the event. As usual, we feel much surer about our knowledge of the replacement histories than about such generalizations as we care to make with regard to the behavior of phones in phonemic change.

With semantic change the same problems recur in an even more drastic form. We have seen earlier how the question of "semantic laws" (that is, of the regularity of semantic change) was vitiated by the wrong parallel. If we formulate semantic changes from the morphemic point of view, they are as regular as the sound changes which indeed we do customarily state in phonemic and not in phonetic language—only we are disappointed, in the case of semantic change, by the relative emptiness of the result. (One of the reasons for this is that there is so much one-to-one replacement, without merger or split, in the lexical and grammatical field.) When we consider morphs instead of morphemes, we start having difficulties with our generalizations. Thus, it will be very hard, if not impossible, to discover any kind of predictability for the movements of individual morphs across the table of morphemes. For the very special cases of analogic change, Kurylowicz' concept of polarization, favoring the better characterized of the two competing allomorphs, is perhaps the most promising attempt. There is, I hope, no need to dwell on the weaknesses of the content-oriented classifications for semantic change; it may suffice to name metaphor as perhaps the most popular quasi universal. There is no doubt that many languages have put portions of their vocabulary through change processes which are similar in essential ways from language to language and for which the term metaphor is a fair label. But the probability that a given morph will be used "metaphorically" is a probability of the same kind (though not necessarily of the same degree) as that for a given phone to undergo a certain sound change. In a sense the chief governing factor is found to be, once again, the synchronic typology. We must not forget that the major content-labels for changes of meaning are at the same time useful in synchronic semantics. Metaphor, in fact, was a rhetorical figure long before it became a term for a class of semantic changes.

We are not surprised, therefore, at the failure to find semantic laws for morphs and their meanings in history. The search for such laws has not been fruitless—for example, Stern's work, particularly his example: "English adverbs which have acquired the sense 'rapidly' before 1300 always develop the sense 'immediately'. This happens when the adverb is used to qualify a verb, etc."[21] Note especially to what extent the "regularity" of this law rests on the semantic (i.e., the morphemic, and not the morphic) identification of the entities affected. But if we are to learn more about the general properties of semantic change, some of the all-too-familiar concepts will have to be abandoned.

6. Conclusion

What is needed in the study of diachronic universals is, of course, more widely based historical and comparative work than was available for many decades; and a great deal of such work is now being done. Furthermore, it must be understood that change has been seen, for many generations of scholarship, in three different ways: as a pattern of (superficial addition or deletions, and of) replacement; as a process culminating in the production of new structures; and as the Saussurian "chessboard" movement, often to no lasting avail, of the counters as they are recognized by their acoustic, articulatory, or otherwise measurable characteristics. Our interest naturally centers on the second and on the third conception of change more than on the first. It is possible that new approaches like transformational grammar which promise to unify synchronic typology in a hitherto unsuspected sense may also bring new principles of importance to an understanding of the universals of change.

ACKNOWLEDGMENTS

In addition to helpful comments by Charles F. Hockett, to be mentioned in the notes, I would like to thank Joseph H. Greenberg, Einar Haugen, Roman Jakobson, and Rulon S. Wells, who have put me in their debt by suggesting changes.

Notes

1. Schwyzer, *Historical Greek Grammar* 1.234ff.
2. See S. C. Gudschinsky, *Word* 12.175ff. On Charmey, see Göttingen *Nachrichten*, Ph.-Hist. Klasse 1929, 195-214.
3. Thanks are due to Charles F. Hockett for his searching comments on this and other points. While none has been ignored, it is impossible here to discuss, adopt, or try to refute all of his comments in full. He takes exception to the notion of quasi-translation as used here, emphasizing that language is a set of habits and not a collection of "texts." But "is" is a difficult word. We are only, after all, trying to analyze the historian's approach, which has essentially been one of matching ("comparing") parts of two or more bodies of utterance; it is not likely that that approach should be irrelevant for an understanding of the habits in question, even granting that habits and texts are things apart. Hockett further objects that that *kinds* of change ought to be rigorously distinguished from *mechanisms* of change in a manner which, if I understand him correctly, goes somewhat beyond the position taken in his *Course* (ch. 52 and elsewhere). This issue needs a full debate.
4. Namely, in economy (Hockett).
5. For the sake of the argument, these words are treated as though they had one morpheme each. Actually, *in-*, *-wit*, *con-* may be said to take part in conditioned replacement processes.
6. "The first and foremost," Hockett suggests, "... is that *replacement occurs*. This is not trivial. There are communicative systems in which it does not, or in which it takes place by mechanisms so totally different ... that the difference is worthy of note."

7. The latter insofar as their relationship to the morphemes are concerned. The morphs themselves are to be thought of as phoneme stretches.
8. Sound changes can apparently not be entirely predicted from internal, systemic stresses and strains, nor can they be explained as the effect of scatter around a target or norm; they have direction and are in that sense specific, much like other happenings in history. The factors which make for prestige differentials, for the development of regional centers, for demographic change, etc., are specific and unique (i.e., not redeemed by the greater simplicity of language structure as contrasted with the often-invoked "world at large") in the sense required.
9. *Language Change and Linguistic Reconstruction*, 38 and 75f.
10. *Indogermanische Forschungen* 45. 105ff.
11. *Language* 33. 538ff.
12. *Psycholinguistics*, 148.
13. Fred W. Householder's watchfulness has saved this sentence from serious misformulation.
14. See Joos, *Readings in Linguistics*, 376.
15. Restricted insofar as vowels are excluded. On the other hand, after the change, "words could end in any of a much larger number of consonants and consonant clusters"—larger, that is, than that of the four vowels (Hockett).
16. *Psycholinguistics*, 148.
17. *Language* 12. 245ff.
18. *Essays in Linguistics*, ch. 8.
19. *Économie des changements phonétiques*, 111.
20. The doctrine of the special unruliness of dissimilations, metatheses, etc., occupies a peculiar position in the history of linguistics. But, in fact, even the dissimilations of liquids familiar from Indo-European and Semitic are much less untypical than they are said to be. They are only in part progressive; their "regularity" is quite considerable (often the counterexamples occur in paradigms only), and even if it were true that graduality is a requirement of ordinary regular sound change, quite a few dissimilatory processes (e.g., the one known as Grassmann's law) may easily be thought of as taking place gradually, while some nondissimilatory and nonmetathetic changes would seem to preclude such a picture. See Hoenigswald, *Phonetica* 11. 202-15.
21. *Meaning and Change of Meaning*, 190.

CHAPTER 3

ASSUMPTIONS ABOUT NASALS: A SAMPLE STUDY IN PHONOLOGICAL UNIVERSALS

CHARLES A. FERGUSON

Center for Applied Linguistics

1. Introduction

Although linguists hesitate to make statements of universal (panchronic, cross-language) validity about the details of phonological structures, they often operate either in their own field work or in their evaluation of others' descriptions as though they held certain assumptions of this kind. Certain common features of the sound systems of human languages are so fundamental, of course, that linguists would exclude from the label "language" a signaling system that lacked them. Such universals may be regarded as definitional; that is, they are implicit in the linguist's concept of language, whether included in his formal definitions or not. For example, the linguist would find it inconceivable that a language should operate without phonemic contrasts, without a small set of distinctive features (or phonetic and distributional classes) in terms of which phonological elements of a segmental sort could be identified, or without differences in frequency of occurrence of such phonological elements.

2. Value of Nondefinitional Assumptions

The present paper is an attempt to formulate several nondefinitional assumptions which the author holds in one section of phonology. Most of them are probably shared with many other linguists; some may be of little validity. No attempt will be made to provide a theoretical framework for the assumptions, but the formulation of a set of statements like this may prove of value in at least three ways.

First of all there is the advantage gained in any field of science from making unspoken assumptions explicit. This process may reveal mistaken or mutually inconsistent assumptions, or may give new insights into the theory of the particular science.

Second, there is the value which universal, nondefinitional statements have for linguistic typology. For example, it is a widely held assumption that a language never has a greater number of phonemic contrasts in the vowels of unstressed syllables than it has in stressed syllables.[1] Any attempt to formulate this assumption carefully and to investigate its validity empirically soon shows that this point classifies languages with distinctive stress into three main types: (1) Languages, typified by Spanish, in which stress has no important effect on the quality of vowels. In languages of this kind, apart from accidental gaps in distribution, there is only one system of vowels appearing in both stressed and unstressed syllables. (2) Languages, like English and Russian, in which stress has the effect of lengthening a vowel and enhancing its characteristic coloration. In such languages the stressed vowels are clearer, and there are in effect two vowel systems, one for stressed syllables and one of fewer contrasts for unstressed syllables, always with some slight tendency for analogical formations to create unstressed vowels from the stressed system (e.g., Russian /e/) or to transfer a neutral vowel of the unstressed system to the stressed system (e.g., English /ɨ/). (3) Languages, like certain Tajik dialects[2] and certain varieties of Syrian Arabic, in which stress has a leveling effect on vowels. In such languages the stressed vowels are not greatly lengthened and are less clear than the unstressed vowels. These languages usually have a greater number of vowel contrasts in unstressed position.[3]

The third value of the formulation of phonological universals lies in the materials it provides for extralinguistic treatment. A nondefinitional universal in linguistics may serve either as an exemplification of principles of some other field of knowledge or as a suggestion toward reformulation of such principles. For example, it is commonly assumed that extensive voiced-voiceless neutralization in a language takes place most commonly in final position and never intervocalically.[4] Or again, in diachronic studies it is generally assumed that a phoneme of [s] type may change to one of [h] type but not vice versa, or of the [k] type to [t] but not vice versa, and so on. Linguistic statements like these suggest interpretation in physiological or psychological terms.

An experienced linguist working in the field of phonology probably operates with many assumptions which could be identified and formulated. This may be shown by the ease with which one can construct an artificial phonemic system which would seem to be perfectly adequate for communication purposes but which the practicing linguist would regard as implausible.[5]

3. Phonological Assumptions — Nasal Phenomena

A full list of phonological assumptions could run well over a hundred. The list of fifteen statements that follows (identified by Roman numerals) is limited to nasal phenomena and is offered as a sample.[6] Three of the statements are diachronic, two are synchronic frequency statements, and the remainder are synchronic existence statements. The statements are generally explained in all-or-none terms, although most are probably only statistically valid; that is, the probability of "exceptions" is very low, and a language showing an exception may be regarded in some sense as abnormal or pathological.

Nasal phonemes are of four general types, which are called here primary nasal consonants, secondary nasal consonants, nasal vowels, and nasal syllabics. These types will be defined, and universal statements will be listed where most appropriate under each type. Two kinds of nasal phenomena have been excluded from the listing: (1) nasal or nasalized allophones or phonemes the most characteristic allophones of which are nonnasal, and (2) prosodic features of nasality. The first are felt to be outside the system of nasal phonemes and not covered by the kinds of universal statements given here. The second are usually analyzable alternatively in terms of segmental phonemes, and in that case the universal statements made here are held to be valid.

3.1. *Primary nasal consonants* (*PNC*)

Definition: A PNC is a phoneme of which the most characteristic allophone is a voiced nasal stop, that is, a sound produced by a complete oral stoppage (e.g., apical, labial), velic opening, and vibration of the vocal cords.

When, in a given language, there are no nasal phonemes of other types with ranges of phonetic values which might conflict with the PNC's, a PNC may have allophones without full oral stoppage, with incomplete velic closure, or without voicing. Even in such a language, however, a PNC in phonological positions or communication situations calling for maximum clarity will have the normal voiced nasal quality. In some languages the PNC's function is in part like that of the vowel phonemes of the language; for example, it may constitute syllable peaks or bear accents, but this is always in addition to consonantal function.

I. Every language has at least one PNC in its inventory. (Complete absence of nasals is reported for three Salishan languages[7] where the PNC's assumed for an earlier period are said to have become voiced stops.)

II. If in a given language there is only one PNC, it is /n/, that is, its most characteristic allophone is apical. When there is no other nasal phoneme in the language with a range of phonetic values which might conflict with the /n/, the /n/ may have labial, velar, or other allophones, but in positions or situations of maximum clarity it has the normal apical value. In the rare instances where a language has only /m/, there seems always to be an apical [n] as an allophone of something else. (In Hockett's analysis of Winnebago [n] is /r/ plus nasality;[8] in Ladefoged's analysis of Yoruba [n] is /l/ next to nasal vowels.[9] Examples of languages with /n/ as the only PNC are chiefly in the Western Hemisphere, for example, Tlingit, a number of Iroquoian languages, Arapaho.

III. If in a given language there are only two PNC's, the other one is /m/, that is, its most characteristic allophone is labial. Languages with /m n/ are extremely common, including examples from Indo-European, Semitic, American Indian (various families), Altaic, Caucasic.

IV. In a given language, the number of PNC's is never greater than the number of series of obstruents. For example, if the language has stops and affricates in four positions (e.g., /p t č k/) the number of PNC's will be four or fewer (e.g., / m n ñ ɳ/, /m n ɳ/, /m n ñ/, or /m n/), never five or more. A number of different arrangements are possible, for example:

Bengali	p t ṭ č k (grouped by a brace)	Nuer	p ṱ t c k
	m n ŋ		m ṋ n ñ ŋ
French	p t k	Fiji	t k
	m n ñ		β ð
			m n ŋ

V. When in a given language there is extensive neutralization among the PNC's, this occurs in prejunctural and/or preconsonantal positions. (Examples include Spanish, Classical Greek; Trubetzkoy cites a number of others.[10])

3.2. *Secondary nasal consonants (SNC)*

Definition: An SNC is a nasal consonant phoneme the most characteristic allophone of which is *not* a simple voiced nasal. In many cases a phone type which may be analyzed as an SNC may alternatively be analyzed as a cluster (e.g., /hn/, /mb/). The statements made here refer to languages where the monophonematic analysis is required either because of contrast with clusters or because of striking parallels of distribution. At least six subtypes occur:

voiceless nasals	(e.g., Kuanyama[11])
aspirated nasals	(e.g., Marathi[12])
glottalized nasals	(e.g., Chontal (Oaxaca)[13])
palatalized nasals	(e.g., Russian)

"emphatic" nasals	(e.g., Syrian Arabic[14])
prenasalized (voiced) stops	(e.g., Fiji[15])
"nasalized clicks"	(e.g., Zulu[16])

VI. No language has SNC's unless it also has one or more PNC's. (Corollary to I.)

VII. In a given language the number of SNC's is never greater than the number of PNC's.

VIII. In a given language the frequency of occurrence of SNC's is always less than that of PNC's.

IX. SNC's are, apart from borrowing and analogical formations, always the result of diachronic developments from clusters. (This assumption is based on the very few cases when the history of SNC's is well known. It is quite probable that other sources exist; in particular, it seems likely that prenasalized stops have developed from voiced stops in certain languages.)

3.3. *Nasal vowels (NV)*

Definition: An NV is a phoneme the most characteristic allophone of which has oral and velic opening and vibration of the vocal cords. When in a given language there are no phonemes with conflicting phonetic values, an NV may have allophones with oral closure, velic closure, or lack of voicing, but clarity positions and situations have normal nasal vowels. (Sample languages: French, Bengali, Taos.)

X. No language has NV's unless it also has one or more PNC's. (Corollary to I.)

XI. In a given language the number of NV's is never greater than the number of nonnasal vowel phonemes.

XII. In a given language the frequency of occurrence of NV's is always less than that of nonnasal vowels. (Reliable frequency counts of phonemes exist for very few languages with nasal vowels. One small count for Bengali[17] shows an oral-nasal vowel ratio of 50:1.)

XIII. When in a given language there is extensive neutralization of NV's with oral vowels, this occurs next to nasal consonants. (Two well-documented examples of this kind of neutralization are Bengali[18] and Yoruba.[19])

XIV. NV's, apart from borrowing and analogical formations, always result from loss of a PNC. (This assumption is based on a small number of languages where the history of the NV's is known. These are chiefly Indo-European—[Indic, Slavic, Romance]—and it is possible that this assumption will have to be modified when more is found out about the history of NV's in other families. One case where an NV may be of quite different origin is in Iroquoian, where one of the NV's posited for the protolanguage seems, on considerations of internal reconstruction, to have derived from earlier /a/ + /i/ or sequences like /awa/.)

3.4. *Nasal syllabics*

Definition: A nasal syllabic is a nasal phoneme which patterns like a syllable rather than like a consonant or vowel in the language (e.g., Japanese /n̄/,[20] Ewe, Xhosa /m/[21]).

XV. A nasal syllabic phoneme, apart from borrowings and analogical formations, always results from loss of a vowel.

Notes

1. Cf. Trubetzkoy, *Principes de phonologie*, 255–256 (Paris, 1949).
2. Cf. Sokolova, *Fonetika tadžikskogo jazyka*, 19 (Moscow, 1949).
3. It is interesting to note that in the Lebanese Arabic spoken in Marjayoun, where the *i-u* contrast which has disappeared in stressed position in much of Lebanese Arabic is still present, the phonetic distance between /i/ and /u/ is less than it is for the *i-u* contrast in unstressed syllables.
4. A fully satisfactory formulation of this would be considerably more complicated and would have to take into account the very rare instances of initial neutralization (as asserted by Trubetzkoy for one variety of Mordvinian) and initial-and-final neutralization (asserted for Kirghiz). Cf. Trubetzkoy, *op. cit.*, 254–255.

5. The author has on a number of occasions reported to fellow linguists a system summarized in the following list of phoneme symbols: č k k^w v s ž ð m' n' ñ' ŋ' l λ y ʔ ü ü· æ æ· ʌ ʌ. ῐ ɔ̃ ũ. The reaction runs from mild surprise to disbelief.
6. Two brief treatments of nasal universals are known to the author, Trubetzkoy, *op. cit.*, 189–196, and Hockett, *Manual of Phonology*, 119–120 (Baltimore, 1955).
7. Cf. Hockett, *op. cit.*, 119.
8. Cf. *ibid.*, 80–81. Even in the absence of further evidence Hockett's analysis seems less convincing than a more traditional one of /n/ and /r/ as separate phonemes; other treatments of Winnebago recognize /m/, /n/, and /r/, with either an additional /n_2/ or certain morphophonemic interchange between /n/ and /r/.
9. Cf. Ladefoged, *A Phonetic Study of West African Languages*, 23–24 (Cambridge, 1964).
10. Cf. Trubetzkoy, *op. cit.*, 193.
11. Cf. Westermann and Ward, *Practical Phonetics*, 65 (London, 1957).
12. Cf. Lambert, *Introduction to the Devanagari Script* (London, 1953).
13. Cf. *IJAL* 16:35 (1950).
14. Cf. *Language* 30:566-567 (1954).
15. Cf. Hockett, *op. cit.*, 124.
16. Cf. Doke, *The Phonetics of the Zulu Language* (Witwatersrand, 1926).
17. Cf. *Language* 36:51 (1960).
18. Cf. *Language* 36:44 (1960).
19. Cf. Ward, *An Introduction to the Yoruba Language*, 13 (Cambridge, 1952).
20. Cf. *Language* 26:112 (1950).
21. Cf. Doke, *The Southern Bantu Languages*, 92 (London, 1954).

CHAPTER 4

PHONEME DISTRIBUTION AND LANGUAGE UNIVERSALS

SOL SAPORTA

University of Washington

1. Language Universals Closely Related to Language Typology

It is clear that the problem of language universals and that of linguistic typology are closely related. Indeed, the two are merely different sides of the same coin. The typological statement that there are languages with a feature *X* and languages without *X* is only as meaningful as the identification and definition of *X* in the abstract, that is, independent of any language. Thus, to say, for example, that all (or many) languages have 'a contrast between nasal and oral consonants' presupposes a universal definition, for terms like *nasal* and *oral.* Universal definitions are, then, a prerequisite for typology, *universal* in this sense meaning 'universally available,' that is, belonging to some metatheory of linguistics.[1] Furthermore, a similar statement to the effect that languages with feature *X* also have feature *Y* is a statement about language universals which may be viewed as a special kind of datum resulting from a typological analysis. Thus, typological classification is a prerequisite for a statement of language universals, where now *universal* means 'universally present.'

There have been two types of objections to work in language typology. The first resolves itself into a lack of criteria for evaluating alternative classifications. The number of possible classifications for any number of languages soon gets large; for the languages of the world the possibilities are unmanageable.

However, the conclusion that consequently any choice is arbitrary seems unnecessarily pessimistic. The fact that one can always find one feature to justify grouping two languages together does not imply that all classifications are equally useful. We view a typology as a device which yields predictions of this type: Given two languages *A* and *B* which are assigned to one type by virtue of sharing a certain feature *X*, and given the occurrence of another feature *Y* in *A*, we predict its occurrence in *B*. Note that this is nothing more or less than the positing of a special kind of universal of the type $X \rightarrow Y$;[2] and, in fact, the most useful typology is exactly the one which provides a maximum of such universals.

The second objection is based on disagreement as to what terms properly constitute a part of the metatheory, since, as we have suggested, some universal definitions are a prerequisite for typology. Now there are two types of terms in the metatheory: those of substance and those of form. The first are terms like *nasal*, *stop*, *length*, etc., or on the level of meaning, like *past*, *dual*, *animate*, etc., which are defined in either phonetic or semantic terms. The formal terms, however, do not require any such 'external' reference. Thus, a term like *infix* is presumably a formal term in the metatheory, that is: (1) universally available—definable without reference to a particular language—and (2) formal—definable without reference to phonetics or semantics. The question arises as to whether a term like *noun*, on the other hand, is a formal term in the metatheory. Most definitions of *noun* are either semantics-oriented (the 'person, place, or thing' type of definition), or specific-language-oriented (the 'noun-in-English' type of definition).[3] It is precisely this fact that has hampered work in typological classification and language universals on the grammatical level. The semantic definition seems inappropriate, or at least undesirably imprecise, in a discipline which claims to be formal and rigorous; the specific-language-based definition makes any cross-language identification on formal terms impossible or, at best, arbitrary. Similarly, the statement that two languages both have /p/ has little meaning. The statement that they both have phonemes which are distinctively voiceless, bilabial, and stops is useful because the last three terms can be given physical (articulatory or acoustic) definitions with considerable precision. In other words, the fact that phonological typologies have proved more feasible than grammatical ones is in part due to the advanced status of theories of universal phonetics as compared to semantics. In any case, an important prerequisite for a precise investigation of language typology and language universals is specifying the terms of the metatheory and the bases for their inclusion, that is, whether their definitions are purely formal or not.

So far, then, we have proposed three two-way distinctions: universal/specific, form/substance, and phonology/grammar. We can illustrate the possibilities as follows, filling in those boxes for which we have cited examples:

	PHONOLOGY		GRAMMAR	
	Substance	*Form*	*Substance*	*Form*
Universal	nasal		animate	infix
Specific				noun

In reference to the figure, there is no need to subdivide the columns headed *Substance*, since phonetic and semantic terms are by definition universals and not specific. However, any such term may theoretically reappear as a formal term in a specific language and, rarely perhaps, as a formal term in the metatheory. Thus the term *vowel* (or *vocoid*) defined in terms of the presence of a certain acoustic or articulatory feature may yield the same class of phenomena, either for a specific language or for all languages, as the definition of vowels as 'the minimum repertory of phonemes such that at least one of these phonemes must occur in every word.'[4] We are familiar with the case where semantically defined terms in the metatheory correspond to formally defined classes in a specific langauge, since it is these terms which yield the familiar grammatical categories, such as the contrasts *animate/inanimate* or *singular/plural*.

But there is a group of terms, such as *endocentric construction*, or *immediate constituent*, which do not readily fit into such a classification as the one proposed here. These terms have usually been identified with the grammatical aspect of language, but this restriction is probably unwarranted, since they seem rather to apply to certain types of rules in a description. A language 'has' *endocentric constructions* if it has rules of the form:

$$X = A \langle B \rangle \text{ or } X = \langle A \rangle B$$

But A and B may represent phonological terms, say, *consonant* and *vowel*, as well as grammatical terms, like *adjective* and *noun*. In short, certain terms are universally available because they refer to aspects of the models of description.[5]

Now, some but not all of the features which are universally available are also universally present. It seems necessary to distinguish, however, those which are present by definition (universally necessary) from those which are not, though the basis for such a distinction is vague. Though every language has a contrast between consonants and vowels, presumably we would not use the absence of such a contrast as sufficient evidence for excluding a particular system of communication from being a language. On the other hand, a system of vocal signs all of which were onomatopoeic would be suspect, violating the requirements of arbitrariness which characterizes language by definition.

We now ask the following sets of questions about the terms *phoneme*, *syllable*, and *phonological word:* (1*a*) Are they terms in the metatheory; that is, can we define *phoneme*, or can we only define *phoneme-in-L*, where *L* is some language? (1*b*) If they are in the metatheory, we ask: Are they formal terms, that is, definable without reference to phonetics? (2*a*) If they are in the metatheory, that is, universally available, we ask: Are they universally present? (2*b*) If they are universally present, we ask whether they are present by definition, that is, universally necessary, or not. To say that they are necessary will mean that they are universally present no matter what model of description is used.

The investigation of these questions presupposes some framework within which the nature of phonological statements can be made explicit.

2. Grammar as a Generative Theory

Adopted here is the view, formulated most clearly by Chomsky,[6] that a grammar is a theory which ideally generates all and only the grammatical sequences of a particular language. A phonological description or generative phonology describes all and only the phonologically acceptable sequences, including the as yet unobserved ones, such as English *fet* but not *fte*. The adequacy of the description is determined in part by the accuracy of its predictions about the acceptability of unobserved sequences.

Chomsky has demonstrated that three models underlie generative grammars or, phrased differently, that there are three different kinds of rules: a Markov-process or finite-state rule, an immediate-constituent or phrase-structure rule, and a transformation rule.

Now, we are concerned here with two notions. The first is the output of such a grammar, that is, the sequences to be generated. The ideal end-product of a phonological description is the smallest unit *X* about which it can be said that all combinations of phonologically grammatical *X*'s are themselves phonologically grammatical. This unit may be called a *phonological word.* Any language which has a phonology has a phonological description, and any description has an output, so that this unit is present in all languages by definition, that is, universally necessary.

Now the acceptable sequences, to the extent that they constitute a finite set, can always be listed. But we are presumably unwilling to accept such a list as the most adequate description for any natural language. That is, we insist that all languages have words which are partially similar in sound, in the form of minimal pairs or rhyme, alliteration, or something of the sort. Consequently any adequate phonology will have to describe the acceptable sequences as combinations of recurring elements or *primes.* During the Conference, I suggested that, for the purpose of stating permissible phonological sequences, the inventory of these recurring elements would correspond closely enough to what we usually call *phonemes* to warrant applying that term.[7] I did not make clear enough, however, that for stating and comparing the phonological inventory of languages independent of the distribution, *features* are more likely to provide a useful basis; typological statements about inventories are inevitably phrased in phonetic terms. In any case, the present argument attempts to demonstrate only that any phonological description must have two kinds of units, one to be the output and the other the elements which combine to form this output.

Now, one difference between a finite-state grammar, on the one hand, and a phrase-structure or transformation grammar, on the other, is the introduction in the latter of intermediate levels between the output and the primes, levels like *onset*, *coda*, and *syllable*, etc. Specifically, *syllable* is to phonology what *phrase* is to grammar, namely a unit intermediate between the output and the primes. Thus, *phoneme*, *syllable*, and *phonological word* are all formal terms in the metatheory, that is, universally available. But it is, in theory, possible to have a language in which all words are exactly one syllable long, in which case the distinction between phonological word and syllable disappears. Similarly, if there were a language in which all syllables were exactly one phoneme long, the distinction between syllable and phoneme would disappear (and, incidentally, so would the distinction between vowel and consonant).[8] Phoneme and phonological word are, therefore, universally present by definition, that is, universally necessary. Syllable, if it is universally present, is so by empirical observation. In other words, to say that a language 'has' syllables is to say that in stating the distribution of phonemes an immediate-constituent model will prove simpler than a finite-state model.

Distributional statements are often phrased in phonetic terms. Elsewhere,[9] we have suggested a universal based on such phonetic statements, namely that the frequency of any C_1C_2 would be a function of the difference between C_1 and C_2 with both extreme similarity and extreme difference tending to be avoided. It is the main point of this discussion that phonological typologies have rarely explored purely formal bases for classification. I do not necessarily imply that these are more fruitful, only that they are different and that it is appropriate that they be investigated.

Hereafter, *universal*, meaning 'universally present,' is used in the broadest sense to include all phenomena of other-than-chance frequency. Ideally, merely a cataloguing of such frequencies would be inadequate without some rationale leading to the identification of what the other-than-chance factors were, the latter often being determined by nonlinguistic considerations. Thus, for example, the frequency of diphthongs in Spanish[10] is a function of stress, so that diphthongs are more likely to occur in stressed syllables than in unstressed. To what extent this applies in other languages is an open question, but some physiological analysis of the relationship between the physical bases of stress and the duration of a vocalic nucleus would presumably provide a basis for suspecting that such a situation is the rule rather than the exception. In short, the most interesting hypotheses are those which relate regularities in linguistic data to regularities elsewhere.

During the Conference this question came up several times in connection with the quotation from Bloomfield that 'useful generalizations ... are inductive.'[11] Some of the participants felt, however, that the most suggestive hypotheses about universals are those which follow from our definition of language as human behavior and as being subject to laws governing such behavior. Indeed, the question of how many languages constitute an adequate sample for a generalization is not a linguistic problem at all, but rather a statistical one.

3. Hypotheses Illustrating Possibilities of Generalization in the Area of Phoneme Sequences

Several tentative hypotheses are presented here. Underlying them may be a general principle of economy whereby the presence of the complex pattern implies the presence of the more simple one. These hypotheses are presented purely by way of illustration of the possibilities of generalization in the area of phoneme sequences.

> *Hypothesis 1.* In languages with both dissolvable and non-dissolvable medial clusters, the former will be significantly more frequent than the latter. (A dissolvable cluster is defined as a sequence whose first part occurs in final position and whose second part occurs in initial position.)

Hypothesis 2. In languages with phonemic stress, the number of phonemic contrasts in stressed syllables will be greater than or equal to the number of phonemic contrasts in unstressed syllables.

Hypothesis 3. The presence of C_1C_2- makes -C_2C_1 as likely as or more likely than -C_1C_2.

Hypothesis 4. For languages with phonemic stress, the presence of n unstressed syllables flanking a stressed syllable implies the presence of $n-1$ unstressed syllables.

Now, there may indeed be languages where Hypothesis 4 is violated and the limitation on this hypothesis may serve to formulate the relation between universals and typology in a different way. Given a general principle such as the one about a more complex → a less complex, which in spite of wide application is not, strictly speaking, a universal, it seems reasonable to suggest that precisely this limitation would provide the basis for a fruitful typological classification. In other words, languages which violate Hypothesis 4 form a type. We posit that these languages will tend to share other features as well, and furthermore that it is just such a clustering of features which characterizes a useful typology. In other words, a good candidate for a diagnostic feature upon which to base a classification is any case where there seems to be a limitation on some general principle which can be established on (physio- or psycho-) logical grounds, the assumption being that deviations in such cases are more likely to affect other aspects of linguistic structure.

It is of some importance to note that the degree of error in typological and universal statements can be no less than the extent to which we permit truly alternative, that is, nonconvertible, solutions.[12] Furthermore, it is not enough, for example, that the unit-phoneme versus cluster analyses of affricates be convertible in some sense. They must, in fact, be converted before any precise statements can be made which relate to numbers of phonemes, types and frequency of clusters, etc. However, once the form of a phonological description is agreed on, evaluation criteria become feasible, and we can eliminate some portion of the nonunique solutions.

Besides the purely phonological types of relationships explored earlier, there are those between phonology and morphology which deserved to be investigated. For example, consider the following data on the length of morphs in phonemes in Spanish:[13]

Number of Phonemes	*Number of Different Morphs*
0	6
1	59
2	97
3	307
4	387
5	327
6	261
7	143
8	64
9	19
10	4
11	1
12	2
13	1
14	1
	1679

The sample is a list of morphs, and it is by no means clear to what extent the results are generalizable to texts.[14] Nevertheless, there is a regularity in the fact that the distribution yields a one-peak curve with the mean (4.4) near the peak. It is not clear that such a distribution would result by chance alone and, if not, what factor other than chance might be operating to produce such a distribution. Nevertheless, one cannot help wondering whether or not such a distribution is universal and, if not, what other factors correlate with different distributions.

Another relation which suggests itself is that between the length of morphs and number of phonemes in the inventory.

Hypothesis 5. The mean length of morphs will be inversely related to the number of phonemes in the inventory.[15]

4. Conclusion

One last thought: There is no reason to include only rules of dependency in a statement of language universals. It is just as interesting to point out factors which are independent. We will not be surprised to find that questions of phonemic inventory have no relation to the presence or absence of certain grammatical categories, say, that the presence of a voiced/voiceless distinction in stops is independent of the presence of a category of person in verbs. This is merely a trivial example of the general rule of the arbitrariness of the linguistic sign, that is, the independence of sound and sense. However, it might be of some interest to find that there is no relation between, say, the number of vowels and the number of consonants, either in the inventory, or in permissible sequences. This would, of course, be a peculiar use of the term *universal*, but such statements result from exactly the same procedures which yield statements about the other-than-chance cooccurrence of features.

Notes

1. Cf. Fred W. Householder, "On linguistic terms," in Sol Saporta (ed.), *Readings in Psycholinguistics* (New York, 1961), pp. 15–25. The author's research is supported in part by grant M 2385 from the National Institutes of Health, Public Health Service, and by grants G2502 and G5555 from the National Science Foundation.
2. The symbol → is to be read 'implies the presence of (but not vice versa).' Rulon Wells pointed out during the Conference that every hypothesis of the form $X \rightarrow Y$ had a diachronic counterpart —namely, given a language with X and no Y, we predict either the disappearance of X or the appearance of Y.
3. Householder now suggests the following as a sketch of such a definition:

   "(*a*) If a language L has a favorite sentence-type of two parts (X and Y) such that personal names occur more frequently as all or the nucleus of one part (say X) than of the other (Y), then X may be called 'noun phrase.'

"(*b*) If there is a (syntactically or morphologically defined) form-class which regularly occurs as head of 'noun phrase', but less often (or never) as head of *Y*, then the members of this form-class are 'nouns.' "

Even the preceding includes one term, *personal names*, which requires some purely formal bases for identification.

See now, however, a more meaningful discussion of such notions by Jerrold J. Katz and Paul M. Postal, *An Integrated Theory of Linguistic Descriptions* (Cambridge, 1964).

4. C. E. Bazell, *Linguistic Form* (Istanbul, 1953), pp. 47-48. A number of the participants in the Conference pointed out that, in fact, the two definitions do not yield the same classes for all languages. Hockett, who commented in writing, cites Bella Coola as an example of a language which has "utterances without vowels." Householder suggests that "if a language has all 'words' of phonetic CVC form, then one V is predictable (and therefore non-phonemic), and the statement will not be true." This is an example of the effect of nonunique solutions on any cross-language comparison.
5. In the original version of this paper, I suggested these were formal terms, presumably in the grammar, but I prefer to modify this view now.
6. Cf. Noam Chomsky, *Syntactic Structures* ('s-Gravenhage, 1957), and "Three Models for the Description of Language," *IRE Transactions on Information Theory*, 1T-2, No. 3. 113-124 (1956). The relevance of these models for phonological descriptions is suggested in Sol Saporta and Heles Contreras, *A Phonological Grammar of Spanish* (Seattle, 1962). Recent work in generative phonology has made clear the need for modification of the view suggested here. See, for example, Morris Halle, "Phonology in Generative Grammar," *Word* 18 (1962), 54-72.
7. The correspondence will not be perfect. It is conceivable, and for some languages perhaps inevitable, that the elements will occasionally correspond, on the one hand, to features and, on the other, to clusters. [Indeed, recent work in generative phonology points out the weakness of this position. The relevance of features in distribution was unexplored in this paper. Similarly, the phonological segments referred to as phonemes are not identical to the now classical position regarding segmentation.]
8. In his written comments, Hockett suggests that "there are languages where one does not need both *phoneme* and *syllable*," and quite correctly points out that "in such languages it is purely a matter of convenience whether one drops the one or the other term."

He concludes, however, that consequently neither unit is a universal. Jakobson, during the Conference seemed to propose, on the contrary, that both *phoneme* and *syllable* were universals and that any distinction is unwarranted. However, there seems to be no a priori reason for positing both, and this suggests that they are entities of a different sort. Languages of the type Hockett mentions are only one kind of evidence that they are different.

9. Sol Saporta, "Frequency of Consonant Clusters," *Language* 31. 25–30 (1955). See, too, Kathryn C. Keller and Sol Saporta, "Frequency of consonant clusters in Chontal," *IJAL* 23. 28–35 (1957); G. L. Bursill-Hall, "Consonant clusters in French," *JCLA* 2. 66-77 (1956); John B. Carroll, "The assessment of phoneme cluster frequencies," *Language* 34. 267-278 (1958).
10. Sol Saporta and Rita Cohen, "The distribution and relative frequency of Spanish diphthongs," *Romance Philology* 11. 371-377 (1958).
11. Leonard Bloomfield, *Language* (New York, 1933), p. 20, cited with apparent approval in the work papers by Hockett and Ullmann.
12. Fred Householder proposed a number of plausible phonemic solutions which affected the validity of certain hypotheses. For example, Hypothesis 3 is almost certainly false for English if one posits /-pl/ in *apple*, etc.
13. Posing the question in these terms assumes an item-and-arrangement model of morphemics. However, some such questions can be framed for any model. For an item-and-process model one could determine the length in morphophonemes of (the basic form of) morphemes.
14. Actually, the sample is restricted to those morphemes with more than one alternant. Sol Saporta, "Morpheme alternants in Spanish," in Henry R. Kahane and Angelina Pietrangeli (eds.), *Structural Studies on Spanish Themes* (Salamanca, 1959), pp. 15–162.
15. Roman Jakobson pointed out a number of "compensatory" alternatives which would relate to a small phonemic inventory: (1) either the morphs might be longer than usual, or (2) a larger than average percentage of possible combinations are in fact utilized, or (3) there are a larger number of homonyms. William Gedney suggested that the presence of phonemic tone or stress might be particularly relevant in any precise formulation of this hypothesis.

CHAPTER 5

SOME UNIVERSALS OF GRAMMAR WITH PARTICULAR REFERENCE TO THE ORDER OF MEANINGFUL ELEMENTS

JOSEPH H. GREENBERG

Stanford University

1. Introduction

The tentative nature of the conclusions set forth here should be evident to the reader. Without much more complete sampling of the world's languages, the absence of exceptions to most of the universals asserted here cannot be fully assured. As indicated by the title, attention has been concentrated largely, but by no means exclusively, on questions concerning morpheme and word order. The reason for this choice was that previous experience suggested a considerable measure of orderliness in this particular aspect of grammar. In the body of this paper a number of universals are proposed. A large proportion of these are implicational; that is, they take the form, "given *x* in a particular language, we always find *y*." When nothing further is said, it is understood that the converse, namely, "given *y*, we always find *x*," does not hold. Where the two sets of characteristics are binary, the typical distribution in a tetrachoric table is a zero as one of the four entries.[1] From the point of view of scientific methodology, there is nothing to apologize for in such results, and this is so for two reasons. First, the lowest-level laws as described in manuals of scientific method take precisely this form.[2] Second, what seem to be non-implicational universals about language are in fact tacitly implicational since they are implied by the definitional characteristics of language.[3] Further, to assert the definitional characteristics themselves is obviously tautologous.

It is perhaps worth while to point out that a number of universals of the second type—that is, those implied by the definitional characteristics of language—although not usually formally stated in this paper, are in fact involved in the notion of the general comparability of languages in the grammatical sphere which underlies the specific statements found here. For example, a whole series of universals in the usual sense are assumed in such a statement as the following: If a language has verb-subject-object as its basic word order in main declarative clauses, the dependent genitive always follows the governing noun. It is here assumed, among other things, that all languages have subject-predicate constructions, differentiated word classes, and genitive constructions, to mention but a few. I fully realize that in identifying such phenomena in languages of differing structure, one is basically employing semantic criteria. There are very probably formal similarities which permit us to equate such phenomena in different languages. However, to have concentrated on this task, important in itself, would have, because of its arduousness, prevented me from going forward to those specific hypotheses, based on such investigation, which have empirical import and are of primary interest to the nonlinguist. Moreover, the adequacy of a cross-linguistic definition of 'noun' would, in any case, be tested by reference to its results from the viewpoint of the semantic phenomena it was designed to explicate. If, for example, a formal definition of 'noun' resulted in equating a class containing such glosses as 'boy', 'nose', and 'house' in one language with a class containing such items as 'eat', 'drink', and 'give' in a second language, such a definition would forthwith be rejected and that on semantic grounds. In fact, there was never any real doubt in the languages treated about such matters. There is every reason to believe that such judgments have a high degree of validity. If, for example, someone were to dispute the specific assignment of order type of a genitive construction given in this paper, it is quite clear on what evidence such an assignment would be accepted or rejected.

For many of the statements in this paper, a sample of the following 30 languages has been utilized: Basque, Serbian, Welsh,

Norwegian, Modern Greek, Italian, Finnish (European); Yoruba, Nubian, Swahili, Fulani, Masai, Songhai, Berber (African); Turkish, Hebrew, Burushaski, Hindi, Kannada, Japanese, Thai, Burmese, Malay (Asian); Maori, Loritja (Oceanian); Maya Zapotec, Quechua, Chibcha, Guarani (American Indian).

This sample was selected largely for convenience. In general, it contains languages with which I had some previous acquaintance or for which a reasonably adequate grammar was available to me. Its biases are obvious, although an attempt was made to obtain as wide a genetic and areal coverage as possible. This sample was utilized for two chief purposes. First, it seemed likely that any statement which held for all of these 30 languages had a fair likelihood of complete or, at least, nearly complete universal validity. Second, less reliably, it serves to give some notion of the relative frequency of association of certain grammatical traits. In this respect, of course, it is not to be taken literally. On some questions I have gone well outside the sample.

The main section of the paper, which follows, is concerned with the establishment of universals on the basis of the empirical linguistic evidence. These are presented with a minimum of theoretical comment. The final section is exploratory, seeking to discover what general principles may exist from which at least some of the generalizations of the earlier sections might be deduced. For convenience of exposition, the universals scattered though the text are repeated for cross reference in Appendix III. The theoretical section is far more speculative and uncertain than the sections devoted to the universals themselves. In a certain sense we would prefer to have as few universals as possible, not as many. That is, we would like to be able to deduce them from as small a number of general principles as possible. However, the establishment of a relatively large number of empirical generalizations must, on the whole, come first. For one thing, it would be embarrassing to deduce a particular universal from what seemed like a valid general principle, only to discover that the generalization was not empirically valid.

2. The Basic Order Typology [4]

Linguists are, in general, familiar with the notion that certain languages tend consistently to put modifying or limiting elements before those modified or limited, while others just as consistently do the opposite. Turkish, an example of the former type, puts adjectives before the nouns they modify, places the object of the verb before the verb, the dependent genitive before the governing noun, adverbs before adjectives which they modify, etc. Such languages, moreover, tend to have postpositions for concepts expressed by prepositions in English. A language of the opposite type is Thai, in which adjectives follow the noun, the object follows the verb, the genitive follows the governing noun, and there are prepositions. The majority of languages, as for example English, are not as well marked in this respect. In English, as in Thai, there are prepositions, and the noun object follows the verb. On the other hand, English resembles Turkish in that the adjective precedes the noun. Moreover, in the genitive construction both orders exist: 'John's house' and 'the house of John'.

More detailed consideration of these and other phenomena of order soon reveals that some factors are closely related to each other while others are relatively independent. For reasons which will appear in the course of the exposition, it is convenient to set up a typology involving certain basic factors of word order. This typology will be referred to as the basic order typology. Three sets of criteria will be employed. The first of these is the existence of prepositions as against postpositions. These will be symbolized as Pr and Po, respectively. The second will be the relative order of subject, verb, and object in declarative sentences with nominal subject and object. The vast majority of languages have several variant orders but a single dominant one. Logically, there are six possible orders: SVO, SOV, VSO, VOS, OSV, and OVS. Of these six, however, only three normally occur as dominant orders. The three which do not occur at all, or at least are excessively rare, are VOS, OSV, and OVS. These all have in common that the object precedes the subject. This gives us our first universal:

Universal 1. In declarative sentences with nominal subject and object, the dominant order is almost always one in which the subject precedes the object.[5]

This leaves us with three common types: VSO, SVO, and SOV. These will be symbolized as I, II, and III, respectively, reflecting the relative position of the verb.

The third basis of classification will be the position of qualifying adjectives (i.e., those designating qualities) in relation to the noun. As will be seen later, the position of demonstratives, articles, numerals, and, quantifiers (e.g., 'some', 'all') frequently differs from that of qualifying adjectives. Here again there is sometimes variation, but the vast majority of languages have a dominant order. Dominant order with adjective preceding noun will be symbolized by A and dominant order with noun preceding adjective by N. We thus arrive at a typology involving 2 × 3 × 2, that is, twelve logical possibilities. The 30 languages of the sample are distributed among these twelve classes as shown in Table 1.[6]

TABLE 1

	I	II	III
Po-A	0	1	6
Po-N	0	2	5
Pr-A	0	4	0
Pr-N	6	6	0

The table has been arranged so that the 'extreme' types Po-A and Pr-N are in the first and fourth row, respectively. It is evident that with respect to these extremes, I and III are polar types, the former being strongly correlated with Pr-N and the latter with Po-A. Type II is more strongly correlated with Pr-N than with Po-A. It is also clear that adjective position is less closely related to types I, II, and III than is the Pr/Po contrast. The table is, I believe, a fair representation of the relative frequency of these alternatives on a world-wide basis. Type II is the most frequent; type III almost as common; type I is a definite minority. This means that the nominal subject regularly precedes the verb in a large majority of the world's languages.

Turning for a moment to genitive order, we note that this characteristic might fittingly have been utilized for typological purposes. The reason for not employing it is its extremely high correlation with Pr/Po, a fact generally known to linguists. It would thus virtually have duplicated the latter criterion. It was not chosen because Pr/Po on the whole is slightly more highly correlated with other phenomena. Of the present sample of 30 languages, 14 have postpositions, and in every one of these the genitive order is genitive followed by governing noun. Of the 14 prepositional languages, 13 have the genitive following the governing noun. The only exception is Norwegian, in which the genitive precedes. Thus, 29 of the 30 cases conform to the rule. If anything, 1/30 is an overestimation of the proportion of exceptions on a world-wide basis. We therefore have the following universal:

> *Universal 2.* In languages with prepositions, the genitive almost always follows the governing noun, while in languages with postpositions it almost always precedes.

Turning once more to the data of Table I, we find striking evidence of lawful relationships among the variables in that of the 12 possibilities 5, or almost half, are not exemplified in the sample. All of these types are either rare or nonexistent.[7] For type I, we see that all 6 languages of the sample are Pr/N. This holds with extremely few exceptions on a world-wide basis. There are, however, a few valid examples of I/Pr/A, the mirror image, so to speak, of the fairly frequent III/Po/N. On the other hand, there are, as far as I know, no examples of either I/Po/A or I/Po/N. Hence we may formulate the following universal:

> *Universal 3.* Languages with dominant VSO order are always prepositional.

Languages of type III are, as has been seen, the polar opposites of type I. Just as there are no postpositional languages in type I, we expect that there will be no prepositional languages in type III. This is overwhelmingly true, but I am aware of several exceptions.[8] Since, as has been seen, genitive position correlates highly with Pr/Po, we will expect that languages of type III normally have GN order. To this there are some few exceptions. However, whenever genitive order deviates, so does adjective order, whereas the corresponding statement does not hold for Pr/Po.[9] We therefore have the following universals:

Universal 4. With overwhelmingly greater than chance frequency, languages with normal SOV order are postpositional.

Universal 5. If a language has dominant SOV order and the genitive follows the governing noun, then the adjective likewise follows the noun.

An important difference may be noted between languages of types I and III. In regard to verb-modifying adverbs and phrases as well as sentence adverbs, languages of type I show no reluctance in placing them before the verb so that the verb does not necessarily begin the sentence. Further, all VSO languages apparently have alternative basic orders among which SVO always figures. On the other hand, in a substantial proportion, possibly a majority, of type III languages, the verb follows all of its modifiers, and if any other basic order is allowed, it is OSV. Thus the verb, except possibly for a few sentence modifiers (e.g., interrogative particles), is always at the end in verbal sentences. It is not logically required, of course, that languages all of whose basic orders involve the verb in the third position should also require all verb modifiers to precede the verb, but this seems to hold empirically. Thus, languages in which the verb is always at the end may be called the "rigid" subtype of III. In the present sample, Burushaski, Kannada, Japanese, Turkish, Hindi, and Burmese belong to this group, while Nubian, Quechua, Basque, Loritja, and Chibcha do not.[10] These considerations permit us to state the following as universals:

Universal 6. All languages with dominant VSO order have SVO as an alternative or as the only alternative basic order.

> *Universal 7.* If in a language with dominant SOV order, there is no alternative basic order, or only OSV as the alternative, then all adverbial modifiers of the verb likewise precede the verb. (This is the rigid subtype of III.)

3. Syntax

Having defined the basic order typology and stated some of the universals that can be most immediately derived from the consideration of its defining properties, we turn to a number of syntactic universals, many but not all of which are associated with this typology. One set of criteria employed in this typology was the order of nominal subject, nominal object, and verb in declarative sentences. One reason for stating the criteria in this manner was that interrogative sentences tend to exhibit certain characteristic differences as compared to declarative statements. There are two main categories of questions, those of the yes-no variety and those involving specific question words. A common method of differentiating yes-no questions from the corresponding statement is by a difference of intonational pattern, as in English. Our knowledge of these patterns still leaves much to be desired. However, the following statement seems to be sufficiently documented:

> *Universal 8.* When a yes-no question is differentiated from the corresponding assertion by an intonational pattern, the distinctive intonational features of each of these patterns are reckoned from the end of the sentence rather than from the beginning.

For example, in English a yes-no question is marked by a rise in pitch in the last stressed syllable of the sentence and the corresponding statement by falling pitch. The reckoning of distinctive patterns from the end of the sentence may well hold for all intonational patterns.

Yes-no questions may likewise be signaled by a question particle or affix. Some languages use both this method and intonation as alternatives. The position of such question markers is fixed by either reference to some specific word, most frequently the verb, or the emphasized word of the question, or it may be fixed by position in the sentence as a whole. In languages of the rigid subtype III, it is of course impossible to distinguish between position after the verb and position at the end of the sentence. In the present sample, there are 12 languages with such initial or final particles. With reference to the basic order typology, these 12 examples are distributed as shown in Table 2.[11]

TABLE 2

	I	II	III
Initial particle	5	0	0
Final particle	0	2	5

The two examples of a final particle in group II are prepositional languages (Thai and Yoruba). The table includes only cases where there is a single such particle or affix in the language, or there are several following the same rule. In two of the languages in the samples, there is more than one such element, each with differing rules. Zapotec (I/Pr) has either an initial particle alone or this same particle in conjunction with a final particle. Songhai (II/Po) has three such particles, two of them an initial and one a final particle. These complications as well as the fact that at least one language outside of the sample belonging to (II/Po), namely, Lithuanian, has an initial particle suggest the following rather cautious statement:

> *Universal 9.* With well more than chance frequency, when question particles or affixes are specified in position by reference to the sentence as a whole, if initial, such elements are found in prepositional languages, and, if final, in postpositional.

Where specification depends on some particular word, the particle almost always follows. Such particles are found in 13 languages of the present sample.[12] Examples of the rigid subtype III are counted in both this and the previous category. Of these 13, 12 are suffixed. They include both prepositional and postpositional languages, but none in group I. The following, therefore, probably holds:

> *Universal 10.* Question particles or affixes, when specified in position by reference to a particular word in the sentence, almost always follow that word. Such particles do not occur in languages with dominant order VSO.

The other basic kind of question, that involving an interrogative word, likewise shows a definite relationship to the basic order typology. In such sentences, many languages have a different word order than that of the corresponding declarative sentence. Characteristically, the question word comes first, except for the possible retention of normal order within smaller units (e.g., phrases). This holds in English, for example, where the question word is first in 'What did he eat?' as against the statement, 'He ate meat'. The second point is illustrated by 'With whom did he go?' as against 'He went with Henry', where the question phrase comes first but the order within the phrase itself is not disturbed. Many languages which put interrogatives first likewise invert the order of verb and subject (e.g., German 'Wen sah er?'). Such languages sometimes invert for yes-no questions, (e.g., 'Kommt er?'). It appears that only languages with interrogatives always initially invert, and only languages which invert in interrogative word questions invert for yes-no questions.[13]

In the present sample, 16 languages put the interrogative word or phrase first. They are distributed as shown in Table 3.

TABLE 3

	I	II	III
Question word first	6	10	0
Question and statement order identical	0	3	11

	Pr	Po
Question word first	14	2
Question and statement order identical	2	12

A definite relationship thus appears, and we have the following universals:

> *Universals 11.* Inversion of statement order so that verb precedes subject occurs only in languages where the question word or phrase is normally initial. This same inversion occurs in yes-no questions only if it also occurs in interrogative word questions.

> *Universal 12.* If a language has dominant order VSO in declarative sentences, it always puts interrogative words or phrases first in interrogative word questions; if it has dominant order SOV in declarative sentences, there is never such an invariant rule.

Verbal subordination to verb will be considered next. Semantically, the concepts to be considered here include time, cause, purpose, and condition. Formally, we have one or more of the following: introductory words (i.e., "conjunctions"); and verbal inflections, whether finite, involving categories of person and number (e.g., subjunctives) or nonfinite forms such as verbal nouns and gerundives. It seems probable that conjunctions are more frequent in prepositional languages, nonfinite verb forms in postpositional languages, and that finite verb forms are found in both, but this point was not investigated. In accordance with the over-all emphasis of the paper, attention was directed to the question of the relative order of subordinate and main verbal forms. Since the subordinate verb qualifies the main verb, we would expect it to precede the main verb in all languages of the rigid subtype of III. Since this subtype was defined merely in terms of the invariable precedence of noun object, the question remains for empirical verification. In fact, this turns out to be true for all the languages of this subtype in the sample and, no doubt, holds generally.[14] In languages of other types certain characteristics of individual constructions appear. The normal order everywhere is for the protasis of conditional constructions to procede the apodosis, that is, for the condition to precede the conclusion. This is true for all 30 languages of the sample. In languages of the rigid subtype of III the protasis never follows, but in other languages it will do so occasionally.

On the other hand, in expressions of purpose and volition the normal order is for these to follow the main verb except in languages of the rigid subtype of III. Here again there are no exceptions in the sample. We have therefore the following universals:

> *Universal 13.* If the nominal object always precedes the verb, then verb forms subordinate to the main verb also precede it.
>
> *Universal 14.* In conditional statements, the conditional clause precedes the conclusion as the normal order in all languages.
>
> *Universal 15.* In expressions of volition and purpose, a subordinate verbal form always follows the main verb as the normal order except in those languages in which the nominal object always precedes the verb.

Another relation of verb to verb is that of inflected auxiliary to main verb. For present purposes, such a construction will be defined as one in which a closed class of verbs (the auxiliaries) inflected for both person and number is in construction with an open class of verbs not inflected for both person and number. For example, in English 'is going' is such a construction. This definition, of course, excludes the possibility of such a construction in languages in which the verb has no category of person and number (e.g., Japanese). In the sample of 30 languages, 19 have such inflected auxiliaries. They are distributed among the order types as shown in Table 4.[15]

TABLE 4

	I	II	III
Auxiliary precedes verb	3	7	0
Auxiliary follows verb	0	1	8

	Pr	Po
Auxiliary precedes verb	9	1
Auxiliary follows verb	0	9

These data suggest the following universal:

> *Universal 16.* In languages with dominant order VSO, an inflected auxiliary always precedes the main verb. In languages with dominant order SOV, an inflected auxiliary always follows the main verb.

Uninflected auxiliaries will be considered later in connection with verb inflections.

In nominal phrases, the position of attributive adjectives in relation to the noun modified is a key factor. The position of the qualifying adjective shows a definite though only statistical relation to the two other bases of the typology. A summary of these data for the languages of the sample is given in Table 5.

TABLE 5

	I	II	III
NA	6	8	5
AN	0	5	6

	Pr	Po
NA	12	7
AN	4	7

In general, then, the tendency is for adjectives to follow the noun in prepositional languages, and most strongly so in languages of type I, which are always prepositional as has been noted. There are a few rare exceptions, not in the sample, of languages of type I with adjective before the noun, as was noted earlier. Hence, we have the following *near* universal:

> *Universal 17.* With overwhelmingly more than chance frequency, languages with dominant order VSO have the adjective after the noun.

From the data of Table 5, it will also be noticed that there are 19 languages with adjective after the noun, as against 11 with the adjective before the noun. This is representative of a general tendency which very nearly overrides the opposite rule to be expected in languages of type III.

The position of demonstratives and numerals is related to that of descriptive adjectives in individual languages. However, these items show a marked tendency to precede even when the descriptive adjective follows. On the other hand, when the descriptive adjective precedes, then the demonstratives and numerals virtually always precede the noun likewise. The data from the sample languages are given in Table 6.

TABLE 6

	NA	AN
Dem. - Noun	12	7
Noun - Dem.	11	0
Num. - Noun	8	10
Noun - Num.	11	0

In one language, Guarani, numbers may either precede or follow the noun, and this case was not included in the table. In Guarani, the adjective follows the noun, as would be expected. In the case of numbers, it should be noted that for languages with numeral classifiers, it was the position of the numeral in relation to the classifier which was taken into account.[16] There seems to be no relation between the position of the numeral and the demonstrative outside of that mediated by adjective position. Languages in which the adjective follows the noun may have numeral preceding while demonstrative does not, demonstrative preceding while numeral does not, both preceding or neither preceding. Outside of the sample, however, there are a small number of instances (e.g., Efik) in which the demonstrative follows while the adjective precedes. It may be noted that other quantifiers (e.g., 'some', 'all') and interrogative and possessive adjectives show this same tendency to precede the noun, as evidenced, for example, in the Romance languages, but those cases were not studied. We have then the following universal:

Universal 18. When the descriptive adjective precedes the noun, the demonstrative and the numeral, with overwhelmingly more than chance frequency, do likewise.

An additional related observation may be noted:

Universal 19. When the general rule is that the descriptive adjective follows, there may be a minority of adjectives which usually precede, but when the general rule is that descriptive adjectives precede, there are no exceptions.

This last universal is illustrated by Welsh and Italian in the present sample.

The order within the noun phrase is subject to powerful constraints. When any or all of the three types of qualifiers precede the noun, the order among them is always the same: demonstrative, numeral, and adjective, as in English, 'these five houses'.

When any or all follow, the favorite order is the exact opposite: noun, adjective, numeral, demonstrative. A less popular alternative is the same order as that just given for the instances in which these elements precede the noun. An example of the latter is Kikuyu, a Bantu language of East Africa, with the order, 'houses these five large', instead of the more popular 'houses large five these'. We have, then, a universal:

Universal 20. When any or all of the items (demonstrative, numeral, and descriptive adjective) precede the noun, they are always found in that order. If they follow, the order is either the same or its exact opposite.

The order of adverbial qualifiers of adjectives in relation to the adjective will now be considered. This order also shows a definite relation to that between the descriptive adjective and the noun, as shown by Table 7. In the third row are cases in which certain adverbs precede and others follow.[17]

TABLE 7

	AN	NA
Adverb - Adjective	11	5
Adjective - Adverb	0	8
Adj. - Adv. and Adv. - Adj.	0	2

From Table 7 it can be seen that there is a tendency for the adverb to precede the adjective, which can be overridden only in some cases when the adjective follows the noun. The situation thus far is similar to that obtaining with regard to demonstratives and numerals. However, if we look further, we note that all of those languages in which some or all adverbs follow the adjective not only have the noun followed by the adjective, but also are all of types I and II. Thus we have a universal:

> *Universal 21.* If some or all adverbs follow the adjective they modify, then the language is one in which the qualifying adjective follows the noun and the verb precedes its nominal object as the dominant order.

One other topic concerning the adjective to be considered is that of comparisons, specifically that of superiority as expressed, for example in English, by sentences of the type '*X* is larger than *Y*'. A minority of the world's languages have, like English, an inflected comparative form of the adjective. More frequently a separate word modifies the adjective, as in English, '*X* is more beautiful than *Y*', but in many languages this is optional or does not exist at all. On the other hand, there is always some element which expresses the comparison as such, whether word or affix, corresponding to English 'than', and obviously both the adjective and the item with which comparison is made must be expressed. We thus have three elements whose order can be considered, as in English *larg(er) than Y*. These will be called adjective, marker of comparison, and standard of comparison. The two common orders are: adjective, marker, standard (as in English); or the opposite order: standard, marker, adjective. These two alternatives are related to the basic order typology, as shown by Table 8.[18] A number of languages are not entered in this table because they utilize a verb with general meaning 'to surpass'. This is particularly common in Africa (e.g., Yoruba): '*X* is large, surpasses *Y*'. Loritja, an Australian language which has '*X* is large, *Y* is small', is likewise not entered.

TABLE 8

	I	II	III
Adjective - Marker - Standard	5	9	0
Standard - Marker - Adjective	0	1	9
Both	0	1	0

	Pr	Po
Adjective - Marker - Standard	13	1
Standard - Marker - Adjective	0	10
Both	0	1

Universal 22. If in comparisons of superiority the only order, or one of the alternative orders, is standard-marker-adjective, then the language is postpositional. With overwhelmingly more than chance frequency if the only order is adjective-marker-standard, the language is prepositional.

A clear relation to the basic order typology is likewise found in constructions of nominal apposition, particularly those involving a common along with a proper noun. A number of semantic and formal subtypes are involved (e.g., titles of address, 'Mr. X,' as against appellations 'Avenue X'). The latter type is, in certain cases, assimilation to the genitive, and may therefore be expected to show a similar order (e.g., 'the city of Philadelphia'). English is somewhat ambivalent, doubtless because of adjective-noun order, as can be seen from '42nd Street' versus 'Avenue A', or 'Long Lake' versus 'Lake Michigan'. Most languages, however, have a single order (e.g., French, 'Place Vendôme', 'Lac Genève', 'Boulevard Michelet'). My data here are incomplete because grammars often make no statement on the subject, and I was dependent on text examples.[19]

In Table 9, contrary to usual practice, the genitive construction is used instead of Pr/Po since it gives more clear-cut results.

TABLE 9

	I	II	III
Common Noun - Proper Noun	2	7	0
Proper Noun - Common Noun	0	2	6

	GN	NG
Common Noun - Proper Noun	8	1
Proper Noun - Common Noun	0	8

Universal 23. If in apposition the proper noun usually precedes the common noun, then the language is one in

which the governing noun precedes its dependent genitive. With much better than chance frequency, if the common noun usually precedes the proper noun, the dependent genitive precedes its governing noun.

As the concluding item in the discussion of nominal construction, we take the relative clause which modifies a noun (e.g., English, 'I saw the man who came', 'I saw the student who failed the examination'). Here again there is considerable diversity of formal means from language to language. All that will be considered here is the order as between nominal antecedent and the verb of the relative clause (e.g., 'man' and 'came' in the first sentence).

Once more the distribution of the rules of order, as set forth in Table 10, shows a clear relation to the categories of the basic order typology.[20]

TABLE 10

	I	II	III
Relational expression precedes noun	0	0	7
Noun precedes relational expression	6	12	2
Both constructions	0	1	1

	Pr	Po
Relational expression precedes noun	0	7
Noun precedes relational expression	16	4
Both constructions	0	2

From Table 10 it is clear that if the relational expression precedes the noun either as the only construction or as alternate construction, the language is postpositional. However, outside of the sample there is at least one exception, Chinese, a prepositional language in which the relational expression precedes the noun. It is plausible to explain this deviation as connected with the fact that in Chinese the adjective precedes the noun. As with adjective-noun order there is a pronounced general tendency for the relative expression to follow the noun it qualifies. This tendency is sometimes overcome but only if (1) the language is prepositonal or (2) if the qualifying adjective precedes the noun.

Universal 24. If the relative expression precedes the noun either as the only construction or as an alternate construction, either the language is postpositional, or the adjective precedes the noun or both.

Thus far nothing has been said about pronouns. In general, pronouns exhibit differences regarding order when compared with nouns. This was the reason for specifying nominal subject and nominal object in the definitions of the basic typology. One peculiarity of pronominal order is illustrated by French where we have, 'Je vois l'homme' but 'Je le vois'; that is, the pronominal object precedes, whereas the nominal object follows. Similar examples are found in a number of languages of the sample. In Italian, Greek, Guarani, and Swahili, the rule holds that the pronominal object always precedes the verb, whereas the nominal object follows. In Italian and Greek, however, the pronoun follows just as does the nominal object with imperatives. In Berber the pronoun objects, direct or indirect, precede the verb when the verb is accompanied by the negative or future particle. In Loritja, the pronominal object may be an enclitic added to the first word of the sentence. In Nubian, the usual nominal order is SOV, but the alternative SVO is fairly frequent. For pronominal object, this alternative never occurs. In other words, the pronominal object always precedes the verb, whereas the nominal object may either precede or follow. In Welsh, in an alternative order with emphasis on the pronoun subject, the pronoun subject comes first in the sentence. In such sentences the pronominal object precedes the verb, but the nominal object follows. Finally, in Masai, whereas normal order for nominal object is VSO, a pronominal object precedes a nominal subject and immediately follows the verb.

No contrary instances occur in the sample of a pronominal object regularly following the verb while a nominal object precedes. We may therefore state the following universal:

Universal 25. If the pronominal object follows the verb, so does the nominal object.

4. Morphology

Before proceeding to the question of inflectional categories, which will be the chief topic of this section, certain general considerations relating to morphology will be discussed. Morphemes within the word are conventionally divided into root, derivational and inflectional. As elsewhere in this paper, no attempt at definition of categories will be attempted. Derivational and inflectional elements are usually grouped together as affixes. On the basis of their order relation to the root, they may be classified into a number of categories. By far the most frequent are prefixes and suffixes. Infixing, by which a derivational or inflectional element is both preceded and followed by parts of the root morpheme, may be grouped with other methods involving discontinuity. Examples of such other methods are intercalation, as in Semitic, and what might be called ambifixing, where an affix has two parts, one of which precedes the entire root, while the other follows. All such discontinuous methods are relatively infrequent, and some languages do not employ any of them. The following universal on this topic is probably valid:

Universal 26. If a language has discontinuous affixes, it always has either prefixing or suffixing or both.

As between prefixing and suffixing, there is a general predominance of suffixing. Exclusively suffixing languages are fairly common, while exclusively prefixing languages are quite rare. In the present sample, only Thai seems to be exclusively prefixing. Here again a relationship with the basic order typology appears.[21]

TABLE 11

	I	II	III
Exclusively prefixing	0	1	0
Exclusively suffixing	0	2	10
Both	6	10	1

	Pr	Po
Exclusively prefixing	1	0
Exclusively suffixing	0	12
Both	15	2

Universal 27. If a language is exclusively suffixing, it is postpositional; if it is exclusively prefixing, it is prepositional.

Where both derivational and inflectional elements are found together, the derivational element is more intimately connected with the root. The following generalization appears plausible:

Universal 28. If both the derivation and inflection follow the root, or they both precede the root, the derivation is always between the root and the inflection.

There are probably no languages without either compounding, affixing, or both. In other words, there are probably no purely isolating languages. There are a considerable number of languages without inflections, perhaps none without compounding and derivation. The following probably holds:

Universal 29. If a language has inflection, it always has derivation.

Turning now to verb inflectional categories, we can state that since there are languages without inflection, there will obviously be languages in which the verb has no inflectional categories. In the far more frequent cases in which the verb has inflectional categories, a partial implicational hierarchy exists.

Universal 30. If the verb has categories of person-number or if it has categories of gender, it always has tense-mode categories.

The greater externality of gender categories in the verb can be seen from the following generalization:

Universal 31. If either the subject or object noun agrees with the verb in gender, then the adjective always agrees with the noun in gender.

Gender agreement between noun (usually noun subject) and verb is far less frequent than agreement in person and number; yet examples of the former without the latter do occur (e.g., in some Daghestan languages of the Caucasus). However, where such gender categories appear, they always seem to be associated with number also. Therefore we have the following:

> *Universal 32.* Whenever the verb agrees with a nominal subject or nominal object in gender, it also agrees in number.

A further observation about noun-verb agreement in number may be made. There are cases in which this agreement is regularly suspended. In all such cases, if order is involved, the following seems to hold:[22]

> *Universal 33.* When number agreement between the noun and verb is suspended and the rule is based on order, the case is always one in which the verb precedes and the verb is in the singular.

Such phenomena as the suspension of agreement are analogous to that of neutralization in phonemics. The category which does not appear in the position of neutralization, in this case the plural, may be called the marked category (as in classical Prague School phonemic theory). Similar phenomena will be encountered in the subsequent discussion.

The three most common nominal inflectional categories are number, gender, and case. Among systems of number, there is a definite hierarchy which can be stated in the following terms:

> *Universal 34.* No language has a trial number unless it has a dual. No language has a dual unless it has a plural.

Nonsingular number categories. are marked categories in relation to the singular, as indicated in the following universal:

> *Universal 35.* There is no language in which the plural does not have some nonzero allomorphs, whereas there are languages in which the singular is expressed only by zero. The dual and the trial are almost never expressed only by zero.

The marked character of the nonsingular numbers as against the singular can also be seen when number occurs along with gender. The interrelations of these two sets of categories are stated in the following universals :

Universal 36. If a language has the category of gender, it always has the category of number.

Universal 37. A language never has more gender categories in nonsingular numbers than in the singular.

This latter statement may be illustrated from Hausa, which has a masculine and feminine gender distinction in the singular but not in the plural. The opposite phenomenon, to my knowledge, never occurs.

Case systems may occur with or without gender systems and with or without the category of number. The unmarked categories of case systems are the subject case in nonergative systems and the case which expresses the subject of intransitive and the object of transitive verbs in ergative systems. Hence we have the following universal:

Universal 38. Where there is a case system, the only case which ever has only zero allomorphs is the one which includes among its meanings that of the subject of the intransitive verb.

As between number and case, where there is a distinct morpheme boundary, the following relation almost always holds:

Universal 39. Where morphemes of both number and case are present and both follow or both precede the noun base, the expression of number almost always comes between the noun base and the expression of case.

The following general statement may be made about agreement between adjectives and nouns:

Universal 40. When the adjective follows the noun, the adjective expresses all the inflectional categories of the noun. In such cases the noun may lack overt expression of one or all of these categories.

For example, in Basque, where the adjective follows the noun, the last member of the noun phrase contains overt expressions of the categories of case and number and it alone has them.

Case systems are particularly frequent in postpositional languages, particularly those of type III. In the present sample, all the languages of this type have case systems. There are a few marginal cases or possible exceptions.

Universal 41. If in a language the verb follows both the nominal subject and nominal object as the dominant order, the language almost always has a case system.

Finally, pronominal categories may be briefly considered. In general, pronominal categories tend to be more differentiated than those of the noun, but almost any specific statement in this regard will have some exceptions. As a general statement we have the following universals:

Universal 42. All languages have pronominal categories involving at least three persons and two numbers.

Universal 43. If a language has gender categories in the noun, it has gender categories in the pronoun.

Gender categories show certain relations to categories of person in pronouns, as might be expected.

Universal 44. If a language has gender distinctions in the first person, it always has gender distinctions in the second or third person, or in both.

There is likewise a relation to the category of number.

Universal 45. If there are any gender distinctions in the plural of the pronoun, there are some gender distinctions in the singular also.

5. Conclusion: Some General Principles

No attempt is made here to account for all of the universals described in the preceding sections and repeated in Appendix III. Some general principles, however, are proposed which seem to underlie a number of different universals and from which they may be deduced. Attention is first directed to those universals which are most closely connected with the basic order typology and the closely associated genitive construction. Two basic notions, that of the dominance of a particular order over its alternative and that of harmonic and disharmonic relations among distinct rules of order, are introduced. This latter concept is very obviously connected with the psychological concept of generalization.

We may illustrate the reasoning involved by reference to Universal 25, according to which, if the pronominal object follows the verb, the nominal object does so likewise. In other words, in the tetrachoric table resulting from the alternative for each of the combinations there is a single blank. Since the nominal object may follow the verb whether the pronoun object precedes or follows, while the nominal object may precede the verb only if the pronoun precedes, we will say that VO is dominant over OV since OV only occurs under specified conditions, namely when the pronominal object likewise precedes, while VO is not subject to such limitations. Further, the order noun object–verb is harmonic with pronoun object–verb but is disharmonic with verb–pronoun object since it does not occur with it. Likewise verb–noun object order is harmonic with verb–pronoun object and disharmonic with pronoun object–verb. We may restate our rule, then, in terms of these concepts as follows:

> A dominant order may always occur, but its opposite, the recessive, occurs only when a harmonic construction is likewise present.

Note that the notion of dominance is not based on its more frequent occurrence but on the logical factor of a zero in the tetrachoric table. It is not difficult to construct an example in which one of the recessive alternatives is more frequent than the dominant. Dominance and harmonic relations can be derived quite mechanically from such a table with a single zero. The entry with zero is always the recessive one for each construction, and the two constructions involved are disharmonic with each other.

Harmonic and disharmonic relations, as noted earlier, are examples of generalization. In similar constructions, the corresponding members tend to be in the same order. The basis for the correspondence in the present instance is obvious, in that pronoun and noun are both objects of the verb, and the other pair verb-verb is identical. In regard to harmonic and disharmonic relations, a fair amount of freedom will be exercised based on transformational and other relations among constructions, not merely the occurrence of a zero in a tetrachoric table.

Proceeding on this basis, we now consider Universal 3. It will be noted that this universal amounts to an assertion of the nonexistence of postpositional languages of type I. Since in all of the types, I, II and III, S precedes O, this is irrelevant for the present context. This leads to the following conclusions:

> Prepositions are dominant over postpositions, and SV order is dominant over VS order. Further, prepositions are harmonic with VS and disharmonic with SV, while postpositions are harmonic with SV and disharmonic with VS.

What distinguishes type II from type III is that in type II the object follows the verb, a characteristic shared with type I. On the other hand, type III has the object before the verb. From Universal 4, which states that with overwhelmingly more than chance frequency SOV is associated with postpositions, the conclusion is drawn that OV is harmonic with postpositions while VO is harmonic with prepositions. The constructional analogies which support this are discussed later with reference to the closely associated genitive constructions. For the moment it may be noted that the relations between types I, II, and III and Pr/Po may now be recapitulated in these terms: Type I has VS which is harmonic with prepositions, and SO which is likewise harmonic with prepositions. Further, prepositions are dominant. All languages of type I, in fact, are prepositional. Type II has SV which is harmonic with postpositions and VO which is harmonic with prepositions, and prepositions are dominant. In fact, a definite majority of languages of type II have prepositions. Type III has SV and OV, both of which are harmonic with postpositions. However, prepositions are dominant. In fact, the preponderant majority of languages which have type III have postpositions, with but a handful of exceptions.

From the overwhelming association of prepositions with governing noun–genitive order and of postpositions with genitive–governing noun order but with a small number of exceptions of both types, the conclusion is drawn that prepositions are harmonic with NG and postpositions with GN.

The close connection between genitive order and Pr/Po is a simple instance of generalization. The relation of possession is assimilated to other relational notions, for example, spatial relations. In English, 'of' which marks possession is a preposition with the same order properties as 'under', 'above', etc. Further, such spatial and temporal relations are often expressed by nouns or nounlike words, for example, English 'in back of'. In many languages 'behind' = 'the back + genitive'; hence: '*X*'s back' = 'in back of *X*' parallels '*X*'s house'; and 'back of *X*' = 'in back of *X*' parallels 'house of *X*'.

The connection between these genitives and the analogous prepositional or postpositional phrases on the one hand, and subject-verb and object-verb constructions on the other, is via the so-called subjective and objective genitive. Note that in English 'Brutus' killing of Caesar started a civil war' has the same truth value as 'The fact that Brutus killed Caesar started a civil war'. The order of elements is likewise similar. In other words, in such transformations, the noun subject or object corresponds to the genitive, and the verb to the governing noun. In fact, there are languages in which the subject or the object of the verb is in the genitive. For example, in Berber *argaz* 'man' is the general form of the noun, and *urgaz* is either the dependent genitive or the subject of the verb, provided it follows immediately. Thus *iffeγ urgaz*, 'went out the man', exactly parallels *axam urgaz*, 'the house of the man'. Berber, it will be noted, is a language of type I, and the genitive follows the noun. It likewise has prepositions rather than postpositions.

A further relationship among the variables of the basic order typology may be posited, that between genitive order and adjective order. Both the genitive and qualifying adjectives limit the meaning of the noun. There are further facts to support this. There are languages like Persian, in which both adjective and genitive dependence are marked by exactly the same formal means. Where pronominal possession is involved, some languages use a derived adjective, while others use a genitive of the pronoun. There are even instances where adjectives are used in the first and second person, while a genitive is used in the third person (e.g., Norwegian).

We may summarize these results by stating that all of the following are directly or indirectly harmonic with each other: prepositions, NG, VS, VO, NA. We have here a general tendency to put modified before modifier, and the most highly "polarized" languages in this direction are those of type I with NG and NA, a considerable group of languages. The opposite type is based on harmonic relations among postpositions, GN, SV, OV, and AN. This is also a very widespread type, as exemplified by Turkish and others in the present sample. On the other hand, the general dominance of NA order tends to make languages of the Basque type (i.e., III/Po/NA with GN order) very nearly as common as the Turkish type. It should also be pointed out that languages being highly complex structures, there are other factors at work in individual cases not included among the five factors cited at this point. One of them, demonstrative-noun order, has already been mentioned.

It is more difficult to account for the dominances than for the harmonic relations, to explain, for example, why the adjective tends to follow the noun. It may be suggested, however, that noun-adjective predominance arises from the same factor as that which makes subject-verb the dominant order. In Hockett's terminology, there is a general tendency for comment to follow topic. There is some evidence that noun-adjective does parallel subject-verb in this way. In many languages all adjectival notions are treated as intransitive verbs. The qualifying adjective is then a relative or participle of the verb. The tendency of relative clauses, it has been seen, is even stronger than that of adjectives to follow the noun. In some languages such as Arapesh in New Guinea, 'The good man came' would be literally translated 'The man is-good that-one he came'. Adjective-noun order, then, is somewhat ambivalent since analogies with other constructions involving modifiers make it indirectly harmonic with VS while the factor of topic-comment order makes it analogous with SV.

All this is far from a complete theory. Nevertheless, it does suggest that one should examine instances in which, contrary to the prevailing rules, the genitive construction is disharmonic with Pr/Po. One would reason that in such cases the genitive construction is, as it were, being attracted by the adjective-noun construction which, as has been seen, has sources of determination that are to some extent outside of the general framework of harmonic relations connected with the order of modifier and modified. For example, if, in spite of the general rule, we find genitive–governing noun order with prepositions, the reason might be the opposing pull of order adjective-noun which is harmonic with genitive–governing noun. Otherwise stated, the genitive construction should only be disharmonic with Pr/Po when Pr/Po is disharmonic with the adjective-noun order. One may include here cases in which a language has two genitive orders, indicating a probable change of type since one must, in all likelihood, be older than the other. One may further conjecture that if there are exceptions, they will be in type II, which, having both SV and VO which are disharmonic, can provide an anchor in either case for deviant genitive order.

It will be noted that Universal 5, insofar as it refers to postpositional languages of type III (the vast majority), gives a particular instance of this hypothesis; for this statement asserts that a language of type III if it has NG will also have NA. If such a language is postpositional, then NG will be disharmonic with postpositions but harmonic with NA. If we include languages with both genitive orders, then there are at least six cases, all favorable (i.e., with NA rather than AN). These are Somali and Maba with both genitive orders, and Kanuri, Galla, Teda, and Sumerian which have SOV, postpositions, NG, and NA.

This hypothesis will, however, produce some further predictions. For prepositional languages of type III, the hypothesis will be that with varying genitive order or with GN, which is disharmonic with prepositions, the adjective-noun order will be AN. I know of only two cases, Tigrinya with both genitive orders, and Amharic with GN. Both have AN in accordance with our hypothesis. For languages of type II which are prepositional and which have GN, and should therefore have AN, we have Danish, Norwegian and Swedish (possibly a single case), and English with two genitive orders. Both fulfill the hypothesis in that they have AN. Among postpositional languages of type II, we have the Moru-Madi group in the Sudan and the fairly distantly related Mangbetu, both of which, with alternative genitive orders, have the predicted NA. We now encounter the only exceptions of which I am aware, Araucanian in Chile, with both genitive orders; and a group of Daghestan languages in the Caucasus, including some like Rutulian with NG, and others like Tabassaran with both genitive orders. Apparently all those languages of the Daghestan group which are of type III have only GN harmonizing with both postpositions and AN. If so, this is an important indication of the general validity of our hypothesis. Finally, since all languages of type I are prepositional, we have only a single case to consider, prepositional languages with GN. I know of only one example, the Milpa Alta dialect of Nahuatl described by Whorf. It has AN as expected.

Another type of relation than those that have just been considered is illustrated by Universals 20 and 29. These may be called proximity hierarchies. What we have is a rule that certain elements must be closer to some central element than some other satellite. The central element may be the root morpheme or base of a word or the head-word of an endocentric construction. Such a proximity hierarchy is likely to be related to an implicational hierarchy in in the instance of inflectional categories. Just as the category of number is almost always closer to the base than expressions of case, so there are many languages with the category of number but without the category of case, and very few with case but without number. Since, by the proximity hierarchy, number is closer, it is more likely to become amalgamated with the base and so become an inflection. These hierarchies are presumably related to degrees of logical and psychological remoteness from the center, but no analysis is attempted here.

These phenomena are likewise related to those of neutralization. The more proximate category, or the implied category, tends to be more elaborate, and it is the less proximate or the implying categories which tend to be neutralized in its presence. Universals 36 and 37 are related in this manner. Number is the implied category. Gender categories are often neutralized in the marked number (i.e. nonsingular). It is much rarer for number to be neutralized in some particular gender (e.g., the neuter in Dravidian languages). With regard to number and case, number is, as has been seen, more proximate and generally present when case is present, while the opposite relation holds far more rarely. It is likewise common for certain case distinctions to be neutralized in number, while the opposite phenomenon perhaps never occurs.

Another principle is evident from Universal 34. We do not have such systems as the following: a particular grammatical category for the trial, while another embraces the dual and all numbers larger than three. In other words, disjunctiveness or lack of continuity in this respect is never tolerated.

Universals 14 and 15 possibly illustrate the same principle. The order of elements in language parallels that in physical experience or the order of knowledge. In the instance of conditionals, although the truth relations involved are timeless, logicians have always symbolized in the order implying, implied exactly as in spoken language. If *modus ponens* is used in proof, then we have a pragmatic example which follows the order of reasoning. No one thinks to write a proof backwards.

Universals 7, 8, and 40, although superficially very different, seem to be examples of the same general tendency to mark the end of units rather than the beginning. For example, in rigid subtype III, the verb marks the end of the sentence. When the inflections occur only with the final member of the noun phrase, this marks the end of the phrase. This is probably related to the fact that we always know when someone has just begun speaking, but it is our sad experience that without some marker we don't know when the speaker will finish.

The existence of a rigid subtype III, whereas there are no examples of a rigid subtype of I, is probably related to still another factor. In general the initial position is the emphatic one, and while there are other methods of emphasis (e.g., stress), the initial position always seems to be left free so that an element to which attention is directed may come first. Here Universal 12 is an example. It seems probable that in all languages expressions of time and place may appear in the initial positions in the sentence.

The discontinuity of the predicate, which commonly appears in such instances (e.g., German, 'Gestern ist mein Vater nach Berlin gefahren'), illustrates a further principle. On the whole, the higher the construction in an immediate constituent hierarchy, the freer the order of the constituent elements. It has been seen that practically all languages have some freedom of order regarding subject and predicate as a whole; whereas only a small minority have variant order in genitive constructions, and then almost always along with other differences, not merely a difference of order. Within morphological constructions, order is the most fixed of all. On the whole, then, discontinuous constituents are far less frequent than continuous ones.

As indicated in the initial section of this paper, the principles described in this section are to be viewed as no more than suggestive. It is hoped that some of them at least will prove useful for further investigation.

ACKNOWLEDGMENTS

In addition to my indebtedness to the work of Roman Jakobson, to be mentioned in the notes, I would also like to thank Fred Householder and Charles F. Hockett for making helpful critical comments on the earlier version of this paper.

Notes

1. I am indebted to the work of Roman Jakobson for directing my attention to the importance of implicational universals.
2. See, for example, the remarks of R. B. Braithwaite, *Scientific Explanation* (Cambridge, 1953), concerning scientific laws. "The one thing upon which everyone agrees is that it always includes a generalization, i. e., a proposition asserting a universal connection between properties" (p. 9).
3. That is, empirically, not logically, implied. All languages are observed to have the characteristics in question. It should be

added that universals in the sense of nondefinitional characteristics, if found only in language, do have the additional logical property of implying as well as being implied by the definitional properties.

4. Some of the ideas regarding the basic order typology are found in nineteenth-century linguistic literature. For example, the relation between genitive position and prepositions versus postpositions and the hypothesis that some languages favor the order modifier-modified and others the opposite order is already a familiar notion in R. Lepsius' introduction to his *Nubische Grammatik* (Berlin, 1880).

   The most systematic treatment is that of W. Schmidt in *Die Sprachfamilien und Sprachenkreise der Erde* (Heidelberg, 1926) and in several other works. Schmidt's basic conclusions may be summarized here. Prepositions go with nominative-genitive order and postpositions with the reverse order. The nominative-genitive order tends to appear with verb before nominal object and genitive-nominative with object-verb. Schmidt says nothing of subject-verb order so that types I and II as treated in this paper are not distinguished. Further, nominative-genitive is associated with noun-adjective and genitive-nominative with adjective-noun. This last correlation, particularly the latter half, is much weaker than the others. Schmidt gives figures based on a world sample which show good general agreement with the results from the thirty-language sample utilized here. It should be added that Schmidt's chief interest in this topic is as a vehicle for the interpretation of culture history. His results there verge on the fantastic.
5. Siuslaw and Coos, which are Penutian languages of Oregon, and Coeur d'Alene, a Salishan language, are exceptions.
6. The manner in which each language has been assigned can be determined from the data of Appendix I.
7. For details, see Appendix II.
8. Iraqw, a southern Cushitic language, Khamti, a Thai language, standard Persian, and Amharic.
9. The single case where it does not hold seems to be Amharic, which has SOV, GN, and AN, but is prepositional.
10. However, Householder informs me that in Azerbaijani, and in most types of spoken Turkish, it is allowable to have one modifier, especially a dative or locative noun phrase after the verb.
11. Languages of type I—Berber, Hebrew, Maori, Masai, and Welsh; II—Thai, Yoruba; III—Burmese, Burushaski, Japanese, Kannada, Nubian. For Yoruba, see further note 12.
12. In the following languages the affix or particle follows: II—Finnish, Guarani, Malay, Maya, Serbian; III—Basque, Burmese, Japanese,

Kannada, Nubian, Turkish, Quechua. It precedes in Yoruba, but may be accompanied by a final particle.

13. The question word is first in Berber, Finnish, Fulani, Greek, Guarani, Hebrew, Italian, Malay, Maori, Masai, Maya, Norwegian, Serbian, Welsh, Yoruba, and Zapotec.
14. Again, this only holds for literary Turkish, according to Householder. See note 10.
15. Auxiliary precedes verb in Finnish, Greek, Italian, Masai, Maya, Norwegian, Serbian, Swahili, Welsh, Zapotec. Auxiliary follows verb in Basque, Burushaski, Chibcha, Guarani, Hindi, Kannada, Nubian, Quechua, Turkish.
16. For details, see Appendix I.
17. Languages with adjective-noun and adverb-adjective order are Burushaski, Finnish, Greek, Hindi, Japanese, Kannada, Maya, Norwegian, Quechua, Serbian, Turkish. Languages with noun-adjective and adverb-adjective order are Basque, Burmese, Chibcha, Italian, Loritja. Languages with noun-adjective and adjective-adverb order are Fulani, Guarani, Hebrew, Malay, Swahili, Thai, Yoruba, and Zapotec. Languages with noun-adjective and the rule that certain adverbs precede and certain follow the adjective are Maori and Welsh. Berber, Masai, Nubian, and Songhai—no data.
18. Languages with adjective-marker-standard are Berber, Fulani, Greek, Hebrew, Italian, Malay, Maori, Norwegian, Serbian, Songhai, Swahili, Thai, Welsh, Zapotec. Languages with standard-marker-adjective are Basque, Burmese, Burushaski, Chibcha, Guarani, Hindi, Japanese, Kannada, Nubian, Turkish. Both constructions are found in Finnish.
19. Languages with common noun–proper noun are Greek, Guarani, Italian, Malay, Serbian, Swahili, Thai, Welsh, Zapotec. Those with proper noun–common noun are Basque, Burmese, Burushaski, Finnish, Japanese, Norwegian, Nubian, and Turkish.
20. The relational expression precedes the noun in Basque, Burmese, Burushaski, Chibcha, Japanese, Kannada, Turkish. The noun precedes the relational expression in Berber, Fulani, Greek, Guarani, Hebrew, Hindi, Italian, Malay, Maori, Masai, Maya, Norwegian, Quechua, Serbian, Songhai, Swahili, Thai, Welsh, Yoruba, Zapotec. Both orders are found in Finnish and Nubian. In Finnish the construction with the relational expression preceding the noun is in imitation of literary Swedish (personal communication of Robert Austerlitz).
21. The exclusively suffixing languages are Basque, Burmese, Chibcha, Finnish, Hindi, Japanese, Kannada, Loritja, Nubian, Quechua, Songhai, Turkish.

22. The reason for specifying order is that there are instances of neutralization of number agreement in which the order of the item is not involved. For example, in classical Greek the neuter plural goes with a singular verb without regard to order.

Additional note : The following facts were learned too late to be included in the paper. According to information supplied by Einar Haugen, Norwegian has both genitive orders. Note that Norwegian had been the only exception in the sample to the generalization on p. 64. In a discussion at the International Congress of Linguistics at Cambridge in August 1962, it was pointed out that Papago, a Uto-Aztecan language, is I/Po. This is therefore an exception to Universal 3. From Mason's data it should probably be assigned to type 7 of Appendix II.

Appendix I

Basic Data on the 30-Language Sample

	VSO	Pr	NA	ND	N Num
Basque	III	–	x	x	–
Berber	I	x	x	x	–
Burmese	III	–	x[1]	–	–[2]
Burushaski	III	–	–	–	–
Chibcha	III	–	x	–	x
Finnish	II	–	–	–	–
Fulani	II	x	x	x	x
Greek	II	x	–	–	–
Guarani	II	–	x	–	0
Hebrew	I	x	x	x	–
Hindi	III	–	–	–	–
Italian	II	x	x[3]	–	–
Kannada	III	–	–	–	–
Japanese	III	–	–	–	–[2]
Loritja	III	–	x	x	x
Malay	II	x	x	x	–[2]
Maori	I	x	x	–	–
Masai	I	x	x	–	x
Maya	II	x	–	–	–[2]
Norwegian	II	x	–	–	–
Nubian	III	–	x	–	x
Quechua	III	–	–	–	–

	VSO	Pr	NA	ND	N Num
Serbian	II	x	–	–	–
Songhai	II	–	x	x	x
Swahili	II	x	x	x	x
Thai	II	x	x	x	–[2]
Turkish	III	–	–	–	–
Welsh	I	x	x[3]	x	–
Yoruba	II	x	x	x	x
Zapotec	I	x	x	x	–

In the first column, I indicates that normal word order is verb-subject-object, II indicates subject-verb-object, and III subject-object-verb. In the second column, x indicates that the language has prepositions, and – that it has postpositions. In the third column, x indicates that the noun precedes its modifying adjective, and – that it follows. In the fourth column, x indicates that the noun precedes its modifying demonstrative, and – that it follows. In the fifth column, x indicates that the noun precedes its modifying numeral, and – that it follows. In any column, 0 means that both orders are found.

Notes to Appendix I

1. Participle of adjective-verb, however, precedes and is probably as common as adjective following.
2. Numeral classifiers following numerals in each case. The construction numeral + classifier precedes in Burmese and Maya, follows in Japanese and Thai, and either precedes or follows in Malay.
3. In Welsh and Italian a small number of adjectives usually precede.

Appendix II

Distribution of Basic Order Types:

1. I/Pr/NG/NA. Celtic languages; Hebrew, Aramaic, Arabic, Ancient Egyptian, Berber; Nandi, Masai, Lotuko, Turkana, Didinga; Polynesian languages and probably other Austronesian languages; Chinook, Tsimshian; Zapotec, Chinantec, Mixtec, and probably other Oto-Mangue languages.
2. I/Pr/NG/AN. Tagabili and probably other Philippine Austronesian languages; Kwakiutl, Quileute, Xinca.

3. I/Pr/GN/AN. Milpa Alta Nahuatl.
4. I/Pr/GN/NA. No examples.
5. I/Po/NG/NA. No examples.
6. I/Po/NG/AN. No examples.
7. I/Po/GN/AN. No examples.
8. I/Po/GN/NA. No examples.
9. II/Pr/NG/NA. Romance languages, Albanian, Modern Greek; West Atlantic languages, Yoruba, Edo group, most languages of Benue-Congo group including all Bantu languages; Shilluk, Acholi, Bari, most languages of Chad group of Hamito-Semitic but not Hausa; Neo-Syriac, Khasi, Nicobarese, Khmer, Vietnamese, all Thai languages except Khamti; many Austronesian languages including Malay; Subtiaba.
10. II/Pr/NG/AN. German, Dutch, Icelandic, Slavonic, Efik, Kredj, Maya, Papiamento.
11. II/Pr/GN/AN. Norwegian, Swedish, Danish.
12. II/Pr/GN/NA. Arapesh (New Guinea).
13. II/Po/NG/NA. No examples.
14. II/Po/NG/AN. Rutulian and other Daghestan languages in the Caucasus.
15. II/Po/GN/AN. Finnish, Estonian, Ijo, Chinese, Algonquian (probably), Zoque.
16. II/Po/GN/NA. Most Mandingo and Voltaic languages, Kru, Twi, Gã, Guang, Ewe, Nupe, Songhai, Tonkawa, Guarani.
17. III/Pr/NG/NA. Persian, Iraqw (Cushitic), Khamti (Thai), Akkadian.
18. III/Pr/NG/AN. No examples.
19. III/Pr/GN/AN. Amharic.
20. III/Pr/GN/NA. No examples.
21. III/Po/NG/NA. Sumerian, Elamite, Galla, Kanuri, Teda, Kamilaroi and other southeastern Australian languages.
22. III/Po/NG/AN. No examples.
23. III/Po/GN/AN. Hindi, Bengali, and other Aryan languages of India; Modern Armenian, Finno-Ugric except Finnish group; Altaic, Yukaghir, Paleo-Siberian, Korean, Ainu, Japanese, Gafat, Harari, Sidamo, Chamir, Bedauye, Nama Hottentot; Khinalug, Abkhaz and other Caucasian languages; Burushaski, Dravidian; Newari and other Sino-Tibetan languages; Marind-Anim, Navaho, Maidu, Quechua.
24. III/Po/GN/NA. Basque, Hurrian, Urartian, Nubian, Kunama, Fur, Sandawe, Burmese, Lushei, Classical Tibetan, Makasai, Bunak (Timor), Kate (New Guinea), most Australian languages, Haida, Tlingit, Zuni, Chitimacha, Tunica, Lenca, Matagalpa, Cuna, Chibcha, Warrau.

Languages with Object before Subject:

Coeur d'Alene: VOS/Pr/NG/NA.
Siuslaw, Coos: VOS and OVS/Po/GN/AN/

Languages with Variant Constructions:

Geez, Bontoc Igorot 1, 2; Tagalog 1, 2, 3, 4; Sango 9, 10; English 10, 11; Lithuanian 11, 15 (prepositions more numerous); Mangbetu, Araucanian 12, 13; Takelma 12, 16 (prepositions more frequent); Moru-Madi 13, 16; Tabassaran 14, 15; Luiseño 15, 16; Tigre 17, 18, 19, 20; Tigrinya 18, 19; Somali, Maba 21, 24; Afar, Ekari 23, 24.

Appendix III

Universals Restated

1. In declarative sentences with nominal subject and object, the dominant order is almost always one in which the subject precedes the object.
2. In languages with prepositions, the genitive almost always follows the governing noun, while in languages with postpositions it almost always precedes.
3. Languages with dominant VSO order are always prepositional.
4. With overwhelmingly greater than chance frequency, languages with normal SOV order are postpositional.
5. If a language has dominant SOV order and the genitive follows the governing noun, then the adjective likewise follows the noun.
6. All languages with dominant VSO order have SVO as an alternative or as the only alternative basic order.
7. If in a language with dominant SOV order there is no alternative basic order, or only OSV as the alternative, then all adverbial modifiers of the verb likewise precede the verb. (This is the "rigid" subtype of III.)
8. When a yes-no question is differentiated from the corresponding assertion by an intonational pattern, the distinctive intonational features of each of these patterns is reckoned from the end of the sentence rather than the beginning.
9. With well more than chance frequency, when question particles or affixes are specified in position by reference to the sentence as a whole, if initial, such elements are found in prepositional languages and, if final, in postpositional.

10. Question particles or affixes, specified in position by reference to a particular word in the sentence, almost always follow that word. Such particles do not occur in languages with dominant order VSO.
11. Inversion of statement order so that verb precedes subject occurs only in languages where the question word or phrase is normally initial. This same inversion occurs in yes-no questions only if it also occurs in interrogative word questions.
12. If a language has dominant order VSO in declarative sentences, it always puts interrogative words or phrases first in interrogative word questions; if it has dominant order SOV in declarative sentences, there is never such an invariant rule.
13. If the nominal object always precedes the verb, then verb forms subordinate to the main verb also precede it.
14. In conditional statements, the conditional clause precedes the conclusion as the normal order in all languages.
15. In expressions of volition and purpose, a subordinate verbal form always follows the main verb as the normal order except in those languages in which the nominal object always precedes the verb.
16. In languages with dominant order VSO, an inflected auxiliary always precedes the main verb. In languages with dominant order SOV, an inflected auxiliary always follows the main verb.
17. With overwhelmingly more than chance frequency, languages with dominant order VSO have the adjective after the noun.
18. When the descriptive adjective precedes the noun, the demonstrative and the numeral, with overwhelmingly more than chance frequency, do likewise.
19. When the general rule is that the descriptive adjective follows, there may be a minority of adjectives which usually precede, but when the general rule is that descriptive adjectives precede, there are no exceptions.
20. When any or all of the items—demonstrative, numeral, and descriptive adjective—precede the noun, they are always found in that order. If they follow, the order is either the same or its exact opposite.
21. If some or all adverbs follow the adjective they modify, then the language is one in which the qualifying adjective follows the noun and the verb precedes its nominal object as the dominant order.
22. If in comparisons of superiority the only order or one of the alternative orders is standard-marker-adjective, then the language is postpositional. With overwhelmingly more than chance frequency, if the only order is adjective-marker-standard, the language is prepositional.

23. If in apposition the proper noun usually precedes the common noun, then the language is one in which the governing noun precedes its dependent genitive. With much better than chance frequency, if the common noun usually precedes the proper noun, the dependent genitive precedes its governing noun.
24. If the relative expression precedes the noun either as the only construction or as an alternative construction, either the language is postpositional or the adjective precedes the noun or both.
25. If the pronominal object follows the verb, so does the nominal object.
26. If a language has discontinuous affixes, it always has either prefixing or suffixing or both.
27. If a language is exclusively suffixing, it is postpositional; if it is exclusively prefixing, it is prepositional.
28. If both the derivation and inflection follow the root, or they both precede the root, the derivation is always between the root and the inflection.
29. If a language has inflection, it always has derivation.
30. If the verb has categories of person-number or if it has categories of gender, it always has tense-mode categories.
31. If either the subject or object noun agrees with the verb in gender, then the adjective always agrees with the noun in gender.
32. Whenever the verb agrees with a nominal subject or nominal object in gender, it also agrees in number.
33. When number agreement between the noun and verb is suspended and the rule is based on order, the case is always one in which the verb is in the singular.
34. No language has a trial number unless it has a dual. No language has a dual unless it has a plural.
35. There is no language in which the plural does not have some nonzero allomorphs, whereas there are languages in which the singular is expressed only by zero. The dual and the trial are almost never expressed only by zero.
36. If a language has the category of gender, it always has the category of number.
37. A language never has more gender categories in nonsingular numbers than in the singular.
38. Where there is a case system, the only case which ever has only zero allomorphs is the one which includes among its meanings that of the subject of the intransitive verb.
39. Where morphemes of both number and case are present and both follow or both precede the noun base, the expression of number almost always comes between the noun base and the expression of case.

40. When the adjective follows the noun, the adjective expresses all the inflectional categories of the noun. In such cases the noun may lack overt expression of one or all of these categories.
41. If in a language the verb follows both the nominal subject and nominal object as the dominant order, the language almost always has a case system.
42. All languages have pronominal categories involving at least three persons and two numbers.
43. If a language has gender categories in the noun, it has gender categories in the pronoun.
44. If a language has gender distinctions in the first person, it always has gender distinctions in the second or third person or in both.
45. If there are any gender distinctions in the plural of the pronoun, there are some gender distinctions in the singular also.

CHAPTER 6

A SEARCH FOR UNIVERSALS IN INDO-EUROPEAN DIACHRONIC MORPHOLOGY

WARREN COWGILL
Yale University

In searching for universals of diachronic morphology, three approaches come easily to mind. One is to make typological studies of the morphologies of several sets of genetically related languages, and then compare the typologies to see what similarities in development are shown by related languages, and whether there are any general rules that apply to all the languages studied regardless of genetic relationship.

Two kinds of similarities can be looked for: similarities in change and similarities in retention. Looking for similarities in change among related languages should be useful in testing the idea of drift—that is, whether or not the imbalances and stresses of the common protolanguage inevitably lead to similarities in the innovations made by the daughter languages, and what parts of the grammar are most likely to undergo such parallel change. Looking for similarities in change among unrelated languages would help to determine whether there are any general rules for the evolution of typologies—for example, would any language similar in type to Proto-Indo-European or Proto-Uto-Aztecan show much the same evolution as Indo-European and Uto-Aztecan have, or are the structural differences determining the future development of a linguistic system too subtle to be caught by any typology yet devised?

Looking for features retained with little change over a long period by all or most of a set of related languages should reveal whether any features of their common protolanguage were more resistant to change than others, and so in some sense more basic to its structure. If there should prove to be such features, one could then look to see whether or not these belong to the same areas of structure in all language families. The results, even if purely negative, should be of interest to psychologists.

A slightly different approach is to compare the changes that have taken place rather than a selection of the states that the language assumes as it undergoes the effect of these changes in its progress through time. That is, instead of stating that language A, spoken in 500 B.C., has prefixes and grammatical gender, while its daughter language B, spoken in 1500 A.D., has neither, we ask what has become of the prefixes and gender markers of A during the intervening two millennia, and then check to see if any other language we know of has treated its prefixes or gender markers in the same way. If enough data of this type could be accumulated, it might become possible to predict the life expectancy of a particular grammatical feature and the relative probability of several alternative ways in which it might be transformed, replaced, or lost without replacement.

More useful, perhaps, for the practicing historical linguist, but also more laborious and exacting would be to look not at the gross over-all changes in structure but rather at the individual, often minute, innovations whose cumulation over centuries results in the gross changes which can be measured by typology. A sufficiently large collection of such individual changes, appropriately classified, should give linguists a measure of the relative plausibility of different solutions for problems in historical grammar. A change which is recorded as having occurred 20 times will be more plausible than one recorded only 5 times, and both will be more plausible than one for which no parallel can be found at all.

At present each linguist judges the plausibility of a newly proposed solution pretty much by what he happens to remember of the morphologic innovations which during his career he has been led, for one reason or another, to accept as plausible. A reasonably objective standard of plausibility should make it easier for historical linguists to agree on solutions for problems of historical morphology that at present are still disputed, or, in the case of many non-Indo-European languages, not yet even attacked.

However, the collection and classifying of parallel morphologic changes would not be easy. The large number of individual cases to be treated would make the work laborious and time-consuming; the decision as to what constitutes an individual case would often be delicate; the construction and application of a system of classification might prove difficult; and the lack of an agreed-on criterion of plausibility to begin with would bias the results in favor of the investigators' preconceived ideas about linguistic change.

As an experiment in looking for universals by comparing typologies, I have compared the typologies of 14 Indo-European languages, using the 10 indices described by Joseph H. Greenberg in *International Journal of American Linguistics* 26.178–194 (1960; reprinted from *Method and Perspective in Anthropology: Papers in Honor of Wilson D. Wallis*, 1954).

As I am well aware, my study is of very limited value except as a preliminary exploration. The lack of data from non-Indo-European languages means that any universal or near-universal tendencies of change or retention found may be valid only for Indo-European. Like Henry Ford and the color scheme of the Model-T, we can say that any uniformities we observe will be true of the descendants of any language, provided that language happens to be Proto-Indo-European. But not even this much generalization is possible, since the failure to include samples from many of the important branches of Indo-European leaves it uncertain how much of the regularity observable in our samples is true of all Indo-European. At least my figures have some negative value: any failure of the languages sampled to develop alike will a fortiori be true of the world's languages as a whole.

Another weakness of the material used here is the small size of the samples, 100 words of text from each language. Although I am ignorant of statistical methods, I strongly suspect that many of the indices calculated from such short samples have little statistical validity. One of the urgent desiderata of current typology is to determine the minimum size of sample needed to be reasonably sure of having an accurate picture of a language.

An expanded and refined list of indices, perhaps along the lines suggested by Voegelin, Ramanujan, and Voegelin (*IJAL* 26.198–205) would no doubt reveal more than the 10 used by Greenberg. However, it seemed outside the scope of this paper to get involved in trying to devise a new typology; besides, I wanted to be able to use the figures already calculated for Indo-European languages by Greenberg.

The Indo-European languages for which Greenberg gives indices are Classical Sanskrit (a passage from the *Hitopadeśa*, date of compilation unknown but certainly before the fourteenth century A.D.); Old English (a passage from the Alfredian translation of Boethius, about 900 A.D.); Modern English (a passage from the *New Yorker*, 1952 A.D.); Modern Persian (a passage from a chrestomathy published in 1889 A.D.).[1] I abbreviate these as ClSk., OE, NE, and NP. I have taken unchanged the figures given in the table on page 193 of Greenberg's article (*IJAL* 26), without trying to repeat his calculations, although discrepancies in the totals of some indices which, according to my understanding of the method, ought to add up to identical figures suggest that there are some inaccuracies. In the following I have marked figures taken over from Greenberg with an asterisk.

The ten languages which I myself sampled were:

1. Vedic Sanskrit (abbreviated RV), *Rig-Veda* 1.32 from the beginning (*indrasya*) to *asya* in stanza 6. Since Greenberg's sample of Sanskrit comes from a period of the language differing significantly in morphology and syntax from Vedic, I thought it would be worth while to put beside it a specimen of genuinely old Sanskrit and see what differences, if any, would be revealed. Although *Rig-Veda* 1.32 is not one of the oldest of Vedic hymns, it seems old enough to be a fair sample of the earliest available Indo-Aryan. Its date is probably somewhere in the first half of the first millennium B.C.

2. Asoka's Rock Edicts (Asoka), in the version of Girnar, from the beginning of Edict I (*iyaṃ*) to the end of the fourth line of Edict II (*katā*), following the edition of Jules Bloch, *Les inscriptions d'Asoka* (Paris, 1950). This was chosen as a sample of early Middle Indic, securely datable to the middle of the third century B.C.

3. Bengali (Bg.), a passage from the 1862 edition of Kaliprasanna Sinha's *Hutom penchār nakshā* as printed in S. K. Chatterji's *Bengali Phonetic Reader* (London, 1928), from *chele bæla* (page 73) to *siṭi* in line 6 of page 75. I chose Bengali to represent modern Indo-Aryan because from my slight acquaintance with modern Indic I suspected that Bengali had diverged more than most of its sister languages from ancient Indic and that it would be relatively easy to learn enough about it to make the judgments needed for a typological analysis.

4. Old Persian (OP), the first column of Darius I's Bisotun inscription, from θ*ātiy* in line 24 to *pasā*- in line 36, following the edition of R. G. Kent, *Old Persian* 117 (second edition; New Haven, 1953). This text is securely dated to the last two decades of the sixth century B.C. Greenberg had already calculated indices for Modern Persian, and therefore as a representative of ancient Iranian I took Old Persian, the dialect closest to being a direct ancestor of Modern Persian.

5. Cuneiform Hittite (Hitt.), *The Apology of Hattusilis*, tablet I, column I, from the beginning of line 9 (*A-BU-YA*) to *-as-* in line 21, as given in E. H. Sturtevant's *Hittite Chrestomathy* 42–45 (Philadelphia, 1935). This text belongs to the thirteenth century B.C. Although Hittite texts older by several centuries are available, my experience with the language leads me to doubt that they would show up very different typologically from the sample here studied. It should be noted that the readings of some of the Hittite words written logographically are unknown, so that sometimes I have had to guess about the number of morphemes in a word and whether they were combined agglutinatively or not.

6. Homeric Greek (Hom.), *Iliad* 1.22 (*enth*') to *para* in line 34, as printed by Walter Leaf in his second edition of the *Iliad* (Lon-

don, 1902). This is possibly from one of the older parts of the Homeric Epic, and is probably not later than the early eighth century B.C. Since the fragments of Mycenaean provide no texts usable for computing typological indices, Homer constitutes the earliest available Greek.

7. New Testament Greek (NT), the seventh chapter of Luke from the beginning (*epeidē*) to *gar* in verse 6, using the text of A. Souter, *Novum testamentum graece* (Oxford, 1910). This text, dating from the first century A.D., seemed a convenient intermediate point between Homer and Modern Greek, and also offered opportunity for comparison of the same passage in Gothic and Old Church Slavic.

8. Modern Greek (NGk.), from the *Khamena logia* (1888) of Jean Psichari, as printed by Albert Thumb, *Handbuch der neugriechischen Volksprache* 254 (second edition; Strassburg, 1910). The specimen starts at the beginning of the second paragraph (*aphēste*) and goes as far as *pia* in the third line from the end of the paragraph.

9. Gothic (Go.), Luke 7.1 (*bi*) to *uf* in verse 6, corresponding (except for a few words at the end) to the sample of New Testament Greek. The Gothic translation of the Bible was made in the fourth century A.D., and so provides a specimen of Germanic about 500 years older than the Old English text studied by Greenberg. I have followed the readings of Wilhelm Streitberg, *Die gotische Bibel* (second edition; Heidelberg, 1919).

10. Old Church Slavic (OCS), Luke 7.1 (*egda*) to *sebe* in verse 7, using the text of the Zographensis manuscript as printed by A. Leskien, *Handbuch der altbulgarischen Sprache* (third edition; Weimar, 1902). The Slavic translation of the Bible, made in the latter part of the ninth century A.D., is the oldest available Balto-Slavic.

Typological studies of several more languages would have been needed to provide an adequate sampling of Indo-European as a whole. Particularly desirable additions would have been Latin (with samples of early and late Latin, for example Plautus and

Jerome) and one or more modern Romance languages; some Celtic, say Old, and Modern Irish and one of the British languages; a modern Slavic language; Lithuanian; Albanian; Classical Modern Armenian; and Tocharian.

Something needs to be said about the methods I have used in calculating the indices. In general I have not tried to make complete and rigorous grammatical analyses, but rather have proceeded very often by rule of thumb in deciding on word and morpheme boundaries and classifying morphemes into radical, derivational, and inflectional. Of the ten languages studied, Bengali and Modern Greek are the least familiar to me, and it is here that I am most likely to have made mistakes out of ignorance. Since I have not made counts of my own for the four languages studied by Greenberg, I do not know how much my personal way of calculating indices differs from his; however, the fairly close agreement between most of his figures for Classical Sanskrit and mine for Vedic suggests that our results for other languages might not be very divergent.

In the matter of word boundaries I have probably been overinfluenced by whether or not a space was left between letters by the editor of the text I was using. Thus I have considered *tha* a word in Modern Greek, although I suspect that more information on its privileges of occurrence might show it to be in fact a verbal prefix.[2] In general, I have tried to apply Greenberg's rule (*IJAL* 26.192) that 'a nucleus boundary is a word boundary if it is possible to insert an indefinitely long sequence of nuclei.' However, I have not followed Greenberg in considering a sequence like Latin *dominúsque* a single word because the accent of *dominús-* differs from the accent of *dóminus* in other positions. Greenberg here seems to be introducing a phonologic criterion into what is really a grammatical problem. Hence I have considered enclitics as independent words, perhaps more liberally than I should have.

In segmenting words into morphemes I have also differed from Greenberg (*IJAL* 26.189) in not segmenting unless at least one of the putative morphs existed elsewhere with a meaning similar to a part of the total meaning of the sequence in question. In practice,

I think this has made a difference only in the case of etymologically polymorphemic sequences which as the result of semantic change have come to have a meaning not containing the meaning of any of their parts.

In segmenting inflectional morphemes I have sometimes found it hard to decide where to posit rather long morphemes with two or three semantic components and where to make use of partial resemblances between forms to segment out shorter morphemes with fewer semantic components. In general, I have not set up separate number morphemes (except in Bengali), but have considered number as combined into single morphemes with the case markers of nouns and the person markers of verbs. In Vedic, Asokan, Homeric, and New Testament Greek, I set up feminine gender markers as morphemes; in Old Persian, Modern Greek, and Gothic, gender seemed best treated as one component along with case and number in the noun-inflecting morphemes; in Bengali and Hittite, this problem did not arise, and the Old Church Slavic sample contained no feminines. In Vedic and Hittite, mediopassive verb endings were analyzed as two morphemes each, the active ending plus a middle voice marker; in other languages with a distinction of voice, the mediopassive endings were considered single morphemes. In Hittite, Vedic, and Homeric, where a difference in the personal ending is sometimes the sole mark distinguishing present from imperfect tense, it had to be decided whether the present endings were different morphemes from the imperfect endings or were composed of personal endings plus a nonpast morpheme; only in the case of Hittite did the structure of the language seem clearly to warrant segmentation.

I have posited zero morphs, but probably fewer than many linguists would. Thus I have not analyzed verbs consisting only of root and personal ending as containing a zero tense formant, or nouns consisting only of root and case-number ending as containing a zero noun-deriving suffix. Present stems of denominative verbs I take to have only a single derivational morpheme, not a derivational morpheme plus zero present-stem formant. On the other hand, I have considered vocatives and second singular active imperatives as containing zero case-number or person-mood endings even where there was no overt vocative or second singular imperative ending in the language.

For agglutination my indices are more likely to be too high than too low, since it is more likely that I forgot (or was ignorant of) nonpredictable allomorphs than that I failed to see how a set of allomorphs could be so described as to be automatically predictable.

In classifying morphemes into roots, derivational affixes, and inflectional affixes, two main problems arose. The first involves the status of morphemes which are uninflected when they are separate words—so-called prepositions and adverbs. When they are parts of larger words, it was not clear to what extent these should be considered derivational prefixes and to what extent the first roots of compound words. On the one hand, their numbers are limited, and their meanings are usually not concrete, which according to Greenberg (*IJAL* 26. 191) makes them prefixes. On the other hand, these morphemes act like noun stems in some of the more archaic Indo-European languages in that they combine into single words with following noun stems but do not do so with verb stems. I have, therefore, decided to treat Vedic and Homeric words like *sam-udrá* and *eú-phēmos* as compounds; in other languages, where these morphemes combine with verb stems as well as with noun stems, I have considered them prefixes. As a result, in all of the ten languages studied by me there are compound nouns (and verbs derived from them), but compound verbs only in Bengali.

The second problem in classifying morphemes was to draw the line between inflection and derivation. Greenberg's rule here is: 'Derivational morphemes [are] morphemes which, when in construction with a root morpheme, establish a sequence which may always be substituted for some particular class of single morpheme ... without producing a change in the construction' (*IJAL* 26.191). Although this is probably a good criterion for arriving at a useful classification of the affixes of the world's languages in general, I feel that Indo-European affixes can be better classified somewhat differently. In Proto-Indo-European there is a contrast between derivational suffixes and inflectional endings. The latter include only case-number morphemes in the nouns, and person-number-voice-nonpast-imperative morphemes and augment in the verbs. All the rest of Proto-Indo-European morphology is derivation, including feminine gender markers and the formants of tense-aspect and modal stems and participles. Greenberg's rule would probably lead to much the same classification.

But one of the characteristic developments shared by all Indo-European languages since about 500 B.C. is that gender, tense-aspect, mood, infinitive, and participle-forming affixes have come to be sufficiently ubiquitous and paradigmatic to justify a change of status which within the frame of Greenberg's typology seems best describable by saying that they have become inflectional. I am not at all sure whether Greenberg's essentially syntactic criterion for distinguishing inflection and derivation would lead to this result.

My treatment of these morphemes was as follows: everywhere that I recognized separate feminine gender morphemes I considered them inflectional, perhaps wrongly. In Vedic, Old Persian, and Hittite, tense-aspect, mood, and participial formants were assigned to derivation. In Homeric, I treated these affixes and infinitive formants as inflectional, although hesitantly. In Asokan, Bengali, New Testament Greek, Modern Greek, Gothic, and Old Church Slavic, they belong clearly to inflection.

In Bengali, where there is no grammatical number concord, the plural formants of nouns were considered derivational.

The counting of prefixes and suffixes presented no problems once the words had been segmented into morphemes and it had been decided what to count as prefixes and what as the first element of compound words. Since the Vedic sample contained three infixes, I added to Greenberg's ten indices an index of infixes per word (Inf/W), numbered 6*a*.

Similarly in counting nexuses and assigning them to isolating, pure inflection, and concord I experienced little trouble. However, my judgments of the number of nexuses were all ad hoc and not rechecked, so that I may have been inconsistent in analyzing different sentences of similar structure. Regarding the assignment of nexuses to the three categories, I considered conjunctions, adverbs, and prepositional phrases as connected outwardly by isolating constructions; the relation of verb or preposition to its object as pure inflection, except in Bengali, where the relation to an object without case ending is isolating; and that of verb to subject as concord. As a result of rounding off to the nearest hundredth, the totals of these three syntactic indices are sometimes 1.01 instead of 1.00.

TABLE 1

	1	2	3	4	5	6	6*a*	7	8	9	10
	M/W	A/J	R/W	D/W	I/W	P/W	Inf/W	S/W	O/N	Pi/N	Co/N
RV	2.56	.08	1.10	.49	.97	.19	.03	1.24	.26	.48	.27
*ClSk.	2.59	.09	1.13	.62	.84	.16	—	1.18	.16	.46	.38
Asoka	2.52	.26	1.22	.44	.86	.07	.00	1.23	.40	.18	.42
Bg.	1.90	.46	1.09	.28	.53	.01	.00	.80	.57	.29	.14
OP	2.41	.20	1.02	.41	.98	.19	.00	1.20	.23	.39	.38
*NP	1.52	.34	1.03	.10	.39	.01	—	.49	.52	.29	.19
Hitt.	1.95	.42	1.00	.24	.71	.01	.00	.94	.35	.32	.33
Hom.	2.07	.10	1.01	.21	.85	.06	.00	1.00	.48	.27	.26
NT	2.45	.12	1.03	.28	1.14	.18	.00	1.24	.34	.32	.34
NGk.	1.82	.40	1.02	.12	.68	.03	.00	.77	.53	.21	.26
Go.	2.31	.19	1.03	.30	.98	.09	.00	1.19	.37	.34	.29
*OE	2.12	.11	1.00	.20	.90	.06	—	1.03	.15	.47	.38
*NE	1.68	.30	1.00	.15	.53	.04	—	.64	.75	.14	.11
OCS	2.29	.20	1.00	.34	.95	.12	.00	1.17	.41	.33	.26

* Figures for these languages were calculated by Greenberg.

The meanings of the index labels in this table are:

M/W: morphemes per word (measuring synthesis)
A/J: agglutinative intraword morph junctures divided by the total number of intraword morph junctures
R/W: roots per word (measuring compounding)
D/W: derivational morphemes per word
I/W: inflectional morphemes per word
P/W: prefixes per word
Inf/W: infixes per word
S/W: suffixes per word
O/N: isolating constructions divided by the total number of grammatical nexuses
Pi/N: pure inflectional constructions divided by nexuses
Co/N: concordial constructions divided by nexuses

Table 1 presents the resulting indices, including those of the four Indo-European languages calculated by Greenberg.

The first two indices, M/W and A/J, can be said to reflect the over-all morphologic complexity of a language; the higher the M/W index and the lower the A/J index, the more complicated the morphology will be. According to a widespread view, Indo-European languages have generally been getting less synthetic and more agglutinative as time goes by. Rearranging the first two columns of Table 1, with M/W indices in descending and A/J indices in ascending order, will help to show how far this view is borne out by our material.

TABLE 2

	M/W		A/J	
1.	*ClSk.	2.59	RV	.08
2.	RV	2.56	*ClSk.	.09
3.	Asoka	2.52	Hom.	.10
4.	NT	2.45	*OE	.11
5.	OP	2.41	NT	.12
6.	Go.	2.31	Go.	.19
7.	OCS	2.29	OP,OCS	.20
8.	*OE	2.12		
9.	Hom.	2.07	Asoka	.26
10.	Hitt.	1.95	*NE	.30
11.	Bg.	1.90	*NP	.34
12.	NGk.	1.82	NGk.	.40
13.	*NE	1.68	Hitt.	.42
14.	*NP	1.52	Bg.	.46

* Languages calculated by Greenberg.

In both columns of Table 2, there is considerable correlation between time and position in the table. In both, the four modern languages are at or near the bottom, and in both Sanskrit is at the top. The differences between Vedic and Classical Sanskrit turn out to be small and probably not significant, suggesting that in this area of its grammar Classical Sanskrit was effectively stabilized at a level not measurably advanced over Vedic.

But between the extremes both lists show several departures from chronological order. Hittite, the earliest attested of the

14, is very far out of place in both columns, being tenth in synthesis and thirteenth in agglutination. This aberrancy has long been noted and discussed by Indo-Europeanists. According to one view, the Anatolian branch of Indo-European (to which Hittite belongs) separated from the rest of the Indo-European family before the development of some of the complications common to or presupposed by all the other Indo-European languages. Others think the difference is due to extremely rapid evolution of Hittite, perhaps influenced by speakers of some language with a simpler or radically different morphology. My own opinion is that although the low index of synthesis may be partly an archaism (which will be discussed later), the high index of agglutination is almost certainly largely the result of innovation, and much of the analytic tendency of the language may be innovation also. Indeed, I would even hazard the speculation that Hittite may be a Creole, that is, the descendant of a pidgin originally used for communication between speakers of Indo-European and non-Indo-European languages in Anatolia. [3]

The M/W list shows two other departures from chronological order. Old Persian follows instead of preceding Asokan and New Testament Greek. If significant, this position probably reflects the relatively rapid linguistic evolution which resulted in Old Persian being no longer clearly understood less than two centuries after the time of Darius: the inscriptions of the late Achaemenid kings show a confusion in grammar and spelling which indicates that the language they spoke was already essentially Middle Persian. I do not know the reasons for this rapid evolution. However, it seems significant that later in its history, for about the last thousand years, the evolution of Persian seems to have been quite slow. [4] This invites speculation. Is the structure of Modern Persian in some sense in a state of equilibrium, relatively free of the imbalances that presumably are the chief cause of structural change? If so, are other Indo-European languages tending to the same sort of structure? Or is the relative stability of Modern Persian the counterpart of its preceding rapid evolution; in other words, is there some more-or-less uniform rate of change in language, such that a period of rapid change is regularly followed by a period in which the language changes more slowly, covering in the end the same ground that another language might travel at a more uniform speed?

The remaining aberrancy is the position of Homeric. Approximately contemporary with Vedic, this language is far down on the list, below Old Church Slavic and Old English of the ninth century A.D. Indeed, Homeric Greek ranks even below its own daughter language, New Testament Greek. That this is no mere accident of the samples counted is suggested by supplementary counts that I made of Hesiod's *Works and Days* (beginning with *Zeùs* in line 143 and ending with *génos* in line 156, according to Rzach's third edition, Leipzig, 1913) and Plato's *Apology* (from *hoûtos* at the end of 20*e* to the first *pote* in 21*b*, following J. Burnet's edition, Oxford, 1900). The first of these is epic poetry, undated, but linguistically clearly later than Homer; Plato is early fourth century B.C. For Hesiod, I found an index of 2.19 and for Plato 2.30, suggesting that there was indeed a steady increase in synthesis within Greek of the first millennium B.C.

These figures show clearly that the popular conception of an uninterrupted decrease in synthesis within the history of Indo-European is too simple. Furthermore, comparative reconstruction suggests that the Indo-European protolanguage was probably less synthetic even than Homer, to judge by its relatively large number of nouns and verbs without derivational affixes (that is, root nouns and athematic root verbs, including injunctives). There is even some evidence that at one time a verb could not contain more than one derivational affix—for example, a verb characterized by a tense-aspect suffix could not add to this a subjunctive or optative mood suffix.

It therefore seems necessary to substitute for the oversimple straight-line decrease in synthesis a curve with at least one inflection. At the earliest period which our reconstructions can reach, the number of morphemes per word was rising in the Indo-European dialects. Within each dialect it reached a maximum, and then turned downward, in which direction it has been moving ever since. (Further data, of course, could easily reveal that this scheme also is too simple.) The low M/W index of Hittite would then be due partly to an early turn downward, partly to a steep rate of fall.

Of the subgroups from which more than one representative is studied here, Indo-Iranian and Germanic evidently reached their maxima before the earliest recorded texts. I suspect that this would prove to be true of most other Indo-European subgroups as well, so that only in Greek are we privileged to see an Indo-European language becoming more synthetic.

If one assumes that the history of Indo-European synthesis here proposed is correct, it would be interesting to know the time range within which the different dialects were at their M/W maxima—that is, was Indo-Iranian abnormally quick in evolving, or was Greek abnormally slow? Unfortunately, the late date at which most Indo-European languages are attested makes this question unanswerable. The only subgroup besides Anatolian, Indo-Iranian, and Greek adequately attested before the writing of the New Testament is Italic. Hence, languages like Germanic, Balto-Slavic, and Celtic may have reached their maxima no earlier than Greek did, or they may have reached them by 1000 B.C. or even earlier.

It is less easy to fit the indices of agglutination into a simple scheme. The high Old Persian index could be correlated with the language's low M/W index, and taken as one more symptom of the accelerated development that Persian was beginning to undergo. But the low index of Old English and the high index of Asokan suggest rather that the index of agglutination was generally subject to much more oscillation than was the index of synthesis. I think this can be plausibly explained: complex morphophonemics is mainly the result of sound changes which cause morphs to develop differently in different environments. A language undergoing no sound change would in time eliminate most of its morphophonemic alternations by analogic spread of one allomorph for each morpheme, and the history of a language's morphophonemics is largely a seesaw between sound change and analogy. Since sound changes presumably operate with little or no regard for morphology, it follows that a language tending to become more and more agglutinative can easily undergo a sound change which will temporarily arrest or even reverse the general trend.

Comparative reconstruction suggests that Proto-Indo-European was, if anything, less agglutinative than any of its descendants here studied. By internal reconstruction a stage can be envisioned in which part of the morphophonemic complexity (namely quantitative ablaut) did not exist, but in general it seems safe to say that if there ever was a maximum of morphophonemic complexity, it was a good deal earlier than the maximum of synthesis.

In the matter of compounding we find a radically different arrangement. Here Indic uniformly has a high R/W index, ranging from 1.09 in Bengali to 1.22 in Asokan. Apparently compounding became early established as a favorite way of joining morphemes in Indic, and remained popular there despite all the changes that the language underwent in other respects. The high index for Asokan is partly due to my having taken as a compound the oft-recurring *devanaṃpriya-* 'dear to the gods'. If this is taken as a phrase, the R/W index sinks to 1.16, still the highest in the corpus. It may be noted also that Asokan yielded the sole example of a three-root compound.

I strongly doubt that there is any significance to the ordering of the remaining ten languages, with indices ranging from 1.00 to 1.03. Whatever real differences there may be among them in frequency of compounds are evidently too small to be revealed by counting only 100 words of text.

In another way the method used here fails to reveal an important feature of Indo-European historical grammar. By not making a distinction (suggested by Voegelin, Ramanujan, and Voegelin, *IJAL* 26.200) between compound verbs and compound nouns, it fails to reveal that in all these languages compound nouns freely occur, but that only in Bengali and Modern Persian are there compound verbs (aside from rarities like English *housekeep*).[5] Considering how common verb compounding is in the world's languages, its slowness to develop in Indo-European suggests that compounding techniques may be a part of the grammar that is especially tenacious of old patterns and slow to develop new ones.

It seems appropriate to mention here an oft-noted archaism of Indo-European noun compounding, the appearance of the first element in its stem form, with no case or number ending. Thus in Russian *klinopis'* 'cuneiform writing', the word *klin* 'wedge' appears in a form which has otherwise disappeared from the language and which ignores the fact that the meaning of the compound would require a plural, probably in the instrumental case ('writing done with wedges'). It is commonly stated, probably correctly, that this feature of Indo-European compounding technique dates from a time before inflection of nouns for case and number had developed. What is usually not stated is that this is no evidence that case and number endings are a particularly late feature of Indo-European; once established, the pattern of compounding could have remained through tens of thousands of years.

Simply ranking the derivational, inflectional, prefixing, and suffixing indices would have little value, since these figures are essentially only a breakdown of information already contained in the M/W index. If a language has a high morpheme-per-word index, it will automatically have high indices in at least two, and probably all four, of the indices 4 through 7.[6] (For this reason, the summation technique used by Kroeber, *IJAL* 26.175, seems unlikely to prove very useful.)

These indices can be put to better use by calculating the ratios in each language of D/W to I/W and of P/W to S/W. In this way we can see whether there is any trend to enhance derivation as compared with inflection, or to change the relative frequency of prefixes and suffixes.

The ratios of derivation to inflection do not reveal to me any obvious tendency of change that might prove to be valid for all of Indo-European. In Indic and English the ratio seems to have increased with time; in Persian and Greek it has decreased. More striking is the tendency for Indic and Greek to cluster at opposite ends of the list, with Germanic tending to be low but not so low as Greek, while Iranian, Slavic, and Hittite occupy the center. This suggests that each subgroup, once a particular ratio of derivation to inflection had been established, tended to maintain that ratio without a great deal of change. But all conclusions from these figures are subject to a great deal of caution, in view of the somewhat uneven way in which I decided what was inflection and what was derivation. For instance, had I treated tense, mood, and participle formants in Homer as derivational, as I did in Vedic, Old Persian, and Hittite, the Derivation/Inflection ratio for Homer would have been .67, well above everything but Classical Sanskrit (in which, to be sure, I strongly suspect that Greenberg in fact treated such morphemes as inflectional).

TABLE 3

	D/W / I/W		P/W / S/W	
1.	*ClSk.	.74	OP	.16
2.	Bg.	.53	RV, NT (2.–3.)	.15
3.	RV, Asoka (3.–4.)	.51		
4.			*ClSk.	.14
5.	OP	.42	OCS	.10
6.	OCS	.36	Go.	.08
7.	Hitt.	.34	Hom., Asoka *OE *NE (7.–10.)	.06
8.	Go.	.31		
9.	*NE	.28		
10.	*NP	.26		
11.	Hom., NT (11.–12.)	.25	NGk.	.04
12.			*NP	.02
13.	*OE	.22	Bg., Hitt. (13.–14.)	.01
14.	NGk.	.18		

* Languages calculated by Greenberg.

The ratios of prefixes to suffixes, on the other hand, seem to show some correlation with the indices of morphologic complexity shown in Table 2, especially the morpheme-per-word index. The four languages with prefix-to-suffix ratios of .14 to .16 have correspondingly high morpheme-per-word indices; Gothic and Old Church Slavic are next in both lists, followed by Homeric Greek and Old English; and Hittite with the four modern languages is at the end. Only Asokan seriously disturbs the picture, being much lower in the prefix-to-suffix list than in the morpheme-per-word list. Also, the rankings within each group are not the same in both lists, and perhaps further data would show the apparent correlation to be illusory. But, tentatively, we can say that in Indo-European a high morpheme-to-word ratio appears to go with a high prefix-to-suffix ratio. Greenberg has suggested

(*Essays in Linguistics*, 89–92) that prefixes may be psychologically more difficult to work with than are suffixes. Although Chomsky (*Word* 15.202–203) has cast serious doubt on most of the reasons advanced by Greenberg for the relative infrequency of prefixes in the world's languages, it does seem possible that there may be some fundamental difficulty about prefixes compared with suffixes, so that a high ratio of prefixes and prevalence of polymorphemic words are just two aspects of a basic trait of 'complexity', and a rise in one could be expected to entail a rise in the other.

The correlation between prefix-to-suffix ratios and indices of agglutination seems best toward the bottom of the list. In both, Bengali and Hittite come at the end, preceded first by Modern Persian and Modern Greek, and then by Asokan and Modern English, and in both lists Gothic is sixth; but the arrangements of the remaining seven languages in the upper part of the list seem unrelated to one another.

It seems worth while to remark that the extremely low prefix-to-suffix ratio of Hittite agrees well with the hypothesis that this ratio is somehow tied up with the general morphologic complexity of a language; otherwise we might expect Hittite to have a prefix-to-suffix ratio comparable to that of Homeric or Vedic.

Infixes were found only in the Vedic sample. Several of the other languages tested have them, but the samples I examined did not happen to contain any. (Whether Greenberg found any at all in his samples he does not say—hence the dashes in Table 1.) As far as the evidence goes, the ratio of infixes to suffixes, like that of prefixes to suffixes, is correlated with the general morphologic complexity of the language. Counts of longer samples ought to show whether this correlation indeed holds good or not.

The three remaining indices are primarily syntactical, and I do not see how they could be used to get information about morphology that cannot be gotten better and more easily in other ways. Thus No. 8, the index of Isolation, is directly proportional to the number of uninflected words in the text, and hence could conceivably be used to estimate the ratio of inflected to uninflected words in the language, or the average number of inflectional morphemes per inflected word. But both these figures can be obtained more simply and more accurately by counts performed on the text itself.

Similarly the Pure Inflection and Concord indices could be compared with each other to give a ratio of concordial to noncon-cordial inflectional morphemes, but again this could be better obtained by simply counting within the sample. And the information obtained would, I think, be considerably less interesting than a study of the Proto-Indo-European concords themselves and the ways in which they have been retained, lost, or replaced by new ones. But this would lead into the second kind of investigation mentioned at the beginning of this paper, in which the changes themselves rather than the states resulting from the changes are compared.

However, not to limit the scope of this paper too severely to morphology, I have calculated the quotients obtained by dividing indices of Concord by indices of Pure Inflection, in order to see if any obvious trend through time would emerge. The results, in descending order, are: Asoka 2.3; NGk. 1.2; NT 1.1; Hitt. 1.0; OP .97; Hom. .96; Go. .85; *ClSk. .83; *OE. 81; *NE, OCS .79; *NP .66; RV .56; Bg. .48. (Again asterisks indicate languages calculated by Greenberg.) I am unable to discover from these figures anything that looks like a consistent direction of change.

It appears, then, that typology, even in its present very imperfect state, reveals well some features of Indo-European drift, namely a general rise in agglutination, an early rise in synthesis followed by a decline, and a general decline in the prefix- (and infix)-to-suffix ratio. The aberrant position of Hittite in all three of these features is at once enough to require some special explanation (whether a protolanguage distinct from the rest or creolization). On the other hand, larger samples are needed to find out what has been happening to compounding, and the comparison of derivation with inflection and of pure inflection with concord suggests that in these areas there has been no general drift in either direction.

To look for uniform retentions within the typology of Indo-European seems of little value until indices for more non-Indo-European languages are available. Using the four non-Indo-

European languages for which indices are given by Greenberg, we can only say such things as that synthesis has not (yet) gotten as low as in Vietnamese (1.52 in Modern Persian, 1.06 in Vietnamese) nor agglutination as high as in Swahili (.46 in Bengali, .67 in Swahili); compounds and prefixes exist in all the Indo-European languages studied (even though the samples of Hittite, Old English, Modern English, and Old Church Slavic happen not to contain any compounds), while Yakut, Vietnamese, and Eskimo lack prefixes altogether and Eskimo has no compounds.[7]

As an example of what might be done comparing the changes that have taken place in Indo-European subgroups without restricting oneself to the presently available typological indices, I shall add here some remarks on the history of the three positional classes of affixes in Indo-European.

Suffixes were numerous and important in Proto-Indo-European, forming the principal machinery of derivation and inflection and responsible for most of the morphophonemic alternation of root morphemes. Suffixes are still numerous in all the Indo-European languages, and to a considerable extent are etymologically derived from Proto-Indo-European suffixes of similar meaning. This is particularly true of the case-number endings of the noun and the personal endings of the verb, the morphemes which in Proto-Indo-European were already fairly well organized into paradigmatic structures. Most of the innovation among these has been the result of sound change (often causing a suffix to disappear altogether), analogic transfer from one class of stems to another, and reductions in the number of distinct grammatical categories recognized by the language. Indo-European derivational suffixes, including the tense and mood formants of the verb, have been somewhat less conservative, partly, I suspect, because derivation is naturally more casual and less paradigmatic than inflection, and partly because the tense-aspect-mood systems of the Indo-European languages have generally evolved structurally much more than the case-gender-number systems of the noun.

The history of prefixes and infixes has been quite different. Proto-Indo-European had only one infix, *-né-* (ablauting with

-n-) inserted between the second and third consonant of three-consonant roots and forming present stems of verbs, for example **k̑l̥-né-w-* to the root **k̑lew-* 'hear', or **yu-né-g-* to the root **yewg-* 'join, harness'. Already in the protolanguage such presents were not common—I should guess there were at most about forty. In most dialects of Indo-European their numbers have been sharply reduced, and no new infixes created (unless, to be sure, one analyze forms like English *feet* and *sang* as containing infixes rather than zero suffixes). As far as I know, only Baltic now possesses a productive nasal-infix formation, of the type Lithuanian *šviñta* 'grows bright', pret. *švìto*. On the other hand, the infixed presents had begun to give rise to nasal suffixes already in the protolanguage: by recutting nasal presents to roots ending in **w* and **A*, new suffixes *-*néw*- (-*nu*-) and *-*néA*- (-*nA*-) were created, of which at least the former enjoyed a fair popularity in several branches of Indo-European.

What little can be said about the origin of the Proto-Indo-European infix does not bear out Greenberg's suggestion (*Essays in Linguistics*, 92) that infixes usually arise from prefixes. At least, I know of no evidence whatever that the Indo-European nasal infix was ever a prefix. On the other hand, it could conceivably have begun as a suffix. According to one view, not entirely satisfactory, an early prestage of Indo-European had typically two-consonant roots, for example, **k̑l* 'hear', **yw* 'join'. To these might be suffixed a nasal, *-*né*-, or some other consonant, for instance, **w* or **g*; if, now, such a consonant is suffixed both to the plain root and to the nasalized form, we get stems like **k̑l-éw-*: **kl-né-w-* or **yéw-g-*: **yu-né-g-*, in which *-ne-*, originally a suffix, has become, so to speak, embedded within the word as an infix.

As for prefixes, Proto-Indo-European had two kinds. One was the so-called augment, a vowel (mostly *e*) that could be prefixed to verbal forms which in themselves were ambiguous as to mood and time (the so-called injunctive) but with the augment were unambiguously indicative and (almost always) preterit. Certain features of the augment's accentuation in Greek and Sanskrit and its failure to occur outside a contiguous group of languages (Greek, Armenian, Indo-Iranian, perhaps Phrygian) suggest that up until late in the prehistory of Indo-European it was an independent word (meaning roughly 'really') which came to be more and more restricted in its freedom of occurrence until finally it disappeared altogether in most of Indo-European, and in the dialects ancestral to Greek, Armenian, and Indo-Iranian was limited to the position immediately preceding a finite indicative verb. The limitation to this one position automatically entailed a change of status from word to prefix.

The subsequent history of the augment in the three subgroups where it is found is generally parallel. At first, in Vedic, it is a meaningful morpheme, marking as preterit indicative forms that without it were unmarked as to time and mood. In Homer the use of such unmarked forms in values other than past indicative has already largely disappeared, so that augment is mostly an optional addition to a form already unambiguously characterized, although it still performs some service in distinguishing a form like *ephéromen* 'we carried' from *phéromen*, which can mean either 'we carried' or 'we carry'. Then there came a period, represented by Classical Sanskrit, Old Persian, and Classical Greek, in which the augment is universally required with certain preterit tenses (even though most of these would have been unambiguously characterized without it), or else is not used at all—so in Avestan. Apparently it was psychologically easier to use an augment consistently everywhere or nowhere than it was to decide in every case whether or not one was likely to be understood without it. Yaghnobi, the one modern Indo-Iranian language to retain any of the old preterits, is apparently still at this stage, using the augment everywhere.

The next stage is that represented in Indo-Iranian by Pali (a Middle Indic language roughly contemporary with Asokan), Modern Greek, and Classical Armenian (fifth century A.D.). The tenses that take augment are now unambiguously marked even without it, and (consequently?) have begun to drop it, especially from the longer words. In most of Indo-Iranian, from Prakrit and Middle Persian onward, the old preterit tenses were replaced by new forms based on the past participle, so that the augment has now completely disappeared. In Classical Armenian the augment is already severely limited, occurring only in aorists that without it would be monosyllabic. A cursory glance at a Modern Armenian grammar indicates that there is now only one aorist with augment, *ekaw* 'came'; since the present, *gay*, has a different consonant, this is presumably a case of suppletion between stems *ga-* and *eka-*, in which *e-* is no longer a separate morpheme. Thus only Yaghnobi and Modern Greek now retain the Indo-European augment.

The other type of prefixation in Proto-Indo-European is the so-called reduplication, in which the initial consonant of a root, followed by a vowel (and sometimes another consonant), is prefixed to the root. Reduplication occurred in the protolanguage mostly as a formant deriving tense-aspect stems from roots. As a formant of present and aorist stems it was in competition with a number of suffixes, and never achieved any great popularity except in Sanskrit, where it was used to form intensive presents, causative aorists, and (in conjunction with a suffix) desideratives. For the most part, reduplicated aorists and presents survived only as isolated irregularities, becoming continually fewer and less transparent in structure. Only in the perfect, where it had no serious competition, did reduplication settle itself firmly, reaching probably its maximum development in Hellenistic Greek. But even in the perfect the reduplication was subject to restructuring and loss in a way that seems quite unparalleled among the suffixes. Thus in Modern Greek the perfect participle (the one form of the tense surviving) regularly lacks reduplication. In Germanic, where the preterit of strong verbs mostly continues the Indo-European perfect, most verbs had lost reduplication already in Proto-Germanic; those that still had it in Proto-Germanic underwent extremely violent remodelings in North and West Germanic, resulting in its disappearance (and the creation of half a dozen new ablaut patterns).

As a result of these changes, the Proto-Indo-European prefixes have almost completely disappeared from modern Indo-European. In the samples of Asokan, Bengali, Hittite, Modern Greek, Gothic, and Old Church Slavic discussed earlier in this paper, not one prefix inherited from Proto-Indo-European occurs, and I doubt strongly that Greenberg found any in his samples of Old English, Modern English, and Persian.

But the stock of prefixes has made gains from another source by a development which seems to have gone on parallel in all the branches of Indo-European except Tocharian that survived the middle of the first millennium B.C. In Proto-Indo-European, as still in Hittite, Homeric, and Vedic, there were combinations of verb and adverb comparable to English expressions like 'go up' or 'come in'. The order of words was not fixed; the adverb normally preceded the verb, but might do so immediately or separated by other words. But by a process similar to that previously assumed for the prehistory of the augment, the order of words came to be more and more fixed, until (with a few exceptions, such as Old Irish) the adverb came to stand always immediately before the verb, forming a single accentual unit with it. The adverb was thus no longer an independent word, but a prefix to the verb. This in turn entailed a restructuring of the existing combinations of such adverbs with noun stems: what had been compounds now became nouns with prefixes.

Such neoprefixes occur already in Old Persian and New Testament Greek, and constitute most or all of the prefixes in the samples of later languages that I discussed earlier in this paper. (Only, as usual, Hittite is aberrant, having besides its free adverbs two verbal prefixes, of which one happens to occur in the sample studied.) To some extent even these new prefixes have by now fused with the following roots on account of semantic or phonologic change, and so ceased to be independent morphemes.

It seems, therefore, that Indo-European prefixes have shown little tenacity compared to suffixes, and have been created anew by only one process, the fusion of two words into one. There is nothing to parallel the creation of new suffixes by combining old ones or by reanalyzing the end of a stem as a suffix (type *ox-en*).

The history of Indo-European prefixing has yet another interesting feature. Of the three kinds of prefixes, reduplication, augment, and adverbs, the origins of the first are lost in the distances of prehistory, the augment probably became a prefix about the time that strong dialectal differences were arising in the protolanguage, and the development of the last dates from the recorded history of Indo-European. The morphophonemic complexity of each of these classes is in direct proportion to its antiquity. Reduplication, the oldest, is thoroughly nonagglutinating. The augment was probably agglutinative in Proto-Indo-European, and is nearly so in Sanskrit and Greek. In Old Persian it may in fact be agglutinative (I have assumed that it is in calculating the Old Persian A/J index), although the writing system does not permit certainty. But adverbial prefixes are almost everywhere agglutinative.

What this means, of course, is simply that the more recently created morpheme sequences have not been in the language long enough to be seriously disrupted by sound change. Applied to non-Indo-European languages, this observation might help to determine the relative age of different sets of affixes: the more morphophonemic alternation a set shows or entails in adjoining morphemes, the longer it is likely to have been in the language.

Notes

1. I have since learned that the text sampled by Greenberg is a story attributed to Saadi, who died in 1291 A.D. But, as H. H. Paper kindly informs me, its grammar is not significantly different from that of present-day colloquial Persian, so that my discussion of it as if it were from the nineteenth century probably makes for no serious distortions. In any case, this sample is later than any of the ten non-Modern samples investigated by Greenberg and me (with the possible exception of Classical Sanskrit). It should be noted that the division between Middle and Modern Persian is generally put in the eighth century A.D.
2. Fred W. Householder tells me that there is in fact good reason to consider *tha* a separate word, and not a verbal prefix.
3. This suggestion is, of course, not new.
4. Cf. note 1.
5. Householder calls my attention to the existence of verbal compounds in Modern Greek of the type *piyenoérkhome* 'come-and-go', but I gather they are not common. Verbs derived from compound nouns are of course common in many Indo-European languages.

6. Unless, as could conceivably happen, it has numerous and complex compounds, and very restricted derivation and inflexion.
7. Householder has sent me M/W and syntactic indices calculated for samples of Latin and Spanish by Heles Contreras. The samples are: Caesar, *De bello gallico* I.2, II.9, V.52; Gregory of Tours, *Historia Francorum* II.7, III.3, III.4; *Peregrinatio ad loca sancta* I.1, XII.1, XXV.1; E. Relaño, *Historia del lenguaje* (1953) p. 8; R. Gallegos, *Doña Bárbara* (1945) p. 96; and S. Reyes, *Mónica Sanders* (1951) p. 76. The figures are:

	M/W	O/N	Pi/N	Co/N
Caesar I.2	2.08	.11	.73	.16
Caesar II.9	2.16	.13	.67	.20
Caesar V.52	2.27	.09	.68	.23
Average	2.17	.11	.69	.20
Gregory II.7	2.11	.14	.69	.17
Gregory III.3	2.11	.16	.63	.21
Gregory III.4		.12	.68	.20
Average	2.11	.14	.67	.19
Peregr. I	1.82	.15	.62	.23
Peregr. XII	1.82	.18	.59	.23
Peregr. XXV	1.83	.19	.61	.20
Average	1.82	.17	.61	.22
Relaño	1.51	.42	.39	.19
Gallegos	1.58	.36	.40	.24
Reyes	1.47	.44	.30	.26
Average	1.52	.40	.36	.23

Householder's typescript lacks a figure for the M/W of the third sample of Gregory.

Contreras' counts invite some comment. In the first place, it seems noteworthy that the figures for different passages of the same Latin author are fairly close together, as are also the M/W indices of the three Spanish authors; but the syntactic indices for Spanish diverge considerably. This suggests that of the figures derived by Greenberg and me from counts of single 100-word passages, the M/W indices are probably fairly reliable, but the syntactic indices may well not be.

The M/W indices fit fairly well into the pattern of my Table 2. The highest index, 2.17, belongs to the oldest text, Caesar's polished first-century B.C. prose. This puts Caesar's Latin, with regard to synthesis, between my sample of Old Church Slavic and Greenberg's of Old English—much later texts than Caesar, but impressionistically of about equal morphologic complexity with Latin, and like Latin typologically fairly close to Proto-Indo-European. Then comes Gregory from the sixth century A.D., doing his best to write in the language of Caesar, and with an index of synthesis (2.11) only a little lower than Caesar's. But the popular language had already changed much more radically, as is shown by the *Peregrinatio*, a century or so earlier than Gregory, but with an index of only 1.82, equal to that of Modern Greek and lower than that of Modern Bengali. Apparently by the fifth century A.D. spoken Romance had already become a 'modern' Indo-European language as far as number of morphemes per word is concerned. Finally, the index of Modern Spanish, 1.52, shows that the trend downward has continued, but is no lower than that of Modern Persian, the least synthetic of the Indo-European languages investigated by Greenberg and me.

The syntactic indices suggest that the proportion of concordial nexuses has remained fairly stable—even rising a little—while the proportion of isolating nexuses to pure inflectional nexuses has risen considerably, especially during the last 1500 years. This is more of a pattern than I have been able to see in the corresponding indices of the other 14 languages.

CHAPTER 7

ON THE SEMANTIC STRUCTURE OF LANGUAGE

URIEL WEINREICH
Columbia University

1. The Nature of Semantic Universals

1.1. *The state of our ignorance*

If challenged to summarize in a nutshell the universal semantic properties of languages on which linguists could agree, one would probably list two:

(*a*) All languages are information-conveying mechanisms of a particular kind, different from other semiotic mechanisms which are not language (cf. Hockett, 1960). Thus, we would rule out, as nonlanguage, systems which use other than vocal sign-vehicles; systems whose sign-vehicles are not composed of discrete recurring units (phonemes); systems which have unrestricted combinability of signs (i.e., no grammar); systems whose signs are iconic; perhaps even such systems—to add a pragmatic criterion—as are not used for interpersonal communication.

(*b*) The semantic mapping of the universe by a language is, in general, arbitrary, and the semantic "map" of each language is different from those of all other languages.

Obviously this is not much to go on. If, in phonology, we had only the two analogous statements—that all languages have phonemes, and that the particular phonological system is different in every language—we would hardly have met for a conference on phonological universals. Where shall we look for additional high-level generalizations about the semantic properties of language?

The following lines of inquiry, it seems to me, might be profitable:

(*c*) From the semiotic point of view, language is not a homogeneous mechanism. What are the semiotic submechanisms utilized in language? Are the several mechanisms analyzed by Wittgenstein as "language games" (1958.77ff.) uniformly distributed throughout the languages of the world? What formal features of languages are correlated with their semiotic strata?

(*d*) What are the effects of sign combination on the meanings of signs? In particular, how do the grammatical and phraseological limitations on the freedom of combination affect the functioning of linguistic signs?

(*e*) Despite the basically arbitrary quality of semantic "mapping" displayed by languages, there are nevertheless remarkable parallelisms between both related and unrelated languages. How are these parallelisms to be formulated and quantified?

(*f*) What generalizations can be made about any vocabulary as a structured set, imperfect as the structuring may be? Can any over-all structural characteristics of a particular vocabulary be formulated, and if so, can the distribution of such characteristics in the languages of the world be studied?

The scarcity of relevant data is in itself a major obstacle to the elaboration of workable hypotheses. As the references scattered in the present discussion show, there is much to read, but no obvious place to look things up. The most important works on semantics, such as those by Ullmann (1951), Zvegincev (1957), Regnéll (1958), Ziff (1960), and Schaff (1960), are on the whole preoccupied with the one semiotic process of naming, that is, with the use of designators in theoretical isolation; they pay relatively little attention to the combinatory semiotics of connected discourse. Linguistic facts are cited as anecdotal illustrations of this or that segment of the theory, but no attempt is made to sample a whole language representatively. The possibly unequal distribution of particular semantic phenomena among the languages of the world is generally not even considered. There exists a fatal abyss between semantic theory and semantic description (Weinreich, 1962), an abyss which dooms the former to emptiness and the latter to atomization. Subtle philosophers of language like Cassirer (1923) have indiscriminately mixed reliable and unreliable evidence about languages, sometimes allowing evolutionary prejudices to come into play; brilliant logicians have shown a lack of curiosity about languages other than their own. The most stimulating writer of all—Hans Reichenbach (1948)—samples human language only by reference to English, German, Turkish, and occasionally French and Latin.

Except for some very brief remarks by the Aginskys (1948), the only outright attempt to approach what might be classed as the problem of semantic universals has been made by Ullmann. In addition to his programmatic paper (1953), we have his exploration of the semantic structure of one language, French (1952). But his generalizations are, by and large, premature (cf. Weinreich, 1955), and culturally restricted by their method (see 4.1). Almost everything still remains to be done.

No reader of this paper will be so naive as to expect sensational solutions to any of the outstanding problems of semantic analysis. Fully to specify the conceptual framework which underlies the following discussion would alone require a monograph. The writer's only hope is that a critical discussion* of his memorandum may help to put certain questions into researchable form. In view of the state of semantic studies so far, even this would be a memorable achievement for our Conference.

1.2. *Some basic terms*

It will be useful to adopt, as a basis of discussion, the scheme of semantics as developed by Morris (1938). We will accordingly

* It is a pleasure to acknowledge the criticisms of the following persons, who read an earlier version of this paper: Robert Austerlitz, Ol'ga S. Axmanova, Edward H. Bendix, Dwight L. Bolinger, Harold C. Conklin, Joseph H. Greenberg, Charles F. Hockett, Fred W. Householder, Jr., Benjamin Hrushovski, Milka Ivić, Pavel Ivić, Roman Jakobson, Lawrence Krader, John Lotz, Wita Ravid, Michael Riffaterre, Rulon Wells, and Karl E. Zimmer.

say that a language is a repertory of signs, and that discourse involves the use of these signs, seldom in isolation. The rules of permitted sign combination (grammar) are formulated in terms of classes of signs (grammatical classes). Languages contain signs of two kinds: every sign is, in general, a designator or a formator [1] (cf. 2.2). A designator consists of a sign-vehicle and a designatum; [2] a formator consists of a sign-vehicle and an implicit instruction for an operation, such as negation, generalization, and the like (see further 2.2). A designatum may be said to constitute a set of conditions; in a situation in which such conditions are actually fulfilled, and the sign is used in reference to the situation, the token of the sign may be said to denote (Morris, 1938:24). [3] Sometimes sign-tokens are used with a claim to denotation, sometimes without (cf. 2.2.1.1 and 3.1.4). All languages also have deictic devices; these are signs used for referring without designation (cf. 2.2.2). Furthermore, languages contain designators and formators for discourse about language (metalinguistic signs in addition to object-language signs).

The analysis of semiotic devices available in a language for designation, referring, shifting of levels, etc., constitutes its semiotic description. The structure of the designata of the signs of a language is the topic of its semantic description in the strict sense; we may also speak of semantic description in the broad sense as including semiotic description. The relation of semiotic type and designatum of a sign to the form of the sign-vehicle is, of course, by and large arbitrary; however, to the extent that recurrent parallelisms can be found, such semantic-phonological intersections are worth describing. (The important problem of sound symbolism is beyond the scope of this paper; but cf. note 65.) The relation between the semiotic type and designatum of a sign and the syntactic class to which it belongs is, on the other hand, often intimate; the intersections of semantics and grammar require even more attention than semantic-phonological parallelisms, for any language and for language in general.

In the debate over the exclusion of semantic considerations from grammatical description, Chomsky's uncompromising stand (1955, 1957: ch. 9) is, in our opinion, entirely correct. In this paper, it will be assumed that the grammatical description of a language is not only autonomous vis-à-vis the semantic one, but is also presupposed by it. We therefore propose to submit to semantic analysis only utterances which are grammatical, and which have a specified grammatical structure. Thus, we consider it productive to ponder what is semantically unacceptable about *enter out*, but not about *into out*, which is disqualified as ungrammatical.[4] Similarly, in analyzing the polysemy of a word like *fair* into (*a*) 'not biased', (*b*) 'pretty good', etc., it is economical to observe first that *fair* (*b*) belongs, unlike *fair* (*a*), to a very special subclass of adjectives (see 3.2.1).[5]

The proposed priority for grammatical over semantic description raises the problem of the congruence between the units of each type of description. Grammatical analysis operates with meaningful elements (morphemes—segmental and suprasegmental—as well as optional transformations), and some meaningless, obligatory processes. Bloomfield (1933:162, 166) was satisfied to posit a unit of meaning for each unit yielded by the grammar ('sememes' for morphemes, 'episememes' for tagmemes ≃ optional transformations). Since then, the identification of grammatical and semantic units has met with a number of objections (e.g., Hjelmslev, 1953:28f., and notably Bazell, 1954). The most important are these: (*a*) Some morphs are meaningless ("empty morphs," e.g., *to* with infinitives, the *-o-* of *drunk-o-meter*). (*b*) It is unnatural to have sign-vehicles without segmental substance, e.g., a meaningful word order. (*c*) There may be meaningful submorphemic segments ("phonaesthemes," e.g., FL-*ow*, FL-*it*, FL-*y*, FL-*oat*). (*d*) In "idioms," the semantic analysis must treat a polymorphemic expression as a whole. But none of these objections seems sufficient. (*a*) "Empty" morphs are an artifact of an Item-and-Arrangement grammar; in an IP grammar, they are not "empty," but are the segmental markers of a transformation process. (*b*) From the point of view of semiotic theory, there is nothing wrong with having a process as a sign-vehicle (e.g., my raising one hand three times as a signal to a confederate). (*c*, *d*) Such phenomena as "phonaestheme" and "idiom" are indeed definable as many-to-one correspondences between grammatical and semantic units. But while identity between the two planes is incomplete, it is a useful starting-point from which to describe the lack of isomorphism actually found. (See also note 65, and cf. Chomsky, 1957:102f.).

1.3. *Full-fledged, subdued, and enhanced semanticity of speech*

In a remarkable passage, Sapir (1921:13) likens language to a dynamo capable of powering an elevator but ordinarily operating to feed an electric doorbell. Language is used, more often than not, in ways which do not draw upon its full semantic capacity. In its "phatic" functions, when speech is used merely to signify the presence of a sympathetic interlocutor, it easily becomes "desemanticized" to a formidable extent. In its various ceremonial functions ("noncasual" language: cf. French, 1958) language may come to be desemanticized by still another mechanism. In general, insofar as utterances are the automatic symptoms of a speaker's state, insofar as they are interlaced with chains of high associative probability, insofar, in short, as they are not subject to the full voluntary control of speakers, they fail to represent the language in its full capacity as a semantic instrument. Now, the various "leakages" that in practice reduce the power of language as a communicative instrument constitute a legitimate psychological problem, to the solution of which the linguist may have something to contribute. But the more pressing task for linguistics, it seems to me, is to explain the elevator, not the doorbell; i.e., avoiding samples of excessively casual or ceremonial speech, to examine language under conditions of its full-fledged utilization—that is, under conditions where no behavior *but* language would fill the bill.

The use of language can also deviate from the norm in the opposite direction, so that the language becomes, as it were, "hypersemanticized." Such use of language is characteristic of much good literature, although it can be found in workaday life as well. There are at least two marks of hypersemanticization: (1) The phonic vehicle of signs assumes an independent symbolic value (whether "impressionistic"—sound-imitative—or "expressionistic," i.e., synaesthetic); a special semantic relation is imputed to signs with similar vehicles (rhyme, etc.); in short, incipient correlations between content and expression are exploited, in contrast to the arbitrariness of this relation in semantically "normal" uses of language. (2) Over the scope of a given text (poem, etc.) meanings are imputed to some signs which are richer than, or otherwise deviant from, the meanings of the same signs outside the text. Whereas in the "standard" use of language the receiver of a message must only decode it, not decipher it (crack the code), in "hypersemanticized" language the common code is modified *ad hoc*, and the favorably inclined receiver of the message must guess the code modification before he can properly decode the message. It would be uneconomical to dally with a semantic theory which is too weak to account for these phenomena (cf. 3.1.2 and the Postcript); but it is equally pointless to concentrate on these special effects, as so many writers on "meaning" have done, without first accounting for the semantic workings of language in its more standard uses.

2. Semiotic Stratification of Language

2.1. *Logical basis of semiotic analysis*

In the following discussion, the grammatical form of sentences will be compared with their semiotic form. In particular, it will be assumed that it is possible to describe all discourse as either (*a*) having the semiotic form 'Ծ$f(x)$', or (*b*) deviating from it in *specified* ways. In this formulation, 'x' stands for an argument—"something talked about"; 'f' for a predicate—"something said about x"; and 'Ծ' is a covering label for any of a number of operations. More will be said about the inner structure of 'x', 'f', and 'Ծ' in 2.2 and 3.1.

The investigation of discourse in its logical aspects is not a fashionable pursuit, but it seems to be one of the most important frontiers of linguistics for the decades ahead. It is a defensible enterprise, I believe, provided certain cautions are observed. First, there must not be a breath of normativism in it;[6] the descriptive linguist has no interest in making language usage "more logical" than it is—on the contrary, he should explain, if possible, why it is not, in effect, more logical (sec. 5). Second, it is useful to keep in mind that only a very limited portion of logic is brought into play; we are concerned mostly with rules of formation and designation, that is, with limited aspects of a functional calculus, which in logic are merely the preparatory steps for the study of deduction, truth, etc. (cf., e.g., Carnap, 1942:24). Third, as mentioned in 1.2, the study of the "logical" aspects of discourse, as part of semantics, must remain autonomous of the grammatical analysis so that their interrelation may be meaningfully compared.[7] Fourth, we must insist on a sufficiently versatile logic and on a wide sampling of languages.[8] Finally, we must carefully avoid the unjust claim that man cannot in his thinking transcend the "logical mold" given by his languages; there is ample evidence to the contrary—if not in Aristotelian logic, then certainly, let us say, in the medieval doctrine of suppositions. But if these cautions are observed, the investigation is both legitimate and promising. For logic is congenial to language. Even experimental language systems constructed by philosophers conform in many essentials of logical structure to that of human language.[9]

It would be considered naive today to attempt, as did Wegener (1885), to describe the semiotic stratification of human language with examples restricted to German, Greek, and Latin. But it is remarkable how well Wegener's theory stands up now that the range of our evidence has been vastly broadened. It takes only a slightly more flexible calculus, I believe, to accommodate all the varieties of semiotic structure evident in ordinary discourse.

2.2. *Formators*

Virtually every semantic theory operates with a dichotomy of signs, corresponding to what we have called designators and formators.[10] In most systems the formators, or "logical" signs, are given by enumeration. In 1942, it was not yet known how the distinction could be defined for semantics in general (Carnap, 1942:59). Reichenbach's attempted definition (1948:318–325) may be objectionable on technical grounds, and further theoretical investigations are needed. But for our purposes we can apply Carnap's working definition of 'designator' (1947:6): "all those expressions to which a semantical analysis of meaning is applied." While there may be controversial cases, it would seem that a rough distinction of designators (e.g., *bread*, *smear*, *fast*) and formators (*or*, *this*) conforms to an intuitive classification.

If we consider as designators those signs which can appear in the place of '*f*' and '*x*' in expressions of the form '$\eth f(x)$', the complementary class of formators would include, roughly, the following kinds (after Reichenbach, 1948:55–57): (1) "pragmatic operators"; (2) indexical signs; (3) signs for propositional operations (*not*, *or*, *same* [?]); (4) quantifiers of various types; (5) signs which organize the expression ("purely syntactic" signs).

There is, in principle, a possibility of mixed signs: those which have both formative and designative components. But the mechanisms of each type must first be analyzed separately.

The descriptive problems which may eventually yield universals of language are basically of three types:

(*a*) With what degree of distinctness are conceivably separate logical operations expressed, or expressible, in the language?

(*b*) To what extent do the formators appear as separate grammatical units; and, contrariwise, to what extent are formator components "built into" the designata of mixed signs?

(*c*) To what extent do formators or mixed signs have characteristic sign-vehicles or characteristic grammatical properties?[11]

2.2.1. PRAGMATIC OPERATORS. The field of "pragmatics" has virtually no conventional content.[12] For the present discussion we propose to include in it that paradigm of discourse features which comprises assertion, and features incompatible with assertion and with each other: question, command , and attitudes to the content of discourse, insofar as they are coded.

2.2.1.1. As a practical measure we take the assertive "mode" for a standard of reference. It will be seen in 3.1.4 that in every language most utterances contain at least one sign linkage in the assertive mode, although they may also contain additional ones in a "neutral" mode. Among the devices which a language has for "neutralizing" the assertiveness of sentences, some are completely specialized for this function; among such are nominalizing transformations, marked, for example, by a case change in the subject and a change in the verb to the "infinitive" or some other subordinate mood. Sometimes, however, the neutralization of assertiveness is at the same time "motivated" by an indication of the speaker's uncertainty or a positive disclaimer of responsibility. The German change from indicative to subjunctive (*Er ist krank* vs. *Er sei krank*) is such a sign; we may also list the Turkish *-miş*, the Hopi "quotative" (Whorf, 1956:119), the Bulgarian non-evidential (Jakobson, 1957:4f.).

In many languages, the suspension of assertion is obvious from the subordination of a sentence to explicitly nonassertive conjunctions (e.g., *if* ...); hence, the marking of suspended assertion by the mood of the verb becomes redundant and may be eliminated, as it was eliminated in Modern English. It is unlikely that there are languages which have a greater stock of assertion-suspending devices for independent sentences than for conditionals.

2.2.1.2. The indication of the imperative seems typically to intersect with deictic categories (2.2.2) and to be more highly developed for second person than for first or third, for future/present tense than for past. The equivalents of the imperative for nonsecond person are often grammatically more analytic and are asymmetrical with the second-person expression (cf. Yiddish *gejn* 'to go': 2. *gejt*, 1. *lomir gejn*, 3. *zoln zej gejn*). In many languages, the imperative is marked in the verb only; often the second person subject is deleted.[13]

2.2.1.3. Questions are a marked pragmatic mode incompatible with assertion,[14] although they are not usually expressed by a form fitting the grammatical paradigm of verb moods. Sentence questions (yes-or-no) are almost universally indicated by intonation changes and nearly as frequently, perhaps, by the addition of a question "particle" (Russian *li*, Hopi *pï'*, Chinese *.ma*); in considerably fewer languages are there also changes in word order. The hierarchy of the devices can probably be formulated more rigorously.

In contrast to assertion-suspension and command, questions (like attitudinal formators—2.2.1.4) constitute pragmatic operations applicable to parts of sentences as well as to wholes. When applied to parts, typical intersections of the question operator with the "part of speech" occur in so-called completion questions, or *wh*-questions. While there appear in general to be special forms of interrogative words depending on the part or the sentence whose completion is desired (cf. English *what?* vs. *when?*), there are interesting gaps. For example, verb interrogatives (e.g., **Whatted he?* = 'What did he do?') sometimes occur (cf. Sapir, 1921:126, on Yana), but they are rather rare; adjective interrogation in a language like English is accomplished periphrastically (*what kind of?* yet cf. Polish *jaki*, Yiddish *vosər*). It is not clear whether there are any languages with prepositional interrogatives, although it is easy to conceive them (e.g., English **whep*, meaning 'on or under or over or...', as in *Wh-ep the table is the book?* 'Is the book on or under or inside [... etc.] the table?'). [15] More transparent is the reason why certain grammatical distinctions typical of a part of speech are neutralized when it is interrogativized: if *what* had separate singular and plural forms, we would have to know the number of the answer before asking the question. On the other hand, the grammatical specialization of interrogative words is not correlated exclusively with the largest parts-of-speech divisions; thus English distinguishes animate/inanimate in the noun interrogative (*who/what*); adverbial interrogatives are particularly overdifferentiated (*where/when/how* and even *why*) in comparison with noninterrogative adverbs, whose subcategories of place, time, and manner are entirely covert. It is likely that such unusual distinctions, reflecting different dimensions of deixis (2.2.2), are typical of most languages.

2.2.1.4. Attitudes toward the content of discourse are always present and form a subject for psycholinguistic research (Weinreich, 1958); they are relevant linguistically insofar as they are coded. The usual attitudes which find coded expression on the subsentence level are approval and disapproval. Other systems are clearly imaginable (e.g., a suffix indicating that the thing designated by the word is feared, longed for, etc.), but it is not sure whether they occur. Within the simple good–bad dimension, it seems that hypochoristic forms are more common than pejorative ones, and are implied by the latter within any one language. It is also clear that such "expressive derivation" is very unevenly distributed among languages (Ullmann, 1953:232); in the European area, English is notoriously poor in this respect, Italian and the Slavic languages (Stankiewicz, 1954) are very rich; Yiddish is the richest of all Germanic languages, probably as a result of convergence with Slavic. As a formator, the expression of endearment seems to intersect with the designatum of smallness; even if this is not a semantic universal, it is quite typical, although theoretically it could have been the other way round.[16] Grammatically, attitudinal formators seem to be distributed unequally in any language which has them, for example, in Yiddish they are standard for nouns and adjectives but rare for adverbs and entirely marginal for verbs (nursery talk only). It is doubtful whether in any language the verbal class is more sensitive to such distinctions than the nominal class. Attitudinal formators are sometimes phonologically characterized, for example, by palatality in Yiddish or by various consonantal modifications in Nootka (Sapir, 1915); but even where such phonological characteristics are absent, or bypassed, certain paralinguistic devices (voice qualification) appear in their place.

Attitudinal formators having whole sentences as their objects are much more richly patterned than the good–bad qualification for sentence parts. Grammatically, the two chief devices for their expression seem to be affixal mood categories of the verb, formed by affixes or auxiliaries (e.g., optative), and special "modal" adverbs or particles (e.g., 'fortunately'). Thus, in Sierra Miwok we find a volitional mood in the conjugation and a set of adverbs meaning 'would that', 'dubitative' (Freeland, 1951); in Potawatomi we find particles meaning 'would that' and 'it is doubtful that', combinable with the conjunct mode (Hockett, 1948:215). In the continental European languages, a particle of "obviousness" seems very common (German *ja*, French *donc*, Russian *ved'* or *-to*, Polish *przecie*[*ż*]). It appears that in many languages such attitudinal formators share specific grammatical and phonological features (monosyllabicity, unstressability, fixed order, etc.; cf. Arndt, 1960).

Summarizing, we can say that formators of the pragmatic category are often combined with designative components into mixed signs; that they tend to monopolize some types of sign-vehicles (intonation contours) and predominate among others (order patterns, enclitic particles); and that they are quite unevenly distributed among the parts of speech.

2.2.2. DEICTIC SIGNS.[17] These are signs (or components of designata) which involve a reference to the act of speech in which they are used. (See Casagrande, 10.3.) Among the factors of the speech situation which are utilized in deixis are the following: the utterer of the discourse ('first person') or the receiver ('second person'); the time of discourse (tense) and its place (varieties of demonstration); and the identity or nonidentity of the act of discourse (anaphora, reflexiveness, obviation, etc.). That this paradigm constitutes a striking universal of language can be appreciated not only from its widespread distribution but also by visualizing further factors of the speech situation which could be, but do not seem to be, utilized in any language: the loudness of speech, its speed, the certainty of the assertion. No language seems to have "adverbs" meaning 'louder than I am now speaking', 'as slow as my speech now', or the like.

2.2.2.1. Person deixis occurs in highly asymmetrical structures which would deserve a fresh cross-linguistic survey. Thus, many languages have forms including speaker and hearer ("inclusive first person"), but perhaps not those including first and third persons ('not-you') or second and third ('not-I'). Person deixis often intersects unevenly also with nonperson distinctions of gender and number (e.g., English *you*, undifferentiated for number). With respect to parts of speech, person deixis is again unevenly distributed. As a distinctive feature it seems to belong characteristically to the noun category, whereas verbs display only concord with the noun; it is not sure whether there are languages with verbs corresponding to **to we* = 'to be us', etc. In the Serbocroatian dialect of Gorski Kotar, according to P. Ivić, the affirmative sentence-substitute *da* 'yes' may take person suffixes: *da-m* 'I yes = yes, I do'; *da-š* 'you yes = yes, you do'. Within the noun class, the formators of person deixis seem to be combinable with designators, namely status labels, only to a limited extent. Thus there are languages with simplex morphemes corresponding to 'you, my superior' or 'I, your inferior', but not to 'you, a teacher', 'we Americans': combinations of the latter type are invariably complex, being either phrases (as in English) or words (cf. the conjugated nouns of Miwok: *míwï·te· -y* 'I am an Indian'; Freeland, 1951:26; also in Hottentot, according to Greenberg).

The distinction between honorific and nonhonorific signs, limited in some languages to a minute place in the pronominal system but cutting across a large part of the basic vocabulary in other languages (Tibetan, Javanese), can be analyzed semantically under different headings. Sometimes the honorific component of meaning is not dependent on the speaker's evaluation and can be considered on a par with any other designational feature (cf. 4.2); thus in Thai *hat*, *bāt* seem to mean 'royal hand, royal foot' (as against *mɨ*, *thao* 'commoner's hand, commoner's foot') regardless of who is talking to whom. If the choice of honorific forms depends on the attitude of the speaker to the listener or to the subject of discourse, the semantic component might best be classed with other attitudinal operators (2.2.1.4); cf. the Tibetan choice between *u* and *go* 'head', *gongpa* and *sampa* 'thought', *chhab* and *chhu* 'water', etc. (Gleason, 1955:156), the first item of each pair being honorific, the second ordinary. [18] But where the use of honorific terms for second person and ordinary, or deprecatory, terms for first person becomes standardized, we observe an intersection between this attitudinal operator and person deixis. Such seems to be the case in Chinese (Chao, 1956:219), where *bih-chuh*, literally 'dilapidated locality', in effect means 'my home town'.

2.2.2.2. Time deixis is generally expressed by signs which modify either the verbs or (as in Chinese) the sentence as a whole. Time deixis seems to be independent of other forms of deixis but yields syncretisms with certain quantifiers of verbs (omission of iterative aspect in the present tense, etc.) and with certain pragmatic categories: fewer tenses may be distinguished in the imperative than in the indicative, and it is quite usual for tenses to be neutralized under nominalization.[19] Nonpresent tense is often combined with suspension of assertion; cf. the use of past for conditional in English, the use of nominalized sentences for distant past in Sierra Miwok (Freeland, 1952:49), etc. There seems universally to be equal or greater discrimination of time distinctions in past than in future. The criteria for degree of pastness vary and deserve to be investigated. Often a language has a tense for the period from morning of the same day to the time of discourse, and a separate tense for time before the day of discourse. Invariably expressions like 'Sunday', 'in summer' refer to the Sunday or summer nearest the speech act.

It is perhaps a universal that time-deictic "adverbs" are never less differentiated than the tense systems (i.e., there are not more past tenses than distinctions of the type *yesterday*, ... *ago*).

Time deixis seems to be most typically associated with verb forms, although it is a perfectly conceivable component of noun designata as well (*the former*, *quondam*, *present*, *future king*, *the then king*, *the ex-king*, *the king-to-be*). In a language like Tupi, as Greenberg has pointed out, there is a conjugation of nouns for tense. Tense formators tend to intersect with designata involving absolute time—cf. the synchronically simplex *etmol* 'yesterday', *šilšom* 'day before yesterday' in Hebrew—but not with other designata.

2.2.2.3. "Place" deixis seems to be organized according to distance from the first or second person (cf. Latin *iste* 'this one, in relation to you'), visibility ('the one I see'), accessibility, or perhaps also direction ('before, behind')—usually in relation to first person. (For theoretical analyses of "indication," see Collinson, 1937; Shwayder, 1961.) Where only one category of deixis exists, it seems to indicate 'obviousness to first and second person' (*this*; *thus*); the reference may be made precise by a coordinated gesture. Place deixis (as shown by Householder), too, seems to be compatible with designata, especially if related to motion; cf. *come* vs. *go*, *bring* vs. *take*. With regard to parts of speech, "place" deixis seems to show asymmetries very similar to those of interrogativity (cf. 2.2.1.3). In many European languages, we find deictic nouns (inanimate *this*), adjectives (*such*), "overdifferentiated" adverbs (place: *here*, time: *now*, manner: *thus*), but not deictic prepositions or verbs (**to this* = 'to do this'); so contrary to some semantic systems is this potential category that in Yiddish, for example, the deictic verb (*dosn*) occurs only in slang and means 'to excrete'.[20] Again, while the nouns and adverbs of time and place distinguish proximate and distal deixis on a binary principle (*this/that*, *now/then*, *here/there*), such a distinction for adverbs of manner and for adjectives is perhaps rarer; cf. Russian distal *tak*, *takoj*—proximate *ètak*, *ètak*(*ij*), Serbocroatian *ovakav/onakav* (Ivić), Chinese *dzèmma/nèmma* (Hockett) with the English *thus*, *such*, undifferentiated as to proximateness. The distribution of such asymmetries requires cross-linguistic investigation.

"Place" deixis easily combines with absolute indications of place, especially in languages which deal with a very narrow geographical area, where 'higher', for example, may come to mean 'northward' because of the direction of the one dominant slope. (On an orientation system of this type, cf. Haugen, 1957.)

2.2.2.4. The greatest variety is apparently found with respect to the distinction between "the same" and "not the same" act of speech. All languages have "pro-forms" such as *he*, which substitute for other forms to avoid their repetition within a unit of discourse considered as "the same." But pro-forms are on the whole very unevenly distributed with respect to the parts of speech. Perhaps all languages have pro-nouns but few have pro-verbs; English is perhaps unique among European languages in having, in *do*, at least the rudiments of a verb-phrase substitute. For a large number of languages pro-adjectives, pro-numerals, and pro-adverbs of various types seem to be the unstressed forms of the corresponding demonstratives (cf. German *er hat solche Haare* 'hair of this kind' = 'hair of the mentioned kind'). But for the pro-nouns and pro-adjectives (definite article), at least, some languages distinguish between demonstrative deixis and "within-the-discourse" deixis: *he/the* distinct from *this*, French *lui (il)* and *le* distinct from *ce*, *celui*, *-ci*, *ça*. German makes the distinction *(er*, *der* vs. *dieser)*, but Yiddish has lost the adjective part *(der/dieser)*, falling back on the device of so many languages—stressed and unstressed demonstratives. It seems to be a universal that under nominalizations certain distinctions of discourse-deixis are neutralized, e.g., *Bill's books* (< *(some) books? the books?).* Such neutralizations are probably more common than the maintenance of the distinction, as in English *a friend of mine*, Yiddish (but not German) *majnər a frajnd.*

The act of discourse considered as a unit generally extends backward from the moment of time, since the purpose of such deixis is to utilize information already conveyed. But it is also possible to have a certain amount of forward deixis, illustrated by such pro-adjectives and pro-adverbs as *the following*, *as follows*, *(let me say) this.*

In most languages there are also grammatical processes which take as their scope a small, well-delimited part of discourse. This may be the sentence, as in rules of concord (e.g., for animateness, person, number) between subject and predicate, or the verb and object noun; there may be concord between verb (tense) and adverb of time within the sentence. The sentence is also the unit of discourse in rules for reflexivity (designation of object noun by special devices if it is the same as the subject of the same verb), or of obviation (use of different "persons," e.g., for different noun objects of the same verb). Apart from its grammaticalized aspect, reflexivity of sentence scope seems also to be a component of such words as English *(one's) own*, *home* (='one's own home'), *along* (with the subject), *enough* ('... for oneself'), etc.

Some utilization of these two scopes for the criterion "the same discourse" seems to be universal.

2.2.3. PROPOSITIONAL OPERATIONS. Under this heading we consider the linguistic equivalents of certain semantic operations applied to propositions. Such operations may be singulary (negation) or binary (disjunction, conjunction, implication, equivalence).

It is faily clear that no language represents such operations with the maximum economy. While it has been shown to be logically possible to define all propositional operations in terms of two primitives (e.g., negation and conjunction) or even a single primitive, it would be interesting to discover what redundancies are practiced in ordinary language. To appreciate the possible differences we need only consider the Latin distinction between *vel* and *aut* (exclusive and inclusive disjunction), unmatched in modern European languages until the rise of *and/or*; or the alternatives to *and not* (e.g., *except*) and *if not... then* (e.g., *unless*) in English. Greek has one negator with a component 'dependence' *(mē)* and another *(ou)* without (Seiler, 1958: 694f.). One of the best logical analyses of certain "operators" of ordinary English is the one given by Strawson (1952:78-92). Such logical operations fuse with pragmatic components, e.g., *but* = 'and, surprisingly'; *yet* = 'and, very surprisingly'; *p although q* = '*q* and surprisingly *p*'; etc. For some operations, it may also be useful to compare languages as to the definiteness and flexibility of the "scope." Thus, in English, we cannot always distinguish unambiguously between negation of the verb and negation of the sentence as a whole; but most other parts of sentences can be negated separately, if not by *not*, then by *un-* or *non-*.[21] In some languages the sign of negation is a member of a special small form class, as in English;[22] in others, it is a member of a large class, typically the verb (**to not*, e.g., Finnish, Yana). A cross-linguistic study of negation would certainly yield important results.

Negation is one formative component which combines very easily with other designata to form paradigms of antonyms; cf. *over* = 'not under': *under* 'not over'; *well* 'not sick'; French *ignorer* 'ne pas savoir', etc. Negation occurs in many (most?) languages combined with signs for variables, with various degrees of grammatico-semantical isomorphism (cf. *some: no, somebody: nobody, sometimes: never* for older *ever: never;* but not *somewhat:* **nowhat*).

An extremely frequent syntactic concomitant of propositional operations is ellipsis; cf. 3.1.5.

2.2.4. QUANTIFIERS. The representation in ordinary language of operations comparable to the binding of variables in logic requires a highly specialized investigation. But even preliminary reflection leads to a number of hypotheses. First, every ordinary language is far more redundant in its representation of quantification than a logical system, which can define all "quantifiers" by means of negation and one primitive. Most obviously, no language represents cardinal number in logistic terms, and a renewal of cross-linguistic studies of numeral systems, from the point of view of universal deviations from logic, would be quite opportune (P. Ivić). Second, generalization is in many languages expressible in a form analogous to the logical form '$(x)f(x)$' (e.g., *whoever*...), but it is always also expressible approximately as if the universal quantifier were a designator *(all books*, like *interesting books)*. Third, quantification is not, as in the simple functional calculus, restricted to "argument-terms" (say, nouns), but is also combinable with "function-terms" and deictic formators. Thus English has universal quantifiers in noun function *(whoever; everything*, *everybody*, *all)*, in adjective function *(whichever; every*, *each*, *all)*, and in various adverb functions *(wherever*, *everywhere; whenever*, *always; however;* but not **everyhow*, despite *anyhow!)*. Yet it has no general verb *(*to all* = 'to do everything'). As in the case of propositional operations (2.2.3), we find some mixture with pragmatic factors, e.g., *only* = 'surprisingly, no more than'. A widespread form of quantification is combined with event names and concerns their frequency or completion. In languages such formators have separate morphemic representation (frequentative, perfective aspects), whereas in others they are lexicalized, that is, combined with designata into mixed signs (cf. English *some*: *all* :: *to carry*: *to fetch*; *one*: *many* :: *to attend*: *to frequent)*. For the quantifications of events, many languages have special subsystems of signs, such as 'once', 'twice', '*n* times', 'every time', 'nonce'.[23] Simplex terms for the quantification of spatiotemporal deixis ('ever before', 'once before', 'time *t* ago', etc.) are more easily imagined than found.

Every language has signs for existential quantifiers. This semiotic class intersects with grammatical divisions into parts of speech and some of their subdivisions. It may be a universal that the grammatical specialization of the signs for existential quantifiers corresponds to that for the interrogatives (2.2.1.3) and the deictics (2.2.2.3). In English, for example, we have indefinite pronouns (animate: *somebody*; inanimate: *something*); indefinite pro-numerals, also serving as pro-adjectives *(some*, *any*, in intricate interrelations), the indefinite pro-adverbs of manner, place, and time *(somehow*, *somewhere*, *sometime*[*s*]— but hardly *somewhen!*), but not of cause (no **somewhy* for *why*). It is to be noted that there is no indefinite pro-verb (**to something* = 'to do something') and that even the existing names of variables are grammatically complex and asymmetrically constructed. These irregularities seem to be typical deviations from a logical model.

Variable names do not seem to combine easily with designata. And yet, if we are permitted to contrast such lexical pairs as *say* with *talk* = 'say something', *await* and *wait* = 'await something', we find examples of mixture in the transitivity of verbs when the object is not specified. In many languages such "expectancy" is explicitly shown in the form of the verb; cf. Hungarian *írok* 'I write', *írom* 'I write the...'.

Perhaps all languages distinguish between "divided" and "undivided" reference (Quine, 1960:90ff.), that is, between nouns which are quantified in the form 'some *x*, a little *x*, much *x*' and those which are quantified in the form 'an *x*, one *x*, many *x*'.[24] But whereas in a language like English the specification of the kind of reference, divided or nondivided, is obligatory for the noun, in most languages it seems to be optionally marked. The distinction also occurs among nonnouns, for example, divided reference of verbs by means of punctual and iterative aspects; the comparison of English with Russian suggests that the grammaticalization of divided reference in one class of words does not presuppose the same in any other class.

A further subclass among "divided-reference" terms are those which denote individuals—often without any designative component: proper names. (On the semiotic nature of proper names, cf. Sørensen, 1958.) In English and many other languages, proper names have a special grammar; we distinguish, for example, proper *Dolly* from appellative *the*/*a dolly*, although the grammatical machinery differs from one system to another.[25] Householder and Hockett surmise that in every language proper names are a semiotic type of sign with a grammatical mark of their own.

It seems that no language refers to individual constants of more than one class, for example, by having "proper verbs" as well as "proper nouns."

The West and Central European languages are perhaps atypical in distinguishing between indefinite descriptions ('a so-and-so, some so-and-so') and definite descriptions ('the so-and-so'), and correspondingly between relative superlatives ('the sweetest') and absolute superlatives ('a most sweet...'). That this is a common innovation in Europe is suggested by the further detail that all these languages use for definite description the same form (definite article) as for "within-discourse" deixis. Definite descriptions are applied only to nouns.

We have surveyed a number of semantic formators; the discussion of purely syntactic formators[26] is postponed for 3.1.3.

2.3. *Metalinguistic signs and operations*

For ordinary purposes languages serve as their own metalanguages. The effort expended by logicians since the Middle Ages to disentangle the use of signs from their mention is in itself evidence of how smoothly ordinary language blurs the distinction between types. It may be useful for certain purposes to isolate from the vocabulary of a given language those terms whose designata are themselves aspects of language, such as *word*, *say*, *conjugate*, *mean*, *true* (cf. Reichenbach, 1948:58), but, on the whole, these have characteristic features of neither grammar nor phonology. What concerns us here is the question of devices equivalent to quoting, that is, devices which may distinguish between the use and mention of a sign of indefinite type. Many cultures (including, according to Hockett, nonliterate societies) use "vocal quotation marks," manifested by pause and occasional intonational or voice-qualifying features. But the marking of type-shift does not, it seems, become explicit and codified except in writing systems, and even in writing traditions the use of quotation marks is a relatively recent innovation, which semiliterates find difficult to use correctly.[27] Many languages have expressions like "so-called" or "to wit" ("say" = 'that' ...),[28] but one wonders whether improvisation does not here prevail over standardized features. Some languages are reported to have special "quotative moods," but one should distinguish mere suspension of assertion (2.2.1.1), which can serve numerous functions, from specifically quotative mechanisms.

Another metalinguistic operation commonly performed in all cultures is definition, for example, as answers to questions of the type "What's an *X*?" So far, it would seem, no language has been reported to mark defining statements as a semiotic class by any overt grammatical means.[29]

For every language, finally, stock must be taken of all metalinguistic operators such as English *true*, *real*, *so-called*, *strictly speaking*, German *eigentlich*, and the most powerful extrapolator of all—*like*—which function as instructions for the loose or strict interpretation of designata.

3. Combinatorial Semantics

3.1. *Semiotic structure of discourse*

3.1.1. TYPES OF SIGN COMBINATION. If we consider the effect of signs when they are grammatically combined to form discourse, we detect two semiotic processes which are not reducible to each other, and which might be called "linking" and "nesting." The linking process has been the subject of a large philosophical literature, but it would seem that it is nesting which offers far greater theoretical difficulties.

Linking may be described as that effect of a grammatical conjunction of two signs[30] which yields a product of their designata. Assuming, for example, that *flower* has the designatum '$c_1 \cdot c_2 \cdot c_3$' (i.e., the conditions under which the *flower* denotes; cf. 1.2) and *yellow* has the designatum '$c_4 \cdot c_5$', then *yellow flower*, being a grammatical expression in English, has the compound designatum '$c_1 \cdot c_2 \cdot c_3 \cdot c_4 \cdot c_5$'. Similarly, in *(to) walk fast*, the designatum of the expression may be considered the sum of the designata of *walk* and *fast*. The semiotic process is equivalent to Boolean class conjunction.[31]

It is possible to show that linking occurs on various levels. We describe the effect of conjoining *dark* + *yellow* → *dark yellow* as a linking; similarly for *yellow* + *flower*. Yet in *dark yellow flower*, although there is one interpretation of the ambiguous phrase which may be described as an extended linking ('something which is a flower and is dark and is yellow'), there is also another interpretation according to which there is something which is yellow and a flower and "something" which is yellow and dark; but the second "something" is not the same as the first: it is a color, that is, a property of the flower. This effect is easily described in terms of the so-called higher calculus of functions, in which it is possible to speak of properties of properties. Such a calculus, in other words, permits not only expressions like '$f(a)$' or '$f(a, b)$', but also '$\varphi(f)$', and even compound expressions like '$f(a) \cdot \varphi(f)$'. To transcribe our example, we write 'F' for 'flower', 'Y' for 'yellow', and δ' for 'dark', and formulate it (following Reichenbach, 1948) as:

$$(\exists x)\ (\exists f)\ F(x) \cdot f(x)\ .\ Y(f) \cdot \delta(f)$$

The epistemological desirability of a higher functional calculus is a matter of debate,[32] but for describing, not criticizing, the semiotic structure of discourse in ordinary language, no superior method has yet been proposed.

If we consider next such expressions as *buy flowers* or *under water*, we cannot say that the effect is an addition of designata at all. It is as if the designata of *buy* and *under* contained open slots which were harmoniously filled by *flowers* and *water*, respectively, but in a nonadditive way. One of the differences between these and the *yellow flower* examples stems from the fact that *buy* and *(be) under* are two-place relations:

$$x \text{ buys } y = B(x, y)$$
$$w \text{ is under } z = U(w, z)$$

But this qualification is insufficient, for some two-place relations, such as 'resemble', 'be married to', *can* be explicated as linking. For cases such as *buy* and *(be) under*, it is apparently necessary to specify further that the two-place relation is asymmetrical, that is,

$$B(x, y) \supset \overline{B(y, x)}$$
$$U(w, z) \supset \overline{U(z, w)}$$

It would seem that in asymmetrical relations, one argument "links" semiotically with the function, while the other "nests." In a semiotic theory involving designation such as was sketched in 1.2, the linking operation can be accommodated in an intuitively acceptable way; the nesting operation must be introduced by a special definitional stratagem. [33]

We might adopt the convention that in a many-place asymmetrical relation, the first and only the first argument "links" with the function; but since it is not usually obvious from the notation whether the relation is symmetrical, it is preferable to introduce a special mark for the nesting argument, such as '$B(x, \acute{y})$'.

Nesting, like linking, may involve a multiplicity of "levels." Consider *Jim observed the counting of votes.* We have O = '*a* observes *b*' and C = '*c* counts *d*'; writing x_1 for 'Jim', y_1 for 'votes' and x for the omitted first argument of C, we have

$$O(x_1, \acute{C}) \cdot C(x, \acute{y}_1)$$

In an example like *Jim liked to observe the manufacture of lawnmowers*, we have four levels of nesting.

It is possible to interpret the operands of all operations represented by formators (2.2) as being in a nesting relation to the operators. The notational difficulties which arise in connection with mixed signs do not seem to be insuperable; and it is hardly the analyst's fault if language is complicated.

We may now test the theory of two kinds of sign combination on some examples. Consider the English sentence, *The three bitterly crying children walked home fast.* We find a three-place function *(walk)* of level 1 which has as its arguments *children*, *home*, and *-ed* ('time previous to the speech act'). *Children* links with *walk;* the others nest. The function-name *walk* itself appears as the linking argument of another function of level 2, *fast.* Whatever is the argument of the 0-level function [*x is a*] *child* is also the argument of another 0-level function, *x cries.* This 0-level function is in turn an argument for a level-1 function, *x is bitter.* We leave open the question whether *three* and *-ed* 'past' should be analyzed as designator functions whose arguments are *children* and *walk*, or as formators, that is, names of nondesignational semiotic operations to be applied to *children* and to *walk*. Certainly *the* involves such an operation ('such children as have been mentioned in this discourse'). Finally, *home* has a covert semantic structure corresponding to 'the children's home', that is, reflecting a nesting function *x has a home* and a proposition, *the x who walked is the x who had a home*. We dispense with the technical formulation of the analysis.[34]

A simpler example is the Korean sentence, *Kim-ən s'ɛ-čɛk-əl p'alli ilkət s'əmnita* 'Kim read the new book fast'. We have a function, f, translatable as 'x reads y at time t'. The arguments are x = *Kim*, y = *čɛk* 'book', and t = *-ət* 'time previous to the speech act'. Here *-ən* is a syntactic formator showing which is the x-argument; *-əl* similarly shows which is the y-argument. The function f = *ilkət* 'read' is itself the argument of the function $\varphi(f)$, where φ = *p'alli* 'fast'. The argument y of $f(x, \acute{y}, \acute{t})$ is also the argument of another function, $g(y)$, where g = *s'ɛ* 'new'. In the one-place functions φ and g, we find a linking effect; in the three-place function f, there is linking between f and x (and perhaps with t; cf. the remarks on *-ed* in the English example) and a nesting of y "in" f.

Finally, we may analyze two famous Nootka sentences. The expression *lash-tskwiq-ista-ma* 'select—result—in a canoe—assertion' is translated by Whorf (1956:236) as "they are in a boat as a crew of picked men." We seem to have a function of the form $f(x, \acute{y})$, in which the linked argument, x, is omittable, as it were: $f(\ , \acute{y})$ or, in technical notation, $f(\hat{x}, \acute{y})$. The function f is *lash* 'select', and *tskwiq*, rendered by Whorf as 'result', is the marker of y. But, interestingly enough, y here remains as a variable, and is "bound" as the argument of another function, g = *-ista-* 'to be in a boat', where it is again in a linking relation to the function. The sentence thus has the form

$$\vdash g(y) \cdot f(\hat{x}, \acute{y})$$

The sentence means, roughly: "It is asserted that the selected are in a boat," or "... that they, the selected, are in a boat"—which is far more transparent than Whorf's tortured translation. A still simpler case, involving no second-level function, is the Nootka sentence: *ƛimš-ja-ʔis-ita-ʔ i-ƛma* 'boil-result-eat-agents-go for-he does', to which Whorf (1956:242) mystifyingly matches the English "he invites people to a feast." Again we have a two-place function $f(x, \acute{y})$, in which $f =$ *ʔiƛ* 'x goes for y', and x is omittable. Another two-place function, $E(x, \acute{y})$, is $E =$ *ʔis* 'x eats y'. A third two-place function, $B(x, \acute{y})$, is $B =$ *ƛimš* 'x boils y', again with x omittable; *-ja-* marks the preceding sign as being the y of B, and *-ita-* marks the preceding as being the x of E. The final *-ma* may be interpreted as an assertion operator. The whole sentence then has this approximate form:

$$\vdash G(\hat{u}, \acute{w}) \cdot E(w, \dot{z}) \cdot B(\hat{u}, \dot{z}).$$

We are now prepared to formulate an important hypothetical universal:

> *In all languages a combination of signs takes the form of either linking or nesting, and all languages use both patterns in kernel sentences. No further patterns are introduced by transformations. While the number of levels is not theoretically limited, linking on more than three and nesting on more than four is very rare.*

3.1.2. COMPATIBILITY OF DESIGNATA. It was assumed up to now, for the sake of simplicity, that any designatum could be linked or nested with any other. Yet the doubtful semantic acceptability of expressions like *yellows songs, sour rights, drink ice*, etc., suggests that the designata fall into various types which are not all equally compatible with each other. [35]

Our concrete knowledge of semantic systems is pitifully inadequate for the formulation of any universals on this point. It does appear that all languages have incompatible types of designata. It appears further that some of the denotative bases of compatibility, such as the sense by which something is perceived, sensory perceptibility in general, spatiality and temporality, number, etc., are very widely shared (cf. Cassirer, 1923) if not universal. When two culturally very close languages such as German and English are compared (Leisi, 1953), it turns out that while the compatibility of certain specific near-equivalents in the two languages differ, the general domains of compatibility are very similar: although German distinguishes *giessen* and *schütten* 'to pour' according to the liquidity of the object, the distinction appears in English in other contexts (e.g., *eat/drink*). But the lack of data on this point is still abysmal.

No semantic theory would be complete without accounting for the effects of combining "incompatible" designata. As B. Hrushovski put it, the combination of otherwise incompatible designata is a standard device of "hypersemanticized" discourse and may be used by a writer/speaker to force the reader/hearer to find some new, uncoded connection between the designata.[36] It would be surprising if in any culture the improvised combination of "incompatible" signs were unknown; but perhaps different cultures, like different literary periods within Western culture, differ as to the matter-of-factness with which this semantic device is regarded. In the urban cultures of Europe and America, the unprecedented semantic experimentalism of modern poetry has perhaps effected an atypical degree of tolerance for semantic incompatibility.

3.1.3. MARKING OF SEMIOTIC ORGANIZATION. If our analysis of sign combinations, or "syntagmatic semiotics," is correct, then it must be completed by an account of a residue of signs anticipated in 2.2(5), corresponding to what Reichenbach (1948:318ff.) called "logical terms in a syntactic capacity." These are signs whose functions is to organize the discourse by marking the argument-names and function-names, the linkings and nestings, the scopes of pragmatic and semantic operations. These include certain elements of word order, concord, certain aspects of conjugation and inflection, as well as the covert, "cryptotypic" (Whorf, 1956: 92ff.) membership of designators in specialized grammatical classes. But it will be noted that while the syntactic operators are identified, in an enumeration such as this, by their grammatical properties, they are not defined by these properties; for the defining criterion is again a semantic one and agrees only in part with the grammar (cf. 1.2). For example, in a declension some cases serve only as syntactic operators, while others have designative content. The nominative may be a sign of the subject, that is, of the function-linked argument, while an illative that contrasts with an elative combines an expression of nesting with a designation. The semantic classification again intersects with the grammatical one when we classify noun-verb linkings together with certain verb-adverb linkings. The failure to distinguish these criteria can lead only to frustration, which in the case of Sapir's typology of languages (1921) reached truly magnificent proportions (cf. Most, 1949).

Among the most controversial problems in this connection is that of so-called "grammatical meaning." There are those who claim that the meaning of certain signs (≅ formators?) is qualitatively different from those of others (≅ designators). To quote but one sample out of scores: "*Paarden* ['horses'] indeed symbolizes 'more than one horse', but *-en* ['-es'] does not symbolize 'more than one'" (Reichling, 1935:353). In present-day Soviet linguistics, too, the "Word-Paradigm" model of analysis (Hockett, 1954:90) holds a monopoly, and the possibility that the semantic role of affixes and stems may be similar is considered an absurdity (e.g., Budagov, 1958:5 and *passim*; Zvegincev, 1957:98f.; Savčenko, 1959:35ff.; Šendel's, 1959). The opposite view is that there is no special kind of meaning such as "grammatical meaning"; there are merely special signs which have the grammatical (not semantic!) property of obligatoriness.[37] It is our contention that only the latter position is tenable, as it is the only one which conforms with the requirement that semantic and grammatical criteria must be autonomous (1.2).[38] The distinction between material and formal meanings, which has dogged linguistics at least since Schleicher (Cassirer, 1923:164), is not only ethnocentric, but is inapplicable even to Indo-European languages, and should be scrapped. The distinction between autocategorematic and syncategorematic signs, in most of its very numerous interpretations, covertly mixes grammatical with semiotic criteria and is also totally untenable. This still leaves open the question of what signs "belong to" the grammar, but whatever the criteria may be—boundness, obligatoriness, etc.—they are *grammatical*, nonsemantic criteria.[39]

The specific grammatical properties of signs which impose on discourse its semiotic organization are a vast subject in themselves, and the topic cannot even be surveyed here. The one problem that we wish to raise is the possibility of ambiguity in semiotic organization.

(*a*) *Summation versus linking.* It was suggested in 3.1.1. that linking is effected whenever signs are conjoined in a grammatical combination. Languages, however, also have explicit linkage markers, such as *and:* cf. *cozy old houses* = *cozy and old houses.* But the sign of linkage, whether an *and*-word or mere conjunction, may be homonymous with a sign standing for another semantic process equivalent to arithmetical summation; cf. *four hundred and twenty.* (On the polysemy of 'and', cf. Bühler, 1934: 317f.; Hockett, 1958:185f.) There may thus be ambiguities as to whether linkage or summation is intended: cf. *old and experienced women:* 'women who are old and experienced'? or 'some women who are old and some who are experienced'? Where summation is signified by mere conjoining, as in early literary Chinese, we also get "paradoxes" like *po ma fei ma* '[a] white horse [is] not [a] horse' = 'white [and] horse [is] not [a] horse' (Maspéro, 1933:52).

(*b*) *Symmetry of linking.* Whereas in a simple calculus of functions the distinction between arguments and relations is crucial (i.e., '$f(x)$' is "grammatical" but '$x(f)$' is ungrammatical), in a higher calculus of functions, such as ordinary language, the distinction is of very minor importance. If '$x(\Theta)$' ('this is an x'), '$f(x)$', '$\varphi(f)$', etc., are all grammatical, it makes little difference for one-place functions, whether we write '$f(x)$' or '$x(f)$'. To be sure, most linguists believe, like Sapir (1921:126), that "there must be something to talk about and something must be said about this subject of discourse once it is selected." But by intrasentence criteria alone, we can only conclude that (barring minor sentence forms; cf. 3.1.5) "there must be at least two things to be said about each other." The determination of which of the "things" is the "topic" or "thème," which the "comment" or "propos," seems to depend on which is more surprisingly introduced in the context of the preceding speech situation.[40]

(*c*) *Asymmetries of nesting.* It is far different when we come to nesting; here the specialization of roles for relation-name and nesting argument-name is semiotically decisive. (We will call 'function status' the role of a sign as an argument-name or a relation-name within a function.) The most usual pattern is apparently the specialized marking of arguments by syntactic formators, such as nominative vs. oblique case (Latin *-us*/*-um*, Korean *-ən*/*-əl*), subject vs. object particle (Japanese *-wa*/ *-ga*), etc.; fixed order is extremely common, even where it is partly redundant with segmental argument markers (e.g., *they consider stopping it* vs. *they stop considering it*). Often a theoretically possible ambiguity of organization is resolved by the semantic absurdity of one of the alternative interpretations, or (as Hockett has hinted) by proportionality with unambiguous portions of the context. Thus, in the German sentence *Die Birnen assen die Kinder* 'it was the children who ate the pears', we conclude that despite the unusual order, '$f(\acute{y}, x)$', x = *Kinder* and y = *Birnen*. We do so not only because of the absurdity of pears that eat children, but also because the preceding context may contain, as a clue, an unambiguous model, such as *Der Vater ass die Kirschen, und....* Many examples of place ambiguities seem to be due to partial syncretism of grammatical categories, for example, between dative and accusative *euch* and *uns* in German; hence, *er hat uns euch empfohlen* ('he recommended us to you' or 'you to us') is ambiguous, but in most instances the case distinction would take care of discriminating the several nesting arguments of *empfehlen*. But in their semiotic functions, grammars are not 100% efficient, and some unresolvable ambiguities do occur, rare as they are. Chao (1959:3f.) cites a Chinese sentence in which a linking argument (equivalent to an English subject) is interchangeable with various nesting arguments (time and place specifications). In the Yiddish *Hajnt iz šabəs* 'Today is Saturday', one cannot tell whether *hajnt* is a subject or an adverb of time; in *s'kumt ajx a dolər* 'you have a dollar coming to you', one cannot tell from overt markers whether *a dolər* is the subject or the object.

It is far more usual for certain distinctions of function-status to become obscure when sentences are nominalized; cf. the ambiguity of Latin subjective and objective genitive (*amor Dei* < *X amat Deum?* or < *Deus amat X-um?*) or of English *visiting relatives*, derivable both from $V(x, \acute{r})$ and from $V(r, \acute{x})$. There also occur ambiguities of the form '$f(a) \cdot g(a)$' vs. '$\varphi(f[a]$'; cf. *He decided to leave immediately* (= *decided immediately? to leave immediately?*).

While the distinction between '$f(x)$' and '$x(f)$' in sentences with one-level and one-place predicates is, as we have said, of minor importance, the prevalence of functions of more than one place, '$f(a, b, c\ldots)$', and of type higher than one, like '$f(a, b\ldots) \cdot \varphi(f, g)\ldots$', imposes on the vast majority of sentences a determinate semiotic structure. As pointed out in (*b*), semiotic considerations alone would permit us to equate '$f(x)$' with '$x(f)$', or even with '$x\ x$' or '$f\ f$'; but the productivity of expansion patterns of sentences (Chomsky, 1957: ch. IV) endows even the simplest sentence with a grammatical structure similar to that of complex ones, which in turn suggests for the simplest sentence a semiotic analysis analogous to that of higher-level and higher-degree functions; it is only the virtually grammarless discourse of pictorial writing (e.g., Février, 1948:40 illustrating Ojibwa incantations; Voegelin, 1961:85 on Delaware mnemonic pictography) or of the gesture language of congenital deaf-mutes (cf. Spang-Thomsen, 1956) that resembles the form '$fff\ldots$' in its semiotic "structure."

3.1.4. MAJOR FUNCTIONS AND THEIR BACKGROUNDING. It is a further near-universal property of discourse that in sentences expressing more than one function, whether homogeneous (i.e., '$f(a) \cdot g(a)$') or heterogeneous (i.e., '$f(a) \cdot \varphi(f)$'), one of the functions is represented as the *major function*. The usual grammatical correlate of the major function is the subject-predicate construction, but in the verb-phrase-sentences of polysynthetic languages the semiotic cut is marked in other ways.[41] It seems, incidentally, that this universal feature of language is also transferred to all logical systems.[42] Each language has its own stock of grammatical devices for "backgrounding" all but the major proposition of the sentence. It appears to be a universal, too, that in the backgrounding of a proposition some information is lost: the most general loss is pragmatic—that is, the backgrounded proposition is not fully "asserted"—but there may also be losses of tense and subject-object distinctions. It is usual for every sentence to show a major function, but some languages also have ways of backgrounding *all* functions in a sentence; cf. English *There was a beating of drums by the natives* (see also below).

Every "major" proposition is perhaps capable of being backgrounded, at least as a nesting argument in a *verbum dicendi* relation; it is much rarer, on the contrary, for a language to have designators which *cannot* participate in a major function at all, and are condemned, as it were, to the background; in fact, it seems plausible that such a sign would be not a designator but a formator.[43]

The high rigidity of '$f(x)$' organization, reinforced by the grammatical requirement to conform to an extremely low number of sentence types within any one language, is universally counterbalanced by the availability of grammatical devices for transforming f-signs into x-signs and vice versa. We are referring to the semiotic effect of deriving verbals from nouns or noun-phrases, nominals from verb-phrases and sentences—the "stativations" and "verbations" so graphically sketched by Whorf (1956:96ff.), the "event splitting" analyzed by Reichenbach (1948:268f.).[44] Related to these are the operations of abstracting a property from a class, of "solving" functions for a particular argument (Reichenbach, 1948:311f.)—semiotic processes expressed in language by relative clauses and their analogs. These are by no means restricted grammatically to the clause or phrase level; the whole process may take place affixally. As an example we take the Fox sentence (Sapir, 1921:76), *-kiwin-a-m-oht-ati-wachi* 'they together kept (him) in flight from them'. We introduce the notation a^* for an argument-name derived from a function. The Fox sentence has the following semiotic form:

f = *-kiwin-* 'indefinite movement'; hence, $f(x)$ 'x moves in an indefinite way'

φ = *-a-* 'flight'; hence, *-kiwin-a-*: $\varphi(f) \cdot f(x)$ 'x moves fleeingly = x flees'

Here we convert the two-level function to an argument:

$$[\varphi(f) \cdot f(x)] = a^*$$

g = 'to cause'
h = 'to be animate'
$g(\ ) \cdot h(x)$ = *-m-* 'to cause to an animate subject'
y = *-wachi* 'they, animate' (the "causer")
$\acute{z}$ = *-oht-* 'for the subject' } (manner
$\acute{w}$ = *-ati-* 'several objects, one to the other' } of causing)
$g(y, \acute{a}^*, \acute{z}, \acute{w})$ = 'they, animate *(wachi)* cause a^* for themselves *(oht-)* to one another *(-ati-)*'

All together:

$$g(y, \acute{a}^*, \acute{z}, \acute{w}) \cdot \{a^* = [\varphi(f) \cdot f(x)]\} \cdot h(x)$$

In many languages, a limited number of grammatical patterns may be called on for changing the function-status of signs in a multiplicity of ways. Consider the ambiguity of English *His dancing was surprising*. If this means, 'the way he danced...', it is of the form '$f(x) \cdot \varphi(f)$', where the first function is merely backgrounded; if it means, "the fact that he danced...", it has the form '$[f(x) = a^*] \cdot \varphi(a^*)$', where the first "proposition" as a whole is converted to an argument. These matters would require a specialized analysis. Yet it is useful at least to point out the perhaps universal asymmetry of grammatical devices for nominalization and verbalization. Despite the exceptional structure of Chinese, where the backgrounding of *chaau fann* 'fry rice' to 'fried rice' involves no overt marking (Hockett, 1954:102), it is safe to say that in most languages conversion of a relation or a proposition to an argument involves intricate grammatical processes and losses of information, whereas conversion of an argument to a function may be accomplished by something as simple as making the argument the complement of a verb or particle 'to be'. In Miwok, for example, nominalization of a sentence requires affix changes in subject and predicate, but any noun can become predicative either by being conjugated directly or by being verbalized and conjugated as a verb (Freeland, 1951: 136). In English we can contrast the complexity of changes involved in the first and second conversion:

$f(x) \rightarrow a^*$ *He often sent flowers* → HIS FREQUENT SENDING OF *flowers...*

$x \rightarrow f(\ )$ *Three truly excellent wines* → *... are three truly excellent wines.*

This grammatico-semantic asymmetry is also evident when we compare derivationally related verbs and nouns of a language. No matter how austerely the derivation is marked—even by zero, as in English—the verb *to X* only exceptionally means 'to be an *X*' (as in *to soldier, to sire*); much more usually *to X* means 'to treat as an *X*', 'to cover by means of *X*', 'to perform *X*' (cf. *to baby, to mother, to people, to police*, not to speak of verbs derived from inanimate nouns). In other words, even "zero" derivation rarely serves the purely syntactic role of converting an argument-name to a relation-name (cf. Martinet, 1960: 140f.).

While all languages thus contain the means for overcoming the specialization of particular designators for particular function-status (and this measure of convertibility may differ from language to language, achieving a peak in English and Chinese), it is more than likely that such operations are learned rather late in childhood; very young children may master '$f(x)$' sentences and very soon thereafter also '$f(x) \cdot \varphi(f)$', but not '$\varphi(f)$' as a major function ("the redness is surprising") or '$\varphi(a^*) \cdot [a^* = f(x)]$' ("it's funny for the eyes to be red"), which require special grammatical transformations. Now the specialization of signs in argument-roles, relation-roles, and operator-roles naturally gives rise to a powerful ontological metaphor (cf. Marcus, 1960). It is out of such specialization that "class meanings" (Nida's "linguisemes," 1953:5) arise for nouns as "substance-names," verbs as "process-names," etc. Predication, a grammatical phenomenon, comes to be correlated with one of its most typical, but certainly non-criterial semantic interpretations—"actor-action."[45] R. W. Brown not only has given proof of the power of children's grammar-based ontology (1957), but has argued that as children grow older they learn derivations and transformations whose semantic and grammatico-semantic isomorphism decreases; that is, as they learn to use higher-level functions as major functions and to change function-roles of the signs, the foundations of their ontology crumble. This brilliant solution to an old impasse raises fascinating prospects for the cross-cultural investigation of juvenile ontologies and their possible blurring during adolescence.[46]

3.1.5. MINOR SENTENCE TYPES. A conscientious separation of semantic and grammatical criteria also allows us to give a precise formulation to the old and treacherous problem of minor sentence types and impersonal verbs. The mere review of the theories that have been advanced concerning such expressions as *Fire!* or *It's raining* would fill a good-sized book.

A reasonable solution should probably begin by distinguishing ellipsis from minor sentence types proper. Ellipsis is to be defined as a family of transformations, with precisely formulated scopes and functions, yielding the isolation of a part of a sentence against the background of a full source sentence.[47] (All languages use ellipsis, under such typical conditions as replies to questions, conjunction of similarly constructed expression by *and*, etc.) A second type are interjectional nominal expressions, always either as vocatives, or as symptoms of emotional stress or its conventional or rhetorical simulation, of the form 'x!'. (In languages which distinguish linking from nesting by overt segmental markers even interjections may distinguish the forms '(x)!' and '($\acute{x}$)!'. Thus the Roman beggar asking for bread probably said *Panem!* (accusative = '($\acute{x}$)!'), but if he found some bread unexpectedly, he might have shouted *Panis!* (nominative = '(x)!').

In contrast to both elliptical and interjectional elements, we encounter truly "stunted propositions" defined by having a form like ' (x,)' or 'f(,)', etc., in a system which not only permits, but generally requires '$f(x, \acute{y})$'. Critical logic, finding such forms inconvenient or conducive to metaphysical pseudoproblems (cf. Reichenbach, 1948:89f., 332), rejects these forms as "meaningless" and prefers to write not '$(\exists f)$' but '$(\exists y)f(y)$'. But in languages such forms do occur (Martinet, 1960:125f.).

What is thus semiotically "stunted" may receive very different grammatical treatment, depending on the language. In English and German, for example, stunted propositions require a dummy subject *it*, or even a dummy subject plus *is* (*It rained*, *It's a boy*, *Es wird getanzt*); but in other cases the stuntedness is marked by the subjectless sentence [*There was a raising of eyebrows* = '$f(\ ,\acute{y})$'] In Yiddish, a dummy subject is required only if no other term occurs in the sentence: *es regnt* 'it's raining', but *hajnt regnt* 'it's raining today'. In most languages (e.g., Latin, Russian, Hungarian; but not English, Hebrew) the verb phrase alone can function as a full-fledged sentence. Its semantic content does not thereby lose its regular propositional form; the linking argument, grammatically deleted, is then a 'he' or 'they' identified by discourse-deixis. Such is the case in Latin *Venit* 'He is coming', and probably also in many polysynthetic languages where the alleged one-word sentences are really only one-word verb-phrases, functioning as a minor sentence type until a subject noun-phrase is added. Finally, languages which use a copula for converting argument names to relation names may have forms which are "minor" both grammatically and semiotically; cf. Russian *Vojna.* 'It's war = There is a war on', *Est' stol.* 'There is a table', Hungarian *Asztal.* 'It's a table', *Asztal van.* 'There is a table';[48] in English this pattern seems applicable only to evaluative adjectives (e.g., *Excellent*). In Chinese, according to Chao (1959:2), minor sentences "are more primary and relatively even more frequent" in two-way conversation than in other languages; but all the examples, including *Feiji.* '[It's an] airplane' and *Yeou feiji.* 'There is an airplane', are easily recognizable types. Many languages seem to lack grammatical distinction between certain major and minor forms, such as Miwok *šóluku-ʔ* 'a bow' = 'it is a bow' (Freeland, 1951:36).

3.2. *Contextual effects on designation*

3.2.1. POLYSEMY AND HOMONYMY. We must now refine the theory of designation to allow for certain contextual effects. In contrast to the "monosemy" case formulated in 1.2, we now say that a designatum may contain disjunctions between its components. Using A, B,... as signs and $(c_1 \cdot c_2 \cdot ...)$ as their designata, we define:

Polysemy
$$\begin{cases} A\ (c_1 \vee c_2) \\ A\ [c_1 \cdot (c_2 \vee c_2)] \text{ etc.} \end{cases}$$
[49]

The polysemy of a sign may be resolved by the context,[50] as follows:

Resolution
$$\begin{cases} \text{Given } A\,\{c_1 \cdot c_2 \cdot [c_3 \vee (c_4 \cdot c_5)]\};\ B;\ C. \\ \text{If } A + B, \text{ then } A(c_1 \cdot c_2 \cdot c_3) \\ \text{If } A + C, \text{ then } A(c_1 \cdot c_2 \cdot c_4 \cdot c_5). \end{cases}$$

In this presentation, the signs A, B, C... need not be words or even lesser segmental elements; grammatical processes, too, are given to polysemy which is resoluble by the context of other processes, for example, the English preterit: '1. past, 2. (in conditions) counterfactual'. It will also be apparent that one of the important types of polysemy and resolution involves compatibility types in the sense of 3.1.2. Thus, *blue* and *purple* have color components in the context of signs for visible objects, but these are replaced by "affective" values in such contexts as... *music*, ... *prose*.

It should be clear that by accepting a theory which permits disjunctions within a designatum, we resolve the controversial notion of *Grundbedeutung* or *Hauptbedeutung* (reviewed, e.g., by Zvegincev, 1957:215ff., and rejected by him; cf. also the refutation by Karolak, 1960:245-247) into clear-cut operational terms.[51]

Before we can think of quantifying the incidence of polysemy and idiomaticity in a language (cf. 4.3.1), we must also formalize the distinction between vagueness and polysemy. In most standard sources these are treated as a matter of degree (e.g., Ullmann, 1951:119). Black (1949) has given an excellent account of vagueness in the Peircian sense.[52] Some vagueness is inherent in every sign, and the vagueness of different signs is not commensurable since vagueness is a pragmatic factor in denotation and hence beyond the province of semantics as the study of designation. Ambiguity, on the other hand, is a linguistic, semantic phenomenon arising from the presence of disjunctions in a designatum.[53] These disjunctions are determinate results of the participation of a sign in more than one paradigm; thus, taking *coat* as $[c_1 \cdot (c_2 \vee c^3)]$, in which c_1 = 'garment', c_2 = 'of arm's length, worn over shirt' and c^3 = 'knee-length, worn as the outermost piece', we have an ambiguity between *coat*^{1} $(c_1 \cdot c_2)$ and *cout*^{2} $(c_1 \cdot c^3)$, since the classes of objects denotable by each are, in our culture, discrete. Similarly for *arrange* 'put in order' and *arrange* 'orchestrate'. We would like to propose the term "(synchronic) homonymy" for pairs or sets of signs having no element of their designata in common, like *cry*^{1} 'shout' and *cry*^{2} 'weep';[54] *fair*^{1} 'not foul', *fair*^{2} 'not biased', and *fair*^{3} 'pretty good'. But even short of homonomy, polysemous designata differ in "smoothness" (cf. Gove, 1957:12f.): the designatum $[c_1 \cdot c_2 \cdot c_3 \cdot (c_4 \vee c_5)]$ is more "smoothly" organized than $[c_1 \cdot (c_2 \vee c_3 \vee c_4 \vee c_5)]$.

In considering the effect of context on polysemy and homonymy, we find that signs in question behave very differently. For *coat*^{1} and *coat*^{2}, for example, the ambiguity probably remains unresolved in most contexts;[55] for *cry*^{1} and *cry*^{2}, on the contrary, it is hard to think of ambiguous contexts in which the homonymy would not be resolved. As for *arrange*^{1} and *arrange*^{2} or the various *fair*'s, it is possible to construct both unambiguous and ambiguous contexts; an example of ambiguity would be: *(Was the weather good or bad?) It was fair.* Often the resolving context can be specified in grammatical terms. Thus, if *cry* appears without a direct object and without *out*, it is *cry*^{2}; if *arrange* appears without a direct object, it is *arrange*^{2}; if *fair* appears in a negative sentence, or modified by *very*, it is either *fair*^{1} or *fair*^{2} but not *fair*^{3} (Ravid, 1961; cf. also N. N. Amosova, *SPLS*, 1960: 16–18; V. I. Perebejnos, *SSM*, 1961:20–23). The grammatical specialization of the disjunct parts of homonymous or polysemous designata thus hints at differences in their semiotic form: for example, *cry*^{1} $= f(x, \acute{y})$ versus *cry*^{2} $= f(x)$.[56] In many other cases, however, the resolving context cannot be stated in grammatical terms and must be specified in terms of designators (e.g., *fair judge* implies *fair*^{2}; *fair weather* implies *fair*^{1}; *fair condition* is indeterminate; *cry-baby* implies *cry*^{2} while *cri-er* implies, generally, *cry*^{1}).[57] The significant structural problem is to classify the resolving context-words by an analysis of the designata rather than by enumeration. Thus, we might want to say that *fair* implies *fair*^{2} if it occurs in the context of *judge*, *game*, *decision*, *warning*, etc., but a complete analysis must find that c_i which is shared by the designata of *judge*, *game*, etc. The widely practiced discrimination of polysemy by "usage labels" (archaic, poetic; mining, zoology; etc.) involves pragmatic or even nonsynchronic criteria of dialect mixture, and —no matter how useful in itself—it is, from a semantic point of view, beside the point (Zvegincev, 1957:235f.).

The reverse of contextual resolution of ambiguity, of equal importance to all languages, consists in the capacity of a sign to evoke a context. The limiting case is the unique constituent: *logan-* necessarily implies *-berry* as *runcible* implies *spoon* and *shrift* implies *short*. But highly limited leeway short of uniqueness is also common. Thus *addle*, though it does not contain 'egg' or 'head' as an actual component of its designatum, nevertheless implies a collocation with *egg* (Haugen, 1957:459) or *head*, *brain*, or *pate*. Similarly, *to neigh* implies *horse* as a subject; and so forth. This may be called phraseological binding or cliché formation. We could compute a coefficient of contextual density in a language based on the incidence of contextual resolution of ambiguity and cliché formation provided we had an adequate dictionary. Very likely such a coefficient would hover fairly close to some mean for all languages of the world. (The coefficient would be similar in construction to a measure of information content for the average morpheme or sign.)

3.2.2. DEPLETION. When we contemplate the variety of "meanings" which a word like *take* has in English (*take offense*, *take charge*, *take medicine*, *take notice*, *take effect*, etc.), we come to the conclusion that this is a case not of abnormally overdeveloped polysemy of a word, but rather of its semantic near-emptiness. In these contexts, *take* may be said to function as little more than a verbalizer, not quite unlike *-ize* and other affixes. It is preferable to consider the contextual effect illustrated here not as a resolution of polysemy, but as a "depletion" of the designatum (Peirce, 1932: 428). Similarly, *white* in the context ____ *wine* is depleted, though perhaps not so drastically, as a result of the limited contrasts of color-adjectives possible in that frame. Depletion, then, may be defined as a type of polysemy in which designata contain relatively large optional parts whose actualization or nonactualization is determined by precisely delimited contexts.

The phenomenon of depletion is surely a semiotic universal, but perhaps its incidence varies in different languages. Ullmann, for example (1952, 1953), without distinguishing it from polysemy, argued that it is more common in French than in German and English.

Perhaps every language has a portion of its vocabulary which is given to depletion. Whether any universals can be formulated here other than with reference to the high-frequency nature of the "depletive" vocabulary is not clear. One is reminded of such phenomena as the verb for 'give' functioning as a preposition equivalent to 'for' (Mandarin, Thai, French Creole), 'say' as a conjunction introducing quotations, 'body' or 'bone' as a mark of the reflexive ('one's self'); 'son', 'eye', 'mouth' functioning as depleted elements in compounds (Hebrew 'son-of-color' = 'nuance'; Malayo-Polynesian 'eye-of-day' = 'sun'; 'mouth-of-the house' = 'door' in various African languages), etc.

A limiting case of depletion would be that in which a given context, E + ____, causes A to lose its designatum altogether: A is then completely predictable and meaningless (see note 39), like the dative-case marker in a German noun-phrase after *mit*.

3.2.3. IDIOMATICITY. An idiom may be defined as a grammatically complex expression A + B whose designatum is not completely expressible in terms of the designata of A and B, respectively.[58] (The expression is nowadays often said to be semantically exocentric, and its meaning is called a "macrosememe": Nida, 1953.)

Idiom $\begin{cases} \text{Given A } (c_1 \cdot c_2 \cdot c_3)\text{; B } (c_4 \cdot c_5) \\ \text{Then } (A + B)\ (c_1 \cdot c_4 \cdot c_6 \cdot c_7) \end{cases}$

Examples: *Finger-hut* 'thimble' ("literally" 'finger-hat'), *Handschuh* 'glove' ('hand-shoe'), *rub noses with* 'be on familiar terms with'. For any language possessing idioms—and this means every language—the semantic description is not complete unless each idiom, whether a compound or a phrase or an incompletely productive "quasi-transformation" (Harris, 1957: 330f.; Šmelev, 1960), appears in the appropriate semantic paradigms on a par with morphological simplicia and productive transformations. Thus *rub* belongs in a "field" with *scratch*, *abrade*, etc.; *nose* with *face*, *nostril*, *etc.*; but *rub noses* with *familiarity*, *intimacy*, etc.—just as /mə́šruwm/ takes its place in the *toadstool—fungus...* "field" regardless of the fact that /məš/ plays a separate role (*pulp—pap—...*) and so does /ruwm/ (*chamber—hall—...*). It is often useful to have a single term for idioms and grammatical simplicia; "lexeme" is today the most widely used name (Goodenough, 1956; Conklin, 1962; A. B. Dolgopol'skij uses "megasign" in *SPLS* 1960:35–42), even though "lexeme" has competing definitions. In this paper we have been using "sign" to include lexemes and their nonsegmental, processual analogs. It would be useful to have statistics on the distibution of the morpheme-to-lexeme ratio (index of idiomaticity) in the languages of the world.

It is of great methodological importance to bear in mind the complementarity of polysemy and idiomaticity.[59] For if, having formulated the designatum of A as $(c_1 \cdot c_2)$ and of B as $(c_3 \cdot c_4)$, we find that A + B has the designatum $(c_1 \cdot c_5 \cdot c_3 \cdot c_4)$, the resulting idiomaticity of A + B may be merely an artifact of our failure to describe A more correctly as $[c_1 \cdot (c_2 \vee c_5)]$, that is, our failure to state that A contains a disjunction leading to polysemy which is resolved in the context ——— + B. For example, if we tentatively define *charge* as 'fill with energy-providing content' (*charge batteries*, *charge guns*), and confront the definition with the expression *charge an account*, we may either call *charge an account* an idiom or revise the description of *charge* to show polysemy: '1. fill..., 2. burden'. The criteria for choosing solutions for maximum economy in descriptive semantics have never been explored, but it is reasonable to suppose that "unilateral idioms" (e.g., *charge an account*) would wisely be avoided, whereas "bilateral idioms" like *rub noses* should be permitted (cf. Mel'čuk, 1960:77f.; I. S. Toropcev in *SSM* 1961:50-54; N. L. Kameneckajte, *ibid.*: 55–57).

Many languages seem to have specialized grammatical patterns for idioms. In English, for example, a preposition plus a count noun without an article (*at hand, by heart*) often signals idiomaticity. [60] But it is also clear that it is not necessary for languages to have their idioms grammatically marked. The relation of idiom-marking patterns to productive patterns in a grammar would be worth investigating on a cross-linguistic basis.

3.2.4. DETERMINATION. When we compare a normal idiom with the "source" expression in its nonidiomatic sense, we find that elements of the component designata have dropped out of the idiom. But there exists a special type of idiom formation which we may call "determination"; in a sense it is the converse of depletion. In this pattern a sign which alone has a highly unspecific or profoundly ambiguous designatum acquires a more determinate designatum in context. The effect is, more often than not, bilateral.

$$\textit{Determination}\ \begin{cases} \text{Given A } (c_1);\ \text{B } (c_2) \\ \text{Then } (\text{A} + \text{B})\ (c_1 \cdot c_2 \cdot c_3 \cdot c_4) \end{cases}$$

The existence of determination is likewise a universal, but again languages differ strikingly in their degree of utilizing the device. In English we find it especially in verb + adverb constructions: *make up, make over, get up, get over*, etc. In cases like *re-fer, receive, con-fer, con-ceive* it is hardly possible to give any designata at all for the constituent parts. In some Sino-Tibetan languages, on the other hand, the use of determination is highly developed: cf. Chinese *shih-* 'lith-', which becomes determinate in context: *shih-t'ou* 'stone', *shih-yin* 'lithography', etc.; [61] *tao-* 'road' and *-lu* 'road'—neither of them semantically determinate or grammatically free—but *tao-lu* 'road' (Maspéro, 1933:55), 'success', *lu-tao* 'road', *lu-t'u* 'road' (Sofronow, 1950:72, 76). Thai has *bā̆t* '1. cut; 2. begging bowl; 3. noose; etc.' and *buaŋ-* 'noose' (grammatically bound); but *buaŋ-bā̆t* 'noose' (free and determinate). In English exact analogs have to be invented, such as **poly-mult* for 'many', **poli-urb* for 'city'. Formulaically, the Sino-Tibetan type of process turns out to be a combination of contextual resolution of homonymous ambiguity with idiom formation:

$$\begin{cases} \text{Given A } (c_1 \vee c_2 \vee c_3);\ \text{B } (c_2 \cdot c_4 \cdot c_5) \\ \text{Then } (\text{A} + \text{B})\ (c_2). \end{cases}$$

4. Semantic Structure and Content of Vocabularies

4.1. *Bases for comparison*

There is hardly anything more tantalizing in the field of semantic universals than the question whether there are signs, or more exactly, designata which are shared by all languages. (The formators, which certainly show a high degree of universality, were treated separately in 2.2.) In the practical problem of the semantic structures of auxiliary international languages or intermediary languages for machine translation, the number of relevant natural languages is small, and the amount of discoverable "universality" is impressive.[62] But a modest amount of ethnological sophistication will persuade us that for the human race as a whole, there are not very many universally shared designata. The story of the shrinking word list of glottochronology (cf. Hymes, 1960:4–7) shows that even experienced anthropologists may overestimate the size of such a list, which has now, as a result of constant reduction, shrunk to about one hundred items.[63]

But for one who takes semantic description seriously, even the items on the emaciated list are not strictly comparable. For can we say that all languages share a word for 'eye' when, in one language, the corresponding word involves polysemy with 'sight', in another with 'middle', in a third with 'power', and so forth? And even where there are parallelisms between the polysemy patterns, the conditions for their contextual resolutions will surely be different for each language. For this reason, too, comparisons of the "degree of motivatedness of signs" (the morpheme/sign ratio) in sets of languages are feasible only where a high degree of inter-translatability (a priori matching of designata) is assured;[64] Ullmann's survey (1953) of a few West European languages from this standpoint is, contrary to his optimism, virtually useless for world-wide typological purposes.

A more fruitful approach might therefore address itself to the distribution, not of complete designata, but of their disjunctive parts. In contrast to whole designata, the occurrence of their monosemous parts will probably come much closer to universality. Many of the items discarded from the glottochronological list because of the noncomparability of designata as wholes could be replaced by more easily compared disjunct parts of designata.

However, if semantic analysis is to be carried to its logical conclusion, we cannot even stop there: we must base our ultimate comparison on the distribution of semantic components, or distinctive features—the various *c*'s, or conditions for denotation—which go to make up the formulation of a given designatum (1.2).

4.2. *Componential structure*

It is hardly necessary any more to analyze or to justify the concept of semantic component. Since the appearance of the tide-turning papers by Conklin (1955), Lounsbury (1956), and Goodenough (1956), we have had an opportunity to see this concept applied effectively to a number of amenable fields. We proceed here on the assumption that covert semantic components are legitimate units of semantic description,[65] and that, while there may be no unfailing procedure for discovering such components, rational decision procedures can be established for selecting between reasonable alternative descriptions.[66]

Since most studies so far have concentrated on particularly favorable fields such as kinship and color, it is important to stress that the actual designata of languages, even apart from the complications of polysemy (3.2.1), depart from the model $(c_1 \cdot c_2 \cdot c_3 \cdot \ldots c_n)$ in various ways. First, the commutability of the several components is not always perfect, so that they may not be as fully discrete as the canonic formula suggests.[67] Second, man makes ample use of his innate capacity for "perceiving universals" and learns many designata by deriving a gestalt from instances of denotata; hence the designatum coded in its canonical form is for many signs a scientific construct imposed with a degree of artificiality which differs for various signs. Components are also distinguished by the degree of their criteriality. Normative terminologies are characterized by the fact that their designata fully conform to the canonical form (cf. Budagov, 1958:23–29). In ordinary language only some areas are marked by a degree of "terminologization." [68] An objective measure of terminologization for a set of signs might be given by the reliability of informants' validation of proposed formulations of the designata. [69] [A third respect in which actual designata deviate from the traditional model is by the presence of nesting within them; cf. the Postscript.]

We may define as "immediate synonyms" any pair of terms, *A* and *A′*, such that their designata differ by one component. [70] (The "perfect" synonym which has been haunting contemporary philosophy is of trivial importance to ordinary language.) Whereas in the highly patterned or "terminologized" domains of vocabulary, such as kinship or color, distinguishing components recur in numerous sets of signs, the bulk of the vocabulary is, of course, more loosely structured and is full of components unique to single pairs, or small numbers of pairs, of synonyms. But the componential structure as such is not impaired. One can therefore anticipate excellent validations for analyses even of nonterminologized lexical fields. A recent paper by Bendix (1961), in analyzing a group of English synonyms for 'give', not only isolated a component common to the entire set (*x* gives *y* to *z* = '*x* causes *y* to have *z*')—a component which recurs in such pairs as *show* : *see* *drop* : *fall*, *make* : *be*—but also separated out features of status differential between giver and receiver, of casualness, etc., which distinguish *give* from *confer*, *grant*, and the like. In an analysis of a group of synonyms for 'shake', components of intensity (*shake* : *quake*), possible voluntariness (*shake*: *tremble*), and others were revealed which recur elsewhere in the vocabulary (cf. *throw* : *hurl*, *jump* : *fall*). [71] Among the most important components to hunt out in any vocabulary are those which define "dead metaphors":

given a designatum $[c_1 \cdot c_2 \cdot \langle c_3 \cdot c_4 \rangle]$ in which $\langle c_3 \cdot c_4 \rangle$ is a noncriterial component, a dead metaphor might be defined as a sign having as its designatum $(c_3 \cdot c_4)$. This describes, for example, the relation of *head* '⟨ most important ⟩ top part of body above the neck' to *head* 'most important part of...' in *head of the table*, *head of government*, etc.

We may now introduce the notion of semantic continuity. A semantic system is continuous if for every sign A $(c_1 \cdot c_2 \cdot \ldots c_n)$ there is a sign A′ adequately defined as A $(c'_1 \cdot c_2 \cdot \ldots c_n)$—that is, by changing one of the components of the designatum of A (Weinreich, 1962). Contrariwise, there is a semantic discontinuity when a change of a component c_i to c'_i fails to yield a designatum of some sign in the given language. Clearly, there are in every language areas of greater and lesser semantic continuity; for example, the color field is more continuous than the field of folk-zoological nomenclature.

4.3. *Applications*

We could now put all this theoretical machinery to work ... if only we had the data. Unfortunately, in the field of vocabulary we have almost no critically compiled, commensurable data to go on. As a matter of fact, the description of any one vocabulary is so vast a task—even for languages not so hypertrophied as the West European ones (Weinreich, 1962)—that we must search for suitable methods of lexical sampling for typological purposes. For the time being, the best we can do is suggest some of the variables for which we should plan to sample.

We may distinguish between general, quantitative coefficients and special statements involving particular semantic components and their combinations.

4.3.1. GENERAL COEFFICIENTS

(*a*) For the average sign of a vocabulary, or a delimited lexical domain, what is the *degree of terminologization?* What is the proportion of criterial to noncriterial components in the average designatum?

(*b*) For the average lexical set in a vocabulary, or in one of its delimited domains, what is the *degree of semantic continuity?*

(*c*) For the average sign, etc., what is the *incidence of polysemy?* What is the incidence of homonymy? What is the average power of contextual effects, such as ambiguity resolution, cliché formation, depletion, idiomaticity, and determination?

(*d*) Is there a typical absolute size to the stock of lexemes of a language spoken by a preliterate community? Is there a universal inverse proportion between the inventory of different words and the number of idioms (Nida, 1958:286)?

(*e*) For a vocabulary or a delimited lexical domain, how many levels of contrast (Conklin, 1962) are there? In English we find perhaps four and very often fewer. The unspecialized, laymen's sectors of language simply do not have the depth of structure of scientific zoological or botanical taxonomy. Is Wallace's hypothesis (1961*b*) correct in stating that regardless of cultural type or level, institutionalized folk taxonomies do not contain more than 64 (= 2^6) entitities (with corresponding limitations on the elaboration of vocabulary), and that this universal limit is related to the human capacity for processing information? Is there any connection between the low number of hierarchic levels of contrast and the low number of types in language viewed as a functional calculus (3.1.1)? Do languages have specific patterns for forming superordinates?[72]

(*f*) For a vocabulary, etc., what is the degree of its circularity? Differently formulated, what is the efficiency of an ordinary language in serving as the metalanguage for its own semantic description (Weinreich, 1962)? What is the relation between this measure of efficiency and the absolute size of a vocabulary?

4.3.2. SPECIAL CHARACTERISTICS

(*a*) What is the stock of semantic components of a given language? What are some of the universal components (e.g., 'generation', 'sex', 'light' vs. 'dark', 'dry' vs. 'wet', 'young' vs. 'old', 'alive' vs. 'dead', 'incipiency' vs. 'steady state')?[73]

(*b*) What components typically or universally recur in combination? In other words, what are the "things" which have names in most or all languages? Is it not the case that, say, 'sex' and 'age', 'causing to perceive' and 'sense modality' typically appear together *(boy : man :: girl : woman; see : hear :: show : tell)?*

(*c*) What are the typical, recurrent patterns of polysemous disjunction affecting particular components? Are there languages which call 'seeing' and 'hearing', 'eye' and 'ear', 'hand' and 'foot', 'elbow' and 'knee' by the same name? Are we correct in assuming that 'arm' and 'hand', 'leg' and 'foot', 'toe' and 'finger', 'smell' and 'taste', 'cheek' and 'chin', 'tongue' and 'language', 'youngster' and 'offspring', 'guts' and 'emotion', 'head' and 'importance', 'heavy', 'hard' and 'difficult' typically participate in polysemy? Will an adequate sampling of languages confirm the findings obtained in Europe that in polysemy among sensory terms, the metaphoric transfer is always from sight to hearing (Ullmann, 1952:297), that space words are always extended to time notions (e.g., *long, short*), and never vice versa?

(*d*) Is it true that among designations for man-made things, the discreteness of semantic components in a designatum reflects the definiteness of the cultural functions of the object?

(*e*) For a given lexical domain, do some languages show a higher degree of terminologization in their vocabulary than other languages, and is this related to differences in the attention paid to the corresponding domain of "things" in the cultures?

(*f*) Is it true that "the vocabulary relating to the focus (or foci) of the culture is proportionately more exhaustive than that which refers to nonfocal features" (Nida, 1958:283)? How is this related to the specificity of designata (designatum/component ratio), the degree of semantic continuity, and the degree of terminologization in the lexical domain concerned?

(*g*) We may think of simplex signs as standing midway on a scale between complex expressions, on the one hand, and factorial, covert components of simplex signs, for the expression of a given "meaning." Is there, for a given semantic domain, an *optimal level for simplex signs*, related perhaps to the neurological and psychological equipment of the human animal? Are there languages, in other words, where 'round', 'bright', 'soft', and the like are expressed not by simplex signs, but have to be rendered by complex expressions or result only from the factoring out of components from among more specific designata?[74]

(*h*) Is there a way for finding objective support for the grand characterization of the semantic "plan" of a language, its "cognitive style" (Hymes, 1961), to replace the highly impressionistic procedures of Whorf and his disciples?

5. Conclusion

We have attempted to suggest a number of universals of language in the framework of a consistent and comprehensive semiotic theory. At many points in the undertaking, especially where designators were concerned, reference data were felt to be so scant as to make the conclusions unattractively general and modest in relation to the conceptual machinery. But certain over-all patterns nevertheless emerge. Perhaps the most impressive conclusion is that languages are universally less "logical," symmetrical, and differentiated than they could be if the components and devices contained somewhere in each system were uniformly utilized throughout that system.

The greatest challenge arising from this finding of a property of "limited sloppiness" in language is to determine what good it does. Man demonstrates somewhere in every language that he is capable of greater symmetry and discrimination than he employs in the average discourse. We want to consider why this should be so.

Very likely the answer will be found in the ratio between memory capacity, attention span, accessibilty to recall, and effort of discriminatory coding. We can imagine a small office with a chair to sit on and a desk to write on; its occupant may prefer, when reaching for a book from a high shelf, to stand on a chair or even to put a chair on top of the table, rather than further clutter up the office with a ladder. A similar economy may account for the unequal utilization of some semiotic potentials of language and the overburdening of others.

But before such interrelations can be studied with precision, we must have large amounts of empirical research. Above all, there must be a clear-cut realization that the province of linguistic semantics is the study not of denotation or reference, but of the designational system proper to each language.[75]

The distinction between denotation and designation, which is at least of medieval origin, was prevalent in nineteenth-century linguistics as the doctrine of "inner form" (cf. Funke, 1932; Zvegincev, 1957: ch. VII) and reappears in (post-)Saussurean linguistics as the distinction between content form ("valeur") and content substance or purport (e.g., de Saussure, 1922:158f., Hjelmslev, 1953:30f., and, in brilliant practice, Lounsbury, 1956, Goodenough, 1956). It also turns up in the modern philosophy of language in many guises (J. S. Mill, Frege, Husserl, Marty; Peirce, 1932: secs. 391ff., Carnap, 1942, 1947, Quine, 1953: ch. II). Although it has a venerable tradition behind it, the emancipation of designation from denotation in our own time has come under attack from various quarters. "Mechanistic" linguists, captivated by early behaviorism, have protested that intensions as psychic states are inaccessible to observation, and that descriptive semantics must wait until further progress in neurology makes them accessible (e.g., Bloomfield, 1933:140); meanwhile, all the linguist can do is observe "co-occurrence" between signs and their assumed denotata (e.g., McQuown, 1956). In the face of the difficulty of defining words by means of other words, linguists have been urged, in the spirit of Wittgenstein (cf. Wells, 1954), to look, not for the meaning of words, but for their "use" in the language. (But "use" with respect to what?) Under the influence of information theory, linguists have been urged to calculate the transitional probabilities between words and to consider these the "linguistic meaning" of the words (e.g., Joos, 1950: 356). Some philosophers have argued the need to eliminate intension (designation) in the interests of ontological economy. This may be a laudable critical proposal for constructing a language of science; still, the workings of ordinary language cannot be described without intension. The philosophers themselves keep running into the crude fact of structured designation. Frege and Peirce faced it in connection with modal-logic problems; it keeps cropping up in more recent literature under the headings of indirect quotation, "oblique discourse," "referential opacity" (Quine, 1960:141ff.), "intensional structure" and "intensional isomorphism" (Carnap, 1947:56f.). All alternatives to the classical theory of language, when applied to ordinary language, turn out either to evade or to obscure the important issues.[76] Bloomfield's neurological "reductionism," apart from its dependence on potential discoveries which may never be made, misses the properly linguistic, "autonomous" structuring of man-made semantic systems (cf. Wells, 1954:118–121); for "circumlocution" is not, as Bloomfield thought, a "makeshift device" for stating meanings, but *the* legitimate device par excellence. The slogans of British philosophy, useful in sensitizing the linguist to certain subtleties in the polysemy of folk-epistemological terms, hardly compel us to abandon the semantic description of large translucent segments of vocabulary.

Decades have been wasted. Linguistic semantics must free itself from the paralysis imposed on it by a misguided positivism insensitive to the specificities of language. Behavioral data? By all means, let us have behaviorism rather than a new scholasticism operating with inaccessible "dispositions to respond" (Morris, 1946; Carnap, 1947; Quine, 1960), let us have the observable, publicly verifiable performance of human beings charged with the metalinguistic task of manipulating signs for the disclosure of their intensional structure.

Postscript 1965

The author's work on semantic problems undertaken since the preceding paper was written in 1961 is reported in several recent articles, references to which have been added to the bibliography (Weinreich, 1964, 1965). The last-mentioned paper also takes issue with some of the recent literature. A special paper (Weinreich, 1963) is devoted to Soviet lexicology.

In the treatment of "combinatorial semiotics," the present chapter parted company with much of traditional as well as modern logic by claiming that complex signs are constituted out of simplex signs, not by a single process ("linking"), but by at least one other irreducible mechanism ("nesting"). The author's most recent paper (1965) not only pursues the differentiation of semantic relations which hold between the components of a complex sign but takes the further step of claiming that many simplex signs contain within their designata components that stand in mutual relations other than linking. The more recent work thus argues for a formal continuity between the definitional sentences of a metalanguage and the sentences of the object language.

The 1965 paper also attempts explicitly to integrate a semantic theory with a generative conception of syntax. It criticizes the unsatisfactory, basically traditionalist approach to combinatorial problems recently taken by Katz and Fodor (1963) and explores a theory in which a sentence draws its semantic components not from its lexical items alone but also from some of the syntactic categories utilized in its formation. It thus suggests an abandonment of the requirement stated in the present paper (sec. 1.2) to the effect that a grammatical description be autonomous vis-à-vis the semantic description of a language. The recent version of the author's theory also deals with the semantic interpretation of deviant expressions; it seeks a way of overcoming the prejudices of generative grammar against deviant expressions and its helplessness in dealing with the situation up to now.

The question of empirical validation of semantic analyses against informants' reactions has recently been considered, along with numerous other methodological matters, by Zimmer (1964) and Bendix (1965). The latter study, which takes a significant stride forward in the componential analysis of general vocabulary, has succeeded in isolating a number of fairly abstract semantic components which recur in several unrelated languages, and may well be universal.

Notes

1. This particular term is adopted from Morris (1946), but without the pseudobehaviorist elements of its definition there.

2. The further "components" of the sign in the Peirce-Morris tradition —"interpreter" and "interpretant"—are dispensable in the present discussion.
3. We consider the distinction between denotation and designation to be essential to any workable program in semantic research. See also sec. 5. For a highly readable version of the theory of conditions, see Ziff (1960), ch. III.
4. The priority of grammatical over semantic description is conceived of as a feature of the theory, not as a necessary sequence of discovery procedures. (Curiosa like "Jabberwocky" aside, linguists in practice describe a grammar on the basis of texts which are, on the whole, understood.) We observe that among the sentences (and certain sentence sequences) generated by a grammar, some are distinguished by being semantically unacceptable. The semantic description of a language is adequate if it so formulates the meanings of signs that we can predict from an inspection of this formulation that a sentence containing certain signs will be semantically unacceptable. In Laxuti *et al.*'s approach (1959), the distinction is between significant *(osmyslennye)* and insignificant well-formed formulas, but for the analysis of real languages, a stronger criterion of semantic unacceptability should be chosen, e. g., literal absurdity, self-contradiction, and tautology. One of the best tools of semantic analysis of a language is therefore a set of skeletal sentences which, if their slots are incorrectly filled, are especially likely to be semantically unacceptable ("——— is a kind of ———," "it's a ——— but it's ———," etc.). The investigator can, of course, also get informants to perform explicitly metalinguistic operations, e. g., arranging terms in semantic paradigms (antonyms as well as multidimensional sets), ranking synonyms for semantic distance, and even supplying (or evaluating) definitions of terms. While the ideal form of a semantic rule is a definition, many significant elements of a natural language lend themselves to definition only partly or awkwardly (cf. Weinreich, 1962); but a place in a semantic paradigm can be formulated even for hard-to-define or undefinable elements. But this leads to problems of method which are beyond the scope of this paper. [See Postscript.]
5. In Karolak's succinct formulation (1960: 246), "the sememe... arises as the result of a given unit's entry into specific paradigmatic functions, but the given unit is empirically a member of as many paradigms as there are syntagmatic positions in which it is able to function."
6. We can, for example, profit from Reichenbach's unexcelled "analysis of conversational language" (1948: ch. VII) without joining him

in his condemnation of the tendencies to "analogy" (p. 278) or "equalization" (p. 263) of ordinary languages, or in his blame of the German language for the "mistake" of deriving adverbs from adjectives without an overt marker (p. 302). Logicians have unfortunately shown little sophistication in distinguishing, among the "defects" of ordinary language which they have been seeking to overcome, those which are universal (e. g., those which lead to the antinomies) and those which are specific to particular languages. Thus the ambiguity of English *is* (class membership vs. predication vs. identity) does not arise in the same form in languages in which "adjectives" are "verbs." The whole problem of definite descriptions would hardly have occurred to logicians starting, let us say, from Russian or Latin or any other language without articles. In order to keep the descriptive and the critical enterprises distinct, we speak of the "semiotic form" of expressions rather than their "logical form," lest we be forced into the awkward conclusion that some logical forms are illogical.

7. Reichenbach's most serious error, of course, is his desire to rewrite grammar on logical principles (e. g., 1948: 255 and *passim*); but his fulminations against "traditional grammar" should not blind us to the incisiveness of his semantic analyses.
8. Thus, Sechehaye (1926) is tremendously disappointing, in view of its title, since only French and a few other European languages are sampled. Nevertheless, Sechehaye did see the equivalence of the semantic relations adjective : noun :: adverb : verb (p. 64) and came close to our own formulation of linking vs. nesting (see 3.1.1) in terms of the distinction between "complément intrinsèque" and "extrinsèque" (61–79, esp. 71f.). Schmidt's logic (1959) is more subtle, but his material is drawn from one language only (German).
9. As Morris puts it (1938: 21), "...the formalized languages studied in contemporary logic and mathematics clearly reveal themselves to be the formal structure of actual and possible languages of the type used in making statements about natural things; at point after point they reflect significant features of language in actual use." Whorf (1956) greatly exaggerated the cultural relativity of logic by overlooking the most general patterns of sign combination at the expense of the arbitrary structure of designators; cf. also 3.1.3. A fascinating attempt to construct a logically economical language (Loglan) is described by J. C. Brown (1960). On a logical language for structural organic chemistry, cf. Laxuti *et al.* (1959); for linguistics, V. V. Ivanov in *Pytannja...* (1960: 5–8); for geometry, Kuznecov *et al.* (1961).

10. Carnap, for example, speaks (1947: 85) of "the customary distinction between logical and descriptive (nonlogical) signs." The various combinatory logics which strive to overcome this distinction (cf. Rosenbloom, 1950: 109ff.), whatever their merit may be, are clearly less similar to language than more traditional logistic systems.
11. The designers of Loglan (cf. note 9) have assigned specialized canonic forms to signs depending on their semiotic function in a manner which strikes the intuition as remarkably familiar and acceptable (cf. J. C. Brown, 1960: 58f.).
12. Of the three subdivisions of semiotics, pragmatics is the least well defined. A reading of Morris (1938, ch. IX) shows the lack of clarity, and every writer since has made his own outline. Carnap in 1955 relegated all descriptive semantics to pragmatics (1956: 233) and argued that "there is an urgent need for a system of theoretical pragmatics" (1956: 250). Lounsbury (1956: 189) and Jakobson (1957) outline more-or-less individual classifications. The delimitation here is perhaps *ad hoc*, too, although it owes much to Reichenbach (1948).
13. In languages where the imperative has no distinctive verb form and the deletion of the subject is its only overt mark, there is ambiguity between assertions and commands in which the subject is "reinstated" for emphasis, as in English *You eat this soup*. A written phrase like PEDESTRIANS KEEP OUT is "pragmatically" ambiguous at least until intonation shows whether *pedestrians* is a separate clause.
14. An alternative formulation, suggested by Bolinger, is that assertions and questions are poles on a gradient scale which also includes hesitant assertion in its middle ranges. Since "No" may be said in response not only to a question but also to an assertion, it is not surprising that the maker of assertions sometimes allows his speech to reflect his anticipation of a negative response.
15. Katz and Postal (1964: 152, note 29) disagree with the observation that interrogative prepositions, although conceivable, do not seem to occur. They claim instead that such things *cannot* occur. Since their theory contains no grounds for such a deduction, the "disagreement" strikes me as spurious; the only scientific advance reflected in their formulation is an increased contempt for facts.
16. Thus, among children there may be the opposite association between bigness and approval. Hockett has pointed out that Potawatomi is actually a language with two productive diminutives—one of endearment on occasion, the other pejorative. A number of interesting remarks on the study of "covert" atti-

tudinal components in mixed signs are made by Sapir (1915) and by Zvegincev (1957: ch. VII).

17. 'Deixis' seems to be the traditional linguistic term, used in the major relevant studies by Brugmann and by Bühler (1934). Morris (1938: 17f.) adopts the Peircian term 'index'. Jakobson (1957) took Jespersen's term, 'shifter'. Reichenbach (1948: 50) speaks of 'token-reflexive words'. On the overriding importance of deixis to communication, cf. Bar-Hillel (1954).
18. In Korean, as Hockett has pointed out to me, there is a six-way differentiation of forms (largely inflectional) depending on the relative status of speaker and addressee; intersecting that, there is a two-way differentiation said to depend on the relative status of the speaker and what is spoken of.
19. Not all languages are equally asymmetrical on this point. While English *his canoe* corresponds both to *he has a canoe* and *he had a canoe*, Potawatomi (according to a comment by Hockett) extends the "preterit" inflection of verbs to that of possessed nouns. But probably no language distinguishes more tenses in nominalizations than in kernel sentences.
20. Nootka does have a verb stem *qwis-* 'to do thus' (Sapir, 1921: 181). In some Serbocroatian dialects, according to P. Ivić, *onoditi* 'to that' is used (*a*) as a euphemism for "unmentionable" verbs, (*b*) as a pause filler, or (*c*) as a pro-verb to avoid repetition. As Hockett has remarked, in Chinese the addition of the "continuative" *-je* also creates verblike forms from deictic adverbs: *dzèmmaje* 'to do it this way', *nèmmaje* 'to do it that way'. But such forms seem quite rare nevertheless; they suggest the one-way implication that no language marks more deictic distinctions in the "verb" than in verb and noun modifiers.
21. On affixal negation, see now Zimmer (1964).
22. Cf. Lees' class Preverb (Lees, 1960: 18ff.). Reichenbach's objection (1948: 308) that "the word 'not' ... is classified by many grammarians as an adverb; but it is a logical term" illustrates all the defects of his book: in which language? by what kind of grammarians? and why cannot a sign be (grammatically) an adverb and (semantically) a logical term?
23. Thus Potawatomi has a verb-forming suffix *-kuwunukut*, which, added to a numeral root, yields a verb 'to be for... years' (Hockett, 1948: 214).
24. A special study is needed concerning grammatical devices used by languages to convert mass nouns to count nouns and for subjecting proper names to specification by definite description. There is no reason to assume that articles are utilized in the English way. For example, while in English the mass/count

difference is neutralized under the definite article (*an/some iron* : *the iron*), in the NE dialect of Yiddish it is maintained by gender differences (*der ajzn* 'the [piece of] iron' : *di ajzn* 'the [kind of] iron'). In Hebrew, though there is a definite article, *ha-*, it cannot be used for constructions like 'the Jerusalem which I remember': a demonstrative has to be substituted (*ota jerušalaim*...).

25. The following illustrations have been supplied by Householder: In both Latin and Ancient Greek, place names have certain special forms. Personal names have "natural" gender, so that, e. g., *Glycerium* is feminine (not neuter). In Greek the article is optional with personal names in many environments where it is obligatory with common nouns; Latin men's names have a special three-part form, one part of which must be selected from a very small closed list. In classical Greek the vast majority of men's names are two-part compounds of a type which almost never occurs except as a name. In Modern Greek many men's names have a special vocative (in *-o*), and all are subject to prefixation by certain elements (*barba-*, *kapitan-*, *kir-*, *ay-*, etc.) which cannot be attached to nonnames. In English, too (and in many modern languages), there are morphemes like *Mr.*, *Mrs.*, *Dr.*, *Prof.*, etc., whose domain is complete personal names or family names, and others (like *Sir*, *Dame*) whose domain is given names. In many languages (not all) names form an infinitely expandable set, such that any phonologically possible stretch will be accepted without hesitation as being a name by all native speakers. This is true of virtually no other class of morphemes (though almost so for plant-names or the like in English). In Turkish and Azerbaijani there are certain constructions from which either personal names or all names are excluded (constructions involving indefiniteness; names are automatically definite, like personal pronouns).
26. Carnap suggested to Reichenbach (1948: 325n.) that semantical and syntactical formators be treated together, but we find it useful here to maintain Reichenbach's original division.
27. American store windows are full of homemade signs like "HOT COFFEE" TO TAKE OUT.
28. So Sanskrit *iti* and Turkish *diye* for all kinds of express or implicit quotations, and Classical Greek *hōs* for many types of implied and a few kinds of express quotations (Householder).
29. It has been suggested that definitions are sentences with an "equational verb" representing a logical equivalence ('$a \equiv b$'), i. e., 'every *a* is a *b* and every *b* is an *a*'. See, for example, Ziff (1960: 168ff.) on the difficulties of this conception as applied to ordinary language [cf. Postscript].

30. We need not take "conjunction" to imply temporal consecutiveness in the speech event. In a conjunction of signs 'A + B', 'B' may be a process "applied" to 'A'.
31. Ever since the logical phenomenon of predication was emancipated, at considerable effort, from certain well-known metaphysical impasses, the semiotic process involved seems to have become perfectly formulable in a theory of designation.
32. Concerning some typical philosophical objections to a higher calculus, cf. Rosenbloom (1950: 87) and Smart (1949).
33. The procedure is roughly as follows: 'Linking' and 'Nesting' are taken as "metarelations" between a relation and an argument (cf. Reichenbach, 1948: 229ff., 320). Writing 'Lk' for 'linking' and 'Ns' for 'nesting', we define, for any formula '$\varphi(f, \ldots)$',

$$\mathrm{Lk}\,(\varphi, f) =_{Df} (\exists z)\ \varphi(z) \cdot f(z)$$
$$\mathrm{Ns}\,(\varphi, f) =_{Df} \overline{\mathrm{Lk}\,(\varphi, f)}.$$

It appears necessary that in a formula of the form '$\varphi(f, g, h \ldots)$', at least one argument link with the function:

$$(\varphi)(f)(g)(h)\ldots \mathrm{Lk}(\varphi, f) \vee \mathrm{Lk}\,(\varphi, g) \vee \mathrm{Lk}\,(\varphi, h) \vee \ldots$$

If the relation is symmetrical, there is no nesting:

$$(\varphi)(f)(g)\ \varphi\,(f, g) \cdot \varphi\,(g, f) \supset \mathrm{Lk}\,(\varphi, f) \cdot \mathrm{Lk}\,(\varphi, g)$$

The linking operation is equivalent to the classical S-P operation. In some respects, of course, the replacement of the Aristotelian sentence formula, 'S is P', by a logistic version which permits polyadic relations; e.g., 'R(a, b)', has brought about, among other technical benefits, a better approximation of the structure of ordinary language; cf., e.g., Reichenbach (1948: 83), Bühler (1934: 370). But to say, as Bühler does, that "das logistische Schema a Rb ... [symbolisiert] zwei Relationsfundamente, die des S- und P-Charakters entbehren," is accurate only for an uninterpreted calculus; in ordinary language, either 'a' and 'R', or 'b' and 'R', or both, remain very much in an S-P relation. This point has been widely overlooked. Quine, for example (1960: 106f.), passes it by; so does Sechehaye (1926: 72). Reichenbach (1948: 229ff., 320) treats the "metarelation" between a relation and its argument as a dispensable constant; but the constant is by no means dispensable, since there are at least two noninterchangeable "metarelations."

A number of interesting problems arise in this connection which have not yet been investigated. It seems, for example, that some languages distinguish by grammatical devices a more permanent, "nomological" linking or nesting of argument with relations from a more fleeting one; cf. Korean *k'oč-ən təl-e p'imnita* '[the] flower grows [by nature] in [the] field' vs. *k'oč-i...* '... happens to grow'; Russian *on bolen* 'he is sick [now]' vs. *on bol'noj* 'he is [a] sick [person]'; English *he is bumming* vs. *he is a bum;* Polish *on śpiewak* 'he is a singer' vs. *on śpiewa* 'he sings' vs. *on śpiewa sobie* 'he is [casually] singing'; Chinese *woo jia* 'my [inalienable] family' vs. *woo de juotz* 'my [alienable] table' (Hockett, 1958: 187). Defining a change of a relation '$f(x, y)$' to a derived relation '$f'(y, x)$', we may study the use, in a given language, of overt and covert devices for representing 'f'' (overt: passive voice, e.g., 'x sees y' → 'y is seen by x'; covert: antonyms, e. g., 'x gives y to z' → 'z receives y from x'; 'x is under y' → 'y is over x'). Defining a change of a relation '$f(x, y)$' to a derived relation with fewer places '$f''(x)$', we may again survey the overt and covert devices used by a language for reducing the transitivity of relation signs (overt: 'x writes y' → 'x writes', 'x is in y' → 'x is inside'; covert: 'x says y' → 'x talks'). Special treatment seems to be given to the semantic paradigm of relation-names which, though asymmetrical, nevertheless link with both arguments (*seem*, *constitute*, *form*, *resemble*, etc.). It also appears that when the designatum of an asymmetrical relation-name of language L is formulated in the metalanguage of semantic description, ML, the corresponding sentence in ML must also contain a nesting relation, although the converse is not true.

34. Reichenbach's formulas are often simplified in that the time argument is omitted in the notation for verbs. The full analysis of the present example would be roughly as follows. We write 'Walk' for '$\hat{x}$ walks to $\hat{y}$ at [time] $\hat{t}$'; 'Fast' for '$\hat{x}$ is fast at $\hat{t}$'; 'Child' for '$\hat{x}$ is a child at $\hat{t}$'; 'Cry' for '$\hat{x}$ cries at $\hat{t}$'; 'Bitter' for '$\hat{x}$ is bitter at $\hat{t}$'; 'Home' for '$\hat{x}$ is a home at $\hat{t}$'; 'Have' for '$\hat{x}$ has $\hat{y}$ at $\hat{t}$'; 'Mention' for '$\hat{x}$ is mentioned in $\hat{y}$' (where '$\hat{y}$' is an act of speech), '3' for 'three'; 'Θ' for 'this discourse'; 'Prec' for '$\hat{x}$ precedes $\hat{y}$'; and 't_θ' for 'the time of Θ'. We now have: $(\exists x)\,(\exists y)\,(\exists t)\,(\exists f)\,(\exists g)$.

$$3\ \mathrm{Child}\,(x, t) \cdot f\,(x) \cdot \mathrm{Cry}\,(f, t) \cdot \mathrm{Bitter}\,(f, t) \cdot \mathrm{Mention}\,(x, \theta)$$
$$\cdot\, g(x) \cdot \mathrm{Walk}\,(g, y, t) \cdot \mathrm{Fast}\,(g, t).$$
$$\cdot\, \mathrm{Home}\,(y, t) \cdot \mathrm{Have}\,(x, y, t).$$
$$\cdot\, \mathrm{Prec}\,(t, t_\theta).$$

[Cf. Postscript.]

35. It is assumed here that the rules that are needed to exclude "semantically" unacceptable expressions are different in nature and in form from grammatical rules; i. e., that a semantic description

of a language is an autonomous enterprise and not merely a continuation of the grammatical description. [Cf. Postscript.]

36. Cf. Jakobson's demonstration (1959) of how a sentence cited for its multiple and profound absurdity *can* be decoded by a sympathetic analyst through *ad hoc* modifications of the code.
37. Cf. Hjelmslev (1953: 28): "Thus we must not imagine, for example, that a substantive is more meaningful than a preposition, or a word more meaningful than a derivational or inflexional ending." Similarly Chomsky (1957: 104f.). But we do not find it possible to accept Hjelmslev's view that "in absolute isolation no sign has any meaning." On the other hand, there remains the legitimate problem of why most languages prefer "grammatical" to lexical devices for the expression of certain meanings (P. Ivić).
38. Weinreich (1959: 335). In the formulation of this view I have profited from stimulating discussions with Karl E. Zimmer. If we have difficulty in seeing how a suffix (e. g., Dutch *-en*) designates plurality, it is for two reasons only: (1) the meaning of grammatical categories is often abstract (though 'many' in a suffix is hardly more abstract than the word *plurality*, and in *entiti-es* the base surely has a more abstract meaning than the suffix); (2) the phonemically slight forms of affixes are conducive to a high degree of homonymy; yet *-s* '1. (with nouns) many; 2. (with verbs) one' is hardly more fractured than, say, the French free form *sã* '1. hundred; 2. without; 3. blood; etc.' It is to be noted that in many languages, formators can be converted to argument names; cf. *dix* → *dizaine*, *and* → *addition*, *or* → *alternative*, *if* → (*an*) *if*.
39. See Gleason (1962). Savčenko's attempt (1959: 43ff.) to replace Sapir's grammatical criteria of parts-of-speech classification by semantic ones seems belated; but his bold formulation of word-class universals, denied by Sapir, may be quite correct. In this connection it is useful to refer to the relation between obligatoriness and meaning. By a well-known principle from information theory, what is completely predictable carries no information. But while we may identify lack of information with meaninglessness, we can identify presence of information only with meaningfulness, not with meaning (Carnap and Bar-Hillel 1953). It is in this sense that we can easily avoid Ziff's dilemma (1960: 182ff.) over the difference between 'having a meaning' and 'having meaning'; it is striking that the negation—'having no meaning'—covers both a grammatical and a substantive syncretism of the distinction. Insofar as a morpheme is completely redundant with respect to some others (as Karolak, 1960: 246, put it, the morpheme lacks paradigmatic function), we would call it meaningless (cf. also

Ziff, 1960: 41). This would imply that the dative case in German, for example, is meaningful when commutable with the accusative (e. g., after *in*) and meaningless otherwise (e. g., after *mit*). Though this invalidates the search for *Grundbedeutungen* of cases, it is a necessary consequence of the autonomy of grammar and semantics.

40. A crude formulation of the greater surprise factor of the "comment" or "propos" would be this: in a sentence of the form '$f_1(x_1)$', the "comment" is 'f_1' if the preceding context was '$f_2(x_1)$', and the "comment" is 'x_1' if the preceding context was '$f_1(x_2)$'. To determine which is the comment by intrasentence criteria would probably amount to a parasitic semantic interpretation of a grammatical fact. (This note was stimulated by an objection of Hockett's to an earlier formulation.)
41. We assume that in the Nootka examples analyzed earlier, there is a distinctive hierarchy of structure, namely 'the selected are in a boat' and not 'those in a boat are selected'; 'there is a going for eaters of boiled stuff' and not 'there is a boiling of stuff for fetched eaters'.
42. In Reichenbach's words (1948: 26), the expression '$a \supset b \supset c$' is meaningless because it has no major operation. But is a semiotic system without major functions inconceivable to human thought?
43. This would be a reason to consider numerals in English, for example, as formators; note the awkwardness of *the boys were five*— a major function—as against *five boys...*—a backgrounded "function" or a propositional operation. The differentiated "adverbial" affixes of polysynthetic languages might be interpreted as designators restricted to minor function—cf. Nootka *-ista-* 'in a boat', Comanche *piʔ-* 'with buttocks', *taʔ-* 'with the foot' (Casagrande, 1954: 148); but these suffixes may also be quasi-allomorphs of nouns for 'boat', 'buttocks', 'foot'.
44. Many interesting examples are adduced by Marcus (1960), although it is surprising to see a metaphysics erected on a linguistic basis where human language is represented by a sample of one (German).
45. So greatly delayed has been our understanding of the relation between grammar and combinatorial semiotics that even Bloomfield, who would hardly have called an adjective a 'quality word', did not mind mixing semantic and grammatical spheres in calling a predication the 'actor-action' construction. (Similar defects mar Nida's treatment of episememes [1957: 10f.].) For this mixture of metaphors, tolerable only so long as the autonomy of semantics is disregarded, Bloomfield has been charged with mentalism (!) in an excellent article concerning the autonomy of grammatical and semantic processes (Buyssens, 1950: 37; the same collection contains a most judicious statement of the problem by Larochette).

Extrapolation from grammatical classes may, of course, create not only abstract ontological types but also concrete designational classes, e. g., extrapolations from gender to sexuality.

46. The increasing approximation of adult semantic behavior in children of various ages has been the subject of recent studies by Z. M. Istomina (Šemjakin, 1960: 76–113), Flavell and Stedman (1961), and Ervin and Foster (1961).
47. For example, Lees (1960: 103f. and *passim*). A useful corollary would be the definition of a word as a minimum free form, "free" implying not a vague "ability to be said alone" but the precise ability to be isolated by the stated ellipsis transformations of the given grammar.
48. All attempts to analyze such sentences in a binary way by means of covert arguments must be adjudged abortive. If, for example, a covert 'now' is a nesting argument of the 'rain' relation, it also occurs in a backgrounded function in every other sentence using a present-tense verb. If the 'rain' relation is linked with the covert argument 'outdoors' or 'this', then every argument in every major sentence form may also be linked with some 'this' by a deictic operation. As Householder has pointed out, some "weather expressions" in some languages may nevertheless have a covert argument; cf. *it is sunny, the weather is sunny;* but only *it rains*, not **the weather rains*.
49. For a formal approach to polysemy as an intersection of semantic fields, see Laxuti *et al.* (1959: 217f.) and I. I. Revzin in *SSM* (1961: 17–19).
50. The fullest treatment appears to be by Zawadowski (1958; 1959). This well-worn idea (cf. Paul, 1880: 56; Wegener, 1885: 84; Bréal, 1897: 141f.) has recently been proposed by Joos (1958) as the foundation of a new science, "semology." It is being studied systematically by the Cambridge Language Research Unit (cf. Masterman, 1959) and by Ju. D. Apresjan (1962).
51. The problem of invariance under polysemy is approached from a formal point of view by S. K. Šaumjan (*SPLS* 1960: 21–25) and by I. I. Revzin (*SSM* 1961: 17–19).
52. "A proposition (or any other symbol) is vague when there are possible states of things concerning which it is *intrinsically uncertain* whether, had they been contemplated by the speaker, he would have regarded them as excluded or allowed by the proposition..." (Black, 1949: 30).
53. Most dictionaries vastly exaggerate the incidence of polysemy at the expense of vagueness or generality, e. g., in listing separate meanings for *fair* as in *fair chance* and *fair* as in *fair health.* On the fallacy of overspecification in semantic description, see

Benvéniste (1954) and Zawadowski (1959); cf. also Zvegincev (1957: 238–244) and Gove (1957).

54. Since it is essential to operate, not with meaning intuitions, but with explicit meaning descriptions (Weinreich, 1962), the question of whether *shout* and *weep* do or do not share a semantic component depends on the verbatim text of their definitions. One could extract a common factor, such as 'emotional discomposure', *ad hoc*; but would it be economical to carry it in the definitions of each term?

55. But not in all; in *rain*——, it is obviously *coat*[2] (P. Ivić). The contexts, in any case, to be legitimate must not involve any metalinguistic operation. Cf. also note 76.

56. The best study of this problem seems to be Kotelova (1957); see also Axmanova (1957: 104–165). Overlapping of grammatical contexts, i. e., the possibility of ambiguity, as a necessary condition for homonymy is stressed by Vinogradov (1960) and in Avrorin *et al.* (1960), the most enlightening discussions of the subject of homonymy. To the references from the older literature cited by Ullmann (1951) should be added Richter (1926).

57. With regard to *arrange*, we find an extended ambiguity: if *music*[1] means 'Musik' and *music*[2] means 'sheet music, Noten', then *arrange music* means either *arrange*[1] *music*[2] or *arrange*[2] *music*[1], but as a whole it still remains ambiguous. It has been suggested (notably by Godel, 1948; Fal'kovič, 1960) that divergent derivational and compounding patterns can function as criteria for resolving polysemy. But while such divergences may be frequent concomitants of polysemy, an unbiased sampling of vocabulary shows that they are not criterial (Kleiner, 1961). In principle, such concomitances could serve only the lexicographic contemplation of the word, in isolation; it cannot help the hearer of living speech. For how could the ambiguity of *j'ai vu des voiles* 'I have seen veils/sails' be resolved, for the given act of speech, by the fact that the singular of one alternative, 'veils', would be *le voile*, while the singular of the other would be *la voile*? (The example is from Ullmann, 1953: 234.)

58. The novel conception of idioms offered by Hockett (1956) is untenable, for reasons explained elsewhere (Weinreich, 1959).

59. Bar-Hillel (1955: 192) justly defines expressions as idiomatic not only for a given language but also "with respect to a given... dictionary." On the problem of the relation between synonymy and polysemy, see also Kuryłowicz (1955); Šaumjan in *SPLS* 1960: 21–25; and I. I. Revzin in *SSM* 1961: 17–19.

60. Cf. Axmanova (1957: 166–191) on grammatical properties of certain Russian idioms; Smirnickij (1956: 203–230) on correspond-

ing patterns in English; and Ožegov's excellent study (1957) of the general problem of idiom and cliché formation. Incidentally, Hockett's specific suggestion (1956) that in English the pattern Á + N is a mark of an idiom is incorrect; actually, Á + N is productively derived from *X has a A N* (e. g., *yellow-belly*) or *N is for... A* (e. g., *plate for* [*keeping things*] *hot* → *hot plate*).

61. The example is from DeFrancis (1950: 149), who issues useful warnings against the exaggeration of Chinese peculiarities.
62. See Axmanova *et al.* (1961: 24ff.). It is a mark of the timeliness of the subject that the problem of semantic universals (*semantičeskie universalii*) was independently raised by Axmanova at exactly the same time as this paper was being written.
63. B. W. and E. G. Aginsky (1948: 170), under universals of conceptualization, appear to list general semantic fields (including 'maturity', 'space', etc.) and not necessarily universal "lexemes." Elaborate thesaurus outlines, such as Hallig and von Wartburg (1952) and Voegelin and Voegelin (1957), are also not intended as anything more than rough tools for eliciting vocabulary or for classifying elicited items by gross topical domains. For a critical discussion of the thesaurus approach to lexicography, see Wüster (1959) and Hiorth (1960).
64. The best discussion of semantic calibration of vocabularies is Becker (1948).
65. It is assumed that the complex expressions such as noun compounds, unless they are idiomatic, can be analyzed as kernel constructions, or as meaning-preserving transforms of kernel constructions, and that their meaning can be formulated in terms of the meanings of the *overt* constituents and the relations of linking, nesting, and backgrounding. It is only for the study of the *covert* components of semantic simplicia (= grammatical simplicia or idiomatic complex expressions) that componential analysis is required. Some scholars, to be sure, are skeptical about the objectivity of such analyses (e. g., N. F. Pelevina, *SSM* 1961: 30–32) and outline instead a program of research of "semi-idiomatic" complex expressions. This domain of semi-idiomatic, semicovert components, standing in a defective one-to-one relation to morphemes, is certainly important, too. Such defective relations appear in idioms and in all cases of sound symbolism, whether impressionistic (*grumble*, *hiss*, *sibilant*) or expressionistic (*teeny; flit—float—...*; Yiddish *pejsax* 'Passover'—*kejsax* 'Easter').
66. Modern logical semantics, which is still in its infancy, has already provided us with a way of talking about combinatorial processes, but it has had little to contribute so far to the componential

analysis of designata. In Reichenbach's book, for example, we find only casual treatment of 'complex' and 'descriptional' functions (1948: 122, 311f.). The roots of our analysis lie in traditional logical (cf. Ziehen, 1920: 459–599) and psychological (Bruner *et al.*, 1956) models of the concept. The warning that concepts cannot be identified with meanings, often voiced in contemporary Soviet linguistics (e. g., Zvegincev, 1957: 147ff.), seems to stem mainly from an appreciation of the fact, accommodated in our theory, that the canonical form of the designatum is only a limiting case, which fully fits only "terminologized" vocabulary (Schaff, 1960: 389ff.). The psychological reality of covert features can be demonstrated by psychophysical experiments (see now Luria and Vinogradova, 1959), but such procedures are probably unnecessarily circumstantial for the study of specific vocabularies. Every semantic description of a sign, of course, constitutes an analyst's hypothesis and is subject to tests of consistency with the description of other signs, and to validation by native informants (Wallace and Atkins, 1960: 78f.; Weinreich, 1962).

67. It may be useful to apply the notion of "family likeness" (Wittgenstein, 1958: 17ff., 43f.) or "polytypic concepts" (Beckner, 1959: 22–25) to semantic analysis. Polysemy of a sign A would then be defined as $[(c_1 \cdot c_2) \vee (c_2 \cdot c_3) \vee (c_3 \cdot c_4) \ldots]$. Budagov (1961: 23f.) has gone so far as to suggest that in some languages, depending on the level of their cultural development, the "factorability" of designata is more thoroughgoing than in others. Unfortunately, his only evidence for an "underdeveloped" language is Sommerfelt's description of Aranta, which has been much criticized for lack of anthropological refinement.

68. Just as structural semantic analysis is gathering momentum, some scholars are looking ahead in cautioning that only a limited, "terminologized" part of vocabulary lends itself to such analysis; cf. A. A. Reformatskij (*SSM* 1961:13) and N. F. Pelevina (*ibid.*: 30–32).

69. In an informal experiment, a graduate class of 17 students at Columbia University was asked to match the eight terms *bound*, *hop*, *jump*, *leap*, *prance*, *skip*, *spring*, and *vault* with their definitions, taken from a much-used reference dictionary but slightly modified so as to eliminate illegitimate clues. Out of 136 answers, only 54 (40%) were correct on a first run, and only 89 (65%) were correct on a second run, when certain additional, contextual clues were added. Treating dictionary definitions as a proposed description, these low scores indicate a poor degree of reliability, i. e., a low degree of terminologization in this lexical set. Surely the group

would have done better with eight kinship terms, which constitute a highly terminologized field. For validation techniques in semantics, cf. also Naess (1957, with references to his earlier work) and Tennessen (1959).

70 A formal approach to synonymy in terms of set theory has been sketched by V. V. Martynov in *Pytannja...* (1960: 11–31).

71. On a componential analysis of a set of German "synonymous" verbs, cf. M. V. Raevskij (*SSM* 1961: 39–41). On recurrent components in nonterminologized vocabulary, see also Collinson (1939).

72. Chinese, for example, has semantic devices of compounding antonyms for the formation of superordinates: *lai* 'come' + *wang* 'go' = *lai-wang* 'traffic'; *shu* 'lose' + *ying* 'win' = *shu-ying* 'result of the game'; *zao* 'early' + *wan* 'late' = *zao-wan* 'interval, time'; *xu* 'false' + *shi* 'true' = *xu-shi* 'state of affairs', etc. (Sofronow, 1960: 81ff.). The device certainly recurs in other languages, though it is perhaps not so fully utilized; cf. Yiddish *tatə* 'father' + *mamə* 'mother' = *tatə-mámə* 'parents'; *gopl* 'fork' + *lefl* 'spoon' = *gopl-léfl* 'cutlery'.

73. Various investigations now in progress [cf. Postscript] are intended to throw light on the possibilities of componential description of vocabulary. Of particular interest seems to be the problem of whether objective distributional methods will yield results equivalent to intuitive-componential notions of meaning. Among the relevant projects is the work of the Cambridge Language Research Unit (Masterman, 1959); the work on a semantic calculus of kinship terminology (Wallace and Atkins, 1960; Wallace, 1961*a*); and the experimental work on semantic analysis in the Machine Translation Laboratory of Moscow's First State Pedagogical Institute of Foreign Languages (I. R. Gal'perin *et al.*, *SSM* 1961: 5–8; A. K. Žolkovskij *et al.*, *SSM* 1961: 60f.; V. V. Ivanov, *SLTM* 1961: 18–26). On universal "semes," cf. also A. B. Dolgopol'skij (*SPLS* 1960: 35–42). Concerning the universality of affective meaning components, see Maclay and Ware (1961) and Osgood (1961).

74. On the vocabulary of "abstract" superordinates in some languages of primitive societies, cf. Moszyński (1956).

75. The study of denotation or reference is, of course, an entirely legitimate pursuit, both for the purpose of a general theory of communication (e. g., Shwayder, 1961) and for the referential "orientation" of certain primitive terms in a description of a particular language as a semantic system (Laxuti *et al.*, 1959: 219). In the cross-cultural study of color naming, there has been a good deal of progress recently; cf. esp. Ervin (1961) and Šemjakin (1960).

76. Attempts to explicate ordinary language without recourse to intensions are bound to lead to oversimplified conceptions. For example, Goodman (1949) wishes to defend a purely extensional theory of synonymy. This at first seems to lead to a difficulty; for words like *centaur* and *unicorn*, the truth-value of a sentence containing one of them is never changed by replacing it by the other; hence, they would be synonymous. In order to save their nonsynonymy, Goodman points out that there are contexts in which they can*not* be interchanged *salva veritate*, e. g., *picture of a* ——. But it is necessary to point out that the differentiating context is of a very special type, for these sentences are of a kind called quasi-syntactical by Carnap (1937: 74). The words *centaur* and *unicorn* would remain interchangeable in the contexts *tail of a* ——, *teeth of a* ——, *stomach of a* ——, but not in *picture of a* ——, *poem about a* ——, *illusion of a* ——, etc. The latter group of contexts involves metalinguistic operations and may be said to demonstrate the reality of the very intensions which the author sought to eliminate.

References

Aginsky, B. W., and E. G. (1948). "The Importance of Language Universals," *Word* 4. 168–172.

Apresjan, Ju. D. (1962). [Distributional Analysis of Meaning and Structural Semantic Fields], *Leksikografičeskij sbornik* 5. 52–72. Moscow.

Arndt, W. (1960). " 'Modal Particles' in Russian and German," *Word* 16. 323–336.

Avrorin, V. A. *et al.* (1960). [Discussion on Problems of Homonymy ...], *Leksikografičeskij sbornik* 4. 35–102.

Axmanova, O. S. (1957). *Očerki po obščej i russkoj leksikologii.* Moscow.

———, I. A. Mel'čuk, E. V. Padučeva, and R. M. Frumkina (1961). *O točnyx metodax issledovanija jazyka.* Moscow.

Bar-Hillel, Y. (1954). "Indexical Expressions," *Mind* n. s. 63. 359–379.

——— (1955). "Idioms," in W. N. Locke and A. D. Booth (eds.), *Machine Translation of Languages*, 183–193. New York and London.

Bazell, C. E. (1954). "The Sememe," *Litera* 1. 17–31.

Becker, H. (1948). *Der Sprachbund*. Berlin and Leipzig.

Beckner, M. (1959). *The Biological Way of Thought*. New York.

Bendix, E. H. (1961). "Componential Analysis of an English Semantic Field," unpubl. seminar paper, Columbia University.

——— (1965). *Componential Analysis of General Vocabulary: the Semantic Structure of a Set of Verbs in English, Hindi, and Japanese*. Ph. D. dissertation, Columbia University, to appear as a supplement to *IJAL*, April, 1966.

Benvéniste, E. (1954). "Problèmes sémantiques de reconstruction," *Word* 10. 251–264.

Black, M. (1949). *Language and Philosophy*. Ithaca.

Bloomfield, L. (1933). *Language*. New York.

Bréal, M. (1897). *Essai de sémantique*. Paris. (Page ref. to English ed., 1900.)

Brown, J. C. (1960). "Loglan," *Scientific American* 202 (June), 53–63.

Brown, R. W. (1957). "Linguistic Determinism and the Part of Speech," *J. of Abnormal and Soc. Psychol.* 55. 1–5.

Bruner, J. S., J. J. Goodnow, and G. A. Austin (1956). *A Study of Thinking*. New York.

Budagov, R. A. (1958). *Vvedenie v nauku o jazyke*. Moscow.

——— (1961). [Toward a Critique of Relativistic Theories of the Word], *Voprosy teorii jazyka v sovremennoj zarubežnoj lingvistike*, 5–29, Moscow.

Bühler, K. (1934). *Sprachtheorie*. Jena.

Buyssens, E. (1950). "Conception fonctionnelle des faits linguistiques," *Grammaire et psychologie*, 35–51. Paris.

Carnap, R. (1937). *The Logical Syntax of Language*. London.

——— (1942). *Introduction to Semantics*. Cambridge, Mass.

——— (1947). *Meaning and Necessity*. Chicago. (Ref. to 2nd ed., 1956.)

———, and Y. Bar-Hillel (1953). "Semantic Information," *Brit. J. Philos. of Science* 4. 147–157.

Casagrande, J. B. (1954). "Comanche Linguistic Acculturation," *IJAL* 20. 140–151, 217–237; 21. 8–25 (1955).

Cassirer, E. (1923). *Philosophie der symbolischen Formen*, I. Berlin. (Ref. to Eng. ed., New Haven, 1953.)

Chao, Y. R. (1956). "Chinese Terms of Address," *Lg.* 32. 217–241.

——— (1959). "How Chinese Logic Operates," *Anthrop. Linguistics* 1. 1–8.

Chomsky, N. (1955). "Semantic Considerations in Grammar," *Georgetown Univ. Monographs* 8. 141–154.

——— (1957). *Syntactic Structures*. The Hague.

Collinson, W. E. (1937). *Indication* (*Lg. Monographs* 17).

——— (1939). "Comparative Synonymics," *Trans. Philolog. Soc.*, 54–77.

Conklin, H. C. (1955). "Hanunóo Color Categories," *SWJA* 11. 339–344.

——— (1962). "Lexicographical Treatment of Folk Taxonomies," in F. W. Householder, Jr., and Sol Saporta (eds.), *Problems in Lexicography* (*IUPAL*, no. 21), 119-141.

DeFrancis, J. (1950). *Nationalism and Language Reform in China*. Princeton.

Ervin, S. M. (1961). "Semantic Shift in Bilingualism," *American J. of Psychology* 74. 233–241.

———, and G. Foster (1961). "The Development of Meaning in Children's Descriptive Terms," *J. of Abnormal and Soc. Psychol.* 61. 271–275.

Fal'kovič, M. M. (1960). [On the Problem of Homonymy and Polysemy], *Vopr. jaz.*, no. 5, 85–88.

Février, J. G. (1948). *Histoire de l'écriture*. Paris.

Flavell, J. H., and D. J. Stedman (1961). "A Developmental Study of Judgments of Semantic Similarity," *J. of Genetic Psychology* 98. 279–293.

Freeland, L. S. (1951). *Language of the Sierra Miwok* (*IUPAL Memoir* 6).

French, D. (1958). "Cultural Matrices of Chinookan Non-Casual Language," *IJAL* 24. 258–263.

Funke, O. (1932). *Innere Sprachform*. Reichenberg.

Gleason, H. A., Jr. (1955). *An Introduction to Descriptive Linguistics*. New York.

——— (1962). "The Relation of Lexicon to Grammar," in F. W. Householder and Sol Saporta (eds.), *Problems in Lexicography* (*IUPAL*, no. 21).

Godel, R. (1948). "Homonymie et identité," *Cahiers F. de Saussure* 7. 5–15.

Goodenough, W. (1956). "Componential Analysis and the Study of Meaning," *Lg*. 32. 195–216.

Goodman, N. (1949). "On Likeness of Meaning," *Analysis* 10. 1–7.

Gove, P. B. (1957). "Problems in Defining," in J. H. Shera *et al.* (eds.), *Information Systems in Documentation*, 3–14. New York and London.

Hallig, R., and W. von Wartburg (1952). *Begriffssystem als Grundlage für die Lexikographie*. Berlin.

Harris, Z. S. (1957). "Co-occurrence and Transformation in Linguistic Structure," *Lg.* 33. 283–340.

Haugen, E. (1957). "The Semantics of Icelandic Orientation," *Word* 13. 447–459.

Hiorth, F. (1960). "Zur Ordnung des Wortschatzes," *Studia Linguistica* 14. 65–84.

Hjelmslev, L. (1953). *Prolegomena to a Theory of Language* (*IUPAL Memoir* 7).

Hockett, C. F. (1948). "Potawatomi IV," *IJAL* 14. 213–225.

——— (1954). "Two Models of Grammatical Description," *Word* 10. 210–233.

——— (1956). "Idiom Formation," *For Roman Jakobson*, 222–229. The Hague.

——— (1958). *A Course in Modern Linguistics*. New York.

——— (1960). "The Origin of Speech," *Scientific American*, Sept.

Hymes, D. H. (1960). "Lexicostatistics So Far," *Current Anthropology* 1. 3–44.

——— (1961). "On Typology of Cognitive Styles in Language," *Anthrop. Linguistics* 3, no. 1, 22–54.

Jakobson, R. (1957). *Shifters, Verbal Categories, and the Russian Verb*. Harvard University.

——— (1959). " Boas' View of Grammatical Meaning," *American Anthropologist* 61, part 2, 139–145.

Joos, M. (1950). "Description of Language Design," repr. from *JASA* in *Readings in Linguistics* (1957), 349–356. Washington.

——— (1958). "Semology: a Linguistic Theory of Meaning." *SIL* 13. 53–70.

Karolak, S. (1960). [Some Notes on the Structure of the Semantic Spectrum], *Lingua posnaniensis* 8. 243–253.

Katz, J. J., and J. A. Fodor (1963). "The Structure of a Semantic Theory," *Language* 39. 170–210.

——— and P. M. Postal (1964). *An Integrated Theory of Linguistic Descriptions*. Cambridge, Mass.

Kleiner, E. (1961). "The Discrimination of Multiple Meaning in English," unpubl. seminar paper, Columbia University.

Kotelova, N. Z. (1957). [Indications of Syntactic Relations ... as a Means of Discriminating Semantic Distinctions], *Leksikografičeskij sbornik* 1. 98–120.

Kuryłowicz, J. (1955). [Notes on Word Meanings], *Vopr. jaz.*, no. 3, 73–81.

Kuznecov, A. V., E. V. Padučeva, and N. M. Ermolaeva (1961). [On an Informational Language for Geometry and an Algorithm for Translating from Russian to the Informational Language], *Mašinnyj perevod i prikladnaja lingvistika* 5. 3–21.

Larochette, J. (1950). "Les Deux oppositions verbo-nominales," *Grammaire et psychologie*, 107–118. Paris.

Laxuti, D. G., I. I. Revzin, and V. K. Finn (1959). [On a Certain Approach to Semantics], S.S.S.R., Ministerstvo vysšego obrazovanija, *Naučnye doklady vysšej školy; filosofskie nauki*, no. 1, 207–219.

Lees, R. B. (1960). *The Grammar of English Nominalizations*. (*IJAL* 26, no. 2, part 2).

Leisi, E. (1953). *Der Wortinhalt; seine Struktur im Deutschen und Englischen*. Heidelberg.

Lounsbury, F. G. (1956). "A Semantic Analysis of Pawnee Kinship Usage," *Lg*. 32. 158–194.

Luria, A. R., and O. S. Vinogradova (1959). "An Objective Investigation of the Dynamics of Semantic Systems," *Brit. J. Psychology* 50. 89–105.

Maclay, H., and E. E. Ware (1961). "Cross-Cultural Use of the Semantic Differential," *Behavioral Science* 6. 185-190.

Marcus, H. (1960). *Die Fundamente der Wirklichkeit als Regulatoren der Sprache*. Bonn.

Martinet, A. (1960). *Éléments de linguistique générale*. Paris.

Maspéro, H. (1933). "La Langue chinoise," *Conférences de l'Institut de Linguistique de l'Université de Paris*, 33–70.

Masterman, M., ed. (1959). *Essays on and in Machine Translation*. Cambridge.

McQuown, N. A. (1956). "Analysis of the Cultural Content of Language Materials," *Language in Culture*, 20–31. Chicago.

Mel'čuk, I. A. (1960). [On the Terms 'Stability' and 'Idiomaticity'], *Vopr. jaz.*, no. 4, 73–80.

Morris, C. W. (1938). *Foundations of a Theory of Signs*. Chicago.

——— (1946). *Signs, Language, and Behavior*. New York.

Most, M. (1949). Comments in *Actes du 6ème Congrès international des Linguistes* (1948), 183–190. Paris.

Moszyński, K. (1956). [The Vocabulary of So-Called Primitive Peoples], *Biuletyn Polskiego Towarzystwa Językoznawczego* 15. 91–112.

Naess, A. (1957). "Synonymity as Revealed by Intuition," *Philosophical Review*, 66. 87–93.

Nida, E. A. (1951). "A System for the Description of Semantic Elements," *Word* 7. 1–14.

——— (1958). "Analysis of Meaning and Dictionary Making," *IJAL* 24. 279–292.

Osgood, C. E. (1961). "Studies on the Generality of Affective Meaning Systems." Urbana, Ill.: Institute of Communications Research, mimeographed.

Ožegov, S. I. (1957). [On the Structure of Phraseology], *Leksikografičeskij sbornik* 2. 31–57.

Paul, H. (1880). *Prinzipien der Sprachgeschichte*. Halle. (Ref. to 5th ed., 1920.)

Peirce, C. S. (1932). *Collected Papers*, II. Cambridge, Mass.

Pytannja... (1960). *Pytannja prikladnoji lingvistyky; tezisy dopovidej mižvuzovs'koji naukovoji konferenciji 22–28.9.1960*. Černivcy.

Quine, W. V. (1953). *From a Logical Point of View*. Cambridge, Mass.

——— (1960). *Word and Object*. Cambridge, Mass., New York.

Ravid, W. (1961). "The Grammatical Behavior of the Adjective 'Fair'," unpubl. seminar paper, Columbia University.

Regnéll, H. (1958). *Semantik*. Stockholm.

Reichenbach, H. (1948). *Elements of Symbolic Logic*. New York.

Reichling, A. (1935). *Het Woord*. Nijmegen.

Richter, E. (1926). "Ueber Homonymie," *FS Paul Kretschmer*, 167–201. Vienna.

Rosenbloom, P. (1950). *The Elements of Mathematical Logic*. New York.

Sapir, E. (1915). "Abnormal Types of Speech in Nootka," reprinted from Canada, Geological Survey, Memoir 62, in *Selected Writings of Edward Sapir*, ed. D. G. Mandelbaum, 1949.

——— (1921). *Language*. New York.

Saussure, F. de (1922). *Cours de linguistique générale*. Paris and Geneva, 2nd ed.

Savčenko, A. N. (1959). *Časti reči i kategorii myšlenija*. Rostov-on-Don.

Schaff, A. (1960). *Wstęp do semantyki*. Warsaw.

Schmidt, F. (1959). *Logik der Syntax*. Berlin, 2nd ed.

Sechehaye, A. (1926). *Essai sur la structure logique de la phrase*. Paris.

Seiler, H. (1958). Comments in *Proceedings of the 8th International Congress of Linguists*, 692–695. Oslo.

Šemjakin, F. N., ed. (1960). *Myšlenie i reč; trudy Instituta psixologii = Izvestija Akademii pedagogičeskix nauk R. S. F. S. R.*, 113. Moscow. [Includes six papers on color terminology in languages of the Soviet Arctic and among preschool Russian children.]

Šendel's, E. I. (1959). [On Grammatical Meanings on the Plane of Content], in T. A. Degtereva, ed., *Principy naučnogo analiza jazyka*, 45–63. Moscow.

Shwayder, D. S. (1961). *Modes of Referring and the Problem of Universals*. Berkeley and Los Angeles.

SLTM (1961). *Tezisy dokladov konferencii po strukturnoj lingvistiki, posvjaščennoj voprosam transformacionnoj grammatiki*. Moscow.

Smart, J. J. C. (1949). "Whitehead and Russell's Theory of Types," *Analysis* 10. 93–95.

Šmelev, D. N. (1960). [On "Bound" Syntactic Constructions in Russian], *Vopr. jaz.*, no. 5, 47–60.

Smirnickij, A. I. (1956). *Leksikologija anglijskogo jazyka*. Moscow.

Sofronow, M. W. (1960). "Die Methoden der Wortbildung in der Sprache des Romans Shuihuzhuan," in P. Ratchnevsky, ed., *Beiträge zum Problem des Wortes im Chinesischen*, 71–94. Berlin.

Sørensen, H. S. (1958). *Word-Classes in Modern English With Special Reference to Proper Names, With an Introductory Theory of Grammar, Meaning, and Reference*. Copenhagen.

Spang-Thomsen, B. (1956). Review of *Structureel analyse van visueel taalgebruik binnen een groep dove kinderen*, by B. T. M. Tervoort, *Word* 12. 459–467.

SPLS (1960). *Tezisy dokladov na 6-om plenarnom zasedanii [Slovarnoj] komissii [O. L. Ja. A. N. S. S. S. R.] posvjaščennom sovremennoj problematike leksikologii i semasiologii* (19–21 oktjabrja 1960 g.). Moscow.

SSM (1961). *Tezisy dokladov mežvuzovskoj konferencii po primeneniju strukturnyx i statističeskix metodov issledovanija slovarnogo sostava jazyka* (21–25 nojabrja 1961 g.) Moscow.

Stankiewicz, E. (1954). "Expressive Derivation of Substantives in Contemporary Russian and Polish," *Word* 10. 457–468.

Strawson, P. F. (1952). *Introduction to Logical Theory*. London and New York.

Tennessen, H. (1959). *Inquiry* 2. 265–290.

Ullmann, S. (1951). *Principles of Semantics*. Glasgow. (2nd ed., 1957.)

——— (1952). *Précis de sémantique française*. Berne.

——— (1953). "Descriptive Semantics and Linguistic Typology," *Word* 9. 225–240.

Voegelin, C. F., and F. R. Voegelin (1957). *Hopi Domains* (*IUPAL Memoir* 14).

——— (1961). "Typological Classification of ... Alphabets," *Anthrop. Linguistics* 3, no. 1, 55–96.

Vinogradov, V. V. (1960). [On Homonymy and Cognate Phenomena], *Vopr. jaz.*, no. 5, 1–17.

Wallace, A. F. C. (1961*a*). "The Psychic Unity of Human Groups," in Bert Kaplan, ed., *Studying Personality Cross-Culturally*, 129–164. Evanston, Ill., and Elmsford, N. Y.

——— (1961*b*). "On Being Just Complicated Enough," *Proceedings of the National Academy of Sciences*, 47. 458–464.

———, and J. Atkins (1960). "The Meaning of Kinship Terms," *American Anthropologist* 62. 58–80.

Wegener, P. (1885). *Untersuchungen über die Grundfragen des Sprachlebens*. Halle a. S.

Wells, R. (1954). "Meaning and Use," *Word* 10. 115–130.

Weinreich, U. (1955). Review of Ullmann (1952), *Lg*. 31. 537–543.

——— (1958). "Travels in Semantic Space," *Word* 14. 346–366.

——— (1959). Review of Hockett (1958), *Romance Philology* 320–341.

——— (1962). "Lexicographic Definition in Descriptive Semantics," in F. W. Householder, Jr., and Sol Saporta, eds., *Problems of Lexicography* (*IUPAL*, no. 21), 25-43.

——— (1963). "[Soviet] Lexicology," in T. A. Sebeok, ed., *Current Trends in Linguistics*, I, 60–93. The Hague.

——— (1964). "Webster's Third: A Critique of Its Semantics," *IJAL* 30. 405–409. Russian version in *Vopr. jaz.* (1965), no. 1, 128–132.

——— (1965). "Explorations in Semantic Theory," in T. A. Sebeok, (ed.), *Current Trends in Linguistics*, III. The Hague, in press.

Whorf, B. L. (1956). *Language, Thought, and Reality*, Cambridge, Mass., and New York.

Wittgenstein, L. (1958). *Preliminary Studies ... the Blue and Brown Books*. Oxford.

Wüster, E. (1959). "Die Struktur der sprachlichen Begriffswelt und ihre Darstellung in Wörterbüchern," *Studium generale* 12. 615–627.

Zawadowski, L. (1958). "La Signification des morphèmes polysèmes," *Biuletyn Polskiego Towarzystwa Językoznawczego* 17. 67–95.

——— (1959). "La Polysémie prétendue," *ibid*. 18. 11–49.

Ziehen, T. (1920). *Lehrbuch der Logik*. Bonn.

Ziff, P. (1960). *Semantic Analysis*. Ithaca.

Zimmer, Karl E. (1964). *Affixal Negation in English and Other Languages: an Investigation of Restricted Productivity*. (Supplement to *Word* 20, no. 2.)

Zvegincev, V. A. (1957). *Semasiologija*. Moscow.

CHAPTER 8

SEMANTIC UNIVERSALS

STEPHEN ULLMANN
University of Leeds

1. Introduction

The quest for universals has played a vital part in the development of semantic studies. The pioneers of modern semantics in the last century saw in the discovery of general "laws" one of the main objectives of the new science. As far back as the 1820's, the German classicist C. C. Reisig had set up "semasiology" as an independent division of linguistics, and had suggested that it should investigate "the conditions governing the development of meaning."[1] Half a century later, in 1883, Michel Bréal was even more categorical. In an article which introduced the term *semantics* into linguistic terminology, he mentioned among the tasks of the new discipline the study of the "laws which preside over the transformation of meanings."[2] In his *Essai de sémantique*, which appeared fourteen years later, Bréal showed how this aim could be achieved, and his example was followed by other linguists who put forward a number of "laws" underlying various types of semantic change. Among some dissenting voices was Saussure, who warned that changes of meaning were often due to unique causes and were no more than isolated accidents in the history of language.[3] Yet the quest continued unabated. It was accepted as axiomatic that, as one linguist, Jespersen, put it, "there are universal laws of thought which are reflected in the laws of change of meaning ... even if the Science of

Meaning ... has not yet made much advance towards discovering them."[4] Even today there are some scholars who hold similar views. Only a few years ago a leading Russian linguist criticized contemporary semantics for having turned away from its principal task: the study of specific laws of linguistic development.[5] Since the early 1930's, however, there has been a significant shift of emphasis in semantics, as in other branches of linguistics: descriptive and structural problems have come to the forefront of research, and the traditional study of changes of meaning, though by no means abandoned, has been relegated to the background. This shift of emphasis has had an important effect on the search for semantic universals. There has been comparatively little work of late on the orthodox type of semantic "law." Instead, attention has been focused on synchronic features of general validity, and also on the principles which determine the structure of the vocabulary.

If one surveys the various semantic "laws" and other universals which have been either implicity assumed or explicitly formulated in the past, one finds that they have one thing in common: nearly all of them are based on insufficient evidence. Only too often have far-reaching conclusions been drawn from inadequate data collected from a limited number of languages. The alleged universals obtained in this way are in many cases quite plausible, but plausibility is no proof unless the proposition is so self-evident that it becomes truistic and trivial. Besides, by the very nature of things, most semantic universals are no more than statistical probabilities, and the likelihood of their occurring in a given language could be determined only if we possessed far more extensive and representative data than we have at present. What Leonard Bloomfield wrote about general grammar is entirely applicable to semantics and deserves to be quoted in full:

> The only useful generalizations about language are inductive generalizations. Features which we think ought to be universal may be absent from the very next language that becomes accessible.... The fact that some features are, at any rate, wide-

spread is worthy of notice and calls for an explanation; when we have adequate data about many languages, we have to return to the problem of general grammar and to explain these similarities and divergences, but this study, when it comes, will be not speculative but inductive.[6]

Since it is one of the aims of this conference to provide precisely such a wide factual basis for the setting up of universals, I shall try in this paper to indicate certain semantic features and processes which might repay investigation on an interlinguistic scale. First, however, it will be necessary to define more closely the two terms "semantic" and "universal." Throughout this paper, "semantic" will be used solely with reference to *word-meaning*. It has been customary since Aristotle to regard the word as the smallest meaningful unit of speech.[7] We now know that this is not so. The "smallest meaningful element in the utterances of a language" is the *morpheme*, not the word.[8] The word itself is defined, in Bloomfield's classic formula, as a "minimum free form"[9] which may consist of one or more morphemes. It follows that semantic problems will arise not only at the word level but also below and above it: below it at the level of bound morphemes (suffixes, prefixes, nonindependent roots, etc.); and above it at the level of phrases and the higher combinations into which they enter. No problems of meaning below or above the word level will be considered in this paper; nor shall I deal with the semantics of so-called "form-words"—pronouns, articles, conjunctions, prepositions, etc.—which, though they behave like words in some respects, have a purely grammatical function and do not therefore belong to the lexical system of a language.[10]

It should also be noted that the word itself is not a linguistic universal in the absolute sense. In so-called "polysynthetic" languages, where a whole series of bound forms is combined into a single term, the word will obviously have a structure and status entirely different from, say, English or Chinese, and many of the tendencies discussed here are therefore inapplicable to such languages.

With regard to the meaning and implications of the term "universal," some flexibility will be needed when applying it to semantic phenomena, which are often fluid, imprecise, and subjective. From the point of view of their validity, the features and processes discussed in this paper will fall into several broad categories:

1. Some of them may turn out to be "unrestricted universals," or "universal implications," according to the terminology of the Memorandum. Even these would be "unrestricted" only in the sense that they occurred in all the languages examined in a large-scale research program. We could, of course, never prove conclusively that they are omnipresent—or "panchronic," as Saussure would say[11]—that they exist in every language at any stage in its development.

2. Most semantic universals are likely to be of the *statistical* variety: they will not be necessarily present in any given language, but one may to some extent predict the probability of their occurrence. It should be added that certain semantic phenomena are not precise enough to be amenable to rigorously statistical analysis, so that no more than a rough estimate of probabilities can be expected.

3. There is yet another type which has some affinities with universals but is far more limited in scope: *parallel developments* which occur in a number of different languages but are unknown elsewhere. Many types of metaphor and other forms of semantic change fall within this category: they are too widespread to be due to mere chance, but not widespread enough to be statistically significant. It is, of course, always possible that such a tendency will turn out to be a statistical universal, and will thus pass into the previous category, if the scope of the inquiry is sufficiently widened.

4. In addition to these tendencies, attention will also have to be paid to *typological* criteria, since, as the Memorandum rightly points out, these have obvious connections with the problem of universals. Very little work has been done so far on semantic

typology;[12] nevertheless, one or two criteria have already been identified, and these will be discussed in the appropriate sections.

In semantics, as in other branches of linguistics, we may expect to find two kinds of universals: *synchronic features* and *diachronic processes*,[13] though in practice it may not always be easy to separate the two. It will also be expedient to distinguish a third class of semantic universals: those which transcend individual words and are bound up with the general structure of the *vocabulary*.

2. Universal Features in Descriptive Semantics

2.1 *Transparent and opaque words*

The relation between sound and sense is a perennial moot point in the philosophy of language. The Greeks were already divided into two camps on this issue: the "naturalists," who argued that words have their meaning "by nature" *(phýsei)*, by virtue of an intrinsic correspondence between form and sense, and the "conventionalists," who claimed that meaning is arbitrary, based on a social convention *(thései)*. Saussure regarded "arbitrariness" as one of the fundamental principles of language,[14] whereas linguists with a different temperament inclined toward the naturalist view and emphasized the importance of onomatopoeia in the structure of our words. The old controversy flared up again some twenty years ago, and during the ensuing debate, the various aspects of the problem were usefully clarified.[15] It seems clear, first of all, that no language is either completely transparent or completely opaque. All of them are likely to contain both conventional and "motivated" terms in varying proportions which will depend on a number of factors, some linguistic, others cultural and social. The existence of two types of words is in all probability a semantic universal. It is hard to imagine a language which would have no onomatopoeic terms and no transparent metaphors, and equally hard to conceive of one which would consist solely of motivated words. This assumption would, of course, have to be empirically tested, together with other, more specific problems raised by motivation.

2. 1. 1. THREE TYPES OF MOTIVATION. In English and many other languages, words can be motivated in three different ways. The verbs *swish*, *sizzle*, and *boom* are *phonetically* motivated because the sounds are a direct imitation of the sense. A compound like *arm-chair* and a derivative like *thinker* or *retell* are *morphologically* motivated: whoever knows their components will understand them at once. Finally, figurative expressions like "the *bonnet* of a car" or "the *pivot* on which a question turns" are *semantically* motivated: they are derived, by transparent metaphor, from *bonnet* "head-dress" and *pivot* "short shaft or pin on which something turns or oscillates." It should be noted that morphological motivation is "relative" in the sense that, while the words themselves are motivated, their ultimate constituents may be opaque, as they are in the preceding examples *arm*, *chair*, *think*, *tell*, and the bound morphemes *-er* and *re-*.[16] The same may be said of semantic motivation: the metaphorical uses of *bonnet* and *pivot* are transparent, but the words themselves, in their literal meanings, are purely conventional.

Can these three types of motivation be regarded as semantic universals? The first and the third types are likely to occur in all languages; the morphological variety, however, will be more restricted in scope since it will depend on the phonological and morphological structure of each idiom. In a language made up entirely of monomorphemic words, there will be little room for such motivation. On the other hand, the existence of infixes in some languages will provide a form of motivation which English does not possess.

2. 1. 2. RELATIVE FREQUENCIES. The proportion of opaque and transparent terms, and the relative frequency of the various forms of motivation, may provide valuable criteria for linguistic typology. This was adumbrated by Saussure when he distinguished between two kinds of languages: the "lexicological" type, where conventionality is prevalent, and the "grammatical" type, which

prefers motivated words. From the examples he gave it is clear that he was thinking primarily in terms of *morphological motivation*. In his view, Chinese represents the extreme form of conventionality whereas Proto-Indo-European and Sanskrit tend toward the opposite pole; English is far less transparent than German, while French, compared with Latin, shows a very considerable increase of the opaque element.[17]

A glance at word-structure in English, French, and German fully confirms Saussure's classification. There are numerous cases where English and French have an opaque, unanalyzable term corresponding to a transparent compound in German: *skate* — *patin* — *Schlittschuh; chive* — *cive* — *Schnittlauch; glove* — *gant* — *Handschuh*, etc. Elsewhere the same idea is expressed in German by a compound, and in English and French by a learned classical formation: *hippopotamus* — *hippopotame* — *Nilpferd; phonetics* — *phonétique* — *Lautlehre; hydrogen* — *hydrogène* — *Wasserstoff*, etc. German can also form derivatives more freely than the other two languages. From the noun *Stadt* it can derive the adjective *städtisch*, whereas English and French have hybrid pairs: *town* — *urban*, *ville* — *urbain*. Similarly *bishop* — *episcopal*, *évêque* — *épiscopal*, *Bischof* — *bischöflich; language* — *linguistic*, *langue* — *linguistique*, *Sprache* — *sprachlich*, etc. It might be possible to devise some statistical test for these relative frequencies. Such a test might be based on samples from dictionaries, on a representative selection of texts, or on both. Such isolated numerical data as are already available seem to be very suggestive. In Old English, for example, which was a more transparent language than Modern English, nearly fifty terms derived from *heofon* "heaven" have been counted, including such picturesque formations as *heofon-candel* "sun, moon, stars," and *heofon-weard* "Heaven's keeper, God."[18] Pending the collection of reliable statistics, the ease with which examples can be almost indefinitely multiplied is symptomatic of the preferences of various languages. Naturally such preferences are merely statistical, and an odd instance can always be found where they do not work, as in the opaque German *Enkel* opposed to the transparent English *grandson* and French *petit-fils*.[19]

The distinction between these two types of word-structure has far-reaching implications which can only be briefly mentioned here. In the teaching and learning of languages it is obviously of great importance whether a given vocabulary is relatively transparent, with many self-explanatory terms and closely knit associative systems, or whether a large proportion of the words is opaque, containing no clue to their meaning. Within a speech-community, the presence of many learned classical terms may create a "language bar" between people with different educational backgrounds.[20] In forming new words, an idiom where compounds and derivatives are easily coined can rely extensively on native resources, as Fichte already emphasized in his *Speeches to the German Nation;* it can also provide ammunition for purism and linguistic chauvinism. Morphological motivation may even tempt philosophers to indulge in gratuitous etymologizing in the vain hope that they may thus discover the "proper" meaning of a word; some of Martin Heidegger's verbal acrobatics can be traced back in no small measure to this factor.[21]

The other types of motivation are less suitable for frequency counts since they are more fluid and subjective than morphological structure. It is commonly believed, for example, that German is richer in onomatopoeic formations than French, but it is hard to think of an objective test which might confirm or disprove this impression.

It has also been suggested that there is a kind of equilibrium between morphological and semantic motivation. Some languages, it is claimed, will tend to fill gaps in vocabulary by forming new words, whereas others add new meanings to existing terms.[22] There may be a grain of truth in this suggestion, but other factors are also involved in the process. If Modern English and Modern French are far less transparent than their older forms, this is due primarily to the introduction of countless foreign words: French and Graeco-Latin into English, mainly Graeco-Latin into French. It would be difficult to prove that semantic motivation, by metaphor or other means, has greatly benefited by the decline of composition and derivation in these languages.

2. 1. 3. PATTERNS OF SOUND-SYMBOLISM. It is common knowledge that onomatopoeic terms, however conventionalized, often show striking similarities in different idioms; they bear witness, in Schuchardt's famous formula, not to historical connections but to "elementary kinship." Here, then, is a strong *prima facie* case for interlinguistic inquiries looking for universals. Since a great deal has been written on the subject, it might be desirable to start with an extensive inventory of what is already known—sorting out scientifically established facts from dilettantish speculations which at times brought the whole matter into disrepute. It will also be necessary to distinguish between "primary" and "secondary" onomatopoeia. Of the two, the primary type, the imitation of sound by sound, is far simpler and less controversial than the secondary type, where nonacoustic experiences—movement, size, emotive overtones, etc.—are represented by the sounds. It is not surprising that in many cases, though by no means in all, the same noise should be perceived and transcribed in much the same way in different languages. The example of the "cuckoo" has often been quoted, and it is no doubt significant that the bird should have closely similar and distinctly onomatopoeic names not only in many Indo-European languages (English *cuckoo*, French *coucou*, Spanish *cuclillo*, Italian *cuculo*, Rumanian *cucu*, German *Kuckuck*, Greek *kókkyx*, Russian *kukushka*, etc.), but even in some Finno-Ugrian idioms (Hungarian *kakuk*, Finnish *käki*, Zyrian *kök*).[23] Similarly, it is only natural that verbs for "snoring" should in many languages contain an [r] (English *snore*, German *schnarchen*, Dutch *snorken*, Latin *stertere*, French *ronfler*, Spanish *roncar*, Russian *chrapét'*, Hungarian *horkolni*, etc.), and those for "whispering" an [s], [ʃ], or [tʃ] (English *whisper*, German *wispern* and *flüstern*, Norwegian *hviske*, Latin *susurrare*, French *chuchoter*, Spanish *cuchichear*, Russian *sheptát'*, Hungarian *súgni*, *susogni*, *suttogni*, etc.). Such correspondences are certainly interesting and worth studying on a broader basis, though they are rather too obvious to throw much light on the fundamental structure of language.

More significant and more delicate are problems raised by secondary onomatopoeia. In this type the connection between sound and sense is less evident than in the previous one; yet even here there exist extensive similarities between various languages. A celebrated example is the "symbolic value" of the vowel [i] as an expression of smallness.[24] This is found in a number of languages: English *little*, *slim*, *thin*, *wee*, *teeny-weeny;* French *petit;* Italian *piccolo;* Rumanian *mic;* Latin *minor*, *minimus;* Greek *mikrós;* Hungarian *kis*, *kicsi*, *pici*, etc. To such adjectives may be added many nouns denoting small creatures or things, such as English *kid*, *chit*, *imp*, *slip*, *midge*, *tit*, *bit*, *chip*, *chink*, *jiffy*, *pin*, *pip*, *tip*, *whit*, and also such diminutive suffixes as the English *-ie*, *-kin*, and *-ling*.[25] By scrutinizing a wide variety of languages it might be possible to establish how general this feature is and whether it is at all formulable in statistical terms. Even then we would, of course, be left with some examples which run counter to the general tendency; indeed there are pairs of antonyms where the onomatopoeic pattern seems to be reversed, with the [i] sound occurring in the term for "large" while its opposite has an open vowel: English *big* — *small;* Russian *velíkij* "great" — *málen'kij* "little, small." The same may be said of German *Riese* "giant," Hungarian *apró* "minute," and Latin *parvus*, though in this last case it is perhaps significant that this adjective has not survived in Romance and has been replaced by words whose phonetic structure was better suited to the idea of smallness.

Onomatopoeia is a popular device in poetry, and there is remarkable consistency in the way certain sound-patterns are used for stylistic purposes in different languages. To cite but one example, a sequence of lateral consonants is particularly well fitted to produce an impression of softness, as in Keats's lines (*Endymion*, Book I, 157–158):

Wi*l*d thyme, and va*ll*ey-*l*i*l*ies whiter sti*ll*
Than *L*eda's *l*ove, and cresses from the ri*ll*.

A famous line in Victor Hugo's poem *Booz endormi* is built on the same pattern:

*L*es souff*l*es de *l*a nuit f*l*ottaient sur Ga*l*ga*l*a.

The device is very old; it is already used in the *Odyssey* (Book I, ll. 56–57):

aieì dè ma*l*akoîsi kaì haimy*l*íoisi *l*ógoisi thé*l*gei.
(and ever with soft and wheedling words she beguiles him.)

It is interesting to find a very similar use of laterals in Finnish and Hungarian poetry;[26] for example, in *Sydämeni Laulu (My Heart's Song)*, by Aleksis Kivi:

Sie*ll*'on *l*apsen *l*ysti o*ll*a,
I*ll*an tu*ll*en tuudite*ll*a.
(It is pleasant for the child to be there,
to swing when evening comes.)

or in *A walesi bárdok (The Welsh Bards)*, by János Arany:

Ah! *L*ágyan ké*l* az éji szé*l*
Mi*l*ford öbö*l* fe*l*é.
(Oh! The night breeze rises softly toward Milford Haven.)

Some at least of these onomatopoeic patterns appear to be deeply rooted in our modes of perception, as has been shown recently by psychological experiments.[27]

It is clear, then, that motivation in its various aspects can suggest several promising lines of research which may well lead to the discovery of linguistic or stylistic universals.

2. 2. *Particular and general terms*

Some languages are remarkably rich in words with specific meanings, while others utilize general terms and neglect unnecessary details. French is usually regarded as a highly "abstract" language,[28] whereas German is fond of "concrete," particular terms. It may be noted that "concrete" and "abstract" are used in this context, not in their usual senses, but as synonyms of "particular" and "general." There are various symptoms of this contrast between the two languages:

1. In some cases, German has three or four specific verbs corresponding to one generic term in French: *gehen, reiten, fahren* — *aller; stehen, sitzen, liegen, hängen* — *être; stellen, setzen,*

legen, hängen — mettre. The detailed particulars expressed by the German verbs will often remain unformulated in French, or will be indicated by the context — unless, of course, there is a specific need to state them, in which case they will be added as supplementary information: *être debout, aller à cheval,* etc.

2. German, as we have seen, is a highly motivated language which uses prefixes lavishly to specify every aspect of the action expressed by the verb. These subsidiary shades of meaning will normally be neglected in French: *setzen, ansetzen — mettre; schreiben, niederschreiben — écrire; wachsen, heranwachsen — grandir.* In English these nuances tend to be expressed by adverbial phrases: *to put on, to write down, to grow up.*

3. French will often use a derivative where German and English have a more specific compound: *cendrier — ashtray, Aschenbecher; théière — teapot, Teekanne; ramoneur — chimney-sweep, Schornsteinfeger.*

4. Outside the lexical sphere proper, there are indications of the same tendency in the German adverbial and prepositional system, such as the distinction between *herein* and *hinein, herunter* and *hinunter,* etc., according to the speaker's position, and the accumulation of adverbs and prepositions to "trace the whole trajectory" of an action: "Wir segelten *vom* Ufer *her über* den Fluss *hin nach* der Insel *zu.*" [29] French and English would leave most of the details unexpressed.

If a sufficient number of languages were examined from this point of view, the relative frequency of particular and general terms might become a useful criterion in linguistic typology, even though it would be difficult to arrive at precise statistical conclusions in this field.

Closely connected with this feature is a problem which has exercised linguists and anthropologists for many years. It has often been asserted that the languages of "primitive" races are rich in specific and poor in generic terms. The Tasmanian aborigines, for example, had no single word for "tree," only special names for each variety of gum-tree and wattle-tree. The Zulus have no word for "cow": they must specify whether they mean a "red cow" or a "white cow," etc. [30] Unfortunately, these reports were based only too often on inadequate evidence such as observations by early missionaries, which were uncritically accepted and reproduced by successive generations of scholars. Only as late as 1952, for example, did an American linguist explode the myth that there is no single term for "washing" in Cherokee.[31] However, the general perpetuation of such assertions has inevitably tended to bring discredit on the whole theory of "prelogical mentality": at a symposium on the Sapir-Whorf hypothesis, held in Chicago in 1953, a philosopher noted that "everyone was apparently quite willing to talk about the primitiveness of a culture but most people were quite unwilling to talk about the primitiveness of language."[32] One may wonder, however, whether there is not at least a grain of truth in the old theory. Certain facts in child psychology and in the history of our own languages seem to suggest that there is. The case of the Zulu speaker who has separate words for red cow and white cow is strangely similar to that of a four-year-old Dutch boy who had special terms for a cow with red spots and one with black spots; it is true that he also possessed a general word for "cow" *tout court*, which was probably due to the influence of his mother tongue.[33] In the same way, the alleged lack of a word for "tree" in the language of Tasmanian aborigines reminds one of the history of Latin *planta* and its modern descendants. The Latin word meant "sprout, slip, cutting." There was in Latin no generic term for "plant" in the modern sense: *arbor* and *herba* were the most comprehensive class-concepts in the botanical field. According to a recent inquiry, the modern meaning of "plant" is first found in Albertus Magnus in the thirteenth century, whereas the French *plante* did not acquire this wider sense until 300 years later.[34]

It should also be borne in mind that what may seem to us a plethora of specific terms may be due, not to faulty powers of abstraction, but to the influence of climate and environment. Thus it is only to be expected that the Eskimos and the Lapps should require a variety of terms to distinguish between different kinds of "snow." Similarly, "the Paiute, a desert people, speak a language which permits the most detailed description of topographical features, a necessity in a country where complex directions may be required for the location of water holes."[35] In the words of Edward Sapir, "language is a complex inventory of all the ideas, interests, and occupations that take up the attention of the community."[36]

In view of the great importance of the problem to linguists and anthropologists alike, it would be most desirable to organize a large-scale research project on the whole question of relations between vocabulary and culture, with special reference to the use of particular and generic terms at different levels of civilization and in different environments. Needless to say, the results of such an inquiry would be of direct relevance to the Sapir-Whorf hypothesis and would throw valuable light on the influence of language upon thought.

2. 3. *Synonymy*

In his *Essai de sémantique*, Michel Bréal put forward a linguistic law which he called "the law of distribution": words once synonymous are subsequently differentiated in various ways and thus cease to be interchangeable.[37] Bloomfield went even further and argued that total synonymy is impossible in language: "Each linguistic form has a constant and specific meaning. If the forms are phonemically different, we suppose that their meanings also are different—for instance, that each one of a set of forms like *quick*, *fast*, *swift*, *rapid*, *speedy*, differs from all the others in some constant and conventional feature of meaning. We suppose, in short, that there are no actual *synonyms*."[38] In fact, it does occasionally happen, in technical nomenclatures, that two synonyms which are completely interchangeable live on side by side for some time, such as for example *spirant* and *fricative* in phonetics, or *caecitis* and *typhlitis* in medicine, both of them denoting an inflammation of the blind gut.[39] Yet it is perfectly true that we automatically tend to discriminate between synonyms, that we tend to assume that two or more words different in form cannot mean exactly the same thing, or cannot mean it in exactly the same manner. Differentiation may work in a variety of ways: it may affect the actual content of the words involved, their emotive overtones, social status, or stylistic register. One linguist has counted no less than nine distinct ways in which synonyms can be differentiated.[40] The "law of distribution" describes an undoubtedly widespread tendency, but not necessarily a universal one. There is every reason to believe that differentiation between synonyms is a sophisticated process which appears relatively late in the development of a language. In Old French, for example, a number of synonymous derivatives could be formed from the verb *livrer: livrage*, *livraison*, *livrance*, *livre*, *livrée*, *livrement*, *livreüre*. Subsequently, this superabundance was felt to be a mere *embarras de richesse* and was reduced to one term: *livraison*.[41]

Another general principle of synonymy is what might be called the "law of synonymic attraction." It has often been found that subjects prominent in the interests and activities of a community tend to attract a large number of synonyms. Some significant concentrations have, for instance, been discovered in Old English literature. In *Beowulf* there are 37 words for "hero" or "prince" and at least a dozen for "battle" and "fight." The same epic contains 17 expressions for "sea," to which 13 more may be added from other Old English poems.[42] An analysis of the vocabulary of the twelfth-century French poet Benoît de Sainte-Maure tells a very similar story: 13 verbs for "vanquish," 18 for "attack," 37 nouns for "fight" and "battle," etc.[43] In slang there are characteristic clusters of synonyms, many among them jocular or euphemistic, for the ideas of "stealing," "drunkenness," and "death," whereas in French dialects there is a profusion of terms for "horse," "rich," "poor," and especially for "mean, avaricious"; the latter vice is described by nearly 200 different expressions, 9 of which are found within a single dialect.[44]

A special form of attraction is the so-called "radiation of synonyms," which was first noticed in French slang.[45] It was found there that when a particular word was given a transferred sense its synonyms tended to develop on parallel lines. Thus the verb *chiquer* "beat" came to be used in the meaning of "deceive," whereupon other verbs for "beat"—*torcher*, *taper*, *estamper*, *toquer*—received the same secondary sense. Such developments are sometimes confined to two words: when the English verb *overlook* acquired the transferred meaning of "deceive," its synonym *oversee* underwent a parallel change.[46] It would be interesting to find out how widespread these processes are in different languages.

2. 4. *Polysemy*

This is the name given, since Bréal, to the use of the same word in two or more distinct meanings. Polysemy is in all probability a semantic universal inherent in the fundamental structure of language. The alternative to it is quite unthinkable: it would mean that we would have to store in our brains a tremendous stock of words, with separate names for any possible subject we might wish to talk about; it would also mean that there would be no metaphors and that language would thus be robbed of much of its expressiveness and flexibility. As a philosopher, W. M. Urban, rightly points out, "this double reference of verbal signs ... is a basal *differentia* of semantic meaning. The fact that a sign can intend one thing without ceasing to intend another, that, indeed, the very condition of its being an *expressive* sign for the second is that it is also a sign for the first, is precisely what makes language an instrument of knowing."[47]

The frequency of polysemy in different languages is a variable depending on a number of factors. The progress of civilization will make it necessary not only to form new words but to add fresh meanings to old ones; in Bréal's formula, the more senses a term has accumulated, the more diverse aspects of intellectual and social activity it represents.[48] This is probably what Frederick the Great meant when he saw in the multiplicity of meanings a sign of the superior quality of the French language.[49] It would be interesting to explore over a wider field the relation between polysemy and cultural progress. Meanwhile, the frequency of polysemy will also depend on purely linguistic factors. As already noted, languages where derivation and composition are sparingly used will tend to fill gaps in vocabulary by adding new meanings to existing terms. Similarly, polysemy will arise more often in generic words whose meaning varies according to context than in specific terms whose sense is less subject to variation. The relative frequency of polysemy in various languages may thus provide a further criterion for semantic typology, though once again it is hard to see how this feature could be exactly measured.

There is, however, another aspect of polysemy which can be more precisely quantified: its relation to *word-frequency.* By systematically comparing the relative frequency of various words with the number of senses in which they are used, the late G. K. Zipf arrived at an interesting conclusion which he termed the "principle of diversity of meanings." According to Zipf, there is a "direct relationship between the number of different meanings of a word and its relative frequency of occurrences." [50] He even tried to find a mathematical formula for this relationship: his calculations suggested that "different meanings of a word will tend to be equal to the square root of its relative frequency (with the possible exception of the few dozen most frequent words)." [51] Put in a different way: $m = F^{1/2}$, where m stands for the number of meanings and F for relative frequency. [52]

Zipf's formula has the great advantage that it can be readily tested in any language where figures for word-frequencies are available. On the other hand, the method should be used with extreme caution. Zipf's count of word-meanings was based on dictionary material, and it is common knowledge that the lexicographer often has to proceed arbitrarily in sorting out the different senses of a term. In numerous cases there are no sharp demarcation lines between these senses; many of our concepts have, as Wittgenstein put it, "blurred edges," [53] and it is impossible to distinguish consistently between several shades of the same meaning and several meanings of the same word. Much will also depend on the comprehensiveness of the various dictionaries, the extent to which they record technical and semitechnical usage. A count based on the Oxford Dictionary would produce a very different result from one founded on a more limited sample. It might even be wiser to refrain altogether from overprecise formulas when dealing with such vague, subjective, and unstable phenomena. The broader correlation between polysemy and word-frequency is, however, more plausible and deserves to be carefully tested in different languages. In fact, it has always been clear that some of the commonest words in a language have a great diversity of meanings: in Littré's dictionary, nearly 40 are listed under *aller*, nearly 50 under *mettre*, and some 80 under *prendre* and *faire*.[54]

Polysemy is a fertile source of *ambiguity* in language. In a limited number of cases, two major meanings of the same word are differentiated by formal means; for example, gender (French *le pendule* "pendulum" — *la pendule* "clock," German *der Band* "volume" — *das Band* "ribbon"); flection (*brothers* — *brethren*, *hanged* — *hung*, German *Worte* "connected speech" — *Wörter* "words"); word-order (*ambassador extraordinary* — *extraordinary ambassador*, French *une assertion vraie* "a true statement" — *un vrai diamant* "a real, i. e., genuine, diamond"); spelling (*discreet* — *discrete*, *draft* — *draught*, French *dessin* "drawing" — *dessein* "design, plan, scheme"); etc.[55] In the vast majority of cases, however, the context alone will suffice to exclude all irrelevant senses. When all these safeguards break down, a conflict between two or more incompatible meanings will ensue, and this may lead to the disappearance of some of these meanings, or even to that of the word itself. In the present state of our knowledge it is impossible to say whether there are any general tendencies at work in these conflicts and in the way they are resolved. A detailed monograph on polysemy in English adjectives suggests that such ambiguities will seldom result in the total eclipse of a word; usually it is sufficient to eliminate one or more of the conflicting meanings. Out of 120 adjectives investigated, only 3—2½%—have disappeared altogether.[55] Further researches may show whether this is or is not a general tendency. Linguistic geographers have also thrown some light on the conditions under which such conflicts are apt to arise. They have found, for example, that "co-ordinated" meanings belonging to the same sphere of thought are often an embarrassment, whereas meanings from different spheres can coexist more easily; thus it is inconvenient to have the same word for both "maize" and "sorghum," but perfectly feasible for the same term to mean "vine-shoot" and "end of a skein." Furthermore, the two meanings will not conflict if there is a clearly perceptible connection between them, as, for instance, in the use of the same word for "head" and, figuratively, for "nave of a wheel." The situation is further complicated by social factors such as the penetration of the Received Standard into dialect areas.[57] When we have more data available from various languages, we shall be in a position to say which, if any, of these tendencies are of general validity.

2. 5. *Homonymy*

Unlike polysemy, homonymy is not necessarily an unrestricted universal. Polysemy, as we have seen, is inherent in the very structure of language, but one could easily imagine an idiom without any homonyms; it would be, in fact, a more efficient medium. Whether such an idiom actually exists could be revealed only by empirical investigations. Even if it does, homonymy is bound to be a statistical universal with a high degree of probability.

Some homonyms arise through *diverging sense-development:* different meanings of the same word move so far away from each other that they come to be regarded as two separate terms. This happened, for example, in English *flower* and *flour* where the difference in spelling underlines the fact that, from a synchronic point of view, they are two distinct words even though historically they have a common origin. Not all cases are so clear-cut; sometimes the lexicographer will hesitate whether he has to do with one word or with two, with polysemy or homonymy.[58] The great majority of homonyms arise, however, in a different way: by *converging sound-development.* This leads to the coincidence of two or more words which were phonetically distinct at an earlier date; thus Old English *mę̄te* and *mētan* have converged and become homonymous in Modern English *meat* and *to meet.* Now the chances of such coincidence will mainly depend on two factors: word-length and word-structure. Languages where short words abound will obviously have more homonyms than those where longer words are prevalent. Hence the relative frequency of homonymy in English and French, as compared, for example, to German or Italian. Even more important than length is the productivity of the various types of *word-structure* in a particular language. For English we have some interesting statistics compiled by B. Trnka, [59] based on an analysis of words included in the *Pocket Oxford Dictionary of Current English*. Trnka distinguishes 14 types of monosyllables, ranging from words with one phoneme to those with 6. His tables show that the commonest type is the CVC sequence which, with 1343 monosyllables out of 3178, represents 42 % of the total figure. The same category also contains the largest number of homonyms, 333. In some of the smaller classes, however, the proportion of homonyms is relatively higher: in the CV combination, for instance, there are 91 examples out of a total of 174 monosyllables. In French, the general pattern of word-structure is very different; there are, in particular, numerous monosyllables consisting of a single vowel or of a vowel preceded by one consonant. Needless to say, the extreme simplicity of this type of word-structure produces a great profusion of homonyms. There are sometimes as many as half a dozen words consisting of the same vowel or consonant + vowel: *au*, *aux*, *eau*, *haut*, *oh*, *os; ceint*, *cinq*, *sain*, *saint*, *sein*, *seing*. [60] If comparable data could be collected for a great many languages, we could find out whether there are any universal, or at least widespread, tendencies in this field; we would also gain a precise typological criterion for determining the relative frequency of homonymy in general, and that of its various types.

Homonyms, like several meanings of the same word, are sometimes differentiated by formal means: gender (French *le poêle* "stove" — *la poêle* "frying-pan," *le vase* "vase, vessel" — *la vase* "mud"); or flection (English *ring*, *rang* — *ring*, *ringed;* German *die Kiefer* "jaws" — *die Kiefern* "firs"). In languages like English and French, *spelling* is employed on a massive scale to differentiate between homonyms, and this is often used as an argument against spelling-reform. Bloomfield was skeptical of the value of spelling as a safeguard against homonymy. "It is wrong to suppose," he claimed, "that writing would be unintelligible if homonyms (e. g., *pear*, *pair*, *pare*, or *piece*, *peace*) were spelled alike; writing which reproduces the phonemes of speech is as intelligible as speech." [61] This is doubtless true, but the point is that writing should be in this respect *more* intelligible than speech. English and French suggest that languages rich in monosyllables, and therefore in homonyms, tend to retain a non-phonetic mode of spelling, and it would not be difficult to establish whether this is a general tendency.

The most important safeguard against homonymic ambiguity is, however, the influence of context. Many homonyms belong to different word-classes; others are so diverse in meaning that they could never occur in the same utterance. Even so, "*homonymic clashes*" happen fairly frequently, and they can be reconstructed with great precision from linguistic atlases. These clashes, and the various ways they are resolved, have been studied so thoroughly by Gilliéron and other linguistic geographers [62] that there is no need to discuss them here. In some cases, it is sufficient to alter slightly the form of one of the homonyms: by giving French *héros* a so-called "aspirate *h*," any possible confusion between *les héros* and *les zéros*, "heroes" and "zeroes," is effectively obviated. Elsewhere, a substitute will have to be found; this may be a derivative, a synonym, a term from the same sphere or from a neighboring sphere, a borrowing from another language, or even a jocular metaphor; when, in part of Southwest France, the words for "cock" and "cat" fell together, the cock was renamed "pheasant" and, more facetiously, "curate." When we have more geographical and historical facts about such conflicts in a number of languages, we shall be able to say how common these various solutions are. It should be noted that clashes between homonyms, or between different meanings of the same word, are synchronic phenomena, whereas the changes to which they give rise are diachronic processes. In this part of linguistics, a rigid separation of descriptive and historical viewpoints would be entirely impracticable. The two must be combined, without being confused. [63]

2. 6. *Semantic typology*

It will have been noticed that four of the five features examined in this section—motivation, generic *versus* specific terms, polysemy, and homonymy—may, if studied on a suitable scale, yield criteria for linguistic typology. All four criteria are statistical: they are concerned with relative frequencies. The precision with which they can be determined will vary with the nature of the phenomena themselves: it will be highest in homonymy and lowest in the distinction between generic and specific words; in the sphere of motivation and polysemy, at least certain aspects of the problem may be amenable to numerical formulation. Two further points are also worth noting. First, some of the preceding features are interrelated: as we have seen, polysemy is closely connected with motivation on the one hand, and with the use of generic terms on the other. Second, all our typological criteria, except, perhaps, motivation, have a direct bearing on the *semantic autonomy* of the word, the degree to which the hearer (or reader) will depend on the context for understanding it. Obviously, a generic term like French *aller* means less in itself, and is therefore more "context-bound," than the more specific German verbs *gehen*, *reiten*, *fahren*. Similarly, a word with many meanings will be highly ambiguous if encountered in isolation, without any contextual support, as, for example, in a newspaper headline or the title of a book or a play, whereas homonyms found in the same isolated position will have no meaning at all. It follows that languages where generic terms, polysemy, and homonymy are prevalent will be relatively "context-bound"; French is a classic example of this type of semantic structure, as I have tried to show in my *Précis de sémantique française*. Naturally, the extent to which we have to rely on context in a given language cannot be stated with any degree of precision; yet it may emerge fairly clearly from close scrutiny of the various factors involved.

3. Universal Processes in Historical Semantics

3. 1. *Metaphor*

3. 1. 1. PARALLEL DEVELOPMENTS. Since metaphor is based on the perception of similarities, it is only natural that, when an analogy is obvious, it should give rise to the same metaphor in various languages; hence, the wide currency of expressions like

the "*foot* of a hill" or the "*leg* of a table." There are, however, less obvious associations which are also remarkably widespread. A well-known example is the figurative use of verbs for "holding" and "grasping" in the sense of "understanding": English *grasp, catch;* French *comprendre* (cf. *prendre*), *saisir;* Italian *capire* (from Latin *capere*); German *begreifen* (cf. *greifen*), etc.[64] The great difficulty about such correspondences is that they may not be genuine cases of parallel development: the various languages may simply have copied each other or some common model. Thus, to take a very recent example, the close similarity between English *skyscraper*, French *gratte-ciel*, Italian *grattacielo*, German *Wolkenkratzer*, etc., is not due to a fundamental identity of vision; the only spontaneous metaphor among them is *skyscraper* which arose in America in the 1890's and was then translated into other languages.[65] When dealing with earlier periods it will often be impossible to distinguish systematically between loan-translation and genuine parallelism.

The only way of solving this difficulty is to collect instances of the same metaphor from widely different languages which cannot possibly have influenced each other. An impressive example of such an inquiry is C. Tagliavini's article on the names of the "pupil of the eye" in various idioms.[66] Among other things, he has examined the metaphor underlying Latin *pupilla* and its modern descendants, where the pupil is compared to a small girl, or sometimes to a small boy, because of the vague resemblance between a child and the minute figure reflected in the eye. This analogy, which may at first seem farfetched, is embodied in the words for "pupil" in various Indo-European languages: Greek *kórē*, Spanish *niña (del ojo)*, Portuguese *menina (do ôlho)*, and many others. But it is equally common in other linguistic groups: Tagliavini has found examples in some twenty non-Indo-European languages as remote from each other as Swahili, Lapp, Chinese, and Samoan.

Such parallel developments are not confined to metaphor: certain metonymic associations can be equally widespread. Thus the use of the word for "tongue," the organ of speech, in the sense of "language" is common to many Indo-European idioms: English *tongue*, Latin *lingua*, Greek *glôssa*, Russian *jazýk*, etc; it is also found in a number of Finno-Ugrian languages, including not only Finnish and Hungarian but even Zyrian, Cheremiss, and others. The same metonymy occurs also in Turkish, in some African idioms, and elsewhere.[67] A collection of such parallel metaphors and metonymies would be of outstanding value since the associations on which they are based seem to be deeply rooted in human experience and largely independent of culture and environment. Hence the importance of a project announced at the London congress of linguists in 1952: the compilation of a "dictionary of semantic parallels."[68]

3. 1. 2. GENERAL TENDENCIES. Over and above these specific developments, the general movement of metaphors appears to be governed by some broad tendencies which are of great potential interest not only to the linguist but also to the psychologist, the literary critic, and others. Only four such tendencies can be briefly mentioned here:

a. Nearly forty years ago, Hans Sperber put forward a "semantic law" inspired by Freudian ideas. He started from the assumption that if we are intensely interested in a subject, it will provide us with analogies for the description of other experiences; in Sperber's terminology, it will become a center of metaphorical "expansion." Thus the terrifying weapons of the First World War suggested to French soldiers various jocular metaphors: beans were described as *shrapnels*, and a woman with many children was facetiously referred to as a machine gun *(mitrailleuse à gosses)*. Sperber summed up his "law" in the following terms: "If at a certain time a complex of ideas is so strongly charged with feeling that it causes *one* word to extend its sphere and change its meaning, we may confidently expect that other words belonging to the same emotional complex will also shift their meaning."[69]

Stated in these terms, Sperber's law is no more than a bold generalization which would have to be extensively tested in different languages and periods. There are certainly cases where the principle is applicable. In sixteenth-century France, torn by religious strife, there were numerous metaphors and similes derived from the sphere of religion.[70] During the French Revolution, analogies inspired by recent progress in physics and chemistry were remarkably popular.[71] Subsequently, the introduction of railways, the spread of electricity and other technological inventions enriched the metaphorical resources of the language.[72] It would seem, however, that Sperber's "law" is too categorical. To take but one example, if there were an automatic connection between emotion and metaphor, then one would expect our air-minded age to have far more images from aviation than are in current use today. The same may be said of the application of this principle to the imagery of a particular writer. While there are some cases where the explanation works, there are others where the major interests and preoccupations of an author have left little or no trace in his metaphors, and an attempt to reconstruct Shakespeare's "inner biography" from the sources of his images has met with a very mixed reception.[73] Nevertheless, there is obviously an element of truth in the theory, and its implications are so interesting that it deserves to be carefully investigated.

b. A very common form of metaphor in the most diverse languages is the *anthropomorphic* type. This was already clearly recognized by the eighteenth-century Italian philosopher Giambattista Vico: "In all languages the majority of expressions referring to inanimate objects are formed by transfers from the human body and its parts, from human senses and human passions.... Ignorant man makes himself the yardstick of the universe."[74] Thus Vico did not hesitate to regard anthropomorphic metaphor as a linguistic universal. Modern linguists will be more cautious, but there can be no doubt that such expressions are extremely common in many languages. They can describe both concrete and abstract experiences: we talk of the *neck* of a bottle, the *mouth* of a river, the *eye* of a needle, the *brow* of a hill, and also of the *heart* of the matter, the *lungs* of a town, the *sinews* of war, etc. Side by side with these metaphors from the human sphere, there are many others working in the opposite direction, where parts of the body are named after animals or inanimate objects: *muscle* (from the Latin *musculus*, literally "little mouse"), *polypus*, *apple* of the eye, *spine*, *pelvis*, and others. If wider investigations were to show that both types are universal, a further question would arise: which of the two is the more frequent? A monograph published in 1948 by a Dutch linguist on the semantics of the body[75] suggests that transfers *from* the human sphere are more common than those directed *toward* it. In Sperber's terminology, our body is a center of both metaphorical expansion and attraction, but it acts more powerfully in the former than in the latter capacity.

c. From concrete to abstract. The fact that, as Bloomfield put it, "refined and abstract meanings largely grow out of concrete meanings"[76] is perhaps too well known and too obvious to require detailed study. It would be most surprising to find a language where metaphors from abstract to concrete are more common than those working the other way round. It might be more profitable to examine the extension of certain specific forms of metaphor within this category. One such form is the wide use of images drawn from *light* and allied experiences, to denote intellectual and moral phenomena: "to throw *light* on," "to put in a favorable *light*," "leading *lights*," *enlighten*, *illuminating*, *brilliant*, *sparkling*, *dazzling*, *coruscating*, *beaming*, *radiant*, etc. Another common pattern is the use of words denoting sense-impressions to describe abstract experiences: "*bitter* feelings," "*sweet* disposition," "*warm* reception," "*cold* disdain," "*even* temper," and others. To us these associations seem obvious and trite; yet only empirical investigations could show how general they actually are.

d. Synaesthesia. Somewhat akin to this last type are the so-called synaesthetic metaphors where words are transferred from one sense to another: from touch to sound, from sound to sight, etc. Since the advent of Symbolism, such transpositions have been erected into an aesthetic doctrine. Baudelaire proclaimed that "les parfums, les couleurs et les sons se répondent" *(Correspondances)*, and Rimbaud wrote a sonnet on the color of vowels *(Voyelles)*. But the modern vogue of synaesthesia should not obscure the fact that this is an ancient and widespread, and quite possibly a universal, form of metaphor. It is found already in

Homer and Aeschylus, and also in some ordinary expressions in Greek, such as *barytone* (from *barýs* "heavy") and *oxytone* (from *oxýs* "sharp"); similarly in Latin *gravis* and *acutus*, which gave our *grave* and *acute* accent. Commenting on such expressions, Aristotle wrote in *De Anima:* "*Acute* and *grave* are here metaphors transferred from their proper sphere, namely, that of touch.... There seems to be a sort of parallelism between what is acute and grave to hearing and what is *sharp* or *blunt* to touch." [77] Synaesthetic metaphors have been found in China and Japan, India, Persia, Arabia, Egypt, Babylonia, and Palestine, [78] and from the language of the Kwakiutl Indians Franz Boas quotes the following powerful image: "the words of speech strike the guests, as a spear strikes the game or the rays of the sun strike the earth." [79] Our own modern languages abound in such metaphors, some of them hardened into clichés: "*cold* voice," "*piercing* sound," "*loud* colors," French *couleur criarde*, Italian *colore stridente*, and many more. [80] There is a rich literature on various aspects of synaesthesia, and by casting the net even wider it would not be too difficult to find out how general the phenomenon is, and whether it is, in fact, a semantic universal.

Further investigations might also reveal that the movement of synaesthetic metaphors is not haphazard but conforms to a basic pattern. I have collected data for the sources and destinations of such images in a dozen nineteenth-century poets, French, English, and American, and have found three tendencies which stood out very clearly: (1) transfers from the lower to the more differentiated senses were more frequent than those in the opposite direction: over 80 % of a total of 2000 examples showed this "upward" trend; (2) touch was in each case the largest single source; and (3) sound was the largest single recipient. [81] The same tendencies have been noted in some twentieth-century Hungarian poets, [82] and it is interesting to learn that the first and most important among them, the "hierarchical" principle, agrees with the findings of experimental psychology. [83] Naturally, the inquiry will have to be considerably broadened, and extended from literary style to ordinary language, before we can begin to generalize; it should also be borne in mind that these tendencies are purely statistical, and there are bound to be deviations from them in particular instances. I myself have found such deviations in the poetry of Victor Hugo, where there are so many synaesthetic metaphors derived from the visual sphere that only the third of the three tendencies is valid: sound is still the main recipient, but sight takes the place of touch as the chief source of transpositions, and there is no significant difference between "upward" and "downward" transfers.[84]

3. 2. *Extension and restriction of meaning*

Ever since the early days of modern semantics it has been known that two opposite tendencies are at work in the development of words: some terms tend to widen their meaning, others to narrow it. The English *bird* has extended its range since Old English times when it was used only in the sense of "young bird." As the logicians would say, its "extension" has been increased, and its "intension" has been reduced: it is now applicable to more things but tells us less about them. On the other hand, an old synonym of *bird*, *fowl*, has developed in the opposite direction: originally it meant "bird" in general (cf. German *Vogel*), as it still does in the Bible: "Behold the *fowls* of the air." Subsequently its range was narrowed down to its present meaning, which is more distinctive and less comprehensive than the older sense.[85]

Both extension and restriction can result from a variety of causes, some purely linguistic, others psychological or social. Nevertheless, several linguists have suggested that restriction of meaning is on the whole more common than extension.[86] This has recently been confirmed by some psychological experiments conducted by Heinz Werner,[87] according to whom there are two main reasons for the disparity. "One is that the predominant developmental trend is in the direction of differentiation rather than of synthesis. A second reason, related to the first, is that the formation of general concepts from specific terms is of lesser importance in non-scientific communication though it is rather a characteristic of scientific endeavor. In other words, language in everyday life is directed toward the concrete and specific rather than toward the abstract and general." The problem is of great interest, but we shall need many more facts from different languages before we can set up the predominance of restriction as a semantic universal.

3. 3. *Taboo*

The term *taboo* is of Polynesian origin, and the very fact that we use such an exotic word to denote a phenomenon which is very common in our own culture is symptomatic of the universality of taboo. Here we are concerned only with the linguistic side of the problem. There is a voluminous literature on the subject, and, as in the case of onomatopoeia, any future research project could best be started by compiling a critical inventory of what is already known. Language taboos seem to spring from three main causes. First, there are those inspired by *fear*, or "holy dread," as Freud preferred to call it:[88] religious restrictions on the use of the name of God, and also superstitious avoidance of any direct reference to the dead, to the devil, and to evil spirits, and the widespread and varied taboos on animals. A second group is dictated by a sense of *delicacy*: when we have to talk of such unpleasant topics as illness and death, physical or mental deficiencies, and such criminal acts as cheating, stealing, or killing, we often have recourse to euphemisms, and this can permanently affect the meaning of the latter: instead of veiling a tabooed subject, the euphemism will become indissolubly linked with it, as has happened with *undertaker*, *disease*, *imbecile* (from Latin *imbecillus* or *imbecillis*, "weak, feeble"), and other similar terms. Third, taboo bans may result from a sense of *decency* and propriety: references to sex, names of certain parts and functions of the body, and swear-words are particularly subject to this form of taboo. While all three types are of wide currency, none of them is an unrestricted universal since they are governed by social and cultural factors and will arise only in certain environments. The first type is bound to become rarer with the progress of civilization, though it will not disappear altogether. The second and especially the third type, on the other hand, will be encouraged, up to a point, by the development of higher moral standards and more refined forms of social behavior, though some of these more sophisticated taboos may be subsequently rejected as prudish and hypocritical: we no longer say *limbs* or *benders* instead of *legs*, or *waist* instead of *body*, as did some Boston ladies a hundred years ago.[89] The growth and decay of the various forms of taboo, in relation to social and cultural development, could be systematically studied in various languages. Many data are already scattered in linguistic, anthropological, and psychological treatises, but they would have to be broadened, classified, and reinterpreted before definitive conclusions could be reached.

Apart from these general tendencies, some specific patterns of taboo and euphemism would also be worth looking into. Perhaps the most striking feature is the frequency and diversity of taboos on names of *animals*. A recent monograph on the subject, by a Brazilian linguist,[90] cites no less than 24 animals whose names have been subjected to such bans in various languages. They range from ants, bees, and worms to bears,[91] tigers, and lions—even butterflies and squirrels appear in the list. One of the most remarkable cases is that of the weasel. The fear inspired by this animal has given rise to a multiplicity of propitiatory euphemisms which are very similar in different languages: in some of them it is described as a "little woman" (Italian *donnola*, Portuguese *doninha*) or as a "pretty little woman" (French *belette*, diminutive of *belle*, Swedish *lilla snälla*), while elsewhere a pretense is made of including it within the family by turning it into a "bride," a "daughter-in-law," or a "sister-in-law."[92] In other forms of taboo, too, there are some interesting parallel developments; thus the same mixture of euphemism and irony which gave *imbecile* its present sense lies at the root of similar changes in the same sphere: French *crétin* is a dialectal form of *chrétien; benêt* comes from *benedictus* "blessed"; English *silly* once meant "happy, blessed" (cf. German *selig*), whereas *idiot* goes back to a Greek word meaning "private person, layman."

As some of these examples show, euphemism, or ironical "pseudo-euphemism," will often lead to a permanent depreciation of meaning. The frequency of so-called *pejorative* sense-development was noticed by many early semanticists;[93] some saw in it a symptom of a fundamental streak of pessimism or cynicism in the human mind. Yet, as Bréal rightly pointed out, "this alleged pejorative tendency is the result of a very human disposition to veil and disguise awkward, offensive, or repulsive subjects."[94] Thus the notorious deterioration which has affected various words for "girl" or "woman," such as English *hussy*, *quean*, French *fille*, *garce*, or German *Dirne*, was no doubt due to genuine or pseudo-euphemism rather than to any antifeminine bias. These and other types of pejorative sense-change—those arising from national or social prejudice or from a simple association of ideas—are sufficiently widespread to be worth investigating on a broad interlinguistic basis. Side by side with these pejorative changes there are also ameliorative ones[95] where an unpleasant meaning is either weakened or even turned into a favorable one. An example of weakening is the English *blame*, which is historically the same word as *blaspheme;* a case of positive improvement is English *nice* from Latin *nescius* "ignorant." One has the impression that such ameliorative changes are less common than pejorative ones, perhaps because the ranks of the latter are swelled by euphemisms and pseudo-euphemisms; but this would have to be confirmed by wider investigations. Another problem which it would be interesting to explore is the development of neutral terms, "*voces mediae*," which often tend to specialize either in a favorable or in an unfavorable meaning. Thus both *luck* and *fate* are in themselves neutral, ambivalent words, but the adjectives *lucky* and *fatal* have become polarized, the former in a positive, the latter in a negative, sense. One wonders whether there is any predominant trend of development in one direction or another.

3. 4. *Implications for linguistic reconstruction*

The processes discussed in this section, to which several others could be added, are of direct relevance to etymology and comparative linguistics. Commenting on the traditional study of semantic changes, Bloomfield stated that, "aside from its extralinguistic interest, [it] gives us some measure of probability by which we can judge of etymologic comparisons."[96] Such probability would be very considerably increased if some of the tendencies involved turned out to be semantic universals. This would help the etymologist and the comparatist in two ways. First, it would tell him what kind of changes to expect, and whether a particular change suggested by his data would be common or infrequent, normal or exceptional. Second, it would enable him to choose between alternative explanations. Let us assume, for instance, that the preponderance of synaesthetic metaphors from the lower to the higher senses was to be shown by further research to be a semantic universal. Let us also assume that an etymologist was faced with two early meanings of a given word, one related to touch, the other to sound. When deciding as to which of the two meanings came first, it would be logical to surmise that the tactile sense preceded the acoustic one, since transfers from touch to sound are far more common than those from sound to touch. It is true, of course, that these tendencies are purely statistical, and it is perfectly possible that in a particular case the process worked the other way round. Nevertheless, a hypothesis which was in harmony with the general tendency would have a better chance of being correct than the alternative explanation; it might even be possible to calculate the margin of error, which might be large in some cases and negligible in others.

4. Universal Principles in the Structure of the Vocabulary

During the last three decades, structuralist methods have been introduced into semantics, and there has been a shift of interest from single words toward higher lexical units. The importance of this new orientation can be seen from the fact that "structural semantics" was on the agenda of the last international congress of linguists, held in Oslo in 1957.[97] The new science is still in its infancy, and it is faced with considerable difficulties. While no one would seriously maintain that the vocabulary is without any organization, it is clear that the methods of structural analysis which have been successfully applied to other branches of linguistics are not immediately applicable to semantics; it is sufficient to remember that, as the Memorandum points out, the number of phonemes in any language does not exceed 70, whereas the Oxford Dictionary is said to contain over 400, 000 words.[98] Despite these difficulties, some encouraging results have already been obtained,[99] and the interest of research workers is turning more and more toward these matters. These studies have already raised several problems with universal implications, three of which will be briefly discussed here. They arise at three distinct levels of linguistic analysis: at the level of single words, that of conceptual spheres, and lastly that of the vocabulary as a whole.

4. 1. *Lexical constants*

A comparison of a wide variety of languages would quickly show whether there is such a thing as a "lexical constant": an object, event, or other feature of such fundamental importance that it must somehow be expressed in any language;[100] whether it is expressed by a nonindependent root, a simple word, a compound word, or even a phrase is of secondary significance. Even if the evidence for such constants were so overwhelming that we could set them up as unrestricted universals, we would still have to allow for differences between various languages. Assuming, for example, that the idea of fatherhood is a lexical constant, we find that in Latin there were two words for "father": *genitor* for the physiological relationship, and *pater*, which carried social connotations (cf. *paterfamilias*).[101] But this does not really affect the status of a lexical constant; it merely means that its various aspects may be expressed by separate words in some languages.

If a list of lexical constants could be established—whether as unrestricted universals or as statistical ones with a high degree of probability—this would be of great interest to comparative linguistics. When studying the vocabulary of Proto-Indo-

European or any other extinct language, we could safely assume that it had some word or other element for the expression of such constants. In some cases these basic words have survived in the idioms descended from the protolanguage, as in English *mother*, Latin *māter*, Greek *mḗtēr*, Sanskrit *mātár-*, etc. Elsewhere they have been replaced by other terms for a variety of reasons. Taboo in particular has often disturbed the pattern of correspondences. Thus the "left hand" is quite possibly a lexical constant, yet there are different words for it in various Indo-European languages. Some have, in fact, been borrowed from a foreign source: French *gauche* from Germanic, Spanish *izquierdo* from Basque. This diversity is obviously connected with the superstitions and taboos which have developed around the left hand in many countries. Another possible lexical constant, the "moon," has also been the object of many superstitions which are still faintly noticeable in our terms *lunatic* and *lunacy*. As Bloomfield points out, "the Indo-European languages use the most varied words for 'moon'; it is notable that Russian has borrowed Latin ['lu: na] as [lu'na], though otherwise it makes scarcely any but highly learned borrowings from Latin."[102] When the name of a lexical constant is struck by a taboo ban or drops out of use for some other reason, a replacement has to be found, and this may lead to the borrowing of words which would not normally pass from one language to another.

4. 2. *Lexical fields*

One of the most fruitful concepts evolved so far in structural semantics is that of the "lexical field," closely associated with Jost Trier and his school. So much has been written of late on this subject[103] that it is unnecessary to go into details. It will be sufficient to recall that lexical fields are highly organized and integrated conceptual spheres whose elements mutually delimit each other and derive their significance from the system as a whole. In each field a sphere of experience, concrete or abstract, is analyzed, divided up, and classified in a unique way which embodies a scale of values and a peculiar vision of the world. Examples of lexical fields are: the system of colors, the network of family relations; or, among abstract experiences, the terms for intellectual qualities, ethical and aesthetic values, religious and mystical experiences.

The numerous articles and monographs which have recently been published on these problems have all tended to emphasize the differences between these fields in various languages; they have concentrated on what is distinctive and idiosyncratic in them rather than on what they have in common. Yet, beneath all the diversity, there is likely to be an underlying unity which a systematic comparison of these fields would no doubt reveal. Thus we are told of striking differences between the number and nature of *color* distinctions:[104] there was no single term for "brown" or "gray" in Latin; Russian has two words for "blue" — *sínij* "dark blue" and *golúboj* "sky-blue"; the Navaho "have two terms corresponding to 'black', one denoting the black of darkness, the other the black of such objects as coal. Our 'gray' and 'brown', however, correspond to a single term in their language and likewise our 'blue' and 'green'."[105] These differences are highly significant, but it would be equally interesting to know whether there are any elements common to all classifications of colors, any distinctions which have to be expressed everywhere and which could therefore rank as lexical constants.

The same point is even more clearly noticeable in another closely organized field which has been extensively studied in various languages: the nomenclature of *kinship* terms. Take, for instance, the words for "brother" and "sister." These two concepts seem so fundamental to us that we find it difficult to imagine any language that could do without them. Yet a glance at other idioms will show that they are not in any sense lexical constants. In Hungarian, there was no single term either for "brother" or for "sister" until well into the nineteenth century;[106] instead, there were, and still are, two pairs of separate words for "elder" and "younger brother" and "elder" and "younger sister." In Malay, on the other hand, there is one collective term for "sibling," which can also mean "cousin." In his report on structural semantics to the Oslo congress of linguists, Professor

Hjelmslev summed up the difference between the three solutions in the following table:[107]

<table>
<tr><th></th><th>Hungarian</th><th>English</th><th>Malay</th></tr>
<tr><td>"elder brother"</td><td>bátya</td><td rowspan="2">brother</td><td rowspan="4">saudara</td></tr>
<tr><td>"younger brother"</td><td>öcs</td></tr>
<tr><td>"elder sister"</td><td>néne</td><td rowspan="2">sister</td></tr>
<tr><td>"younger sister"</td><td>hug</td></tr>
</table>

The three arrangements, though very different, have one thing in common: the general relationship of "siblings" (children of the same parent or parents) is expressible in each of them, either in itself or combined with other criteria. A comparison of the same field in a number of languages would reveal whether this relationship is a semantic universal. It would also show how many ways there are of "structuring" this part of the field, and how frequent these various solutions actually are. The same method could then be applied to other sections of the field. Even languages belonging to the same family and culture will sometimes show remarkable discrepancies. Thus there is no single term for "grandfather" or "grandmother" in Swedish: a distinction is made between *farfar*, the father's father, and *morfar*, the mother's father, and similarly between *farmor* and *mormor*. Latin had no single word for "uncle" or "aunt": it distinguished between the father's and the mother's brother *(patruus — avunculus)* and between the father's and the mother's sister *(amita — matertera)*; only the two middle terms have survived in English *uncle* and *aunt*. In languages with a different social and cultural background, these discrepancies will be even more marked. In Dravidian, for example, there is an intricate hierarchy of kinship terms based on four sets of distinctions: sex, generation, alliance, and age, of which the third, the only nonbiological one, is the most important.[108] In Malay, the collective term *saudara* "sibling or cousin," which has already been mentioned, can be subdivided into "younger" and "elder sibling or cousin," and the latter again into "elder sister or female cousin" and "elder brother or male cousin."[109]

It may be noted in passing that the theory of lexical fields has certain affinities with the *Sapir-Whorf hypothesis.* Trier and his followers would readily agree with Whorf that each language contains a "hidden metaphysics" and that "we dissect nature along lines laid down by our native languages."[110] There are, however, two important differences between the two schools: (1) lexical fields have so far been explored mainly in the best-known European languages, whereas Whorf deliberately turned away from "Standard Average European" and concentrated on totally different linguistic systems, notably the American Indian ones; (2) the theory of lexical fields is focused on vocabulary, while Whorf's most impressive successes were obtained in the grammatical sphere. It would seem, then, that the two approaches, which have developed independently of each other,[111] could usefully supplement each other, and the time may come when they can be combined into a unified theory.

4. 3. *The classification of concepts*

Experiments have been made time and again to devise a more rational arrangement for dictionaries than the customary one in alphabetical order. Roget's *Thesaurus* was an early attempt in this direction. In recent years, some closely reasoned schemes for conceptual dictionaries have been put forward,[112] and the subject has become so topical that it was placed on the agenda of the London congress of linguists in 1952.[113] At that congress, Professor von Wartburg presented an even more ambitious project which he and R. Hallig had worked out over a number of years: a broad classification of concepts applicable to any vocabulary.[114] Under three main headings: "The Universe," "Man," and "Man and the Universe," concepts are classified and arranged in such a way that they form an articulate structure of interdependent elements. The aim of the project is practical: if a series of monographs on the vocabulary of different languages, or different periods of the same language, could, within reason, all conform to the same pattern, the results could be easily compared and any differences quickly noticed. Before and since the publication of the Hallig-Wartburg scheme, a number of studies on the vocabulary of French writers from various periods have been based on this system:[115] it has also been applied to a text in Romansh.[116] While no one would claim special virtues for this particular classification, it would be an important step forward if a system of concepts could be generally accepted as a uniform yet flexible framework for further lexical studies.[117]

5. Conclusion

The list of topics discussed in this paper is not meant to be exhaustive in any way. I have merely tried to suggest some directions in which we may look for universals or, more modestly, for general tendencies in semantics. If a co-ordinated research program could be organized to explore some of these problems, then we would have to establish a rough *order of priorities*, starting with relatively simple questions and gradually working our way toward more complex ones. From this purely practical point of view, the subjects listed previously fall into four broad categories:

1. It would be best to begin with some clearly defined problems which could be formulated in precise numerical terms. Such problems are, for instance, the relation between polysemy and word-frequency; connections between homonymy and word-structure; the sources and destinations of synaesthetic metaphors; the number and nature of lexical constants.

2. In the next phase of the program we could proceed to the study of certain phenomena which are more complicated in themselves, but about which extensive data are already available from many languages. Onomatopoeia, taboo, and parallel metaphors would belong to this category.

3. At a later stage we might be ready to tackle such intricate matters as the ratio of transparent and opaque words; the preponderance of specific or generic terms; the frequency of pejorative and ameliorative sense-change and of extension and restriction; the structure of the same lexical field in various languages.

4. Finally, some important research projects will have to wait until we have the means of collecting the necessary data. Thus, if there are any general tendencies behind the conflicts caused by polysemy and homonymy, we shall be in a better position to discover them when linguistic atlases are available for many more languages than at present.

If, in the course of such a program, some semantic universals could be precisely identified, this would be of great significance not only for linguistics but also for other branches of study. While some of the problems discussed earlier are of purely linguistic interest, others clearly have wider implications. To mention but a few, the distinction between transparent and opaque words raises important educational issues; onomatopoeic and metaphorical patterns are of direct relevance to stylistics; synaesthesia is basically a psychological phenomenon, with wide ramifications in language and literature. Such problems as taboo and lexical fields could best be attacked by a concerted effort of linguists, anthropologists, ethnologists, psychologists, and sociologists. The study of lexical fields, and of the structure of the vocabulary in general, would also supplement the Sapir-Whorf hypothesis and throw light on the impact of language upon thinking, which is one of the main themes of contemporary philosophy. Among all branches of linguistics, semantics undoubtedly has the most varied and most intimate contacts with other disciplines, and the discovery of universals in this field would have far-reaching repercussions in neighboring spheres.

Acknowledgments

I am indebted to the following colleagues for information and critical remarks: Professors Harold C. Conklin, Charles F. Hockett, Fred W. Householder, and Dell H. Hymes.

Notes

1. See H. Kronasser, *Handbuch der Semasiologie*, Heidelberg, 1952, p. 29, and K. Baldinger, *Die Semasiologie*, Berlin, 1957, pp. 4f.

2. M. Bréal, "Les lois intellectuelles du langage," published in *L'Annuaire de l'Association pour l'encouragement des études grecques en France*; quoted by A. W. Read, "An Account of the Word *Semantics*," *Word*, IV (1948), 78–97.
3. F. de Saussure, *Cours de linguistique générale*, 4th ed., Paris, 1949, p. 132.
4. O. Jespersen, *Mankind, Nation, and Individual from a Linguistic Point of View*, Oslo, 1925, p. 212.
5. V. A. Zvegintsev, *Semasiologija*, Moscow, 1957, p. 46.
6. L. Bloomfield, *Language*, New York, 1933, p. 20.
7. See R. H. Robins, *Ancient and Mediaeval Grammatical Theory in Europe*, London, 1951, pp. 20f.
8. C. F. Hockett, *A Course in Modern Linguistics*, New York, 1958, p. 123.
9. Bloomfield, *op. cit.*, p. 178.
10. Cf. S. Ullmann, *Principles of Semantics*, 2nd ed., Glasgow and Oxford, repr. 1959, pp. 58f.
11. Saussure, *op. cit.*, pp. 134f.
12. Cf. Ullmann, "Descriptive Semantics and Linguistic Typology," *Word*, IX (1953), 225–240, and Dell H. Hymes's comments in *Anthropological Linguistics*, III (1961), p. 27.
13. Cf. A. Sommerfelt, "Points de vue diachronique, synchronique, et panchronique en linguistique générale," *Norsk Tidsskrift for Sprogvidenskap*, IX (1938), 240–249.
14. Saussure, *op. cit.*, p. 100.
15. For references, see Ullmann, *Principles of Semantics*, pp. 83f., 305.
16. Cf. Saussure, *op. cit.*, pp. 180ff. On this problem see, recently, L. Zawadowski, "The So-called Relative Motivation in Language," *Omagiu lui Iorgu Iordan*, Bucharest, 1958, pp. 927–937.
17. Saussure, *op. cit.*, pp. 183f.
18. See V. Grove, *The Language Bar*, London, 1949, pp. 45f.
19. Cf. U. Weinreich, *Language*, XXXI (1955), 538. On the need for statistical data, see *ibid.* and G. Mounin, *Bulletin de la Société de Linguistique de Paris*, LV (1960), 50.
20. See Grove, *op. cit.*
21. See M. Wandruszka, "Etymologie und Philosophie," *Etymologica. Walther von Wartburg zum 70. Geburtstag*, Tübingen, 1958, pp. 857–871: pp. 858ff. On Fichte see *ibid.*, pp. 866f.
22. See C. Bally, *Linguistique générale et linguistique française*, 3rd ed., Berne, 1950, p. 343.
23. See Z. Gombocz, *Jelentéstan* ("Semantics"), Pécs, 1926, p. 12.
24. Cf., recently, M. Chastaing, "Le symbolisme des voyelles. Significations des *I*," *Journal de Psychologie*, LV (1958), 403–423, 461–481.

25. Cf. Jespersen, *Language: Its Nature, Development, and Origin*, London, repr. 1934, p. 402.
26. See I. Fónagy, *A költöi nyelv hangtanából* ("From the Phonetics of the Language of Poetry"), Budapest, 1959, pp. 24ff., 71.
27. See H. Wissemann, *Untersuchungen zur Onomatopoiie*, I, Heidelberg, 1954.
28. V. Brøndal, *Le français, langue abstraite*, Copenhagen, 1936; Bally, *op. cit.*, pp. 346ff.; J. Orr, *Words and Sounds in English and French*, Oxford, 1953, ch. VIII. Cf. on these matters C. F. Hockett, "Chinese versus English," in H. Hoijer, ed., *Language in Culture*, Chicago, 1954, pp. 106–123.
29. See Bally, *op. cit.*, p. 350.
30. See Jespersen, *Language*, p. 429.
31. A. A. Hill, "A Note on Primitive Languages," *International Journal of American Linguistics*, XVIII (1952), 172–177.
32. A. Kaplan in *Language in Culture*, *op. cit.*, p. 219.
33. W. Kaper, *Kindersprachforschung mit Hilfe des Kindes*, Groningen, 1959, p. 11.
34. W. von Wartburg, quoted by K. Baldinger, "L'étymologie hier et aujourd'hui," *Cahiers de l'Association Internationale des Études Françaises*, XI (1959), 233–264; p. 259 cited.
35. P. Henle, ed., *Language, Thought, and Culture*, Ann Arbor, 1958, p. 5.
36. *Ibid.*
37. M. Bréal, *Essai de sémantique*, 6th ed., Paris, 1924, p. 26.
38. Bloomfield, *op. cit.*, p. 145.
39. Cf. C. Schick, *Il Linguaggio*, Turin, 1960, p. 188.
40. W. E. Collinson, "Comparative Synonymics," *Transactions of the Philological Society*, 1939, pp. 54–77.
41. See F. Brunot and C. Bruneau, *Précis de grammaire historique de la langue française*, 3rd ed., Paris, 1949, p. 172.
42. See O. Jespersen, *Growth and Structure of the English Language*, 6th ed., Leipzig, 1930, p. 48.
43. See W. von Wartburg, *Problèmes et méthodes de la linguistique*, Paris, 1946, pp. 175f.
44. *Ibid.*, p. 135.
45. See M. Schwob and G. Guieysse, "Études sur l'argot français," *Mémoires de la Société de Linguistique de Paris*, VII (1892), 33–56, and more recently B. Migliorini, "Calco e irradiazione sinonimica," *Boletín del Instituto Caro y Cuervo*, IV (1948), 3–17, repr. in *Saggi Linguistici*, Florence, 1957. As Professor Hockett rightly points out, "radiation of synonyms" is a special form of analogy.
46. See S. Kroesch, "Analogy as a Factor in Semantic Change," *Language*, II (1926), 35–45.

47. W. M. Urban, *Language and Reality*, London ed., 1939, pp. 112f.
48. Bréal, *Essai de sémantique*, p. 144.
49. *Ibid.*
50. G. K. Zipf, "The Repetition of Words, Time-Perspective, and Semantic Balance," *The Journal of General Psychology*, XXXII (1945), 127-148; p. 144 cited. Cf. also the same author's *Human Behavior and the Principle of Least Effort*, Cambridge, Mass., 1949.
51. "The Meaning-Frequency Relationship of Words," *The Journal of General Psychology*, XXXIII (1945), 251–256; p. 255 cited.
52. J. Whatmough, *Language, A Modern Synthesis*, London ed., 1956, p. 73.
53. L. Wittgenstein, *Philosophical Investigations*, Macmillan, 1953, p. 34.
54. See Kr. Nyrop, *Grammaire historique de la langue française, IV: Sémantique*, Copenhagen, 1913, p. 26.
55. Cf. A. Rudskoger, "*Fair, Foul, Nice, Proper*"*: A Contribution to the Study of Polysemy*, Stockholm, 1952, pp. 473ff.
56. *Ibid.*, p. 439. Cf. also R. J. Menner, "Multiple Meaning and Change of Meaning in English," *Language*, XXI (1945), 59–76.
57. See K. Jaberg, *Aspects géographiques du langage*, Paris, 1936, p. 64.
58. On the boundary between polysemy and homonymy, see R. Godel, "Homonymie et identité," *Cahiers Ferdinand de Saussure*, VII (1948), pp. 5–15; P. Diaconescu, "Omonimia și polisemia," *Probleme de Lingvistică Generală*, *I*, Bucharest, 1959, pp. 133–153; M. M. Falkovich, "K voprosu ob omonimij i polisemij," *Voprosy Jazykoznanija*, 1960, no. 5, pp. 85–88. Cf. also Weinreich, *Language*, XXXI (1955), 541f.
59. B. Trnka, *A Phonological Analysis of Present-Day Standard English*, Prague, 1935, pp. 57–93. See also Jespersen, "Monosyllabism in English," *Linguistica*, Copenhagen and London, 1933, pp. 384–408. As Professor Hockett points out, Trnka's figures would have to be revised in the light of current methods of phonemic analysis.
60. See Bally, *op. cit.*, pp. 269f.; L. C. Harmer, *The French Language Today*, London, 1954, ch. IV; A. Schönhage, *Zur Struktur des französischen Wortschatzes. Der französische Einsilber*, Bonn, 1948, unpubl. thesis reviewed by G. Gougenheim in *Le Français Moderne*, XX (1952), 66–68. Cf. P. Miron, "Recherches sur la typologie des langues romanes," *Atti dell'VIII. Congresso Internazionale di Studi Romanzi*, Florence, 1960, vol. II, pp. 693–697.
61. Bloomfield, *op. cit.*, p. 502.
62. See esp. Wartburg, *op. cit.*, ch. III; Orr, *op. cit.*, chs. XII–XIII; I. Iordan and J. Orr, *An Introduction to Romance Linguistics*,

London, 1937, ch. III. On homonymic clashes in English, see R. J. Menner, "The Conflict of Homonyms in English," *Language*, XII (1936), 229–244, and E. R. Williams, *The Conflict of Homonyms in English*, Yale Studies in English, 100 (1944).

63. Cf. Wartburg, *loc. cit.*, and Ullmann, *Principles of Semantics*, pp. 144ff.
64. See Gombocz, *op. cit.*, pp. 6f. On parallel metaphors see, recently, A. Sauvageot, "A propos des changements sémantiques," *Journal de Psychologie*, XLVI (1953), 465–472.
65. See B. Migliorini, "Grattacielo," *Lingua e cultura*, Rome, 1948, pp. 283f.
66. C. Tagliavini, "Di alcune denominazioni della pupilla," *Annali dell' Istituto Universitario di Napoli*, N. S., III (1949), 341–378, esp. pp. 363ff.
67. See Gombocz, *op. cit.*, p. 94; B. Collinder, *Fenno-Ugric Vocabulary*, Stockholm, 1955, pp. 25 (*s. v.* Finnish *kieli*), 43 (*s. v.* Hungarian *nyelv*); G. Révész, *The Origin and Prehistory of Language*, London, 1956, pp. 56f.
68. See J. Schröpfer, "Wozu ein vergleichendes Wörterbuch des Sinnwandels? (Ein Wörterbuch semasiologischer Parallelen?)," *Proceedings of the Seventh International Congress of Linguistics*, London, 1956, pp. 366–371.
69. H. Sperber, *Einführung in die Bedeutungslehre*, Bonn and Leipzig, 1923, p. 67. The English translation is the one given by W. E. Collinson in *Modern Language Review*, XX (1925), 106.
70. See E. Huguet, *Le langage figuré au XVIe siècle*, Paris, 1933, pp. 1–18.
71. See F. Brunot, *Histoire de la langue française*, *X*, *1*, pp. 64ff.
72. Cf. Ullmann, *The Image in the Modern French Novel*, Cambridge, 1960, pp. 140ff.
73. On this problem see Wellek and Warren, *Theory of Literature*, London ed., repr. 1954, pp. 214ff., and Ullmann, *Style in the French Novel*, Cambridge, 1957, pp. 31ff.
74. Quoted by Gombocz, *op. cit.*, p. 73.
75. J. J. de Witte, *De Betekeniswereld van het lichaam*, Nijmegen, 1948.
76. Bloomfield, *op. cit.* p. 429.
77. Quoted by W. B. Stanford, *Greek Metaphor*, Oxford, 1936, p. 49; cf. *ibid.*, pp. 53 and 57.
78. See A. Wellek, "Das Doppelempfinden im abendländischen Altertum und Mittelalter," *Archiv für die gesamte Psychologie*, LXXX (1931), 120-166.
79. F. Boas, "Metaphorical Expressions in the Language of the Kwakiutl Indians," *Donum Natalicium Schrijnen*, Nijmegen and Utrecht, 1929, pp. 147-153: p. 148.

80. Cf. Gombocz, *op. cit.*, p. 7.
81. See Ullmann, *Principles of Semantics*, pp. 266ff.
82. See A. H. Whitney, "Synaesthesia in Twentieth-Century Hungarian Poetry," *The Slavonic and East European Review*, XXX (1951–1952), 444–464.
83. Cf. H. Werner, *Language*, XXVIII (1952), 256.
84. See Ullmann, "La transposition dans la poésie lyrique de Hugo," *Le Français Moderne*, XIX (1951), 277–295: pp. 287f.
85. See H. Schreuder, "On Some Cases of Restriction of Meaning," *English Studies*, XXXVII (1956), 117–124.
86. Bréal, *Essai de sémantique*, p. 107; Bloomfield, *op. cit.*, p. 151; J. Vendryes, *Le langage*, Paris, 1921, p. 237.
87. H. Werner, "Change of Meaning: a Study of Semantic Processes through the Experimental Method," *The Journal of General Psychology*, L (1954), 181-208; p. 203 cited.
88. S. Freud, *Totem and Taboo*, London, Pelican Books, repr. 1940, p. 37.
89. Jespersen, *Growth and Structure*, p. 226.
90. R. F. Mansur Guérios, *Tabus Lingüísticos*, Rio de Janeiro, 1956, ch. XVIII.
91. Cf. A. Meillet, "Quelques hypothèses sur des interdictions de vocabulaire dans les langues indo-européennes," *Linguistique historique et linguistique générale*, 2 vols., Paris, 1921–1938, vol. I, pp. 281–291, and M. B. Emeneau, "Taboos on Animal Names," *Language*, XXIV (1948), 56–63.
92. Mansur Guérios, *op. cit.*, pp. 152ff.; Nyrop, *op. cit.*, pp. 275f.
93. On these processes see esp. H. Schreuder, *Pejorative Sense-Development in English, I,* Groningen (1929), and K. Jaberg, "Pejorative Bedeutungsentwicklung im Französischen," in *Zeitschrift für romanische Philologie*, XV (1901), XVII (1903), and XIX (1905).
94. Bréal, *Essai de sémantique*, p. 100.
95. See G. A. van Dongen, *Amelioratives in English, I*, Rotterdam, 1933.
96. Bloomfield, *op. cit.*, p. 430. On these problems see esp. G. Bonfante, "On Reconstruction and Linguistic Method," *Word*, I (1945), 132–161; E. Benveniste, "Problèmes sémantiques de la reconstruction," *Word*, X (1954), 251–264; H. M. Hoenigswald, *Language Change and Linguistic Reconstruction*, Chicago, 1960.
97. See the *Proceedings of the Eighth International Congress of Linguists*, Oslo, 1958, pp. 636–704. It appears again on the agenda of the next congress, to be held in Cambridge, Mass., in 1962.
98. S. Potter, *Modern Linguistics*, London, 1957, p. 101.
99. For a brief account of these results, see the Supplement to the second ed. of Ullmann, *Principles of Semantics*.

100. Cf. H. J. Pos, "The Foundation of Word-Meanings: Different Approaches," *Lingua*, I (1947–1948), 281–292: pp. 289ff.
101. See Meillet, *op. cit.*, vol. I, p. 41.
102. Bloomfield, *op. cit.*, p. 400.
103. For a general survey see S. Öhman, "Theories of the 'Linguistic Field'," *Word*, IX (1953), 123–134, and her book, *Wortinhalt und Weltbild*, Stockholm, 1951. Various aspects of the field theory are discussed in *Sprache-Schlüssel zur Welt. Festschrift für Leo Weisgerber*, Düsseldorf, 1959. Cf. also Ullmann, *Principles of Semantics*, pp. 152ff. and 309ff.
104. See esp. I. Meyerson, ed., *Problèmes de la couleur*, Paris, 1957.
105. Henle, *op. cit.*, p. 7.
106. The word *fivér* "brother" and *növér* "sister" are neologisms formed in the late 1830's and early 1840's; see G. Bárczi, *Magyar Szófejtö Szótár* ("Hungarian Etymological Dictionary"), Budapest, 1941 (*s. v. fiú* and *nö*, *né*).
107. Hjelmslev, "Pour une sémantique structurale," repr. in *Essais linguistiques*, Copenhagen, 1959, pp. 96–113; p. 104 cited. I have replaced the French terms by English ones and the Malay form *sudarā* by *saudara*, as suggested by Professor Conklin.
108. See L. Dumont, "The Dravidian Kinship Terminology as an Expression of Marriage," *Man*, LIII (1953), 34–39; "Hierarchy and Marriage Alliance in South Indian Kinship," *Occasional Papers of the Royal Anthropological Institute of Great Britain and Ireland*, no. 12 (1957).
109. I am indebted to Professor Harold C. Conklin for the Malay data. Cf. also H. Galton, *Zeitschrift für Ethnologie*, LXXXII (1957), 121–138; W. H. Goodenough, *Language*, XXXII (1956), 195–216; F. G. Lounsbury, *ibid.*, pp. 158–194; O. N. Trubachov, *Istorija slavianskich terminov rodstva*, Moscow, 1959; L. Weisgerber, *Vom Weltbild der deutschen Sprache*, 2 vols., 2nd ed., Düsseldorf, 1953–1954: vol. I, pp. 59ff., and vol. II, pp. 81f.
110. *Language, Thought, and Reality. Selected Writings of Benjamin Lee Whorf*, ed. J. B. Carroll, Cambridge, Mass, and New York, 1956, pp. 212f.
111. Cf. Weisgerber, *op. cit.*, vol. II, pp. 255ff.
112. See esp. F. Dornseiff, *Der deutsche Wortschatz nach Sachgruppen*, 5th ed., Berlin, 1959. See also two articles by K. Baldinger: "Die Gestaltung des wissenschaftlichen Wörterbuchs," *Romanistisches Jahrbuch*, V (1952), 65–94, and "Alphabetisches oder begrifflich gegliedertes Wörterbuch?", *Zeitschrift für romanische Philologie*, LXXVI (1960), 521–536.
113. See the *Proceedings of the Seventh International Congress of Linguistics*, pp. 77–89, and 343–373.

114. R. Hallig and W. von Wartburg, *Begriffssystem als Grundlage für die Lexikographie. Versuch eines Ordnungsschemas*, Abhandlungen der deutschen Akademie der Wissenschaften zu Berlin, Klasse für Sprachen, Literatur und Kunst, Heft 4, 1952.
115. See the works listed in Wartburg, *Problèmes et méthodes*, p. 161, and H. E. Keller, *Étude descriptive sur le vocabulaire de Wace*, Berlin, 1953.
116. M. H. J. Fermin, *Le vocabulaire de Bifrun dans sa traduction des quatre Évangiles*, Amsterdam, 1954.
117. Cf. *Language in Culture*, p. 193.

CHAPTER 9

IMPLICATIONS OF LANGUAGE UNIVERSALS FOR LINGUISTICS

ROMAN JAKOBSON

Harvard University, Massachusetts Institute of Technology

No doubt, the linguists who are present have responded to the scientific gain of this stimulating conference with a feeling of joyful relief. It has often been said that linguistics is a bridge between the sciences and the humanities, but it was a long time before the unity of linguistics with the exact sciences became definitely consolidated.

Hermann Helmholtz (II, 25f.[3])* predicted that "students will find themselves compelled to go through a stricter course of training than grammar is in a position to supply." This great German scientist of the last century was aghast to find evidence of a "certain indolence and vagueness of thought" in his compatriot students of grammar, and particularly to note their "laxity in the application of strictly universal laws. The grammatical rules, in which they have been exercised, are for the most part followed by long lists of exceptions; accordingly they are not in the habit of relying implicitly on the certainty of a legitimate deduction from a strictly universal law." According to Helmholtz, the best remedy for these defects "is to be found in mathematics, where there is absolute certainty in the reasoning, and no authority is recognized but that of one's own intelligence."

Our century has witnessed the gradual stages of a spectacular *rapprochement* between linguistic and mathematical thought. The

* References are cited by number of appearance in the bibliography.

gratifying concept of invariance, which in synchronic linguistics had been first applied for an intralingual comparison of variable contexts, was finally expanded to an interlingual comparison. Typological confrontation of diverse languages reveals universal invariants; or—to quote the inaugural chart of the present conference, the "Memorandum Concerning Language Universals" prepared by J. H. Greenberg, C. Osgood, and J. Jenkins—"Amid infinite diversity, all languages are, as it were, cut from the same pattern." We see emerging ever new, unforeseen, but henceforth perfectly discernible "uniformities of universal scope," and we are happy to recognize that the languages of the world can actually be approached as manifold variations of one worldwide theme—human language.

This outlook is particularly agreeable after the stern opposition to any TYPOLOGICAL comparison of languages which was current among American linguists during the 1940's and *mutatis mutandis* corresponded to the simultaneous Soviet Russian ban on comparative HISTORICAL studies by the then dictatorial Marrist dogma.

The tension between two polar trends—parochial particularism and all-embracing solidarity—which Saussure observed in language (205ff.[15]), is true for linguistics as well: "individual-language-oriented definitions" and concentration on differentials alone alternate here with a search for common denominators. Thus among scholastic theoreticians of language the renowned Paris savant of the twelfth century, Pierre Hélie, declared that there are as many kinds of grammar as there are languages; whereas in the thirteenth century, *grammatica universalis* was considered indispensable to give grammar a scientific status. Roger Bacon taught: "Grammatica una et eadem est secundum substantiam in omnibus linguis, licet accidentaliter varietur" (43[17]). Only today, however, does linguistics have at its disposal the necessary methodological prerequisites for constructing an adequate universal model.

The strictly relational, topological character of the cross-language invariants under study has been repeatedly pointed out in the course of our deliberations. Previous endeavors to define the interlingual invariants in ABSOLUTE metrical terms could only fail. There is an inventory of simple relations common to all tongues of the world. Such relations pertain both to the early acquisitions of children's language and to the most stable verbal properties in those types of aphasic regress which display a mirror picture of infants' development. This repertory (484ff.[6]) may be exemplified in phonemics by such simple relations as compact/diffuse (universally displayed in vocalism, and for most languages also in consonantism), grave/acute (universally displayed in consonantism and/or in vocalism, in the former almost universally), and nasal/nonnasal (near-universal in consonantism). To instance simple relations among grammatical universals, we may cite the difference between the classes of nouns and verbs (which assign to their referents the roles of 'existents' and 'occurrents' respectively, as Sapir used to call them: p. 1[13], p. 123[14]). This difference is correlated but never merges with the likewise universal difference of two syntactic functions—subject and predicate. A few more examples: the particular class, pronouns (or in Charles Peirce's terms, 'indexical symbols': 275ff.[10]); the category of number, with its basic distinction between singular and plural; and the category of person, with its opposition of impersonal ('third person') and personal forms, which in turn include an opposition of addressee ('second person') and addresser ('first person'): the two numbers and the three persons are universally displayed by pronouns, as J. H. Greenberg states.

Another and much richer inventory of universals consists of implicational rules which set a compulsory connection between two different relational properties of language. Thus in phonemics the combinability of distinctive features into bundles or sequences is restricted and determined by a considerable number of universal implicational rules. For instance, the concurrence of nasality with the vocalic feature implies its concurrence with the consonantal feature. A compact nasal consonant (/ɲ/ or /ŋ/) implies the presence of two diffuse consonants, one acute (/n/) and the other grave (/m/). The acute/grave opposition of compact nasal consonants (/ɲ/ vs. /ŋ/) implies an identical opposition of compact oral stops (/c/ vs. /k/). Any further tonality opposition of nasal consonants implies a corresponding opposition of oral consonants; and any opposition of nasal vowels implies a corresponding opposition of oral vowels (cf. C. A. Ferguson's "Assumptions about Nasals").

The present-day inquiry into the hierarchical arrangement of phonemic systems enables us to uncover the basis for each of the implicational rules stated. The more complex a phonemic entity, the less susceptible it is of further fissions. The important role assigned by the late Viggo Brøndal to the laws of compensation in the grammatical structure of languages (105ff.[1]) is perhaps even more significant for their phonemic patterning (491ff.[6]). For example, the marked character of nasals in their relation to orals results in the lower combinability of nasality with further features. The marked character of compactness in the diffuse/compact opposition of consonants explains the near-universal character of compact nasals and the limited spread of their diffuse counterparts. Inversely, the marked character of diffuseness in the diffuse/nondiffuse opposition of vowels explains why there are fewer diffuse than nondiffuse phonemes among the nasal vowels of the world (cf. Issatschenko[5]). On the other hand, of the two oppositions—grave/acute and compact/diffuse—the former takes primary place in the phonemic stratification of the consonantal pattern; therefore the compact/diffuse opposition of nasals implies their grave/acute opposition, as shown earlier (cf. Greenberg's forcible conclusions relevant to the distinctions present in an unmarked morphological category but neutralized in its marked counterpart).

The grounds for phonemic universals invariably lie in the relational structure of the sound pattern. Thus, for instance, in languages without the opposition of stops and corresponding continuants, the obstruents are always implemented exclusively or primarily as stops, because it is precisely the stops which stand in maximum contrast to vowels.

When we examine the few ultimate oppositions which underlie the whole phonemic structure of language and deal with the laws of their interrelation, we necessarily resort in the search for interlingual invariants to the same isomorphic principle as in eliciting intralingual invariants, and thus easily proceed in tracing the typology of existing phonemic patterns and their universal foundations. The tenacious belief that maintains the diversity of languages to be wider in phonemics than in grammar proves at variance with the facts observed.

The 'logical operations' which H. J. Pos, the outstanding Dutch theoretician of language, apprehended in the binary oppositions of distinctive features[12] do indeed give the purely formal bases for a precise investigation of language typology and universals. Sol Saporta's segregation of references to vowels, as "a class defined in formal terms," from references to nasals, as a "class of phenomena defined in substance terms," is groundless, because any distributional definition of vowels presupposes that we identify phonemes in a given position as those possessing one common oppositive feature, vocality, just as the nasal phonemes are for us those which carry the oppositive feature of nasality. In both cases we must deal with relational concepts superimposed on sensuous data.

The distinction of phonemic entities "universally present by definition, i.e., universally necessary," like the phoneme, from those "universally present by empirical observation," like the syllable, makes no sense whatever. Saporta affirms that "in a language in which all syllables are exactly one phoneme long, the distinction between syllable and phoneme disappears"; but such a language is absolutely impossible, because the only form of syllable universally admitted is the sequence "consonant plus vowel." Saporta's assumption is as aimless and arbitrary as if he referred to some imaginary language where all words were one phoneme long, or where each phoneme contained but one feature. The hierarchy of universal linguistic units, from the utterance to the distinctive feature, must be a formal definition applicable to world-wide verbal experience. We are faced with the question of general laws which govern the relations between linguistic units differing in their rank. Thus, with regard to both phoneme and word, the smaller the number of phonemes and their combinations and the shorter the word pattern in a given language, the higher is the functional load carried by the phonemes. According to J. Krámský,[7] the higher the percentage of consonants in the code, the lower is the rate of their occurrence in the corpus. Should this affirmation prove correct, it would mean that distinctive features tend toward a universally constant frequency in the corpus.

On the grammatical level, J. H. Greenberg's list of 45 implicational universals is an impressive achievement. Even if advancing research somewhat reduces the number of exceptionless universals and increases the sum of near-universals, these data will remain invaluable and indispensable preliminaries to a new typology of languages and to a systematic outline of the universal laws of grammatical stratification. Skeptical reminders of numerous as-yet-unexplored languages are hardly convincing. First, the number of languages analyzed or available to analysis is enormous, and, second, even if there may possibly occur a further increase of near-universals to the corresponding diminution of exceptionless universals, this result cannot shake the momentous interest of the inquiry. Statistical uniformities with a probability slightly less than one are no less significant than uniformities with probability of one. We may expect, however, that with the progress of this search and with the refinement of its methods there will be discovered many new grammatical universals along with new near-universals.

Greenberg's statements on universals in the "order of meaningful elements" rightly put forward the notion of a "dominant" order. We are reminded that the idea of dominance is not based on the more frequent occurrence of a given order: actually what is here introduced into the "order typology" by the notion of dominance is a stylistic criterion. For example, of the six mathematically possible relative orders of nominal subject, verb, and nominal object—SVO, SOV, VSO, VOS, OSV, and OVS—all six occur in Russian: The sentence, "Lenin cites Marx," can be rendered as SVO *(Lenin citiruet Marksa)*, SOV *(Lenin Marksa citiruet)*, VSO *(Citiruet Lenin Marksa)*, VOS *(Citiruet Marksa Lenin)*, OSV *(Marksa Lenin citiruet)*, and finally OVS *(Marksa citiruet Lenin);* yet only the order SVO is stylistically neutral, while all the 'recessive alternatives' are experienced by native speakers and listeners as diverse emphatic shifts. SVO is the only word order initially used by Russian children; and in a sentence like *Mama ljubit papu* 'Mama loves papa', if the order of words is inverted—*Papu ljubit mama*, small children are prone to misinterpret it: "Papa loves mama," as if one had said, *Papa ljubit mamu*. Correspondingly, Greenberg's first universal could be restated as follows: In declarative sentences with nominal subject and object, *the only or neutral (unmarked)* order is almost always one in which the subject precedes the object. If in a language like Russian the nominal subject and object are not distinguished by morphological means, the relative order SO is compulsory—*Mat' ljubit doč'*, 'Mother loves daughter'; inversion of the nouns would mean 'The daughter loves the mother'. In languages without distinctive characteristics of object and subject, the order SO is the only one admissible.

The cardinal task of deducing empirical universals "from as small a number of general principles as possible"—already achievable by and large in phonemics—has been courageously approached by Greenberg on the grammatical level with more than promising conclusions. Particularly fruitful are his remarks on what we would call, in Charles Peirce's terminology (l. c.), the 'iconic' aspect of word order: "The order of elements in language parallels that in physical experience or the order of knowledge." The initial position of a word in unemphatic speech can reflect not only precedence in time but also priority in rank (the sequence "President and Secretary of State" is far more usual than the reverse), or it may reflect a primary, irremovable role within the given message. In the sentences *Lenin citiruet Marksa* 'Lenin cites Marx' and *Marks citiruetsja Leninym* 'Marx is cited by Lenin' (with the recessive alternatives *Marks Leninym citiruetsja*, *Citiruetsja Marks Leninym*, *Citiruetsja Leninym Marks*, *Leninym Marks citiruetsja*, and *Leninym citiruetsja Marks*—each variety with its own stylistic shade), only the first of the two nouns, the subject, is unomissible, but the oblique term, the accusative *Marksa* and instrumental *Leninym* may be left out. The nearly universal precedence of the subject with regard to the object, at least in unmarked constructions, points to a hierarchy in focusing. It is not by chance that Greenberg's paper treats the universals of grammar "with particular reference to the order of meaningful elements" (syntactic or morphological constituents).

In general, the 'iconic symbols' of language display a particularly clear-cut universalistic propensity. Thus, within a grammatical correlation the zero affix cannot be steadily assigned to the marked category and a 'nonzero' (real) affix to the unmarked category. For example, according to Greenberg, "There is no language in which the plural does not have some nonzero allomorphs, whereas there are languages in which the singular is expressed only by zero. The dual and trial are almost never expressed only by zero." In a declensional pattern, the zero case ("which includes among its meanings that of the subject of the intransitive verb") is treated like the singular in respect to the other numbers. Briefly, language tends to avoid any chiasmus between pairs of unmarked/marked categories, on the one hand, and pairs of zero/nonzero affixes (or of simple/compound grammatical forms), on the other hand.

Phonemic experience may yield some useful stimuli for the investigation and interpretation of grammatical universals. In particular, one may expect the order of children's acquisitions and of aphasic losses to throw new light on the stratification of morphological and syntactic systems.

As we have already observed, the unaccountable fear of a slip into the phonetic substance may hamper the phonemic typology of languages and the discovery of general phonological laws. Likewise, the exclusion of semantic considerations (which has been a tantalizing experiment in grammatical descriptions) would be, with respect to typology, a flat contradiction in terms. One must agree with Greenberg that it would be impossible to identify grammatical phenomena in languages of differing structure without "employing semantic criteria." Morphological and syntactic typology and universal grammar as its groundwork deal primarily with 'grammatical concepts', by Sapir's designation. It is obvious that in grammar there is no conceptual opposition without a corresponding formal distinction, but neither on the intralingual nor on the interlingual level is this distinction supposed to use one and the same 'grammatical process'. Thus in English the one opposition singular/plural is expressed either by suffixation or by vocalic alternation *(boy: boys; man: men)*. If one language expresses this opposition by suffixation only and another only by vowel alternation, the basic distinction of two grammatical numbers nonetheless proves to be common to both languages.

Not only grammatical concepts but also their interconnection with grammatical processes (exemplified earlier by the analysis of word order), and, finally, the structural principles of such processes, call for an extraction of implicational universals.

Fortunately, in his quest for the universals of grammar Greenberg does not share the whimsical prejudice against "semantics-oriented definitions," which, strange as it seems, may have filtered even into our Conference on Language Universals. One must fully approve Uriel Weinreich's witty remark, that if in phonology we had only a couple of commonplace statements on all-language properties, "we would hardly be meeting for a conference on phonological universals," and, again, that isolated truisms about the universal semantic properties of languages offer "not much to go on." A realistic approach to this field, however, opens an ever-widening prospect for new high-level generalizations. A *conditio sine qua non* of such inquiry is the consistent distinction between grammatical and lexical meanings (or, in Fortunatov's terms, the formal and the real meanings: see ch. 7[11]), which, despite methodological itineraries traced particularly by the outstanding American and Russian pathfinders in linguistics, still bewilders and confuses some students of language. Some of them even seem to be nonplused by rudimentary questions: What, for example, does the plural or the past tense or the inanimate gender actually mean in a verbal code? and does it possess in general any meaning?

A cautious and unremitting search for the intralingual and therewith interlingual semantic invariants in the correlations of such grammatical categories as, for example, verbal aspects, tenses, voices, and moods becomes indeed an imperative and perfectly attainable goal in present-day linguistic science. This inquiry will enable us to identify equivalent grammatical oppositions within "languages of differing structure" and to seek the universal rules of implication which connect some of these oppositions with one another. The great mathematician A. Kolmogorov, an expert also in the science of language, has judiciously defined grammatical cases as those classes of nouns which express "wholly equivalent states" in regard to their referent *(absoljutno èkvivalentnye sostojanija otnositel'no dannogo predmeta*[16]*)*. We analyze a grammatical case into its componential semantic properties and treat these componential properties just as we do distinctive features in phonemics: that is, we define both as terms of INVARIANT oppositions and, correspondingly, as VARIABLES, dependent on different contexts or on different subcodes (styles of language). Incidentally, though it happens that in certain contexts the use of a given case is compulsory and that in this instance its meaning turns out to be redundant, this circumstance does not allow us to equate even so predictable a meaning with meaninglessness. It would be a sheer misunderstanding to imagine that these occasional redundancies might invalidate to any extent the search for the general meanings of grammatical cases. It is true that the Russian preposition *k* 'to' implies the dative case subsequent, but the Russian dative does not imply an antecedent preposition *k* and thus preserves its own general meaning of 'direction toward', just as the Russian noun *xleb* 'bread' does not lose its meaning when preceded by the adjective *peklevannyj* 'wholemeal', although *xleb* is the only noun one can expect after this attribute. In a sequence of two English obstruents, if the first is voiceless, the second too must be voiceless: [kukt] *cooked.* In this instance, however, the apparent analogy between the grammatical and phonemic sequences is misleading. Redundancy does deprive the phonemic feature of its distinctive value, but it cannot rob meaningful units of their proper sense.

Naive attempts to deal with variations without attacking the problem of invariants are condemned to failure. Such ventures change the case system from a hierarchic structure to a summative aggregate and hide the implicational universals which actually form the pivot of the declensional pattern. An interlingual difference in contextual variants does not affect the equivalence of invariant oppositions. Though the genitive of negation exists in Polish and Gothic but not in Czech or Ancient Greek, the genitive does act as a quantifier in all four of these languages.

At present "there is an ineradicable conviction," as H. M. Hoenigswald noted in his thoughtful paper, "that universals may form some sort of system in their own right." The high number of grammatical universals based on "semantic criteria" eloquently proves the failure of the traditional belief cited by Weinreich, that "the semantic mapping of the universe by a language is, in principle, arbitrary."

The most profitable part of Weinreich's paper "On Semantic Universals" is his effort to answer the question, "What generalizations can be made about any vocabulary as a structured set, imperfect as the structuring may be?" The thoughts on language by Weinreich's six-year-old daughter (transmitted to us by her father between conference meetings) offer a particularly valuable and realistic supplement to his argumentation. "The standard works on semantics," Weinreich states, "are on the whole preoccupied with the one semiotic process of naming." His daughter, surprised to learn that there are thousands and thousands of words in a language, surmises that most of them must be "names" (she means nouns), and, on the other hand, grants that this high number of words is not so overpowering, since they go by pairs (of antonyms), as *up* and *down*, *man* and *woman*. *Water*, the little Shifra reasons, must be countered with *dry*, and *to buy* with *to make oneself* (since she is accustomed to buying but not to selling, there is no word alternation *buy—sell* in her thought). The astute child has observed two important properties of vocabulary: its structured arrangement, and the different status of diverse word classes, especially the more open, expandable character of the noun class.

The study of lexical patterning would be easier and more productive if it began not, as usual, with nouns but with more closely circumscribed word classes. Then the bonds between semantic subclasses and their different syntactic treatment would prove particularly revealing. Thus the research started by Professor Gerta Worth (U. C. L. A.) within the frame of our Harvard teamwork (Description and Analysis of Contemporary Standard Russian) shows that the division of all Russian primary (unprefixed) verbs into those which *must* or *may* or *cannot* be combined with a given case or with an infinitive results in a set of verbal classes, substantiated both formally and semanticaly. A similar twofold delineation of nominal classes is more laborious but still feasible. For instance, in Slavic and many other languages, the class of nouns designating an extent of time is syntactically grounded by the fact that only they can be used in the accusative with intransitive verbs (Russian *bolel nedelju* 'was ill a week') and as a second accusative with transitive verbs (Russian *gody pisal knigu* 'for years was writing a book'). An intralingual classification of words which would at last tie together the problems of lexicology and grammar is an essential prerequisite to the cross-language investigation of lexical uniformities.

We have observed that the common joy at the universal outlook of this conference threatened to change into a feeling of frustration when the final debates over the prospective organization and further advancement of research proved inconclusive. Since it is clear that typology and universals cannot be removed from the agenda, and since without continuous collective effort this research cannot be adequately promoted, I shall propose at least one concrete measure.

We most urgently need a systematic world-wide mapping of linguistic structural properties: distinctive features, inherent and prosodic—their types of concurrence and concatenation; grammatical concepts and the principles of their expression. The primary and less difficult task would be to prepare a phonemic atlas of the world. Preliminary discussions aiming toward such an atlas had been undertaken at an international meeting of phonologists in Copenhagen, August 29, 1936, and were extended in 1939–1940 by the remarkable community of Oslo linguists, but were suspended at the German invasion. Today our linguistic section of the Center for Communication Sciences at M. I. T. is desirous of inaugurating work on this atlas, but to realize this project would require the wide cooperation of the Social Science Research Council and of its Committee on Linguistics and Psychology. Linguists of different centers in this country and abroad are to be enlisted in the work of our team.

The number of languages and dialects whose phonemic makeup is already accessible to linguists is fairly high, but—let us admit—at the beginning there will be controversial questions, and some blanks will remain on our maps. Nevertheless, the existence of unexplored areas can never be used as an argument against mapping. The isophones obtained, even if they should be only approximate, will be immensely useful to linguistics and anthropology. Matched with one another, these isoglosses will, no doubt, reveal new implicational rules and present the phonemic typology of languages in its geographical aspect. The phonemic affinities of contiguous languages due to the wide diffusion of phonemic features will be exhaustively displayed by the atlas. Work on phonemic and grammatical atlases of the world will be only a part of that vast international cooperation which is necessary to reach the grand aims advanced by our conference.

To conclude: We all seem to agree that linguistics is passing from the bare study of variegated languages and language families, through systematic TYPOLOGICAL research and gradual INTEGRATION, to become a thoroughly universal science of language. For centuries this field has been a no-man's land, and only a few philosophical contributions—from the medieval treatises on *grammatica speculativa*, through John Amos Comenius' *Glottologia*[9] and the rationalist essays of the seventeenth and eighteenth centuries, to Husserl's[4] and Marty's[8] phenomenological meditations, and finally to the modern works in symbolic logic—have ventured to lay the foundations for a universal grammar.

When questioned by my examiner in Moscow University about the possibility of a universal grammar, I answered by quoting that professor's negative view of Husserl's *reine Grammatik*. There followed a demand for my own attitude; to the questioner's vexation I replied by advancing the necessity for linguists' research in this field.

If present-day linguists finally turn to these problems, equipped as they are with a strict methodology of their own and a rich factual knowledge, they should revise and correct the extant theoretical constructions; but by no means are they justified in ignoring or in underrating the abundant philosophical hints of the past and of the present with the dubious excuse that in this literature one meets now and then with a priori statements and with inattention to verifiable realities. Thus Weinreich's indiscriminate rejection of the allegedly "new scholasticism" in Carnap's and Quine's recent writings is hardly warrantable. Likewise, the philosophers' distinction between autocategorematic and syncategorematic signs remains vital for the construction of a universal grammar even if some of its traditional interpretations have proved to be "totally untenable." A careful empirical check of the various general principles introduced by philosophical grammar may be an effective auxiliary in the linguistic investigation of universals and a welcome preventive measure against uneconomical, superfluous rediscoveries and against the dangerous fallacies with which the so-called creeping empiricism is too often menaced.

This conference has eloquently testified that isolationism in its various shapes vanishes from linguistics when the device of technical separation has served its useful experimental end. The particular and the universal emerge as two correlated moments, and their synthesis reaffirms the irresolvable unity of the outer and inner side of any verbal sign. Linguistics is becoming aware of its interconnection with the adjacent sciences of language, thought, and communication, and it strives to define both the particular characteristics of language and its intimate affinities with other sign systems. The question of language universals inevitably raises the wider problem of the over-all semiotic constants. The inside view of language is now supplemented by a comparison of the verbal pattern with other vehicles of human communication. The intensive collaboration of linguists with cultural anthropologists and psychologists in the Conference on Language Universals indicates that the present-day linguist is about to reject the apocryphal epilogue which the editors of Saussure's *Cours* added in italics: "*The true and unique object of linguistics is language studied in and for itself.*"[15,2] Do we today not conceive language as a whole "in and for itself" and simultaneously as a constituent part of culture and society? Thus linguistics becomes a two-fronted science persistently concerned with the interrelation of whole-and-part aspects. Finally, the question acutely raised by H. M. Hoenigswald and vividly discussed here—"Are There Universals of Linguistic Change?" —has enabled us to expose the most rigid of the habitual segregations, the fictitious chasm between the study of constancy and changes. The quest for universals is organically linked with all other manifestations of a unitary attitude toward language and linguistics.

References

1. Brøndal, V. (1943). *Essais de linguistique générale.* Copenhagen.
2. Godel, R. (1957). *Les sources manuscrites du Cours de linguistique générale de F. de Saussure.* Genève.
3. Helmholtz, H. (1900). *Popular Lectures on Scientific Subjects.* New York.
4. Husserl, E. (1913). *Logische Untersuchungen,* II. 2nd ed., Halle a. S.
5. Issatschenko, A. (1937). "A propos des voyelles nasales," *Bulletin de la Société de Linguistique de Paris,* 113. 267ff.
6. Jakobson, R. (1962). *Selected Writings,* I. The Hague.
7. Krámský, J. (1946–1948). "Fonologické využití samohláskových fonémat," *Linguistica Slovaca,* 4–5. 39ff.
8. Marty, A. (1908). *Untersuchungen zur Grundlegung der allgemeinen Grammatik und Sprachphilosophie.* Halle a. S.
9. Miškovská, V. F. (1959). "La Panglottie de J. A. Komenský," *Philologica Pragensia,* II. 4. 97ff.
10. Peirce, C. S. (1932). *Collected Papers,* II. Cambridge, Mass.
11. Porzeziński, W. (1913). *Vvedenie v jazykovedenie.* 3rd ed., Moscow.
12. Pos, H. J. (1939). "Perspectives du structuralisme," *Travaux du Cercle Linguistique de Prague,* VIII. 71ff.
13. Sapir, E. (1930). *Totality* (LSA, Language Monographs, 6).

14. Sapir, E. (1949). *Selected Writings.* Berkeley and Los Angeles.
15. Saussure, F. de. (1959). *Course in General Linguistics.* New York.
16. Uspenskij, V. A. (1957). "K opredeleniju padeža po A. N. Kolmogorovu," *Bjulleten' Ob"edinenija po problemam mašinnogo perevoda*, 5. 11ff. Moscow.
17. Wallerand, G. (1913). *Les œuvres de Siger de Courtrai.* Louvain.

CHAPTER 10

LANGUAGE UNIVERSALS IN ANTHROPOLOGICAL PERSPECTIVE

JOSEPH B. CASAGRANDE

University of Illinois

1. Introduction

Ever since the early days at Columbia University of our common progenitor, Franz Boas, anthropology and linguistics have in the United States been regarded as kindred disciplines. Boas' students were regularly exposed to the intricacies of American Indian languages in one of the main courses he regularly offered, the other being one in "Statistical Theory" (Steward, 1961, p. 1042). Thenceforth linguistics has always figured importantly in the graduate training of American anthropologists. Linguists are fully accredited members of most of the larger departments of anthropology, and many anthropologists have contributed significantly to both fields—one need only mention Sapir and Kroeber—a tradition that is at least as alive today in the work of many younger people as it was in the past. And Boas also stands secure among the intellectual forebears of American linguistics. Indeed, Emeneau (1943, p. 35) has characterized Boas as "the *guru*, the ancestor in learning, of all those in this country who work in descriptive linguistics." But beyond this historical and cognatic link, there are good substantive, theoretical, and methodological reasons for the close and continuing affinity between the two fields. I say "two fields" because, while many might regard linguistics as a subfield of anthropology, or as a special kind of ethnography, the two have had, particularly abroad, quite independent if sometimes merging traditions. Anthropological linguistics is primarily an American phenomenon.[1]

Despite the relative autonomy of language as a subsystem and the fact that it can have a separate historical career, we are widely agreed that language is a part of culture, perfectly meeting the criteria for anyone's definition of culture. In fact, language and the ideological components of culture for which language is prerequisite can be thought of as culture in its "purest" form, that is, a kind of behavior unique to man, discontinuous with other species, and for which there are not readily identifiable behavioral analogues traceable to biosocial imperatives shared with other animals. If, then, language is of the essence of culture, it behooves us as general anthropologists to attend to what the linguist has to say, and to ask linguists what light their studies can throw on the nature of man, and especially on man as a symbol maker and user. Anthropologists may perhaps need to be reminded from time to time that as students of culture they are *bound* to have an interest in linguistics despite their oft-expressed dismay with the technical demands of the subject. Both fields stand to lose if they follow separate paths. These are, of course, all familiar views. I rehearse them here only to suggest that anthropologists can be expected to have a natural interest in language universals and their ramified implications.

2. Universals in Language and Culture

Among many parallel problems, anthropology and linguistics share that of a dual concern with the particular and the general in culture and in language. We both have the task of uncovering the common pattern, or the universal design, that underlies the exuberant variety of the particular configurations that we call cultures and languages, as well as that of accounting for the latter themselves.[2] That there exist general designs for languages and for cultures is a belief frequently affirmed by anthropologists and linguists alike if seldom demonstrated in detail. Linton's statement (1952, p. 646) is typical: "Behind the seemingly endless diversity of culture patterns there is a fundamental uniformity."

Clearly, the existence of these uniformities is implied in the methods, concepts, and categories that are applied cross-culturally and cross-linguistically by both anthropologists and linguists. And in common-sense terms the reality of a universal pattern is attested to by the fact that men can and do learn each other's languages and, although perhaps with greater difficulty, can come to appreciate each other's cultures, if only by imaginative participation.

It is also interesting to note that the *relative* concern with the particular and the general has shown the same vicissitudes in anthropology and linguistics. The "three stages" of ethnocentricism, descriptive empiricism, and now of comparative structuralism, to give them somewhat arbitrary labels, that Hoenigswald (p. 30) describes for linguistics are equally applicable for anthropology. Boas in anthropology, as Bloomfield in linguistics, marks the watershed; and both were looming figures on this intellectual continental divide. Indeed, if one were to substitute the word "culture" for "language" in the passage from Bloomfield quoted by Ullmann (p. 218), one can virtually hear Boas uttering it in the classroom. Among his students, perhaps only Sapir's attention would be wandering.

This is not the place to recount in detail the history of anthropological concern with universals—it goes back well into the last century—but let me mention briefly a few more recent writings, particularly as they touch on language. Wissler in *Man and Culture* (1923) called attention to what he termed the "universal culture pattern" and the "skeleton of culture," a set of categories which, taken together, Wissler believed, cover the entire range of culture content. In discussing speech, which constituted one of these nine "complexes"[3] in "the culture scheme," he observed that "not only are all languages set up on the same lines, like so many watches in the jeweler's show-case, but ... they are based upon that which is fundamental in the mind" (p. 84).

More recently, Murdock (1945) and Kluckhohn (1953) have written on the problem of cultural universals. Noteworthy, too, is the *Outline of Cultural Materials*, now in its fourth edition (1961), developed by Murdock and his colleagues as a set of categories under which the massive materials in the Human Relations Area

Files are exhaustively catalogued. Murdock and Kluckhohn agree that cultural universals are essentially similarities in *classification*, not content. Kluckhohn describes universals as "invariant points of reference for description and comparison" and as "substitutive uniformities or near-uniformities." Both give some attention to linguistics. Thus Murdock lists as "common denominators of culture" greetings, joking, kinship nomenclature, personal names, numerals, and language itself. Kluckhohn gives more attention to linguistics, both by citing examples of linguistic universals (e.g., "possession or the genitive is expressed in all languages," p. 517), and by referring to linguistics as a model to be emulated in the quest for cultural universals. He notes that "Linguistics alone has discovered elemental units which are universal, objective, and theoretically meaningful" (p. 507). And, he adds, "In cultural anthropology we are still too close to the phase in linguistics when non-European languages were being forcibly recast into the categories of Latin grammar" (p. 508).

On reading these several anthropological treatments of universals, one is immediately struck by the fact that they parallel to a great degree the discussion at this Conference. Clearly, here is a common *anthropological* problem embracing both language and culture. The several types of universals discussed in the Memorandum, while not identified as such or similarly classified, are adumbrated in Kluckhohn's review article. And it is evident that, understood in the sense of the Memorandum, the quest for universals is the chief inspiration of current cross-cultural research, whether synchronic or diachronic, as, for example, represented by Murdock (1949) and his students (Whiting and Child, 1953; Whiting, 1954) and Steward (1949), respectively. However, in the case of anthropology, *universals* is usually taken to refer to true or "unrestricted" universals rather than "statistical universals," and in reference to the latter one speaks in terms such as cross-cultural regularities, covariation, correlations, adhesions, types (as in Omaha- or Crow-type kinship system), and the like.

One additional similarity in approach may be noted. This is the fact that explanations for the occurrence of universals in both language and culture, as touched upon in Lamb's and Osgood's comments at this Conference and as discussed by Murdock and Kluckhohn in the works cited previously, are couched in terms of *underlying* determinant factors and not in terms of the phenomena of language or culture per se. Thus Kluckhohn writes, quoting a memorandum of which he was a co-author, "These [*invariant points of reference*] are to be found in the nature of social systems, in the biological and psychological nature of the component individuals, in the external conditions in which they live and act, in the nature of action itself, in the necessity of its coordination in social systems" (1953, p. 513). In a sense, then, and as Osgood has suggested in his summary statement, these underlying factors become the universals, and cultural and linguistic universals are epiphenomena. Presumably, many of the same or analogous factors operate to determine both cultural and linguistic universals, although one might want to specify some of them a bit differently, for example, in the case of linguistic universals, in terms of neurological, physiological, and psychological capabilities and capacities, and of the nature, functions, and content (including cultural content) of communication itself.

Cultural anthropologists will doubtless be most interested in semantic universals since it is in this domain of language that the influence of culture is most transparent. Yet universals at all levels can teach us something about the nature of man, and we may also assume that physical anthropologists, anatomists, and neurologists (e.g., Spuhler, 1959; Penfield and Roberts, 1959; Du Bruhl, 1958) will also be interested in universals insofar as they throw light on the structural requirements for a brain and speech apparatus capable of creating and using language of a level of complexity that is consistent with minimal cultural needs, a topic to which we shall return later. Moreover, what we do know, or can reasonably infer, about the nature of man and his culture may help to elucidate the universals we can discover, even at the phonological level, which at first blush may seem far removed from sociocultural influences. Thus the universality of the nuclear family and commonalities in teaching-learning processes during the early years of human socialization may work in concert with the phasing of the maturational processes and the relatively long period of infant dependency to produce phonological universals such as bilabials, nasals, and reduplication in primary kinship terms and baby words (Casagrande, 1949; Murdock, 1959). It is conceivable that these universals might even have been shared with our early Hominoid precursors.

As we have previously noted, semantic universals are of prime anthropological interest because of their cultural content and implications. The universal features in descriptive semantics as discussed in Ullmann's contribution are a case in point. For example, the proliferation and specificity of terms, the higher degree of codability, and the greater number of synonyms in areas of special cultural interest are matters of perduring anthropological concern. Similarly, anthropologists will find Ullmann's comments regarding the relations between semantics and civilization (e.g., the correlation of polysemy and progress, particularism and primitiveness) suggestive if debatable. Other topics taken up by Ullmann, such as the widespread parallelisms in metaphors of various types and in metonymy, and the role of language taboos, are of obvious anthropological interest. One is reminded here of what Bastian years ago called *Elementargedanken*. And as we shall discuss in more detail later, the common structural principles underlying these more superficial semantic phenomena are, I believe, of fundamental interest to anthropologists, especially to those concerned with new developments in the comparative study of cognitive processes.

Given their predilection for history, many anthropologists will doubtless show keen interest in diachronic universals. That this is so is evident from the eager if uncritical reception accorded glottochronology by archaeologists and ethnohistorians who seized upon the proposition that basic vocabulary is replaced at a constant rate as another time-clock comparable to C^{14} dating and the like. If it could be shown, with perhaps greater reliability, that phonological changes occur at a constant rate, or within a fairly limited range of rates, clearly such a finding would be a boon to historically minded anthropologists. In fact, a priori one might conjecture that the rate of phonological change might be more regular than that of lexical substitution since it is less immediately susceptible to the vagaries of cultural interference. Moreover, phonological change is less discontinuous than lexical change, increments of change are doubtless smaller (perhaps involving only a single distinctive feature at a time), and tend to occur throughout a phonological system rather than affecting discrete components of it, as is more apt to be the case in lexical substitution. Moreover, the direction of change is more predictable and hence more "discoverable" as one moves backward in time; that is, given a particular phonological feature, the probability is high that it developed out of one of a limited number of possible antecedent features.[4] Here, then, is an intriguing problem for some aspiring phonochronologist.

Further, with regard to diachronic universals, it is evident that processes of change in language parallel those in culture. Indeed, some lexical changes are quite simply "mirror effects" of culture changes as when terms for obsolete items in the cultural inventory drop out of colloquial speech. Change due to replacement as well as simple deletion and addition, as these are discussed in Hoenigswald's paper, operates in other areas of culture as well as in language.[5] Methodologically, the problems raised in tracing the provenience of specimens in an archaeological assemblage are closely akin to those confronted in historical linguistics when dealing with the sources of a lexicon at a particular point in time. From a somewhat different point of view, one may also discern two universal types of change in both language and culture, cumulative or noncyclical, and cyclical change. Examples of the latter are not plentiful, but in the realm of language one might cite Saporta's (Osgood and Sebeok, 1954) study on the phonemes of Spanish which suggests that the efficiency of use of distinctive features oscillates around the 50% point over time. In the sphere of culture, Kroeber and Richardson's classic study (1940) of periodic fluctuations in women's dress fashions is a prime example.

3. Language Universals and Cultural Origins

The origins of culture and the role of language in the emergence of a cultural mode of adaptation are related questions of abiding interest to anthropologists. With his customary perspicacity Sapir addressed himself to these problems in several telling passages. On the antiquity of language he writes:

> The universality and the diversity of speech leads to a significant inference. We are forced to believe that language is an immensely ancient heritage of the human race, whether or not all forms of speech are the outgrowth of a single pristine form. It is doubtful if any other cultural asset of man, be it the art of drilling for fire or of chipping stone, may lay claim to a greater age. I am inclined to believe that it antedated even the lowliest developments of material culture, that these developments, in fact, were not strictly possible until language, the tool of significant expression, had itself taken shape [1921, pp. 22–23].

Now, if language is very ancient in human history, and if we succeed in identifying a universal groundwork, hopefully in some detail, we may ask whether this ancient tongue or tongues might also be expected to conform to this universal design. In other words, has this basic design come down to us through the centuries, or is it the product of convergent or parallel development? Lenneberg (1960), in a very interesting paper, has taken the former view. If the latter, then what was language at its earliest stage like? These questions are perhaps unanswerable in any final way, yet they will certainly continue to intrigue anthropologists for years to come. Sapir, again, has suggested one answer. He writes, "The fundamental groundwork of language, the development of a clear-cut phonetic system, the specific association of speech elements with concepts, and the delicate provision for the formal expression of all manner of relations—all this meets us rigidly perfected and systematized in every language known to us" (1921, p. 22). And in another place he has stated that "... language is an essentially perfect means of expression and communication among every known people. Of all aspects of culture, it is a fair guess that language was the first to receive a highly developed form and that its essential perfection is a prerequisite to the development of culture as a whole" (1949, p. 7). Other arguments tend to buttress

Sapir's position. Thus, there appears to be little evidence that the basic design features of language depend on elaboration or complexity in other aspects of culture, or that any evolutionary trends can be discerned in natural languages (Greenberg, 1957, pp. 56–65). Hoenigswald as well remarks in his contribution to this volume that "these processes [of change by replacement] lead very rarely, if ever, to alterations of fundamental importance for the species" (p. 45).

If one subscribes to the general point of view just suggested, it then follows that what is universal in language may indeed be very old; and the more precisely we are able to specify what is universal in language, the greater insight into the pristine form of language and speech we may hope to achieve.

It is commonplace for anthropologists to assert their belief that language is a prerequisite for culture, but few go further to specify in any but the most general terms just what would be required of language if it is to do the work of culture. We might, then, ask the cultural anthropologist what his specifications would be for a language adequate to serve minimal or, perhaps better, basic cultural needs. Among anthropologists, Hallowell (1955) virtually alone has offered us some penetrating observations in his brilliant articles, "Personality Structure and the Evolution of Man" and "The Self and Its Behavioral Environment." In the latter he writes, "If it be assumed that the functioning of *human* [his italics] societies depends in some way upon this psychological fact [man's capacity for self-awareness], it is not difficult to understand why all human cultures must provide the individual with basic orientations that are among the necessary conditions for the development, reinforcement, and effective functioning of self-awareness" (p. 89). Among these basic orientations are self-other orientation, spatiotemporal orientation, and object orientation.

Hallowell calls attention to the *generic* function of language in providing linguistic means of orienting the individual to the culturally constituted world he apprehends. Thus, he quotes Boas' observation (1911) that "the three personal pronouns—I, thou, and he—occur in all human languages," and that "the underlying idea of these pronouns is the clear distinction between the self as speaker, the person or object spoken to, and that spoken of" (1955, p. 89). In similar fashion, Hallowell calls attention to language universals other than pronominal systems that serve to orient the individual in a self-other dimension. Among these are kinship terms (which we can regard as one subset of a larger set of status terms) and personal names. To these one might perhaps add the notion of personal possession however expressed, and terms for grosser body parts and noncontinuous psychophysiological processes (i.e., those capable of being disrupted) that can be brought into conscious awareness, for example, sleeping, eating, dreaming, copulating, and listening.

As the second basic orientation, Hallowell notes that if the self is to be prepared for action, all cultures must provide some kind of *spatiotemporal* frame of reference. "Just as personal names mediate self-identification and personal reference, in the same way names for places and significant topographical features are a universal linguistic means for discriminating and representing stabilized points in space which enable the self to achieve spatial orientation" (1955, p. 93). Similarly, although the units may of course vary, temporal intervals must be discriminated. If man by virtue of his culture is emancipated from the here and now, then he must be prepared to deal at the symbolic level also with the past and the future. Pertinent to both types of self-orientation mentioned here is Weinreich's discussion (Section 2.2.2., p. 154) of the universality of person, time, and place deixis.

A third universal function of culture is the orientation of the self to a phenomenological world of objects that are "discriminated, classified, and conceptualized with respect to attributes which are culturally constituted and symbolically mediated through language" (1955, p. 91). And Hallowell adds, "It is this objectifying function of speech that enables man to live and act in an articulated world of objects that is psychologically incomparable with that of any other creature." Now if anthropology has taught us anything, it is that these multifarious culturally constituted worlds of objects are not semantically equivalent in any simple way, and that there is no one-to-one correspondence between designata in any two of these worlds. But neither, as we have also learned, is there complete noncorrespondence. In Section 4 of his paper Weinreich has given us some suggestions about how we might deal with the problem of partial correspondence; the question here, from the point of view of the anthropologist, is what kind, where, and at what level might we expect there to be correspondences, and, indeed, given the observable broad similarities in the nature of man, his environment, his social life, and his culture, what correspondences *must* there be.

While Hallowell has not, of course, provided a total semantic design for language, he does suggest some major components for such a design in a manner that, I believe, goes far beyond mere speculation.

Another related approach that takes us a bit further down the same road is that of Wallace, wherein he asks what functional specifications for a human brain might be written based on the anthropologist's knowledge of the tasks which a cultural mode of existence requires that brain to perform (1961*a*, p. 132). Basic to his argument is the concept of "mazeway," which he defines as the "meaningfully organized totality of learned cognitive representations of people, things, processes, and values held at a given time by an individual" (1961*a*, p. 139). Within a society (a culturally organized human group) people act in mutually predictable ways on the basis of semantic equivalences among individual mazeways. A culture, then, may in Wallace's terms be described as a set of mazeway equivalence structures shared by the component members of a society. It is important to note that these mazeways are *equivalent*, not *identical*. In fact, Wallace argues that mazeway identity would be inimical to the development of cultural complexity. Whereas Wallace assumes that mazeway equivalence is a necessary condition of cultural behavior, he flatly asserts that shared motivations are not.

Wallace's discussion is relevant to a consideration of universals in several respects. First, his general description of the structure of a mazeway (1961*b*, pp. 17–19) can be regarded as a tentative and schematic statement of cultural universals at the *cognitive* level, and following Hallowell, and of course many others, we see language as of central importance in shaping this widely shared cognitive structure. Second, while Wallace does not dwell at length on the role of language both in constituting the mazeway or as the device par excellence for achieving mazeway equivalence, he clearly regards it as having a central role in these essential tasks. Thus he suggests that the fundamental cognitive processes of perceiving and learning the meaning of stimuli and of relating these meanings in problem-solving, although differing in cultural content, may follow constant laws irrespective of culture or even of species. And he sees componential analysis, "a recent development of major importance to anthropology," as a powerful operational tool in revealing the complex semantic structure of the mazeway.

In his paper, "Cultural Causality and Law: A Trial Formulation of the Development of Early Civilization," Steward writes: "*If the more important institutions of culture can be isolated from their unique setting so as to be typed, classified, and related to recurring antecedent or functional correlates, it follows that it is possible to consider the institutions in question as the basic or constant ones, whereas the features that lend uniqueness are secondary or variable ones*" (his italics) (p. 6). A similar statement might with at least equal appropriateness be made about language. The phonology of a language and the phonetic shapes of words, being but the instruments of meaning and not in themselves meaningful, are *free* to vary, and this variety serves in a sense to mask what may be basic similarities. Similarly, as so beautifully exemplified in Greenberg's paper in this volume on grammatical universals, there are *alternative* solutions to *common* grammatical problems that again mask underlying uniformities. Indeed, although it may appear to be a contradiction in terms, one might with some justice speak of "universal alternatives," that is, a limited set of alternative solutions to a problem, one or more of which may be used in a particular language.

It appears, then, that there are discoverable universal principles governing human behavior that lie at a deeper subphenomenal level. Some might disdainfully comment that this is to rediscover psychology, and others protest that this is unwarranted reductionism. To the latter I would say that we still are left with the largely historical task of accounting for the particular phenomena of specific languages and cultures, but I would ask whence come the explanatory principles in terms of which these accountings are cast, and in the case of comparative studies, whence come the categories and concepts that permit valid comparison. To the former I would say only that this is precisely the direction in which work in a number of fields of anthropology has been moving. To use a biological metaphor, the genotypical approach is gaining a certain ascendancy over the phenotypical approach in many quarters in both analytic-descriptive and in comparative studies.

Examples of the genotypical approach may be seen in the application of componential analysis to various aspects of culture, most notably kinship.[6] A similar approach has been used by Conklin (1955) with respect to color terms in Hanunóo, by Frake (1961) in the analysis of medical concepts, and presumably it could be extended to other spheres of culture as well. Related efforts are those of Kluckhohn to handle values in terms of binary oppositions [an effort in which he was inspired by the work of Roman Jakobson], of Frake (1962) with respect to settlement patterns, and of Lévi-Strauss in the analysis of myths. And although its source is mathematical, one might also cite in this connection the recent attempt by Davenport (1960) to apply what in game theory is called minimax utility to the observed behavior of Jamaican fishermen.

In many of these studies the ties with linguistic methods and linguistic data are strong, and in reviewing them one has the sense that here is an approach that promises to be equally productive in dealing with problems of language universals as it has proved to be in other spheres of culture. Frake (1962, p. 54) has clearly described the essence of the approach:

> A successful strategy for writing productive ethnographies must tap the cognitive world of one's informants. It must discover those features of objects and events which they regard as significant for defining concepts, formulating propositions, and making decisions. This conception of an ethnography requires that the units by which the data of observation are segmented, ordered, and interrelated be delimited and defined

according to contrasts inherent in the data themselves and not according to *a priori* notions of pertinent descriptive categories.

As we have already suggested at several points in this summary statement, the further problem then becomes: To what extent are these features whereby the world of experience is cognitively constituted universal? This question leads quite naturally to the final topic that I wish to discuss.

4. Language Universals and Linguistic Relativity

Among the many problems of common interest to students of human behavior perhaps none stand to gain greater clarification through systematic work on language universals than those deriving from the linguistic relativity hypothesis. Although adumbrated in the work of several intellectual forebears, notably Franz Boas (1911*a*) and Edward Sapir (1949, e.g., p. 162), the theory of linguistic relativity has been developed most fully and persuasively in a series of influential articles by the late Benjamin Lee Whorf (Carroll, ed., 1956). One cannot hope to improve on Whorf's own eloquent statement of his position:

> Actually, thinking is most mysterious, and by far the greatest light upon it we have is thrown by the study of language. This study shows that the forms of a person's thoughts are controlled by inexorable laws of pattern of which he is unconscious. These patterns are the unperceived intricate systematizations of his own language—shown readily enough by a candid comparison and contrast with other languages, especially those of a different linguistic family. His thinking itself is in a language—in English, in Sanskrit, in Chinese. And every language is a vast pattern-system, different from others, in which are culturally ordained the forms and categories by which the personality not only communicates, but also analyzes nature, notices or neglects types of relationships and phenomena, channels his reasoning, and builds the house of his consciousness [p. 252].

The implications of language universals for such a theory, patently, are far-reaching.

In dealing with the Whorfian theory, one must distinguish carefully between two different but related approaches to the study of the determining influences of language on cognitive processes and other symbolically mediated behavior. One approach grows essentially out of work in the psychological tradition, the other out of an anthropological tradition; these are the fields we have come to call respectively psycholinguistics and ethnolinguistics. The former most characteristically deals with the *generic* function of language in shaping cognitive processes, while the latter is typically concerned with the *comparative* problem of how structural differences among languages, in both their lexical and grammatical aspects, systematically relate to differences in the cognitive processes or other behavior of their speakers. The two approaches are complementary. In fact, the latter presupposes the former, but they approach the problem at different levels, using different kinds of linguistic data, and, at least in part, employing different research strategies.[7] It is of paramount importance, I feel, in working on these problems to be clear about which of these approaches is at issue or in what combination they are involved.

If the linguistic relativity hypothesis is to be put in proper perspective, it becomes crucially important to specify wherein languages are alike as well as wherein they differ. Logically, the very notion of variation assumes knowledge of the base from which phenomena vary. Indeed, it has been said that the ultimate task of science is precisely to account for variation.

It may well turn out that what is universal in language functions much more powerfully, and in a more fundamental way, to shape men's thoughts than what is different. There is some recent experimental work that suggests that this may indeed be so, for example, by Osgood and his associates. Some of this research has already been reported (1960), and some, on the cross-cultural and cross-linguistic generality of the basic dimensions of connotative meaning, is still largely unreported. Wallace is also suggestive on this point:

> The Whorfian and other hypotheses of extreme cultural relativism assert a radical dependence of the very form of rationality upon the local structure of language. But it seems more likely that the elemental notions which are the common base of the various logical and semantic calculi—notions of 'not', of 'and', of 'and/or', of 'identically equal', of 'equivalent', of 'order', and the like—are symbolic representations of processes intrinsic to such evidently universal psychic functions as discrimination, conditioning, and the generalization of learning. Indeed, a radical linguistic relativism would probably be, by its own axioms, not only incapable of proof but incapable of being described [1961*a*, p. 142].

The problem for future research on linguistic relativity is to reconcile the two positions represented above in the quotations from Whorf and Wallace.

5. Conclusion

If individual men or whole peoples dwelled alone in incommensurate worlds constituted only by their unique experiences or by those shared within the bounds of isolated communities, communication among men or among peoples would be impossible. Clearly, this is not so, but the matter is still naggingly indeterminate. We are left, then, with what has long been the essential question for anthropology as it has been for this symposium: How do we account for the simultaneous sense we have of the unique and the universal in our fellow men? What we have done in this symposium, and future work on language universals, will bring us a bit closer to the answer. And what knowledge we can gain of language universals will surely bring the intriguing but recalcitrant problem of linguistic relativity into sharper focus.

Notes

1. It is paradoxical that the anthropological approach most closely approximating the methods of present-day structural linguistics, that of French-British social anthropology, was developed abroad rather than in the United States, where linguistics and anthropol-

ogy have had such close relations over the years. However, this apparent paradox is diminished when one is reminded, as I have been by Dell Hymes and Thomas Sebeok, of the close links between linguistics and anthropology on the Continent. De Saussure, Durkheim, Mauss, Meillet, and, today, Lévi-Strauss, who self-consciously uses linguistics as a model, all share in this intellectual tradition. Nevertheless, the influence of linguistics on British social anthropology is largely derivative; and it is further remarkable that, except for Malinowski, British social anthropologists have shown so little interest in linguistics. A thoroughgoing account of the mutual relations between anthropology and linguistics both in this country and abroad, clearly, would be most illuminating of the joint history of our two disciplines.

2. In an early statement Kroeber (1916, p. 93) eloquently called attention to this dual task. Because of both its content and historical interest the passage is worth quoting at length:

   > ... the determination of what they [Algonkin and Indo-European] have in common, involving as it does the recognition of that in which they are different, is an essential purpose of the study of both; for whether our interest lies in the problem of the nature or that of the origin of human speech, a classification is involved. In its widest ultimate aspect philology is concerned not with Algonkin as such nor with Indo-European as such but with all languages. Only when speech in general, its scope and its methods, are better understood will both Algonkin and Indo-European, or for that matter any particular group of languages, be more truly understandable. The real aim of the study of any American tongue, as well as the aim of any deeper research in Indo-European philology, must therefore be the more precise and fundamental determination of their relations to all other languages; and this necessitates concepts and terms which are applicable in common. It is impossible to characterize the wolf in terms of his skeleton, the elephant of his embryology, the whale of his habits, and then to construct a classification which will help to reveal the inherent nature, the development, or the origin of the animal kingdom.

   I am indebted to Dell Hymes for calling my attention to this quotation.

3. These nine are: speech, material traits, art, mythology and scientific knowledge, religious practices, family and social system, property, government, and war.
4. In conversation with my colleague Kenneth L. Hale, I find that he had independently arrived at similar conclusions.

5. Moore's (1954) treatment of cultural accumulation, for instance, raises many of the same questions covered in Hoenigswald's paper.
6. See Goodenough (1956), Lounsbury (1956), Romney and Epling (1958), Wallace and Atkins (1960), Epling (1961), and Grimes (1962).
7. For an excellent discussion of various levels of approach to the linguistic relativity hypothesis see Fishman (1960).

References

Boas, F. (1911*a*). "Introduction," *Handbook of American Indian Languages*, Part I, Bureau of American Ethnology, Bul. 40. 1–83.

——— (1911*b*). *The Mind of Primitive Man*. New York.

Carroll, J. B. (ed.) (1956). *Language, Thought, and Reality: Selected Writings of Benjamin Lee Whorf*. New York, and Cambridge, Mass.

Casagrande, J. B. (1948). "Comanche Baby Language," *International Journal of American Linguistics* 14. 11–14.

Conklin, H. C. (1955). "Hanunóo Color Categories," *Southwestern Journal of Anthropology* 11. 339–344.

Davenport, W. (1960). "Jamaican Fishing: A Game-Theory Analysis," *Papers in Caribbean Anthropology*. Yale University Publications in Anthropology, No. 59.

Du Bruhl, E. L. (1958). *Evolution of the Speech Apparatus*. Springfield, Ill.

Emeneau, M. B. (1943). "Franz Boas as a Linguist," *Franz Boas, 1858–1942*, American Anthropological Association, Memoir 61.

Epling, P. J. (1961). "A Note on Njamal Kin-Term Usage," *Man* 66. 152–159.

Fishman, J. A. (1960). "A Systematization of the Whorfian Hypothesis," *Behavioral Science* 5. 323–339.

Frake, C. O. (1961). "Diagnosis of Disease Among the Subanun of Mindanao," *American Anthropologist* 53. 113-132.

——— (1962). "Cultural Ecology and Ethnography," *American Anthropologist* 64. 53–59.

Goodenough, W. (1956). "Componential Analysis and the Study of Meaning," *Language* 32. 195–216.

Greenberg, J. H. (1957). *Essays in Linguistics*, Viking Fund Publications in Anthropology, No. 24. New York.

Grimes, J. E. and B. F. (1962). "Semantic Distinctions in Huichol (Uto-Aztecan) Kinship," *American Anthropologist* 64. 104–114.

Hallowell, A. I. (1955). *Culture and Experience*. Philadelphia.

Kluckhohn, C. (1953). "Universal Categories of Culture," *Anthropology Today*, A. L. Kroeber (ed.). Chicago.

Kroeber, A. L. (1916). *Arapaho Dialects*, University of California Publications in American Archaeology and Ethnology 12. 3. 71–138. Berkeley, Calif.

———, and Jane Richardson (1940). *Three Centuries of Women's Dress Fashions; A Quantitative Analysis*, Anthropological Records 5.2.111-153. Berkeley, Calif.

Lenneberg, Eric H. (1960). "Language, Evolution, and Purposive Behavior," in *Culture in History: Essays in Honor of Paul Radin*, S. Diamond (ed.), 869–893. New York.

Linton, R. (1952). "Universal Ethical Principles: An Anthropological View," *Moral Principles of Action*, Ruth Anshen (ed.). New York.

Lounsbury, F. G. (1956). "A Semantic Analysis of the Pawnee Kinship Usage," *Language* 32. 158–194.

Moore, Harvey C., Jr. (1954). "Cumulation and Cultural Processes," *American Anthropologist* 56. 347–357.

Murdock, G. P. (1945). "The Common Denominators of Culture," *The Science of Man in the World Crisis*, R. Linton (ed.). New York.

——— (1949). *Social Structure*. New York.

——— (1959). "Cross-Language Parallels in Parental Kin Terms," *Anthropological Linguistics* 1. 9. 1–5.

Osgood, C. E. (1960). "The Cross-Cultural Generality of Visual-Verbal Synesthetic Tendencies," *Behavioral Science* 5. 146–169.

———, and T. A. Sebeok (1954). *Psycholinguistics, A Survey of Theory and Research Problems*. Baltimore.

Penfield, Wilder, and L. Roberts (1959). *Speech and Brain-Mechanisms*. Princeton, N. J.

Romney, A. K., and P. J. Epling (1958). "A Simplified Model of Kariera Kinship," *American Anthropologist* 60. 59–74.

Sapir, E. (1921). *Language*. New York.

——— (1949). "Language," *Selected Writings of Edward Sapir*, D. Mandelbaum (ed.). Berkeley, Calif.

Spuhler, J. N. (1959). "Somatic Paths to Culture," *The Evolution of Man's Capacity for Culture*, J. N. Spuhler (ed.). Detroit.

Steward, J. H. (1949). "Cultural Causality and Law: A Trial Formulation of the Development of Early Civilization," *American Anthropologist* 51. 1–27.

——— (1961). "Alfred Louis Kroeber, 1876–1960," *American Anthropologist* 63. 1038–1060.

Wallace, A. F. C. (1961*a*). "The Psychic Unity of Human Groups," *Studying Personality Cross-Culturally*, B. Kaplan (ed.). Evanston, Ill., and Elmsford, N. Y.

——— (1961*b*). *Culture and Personality*. New York.

———, and J. Atkins (1960). "The Meaning of Kinship Terms," *American Anthropologist* 62. 58–80.

Whiting, J. W. M. (1954). "The Cross-Cultural Method," *Handbook of Social Psychology*, G. Lindzey (ed.). Cambridge, Mass.

———, and I. L. Child (1953). *Child Training and Personality*. New Haven.

Wissler, C. (1923). *Man and Culture*. New York.

CHAPTER 11

LANGUAGE UNIVERSALS AND PSYCHOLINGUISTICS

CHARLES E. OSGOOD

University of Illinois

1. On Linguistics as a Science

At this conference we have been witness to a bloodless revolution. Quietly and without polemics we have seen linguistics taking a giant step from being merely a method for describing language to being a full-fledged science of language. Of course, as is true of any revolution, the step is only "in progress," and the participants do not see themselves as revolutionary; but in the eyes of a sufficiently remote observer, the change can be noted and its significance recorded.

Linguistics is shifting its concern from the uniquely differential to the broadly general. All of the papers prepared for this conference, and the discussion that completed it, take this revolution for granted. Twenty, even five, years ago, this could not have happened—without bloody eyes and heads. Today it happened quietly. Of course, what is happening in linguistics is also happening in the other sciences of man. There are pervasive swings in the purposes and viewpoints of the social sciences. While Bloomfield was forming the objectivity and operationalism of descriptive linguistics, Watson and Weiss were setting the framework for an objectively descriptive psychology. Ghosts, like *mind* and *meaning*, were laid; methodology became king. Uniquenesses were sought, and found, and empiricism reigned.

But pendulums have a way of reversing their direction. In the very process of describing languages and behavior, linguists and psychologists could not deny the evidences of generality that kept presenting themselves. Beneath the surface of uniqueness, a bedrock of commonness has begun to impress itself upon us again. It is a commonness that is *not* arbitrary, and therefore it is interesting scientifically. What does being *a science* imply?

At the lowest level, a science is merely a new way of talking about familiar phenomena. It is an argot which binds the elite in a warm embrace and separates them from the *hoi polloi*. Working within their own discipline and following the rules, the members of the cult may reach a higher level—of descriptive rigor and carefully defined constructs. Linguistics did this with a sureness and aplomb that embarrassed the other social sciences. Of course, it was assisted by the "chunkiness" of language, and the aptness of its disciples in creating "chunks" where only amorphous continua may exist. But there is a higher level of description—quantification. Here, I think, the courtship with psychology over the past decade or more has been having a significant impact. It is clearly evident in Sol Saporta's paper, for example.

But rigorous, quantitative description of a defined set of phenomena still does not represent a full-blown science. There are two more facets to the whole, and these linguistics undertook here at the Conference. First, there are general empirical *functions* relating construct to construct—the more of this, the more (or less) of that. Empirical science piles function upon function. Psychologists have spent fifty years or more striving to make their empiricism secure. However, an impressive structure of empirical functions invites interpretation—*theory.* Without theory, the massive collection of functions remains that—an incredible challenge to analysis and simplification. Theory is thus a higher-level description; it is a set of principles which, economically and elegantly, encompasses the whole set of functions. Linguistics hasn't arrived, but it now seems well on the way.

What will be the character of the basic principles of linguistic science? Of course I am biased, and I am well aware of the dangers in reductionism, but as a psycholinguist I am equally aware of the fact that language behavior is part of human behavior in general. Just as psychologists are now again reaching out toward universals that cross the barriers of both language and culture, so am I sure that linguists will find their basic principles in the universals of humanness. There will be no special theory of language behavior in psychology, nor should there be in linguistics. Even the hierarchical structure of language is replicated in nonlanguage behavior. The phonic fingers that grasp the doorknob are a unit within the morphic act of opening the door, which in turn is a unit within the larger complex of "going to the store"—a sememe? By virtue of its rigorous description, linguistics has thrown down the gauntlet to psychology; it is a challenge for psychology to try to comprehend and systematize within its principles the neatly ordered universals of language behavior.

It is precisely at the level of language universals that psycholinguistics has meaning and that a true science is a-borning. I recall with deep pleasure the summer seminar at Indiana in 1953, where linguists and psychologists shared themselves freely both in being educated and in educating. While the linguists were pressing the psychologists toward greater rigor in their descriptions of behavior, the psychologists were pressing the linguists toward greater universality in their conceptions. The psychology of language behavior can be useful only in terms of universals. Here are the nexuses between our fields. Where languages commonly use bilabial nasals for "mamma" terms, where they are commonly more susceptible to change in antecedent rather than subsequent positions, where they display a regular ebb and flow in the ratio of phonemes to features—*here* psychology can find a purchase.

But of what kind are the useful universals of language? As one who has been exposed to this conference, I must stress a distinction whose omission will lead us toward dust-bowl empiricism rather than toward a productive science. There are two kinds of universals:

> U_1. *Phenotypes: empirical generalizations that hold for all languages.* As Hockett pointed out, many of these are useful in a definitional sense—they would help a Martian linguist distinguish between human language and organismic communication more generally. But the very fact that *all* human

languages display property *X*, even if it is not definitional, renders property *X* mainly interesting, not particularly useful in science-making.

U_2. *Genotypes: theoretical generalizations, principles in a theory of language behavior, that hold for all languages.* These will be the guts of a science of linguistics. They are the fundamental laws governing the production of semantic regularities, the production of grammatical regularities, the source of language change.

And here we come to one of the nubs of conflict in our conference. There are some who have clung to the traditional notion that *only* the truly universal universals are significant. Traditional? Yes. I have been a walking pincushion for the barbs of linguists who have gleefully blunted my probes for psycholinguistic universality with counter-points of "exceptions." I say that, as a matter of psycholinguistic theory, there will be greater diversity among prefixes than among suffixes in languages. My linguist friend says yes—*but* there is language *Z*, with which he happens to be familiar, where the reverse holds true. The point is that scientific laws are not merely honored by their exceptions—they are literally manufactured out of their exceptions. Exceptions reflect interactions among the whole set of functional laws. Language *Z* does not display regularity *X because* laws 1, 2, and 3 operate in one way under condition alpha and quite differently under condition beta. In other words, it is the nonuniversal, *statistical* universals that are the most interesting to a science of language behavior. Out of the complex patterning of nonuniversal (but lawful) phenomena we will draw forth the underlying principles of a science of language.

However, the search for universal universals—and the failure to find them (quantitatively described)—is essential to the building of a science of language. As this conference has made abundantly clear, there are literally thousands of potential universals—or quasi universals. The important thing at this point is to expand the search for universals of language behavior *and to systematize them in the context of psycholinguistic theory*. When Bloomfield said "the only useful generalizations about language are inductive generalizations," he was telling only one part of the story of science; the other part is the hypothetico-deductive system of principles in which inductive generalizations are organized into predictive theory. Thoughtful analysis of the array of quasi universals, and their interactions, will generate general principles which can then be tested against the whole set of human communication systems. As both Murdock and Lounsbury implied, the sample of languages need not be exhaustive, but it must be representative if these tests are to be adequate.

How should the universals of human language be systematized? Here I can do no more than suggest that their ordering be relevant to what we now think are the underlying principles of language behavior. Of course, these principles will be wrong—if not in fundamental assumption, then certainly in detail—but this is the stuff of which science is made. For the present, I think our search for universals and our presentation of them should be guided by (1) our general methodology and its constructs, and (2) our present assumptions about their bases, for example, in what we know about human perceptual organization, in what we know about human concept formation, in what we know about human skills, and in what we know about human meaning systems. So we look for universalness in the phonemic and morphemic system, for universalness in rules of transformation, for universalness of the semantic map of the world—and in doing so we certainly miss many potential universals that the linguistic science of another age would seek and record. But science-making is a slow and dubious process.

There are, however, some fundamental divisions of the plot that we can make a priori grounds. We should make a distinction between *semantic and structural* universals (I persist with this word, but I am referring to *regularities*). The former will probably relate to the psychology of symbolic processes and the latter to skill and integrational mechanisms. We should also distinguish between *synchronic and diachronic* universals. Again, the psychological principles governing language patterning or structure will probably not be entirely the same as those governing language change—which is primarily a learning process. And the fundamental methodological distinctions between *phonological, morphological, and syntactical* levels of language must not be forgotten. This gives us a 2 × 2 × 3 framework within which to pattern our search for universal laws of language behavior—synchronic/diachronic; semantic/structural; and phonological/morphological/syntactic—a neat space with twelve regions within which to allocate our universal (or quasi-universal) phenomena.

Without trying in every case to specify the Conference papers which gave rise to these notions, but reacting to their sum, let me now suggest four fundamental psycholinguistic generalities that, on the most naive and unresearched level, seem to offer starting points for a science of language behavior.

1. *At all levels* (phonological, morphological, and syntactic), *language systems like other behavioral systems will follow a principle of progressive differentiation in their development*. This underlying law will be reflected in a large number of empirical universals of the following general type: if a language displays characteristic *c*, then it will also display characteristics *b* and *a*; and if it has *b*, it will also have *a*; but not vice versa. Many years ago, Roman Jakobson pointed to such unidirectional dependencies in the development of phonemic distinctions in child language; at the Conference we have added Ferguson's analysis of the development of nasals and Greenberg's analysis of the unidirectional dependency of the dual upon the prior differentiation of singular and plural, for example. It may be noted in passing that the same principle of progressive differentiation has long been a major operating notion in developmental psychology, as in the development of motor skills.

2. *At all levels of units in a language, the competing alternatives will be organized hierarchically in terms of frequency of occurrence and with a relatively low-entropy distribution approximating the Zipf function.* Greenberg's data on the relative frequencies of sentence-types, on the relative frequencies of suffixing versus prefixing versus infixing, and so forth, based on a sample of thirty languages provide the beginnings for such an analysis at the

syntactical level. Saporta's present data on the relative frequencies of alternative morpheme lengths in Spanish and his previous data on the relative frequencies of consonantal clusters in English provide suggestive beginnings at the phonological level. In some research of my own on the cross-linguistic and cross-cultural generality of meaning systems (to which I will return later), we have found rather remarkable stability of the slope of the frequency-diversity functions for qualifiers elicited by standard associational procedures in some nine language/culture communities. All of these "universals" suggest that when the human organism must choose repeatedly among a set of alternatives, it tends to choose a few alternatives with very high frequencies and many alternatives only rarely. And this pervasive law is not restricted to humans, either; rats tested in a "checkerboard" maze where all alternative routes are equally long and equally rewarded display the same lopsided distributions of preference. Living organisms seem to be antientropic in nature.

3. *At all levels of language organization, whenever there are competing means of achieving some criterion of communication performance, these competing means will be related inversely as a compensating system.* In other words, if both characteristics x and y are alternative means of achieving the same communicative end, as x increases y will decrease, both in one language over time and across many languages synchronically. We have seen suggestive (if not sufficient) evidence for several compensating systems of this sort. In maintaining an optimum balance between the discriminatory capacities of speakers and of hearers, the ratio of number of phonemes to number of distinctive features (and hence the maximum possible number of phonemes) seems to oscillate about an efficiency value of 50%; if a code becomes too tightly efficient, speakers will begin to add in redundant features in order to be understood, but as this process inevitably overshoots its mark, and the code becomes too redundant, speakers will begin to drop out certain features and "get away with it"—and the cycle begins again. Other compensating systems have been mentioned here: Inflection seems to compensate with word-order as an alternative means of keeping the syntactical house in order;

size of phonemic inventory seems to bear a compensatory relation to average length of morphemes. Relations of this kind can be studied either synchronically (across representative samples of the world's languages) or diachronically (across historical time-samples of a single language).

4. *At all levels, the laws of language change (diachronic universals) will be found to reside in the principles and conditions of learning as they operate upon individual speakers and hearers.* Given the whole tenor of our conference, this may seem rather obvious, but I think it needs stress. For one thing, it leads us to look more closely into the diachronic aspects of the language behavior of individuals for our general principles of language change—the child learning his first language, the adult learning a second language, the aphasic losing and then recovering language, the effects of fatigue, alcohol, and various drugs upon language performance. Although the structure of a language as it exists at a particular moment in time provides the conditions for learning (points of discrimination difficulty, loci of competing divergent hierarchies as opposed to loci of facilitating convergent hierarchies, regions of overabundance or underabundance of the lexicon, for example), it is the performance of hundreds of thousands of individual speakers and hearers under these common conditions that generates diachronic change. The relation of the efficiency of the phonemic code (already mentioned) to phenomena of language learning in children should be particularly interesting in this respect.

2. On Semantic Universality

All of the preceding was an attempt to write down the essence of what I said informally, and probably better, on the last day of the Conference. Now I would like to say something about research on the generality of affective meaning systems that is presently in progress at The Institute of Communications Research at Illinois. This can be viewed as a footnote to Stephen Ullmann's paper on "Semantic Universals."

Over the past decade we have made a dozen or more factor-analytic studies of the structure of meaningful judgments of

American English–speaking subjects, and we have kept finding the same three dominant factors or dimensions: an Evaluative Factor (represented by scales like *good-bad*, *pleasant-unpleasant*, and *positive-negative*), a Potency Factor (represented by scales like *strong-weak*, *heavy-light*, and *hard-soft*), and an Activity Factor (represented by scales like *fast-slow*, *active-passive*, and *excitable-calm*).

The problem before us now is this: how common is this semantic framework across the range of people doing the judging and across different kinds of concepts being judged? Is it limited to Americans speaking the English language, or is it shared by all humans regardless of their language or their culture? Is it the same for all concepts, be they aesthetic or political, familiar or unfamiliar, words or pictures? Let me anticipate our conclusion from a large number of studies—we find that the evaluation-potency-activity system is remarkably stable across people but quite unstable across the concepts being judged. We will want to inquire into *why* this should be so. But first, some evidence.

When a group of people judge a set of concepts against a set of scales, representing what we call "a semantic differential," a cube of data is generated. Each cell in this cube represents how a particular person judged a particular concept against a particular scale, using a number from 1 to 7. For example, in one cell we might have a number 7, this being one man's judgment of the concept TORNADO against a *slow-fast* scale (indicating that he thinks of TORNADO as *extremely fast*). In the next cell down in the cube we find a number 4, this being his judgment of TORNADO in terms of *honest-dishonest* (the number 4 showing that he feels neither one way nor the other on this scale). Each person, as a subject, is a slice of this cube from front to back; each concept being judged, like TORNADO or MY MOTHER, is a slice of the cube from left to right; and each semantic scale is a horizontal slice or row from top to bottom. In analyzing these data we usually are interested in the correlations between scales—that is, in determining how the semantic dimensions cluster together—but we can rule these correlations either across subjects or across concepts, and we can do it either for all subjects or concepts as a group or for individual subjects or concepts. In other words, there are many ways we can slice our semantic cake, and each method of slicing serves to answer a different kind of question.

The most critical test for generality of these semantic factors clearly would be *between people differing widely in both language and culture*. We have already made a number of cross-cultural comparisons—involving Japanese, Koreans, Greeks, and Navajo, Zuni, and Hopi Indians in the American Southwest—and the similarities in factor structure have been striking. But, for the most part, these studies have involved simply translating English scales into the various languages, and we are open to the criticism that we have forced people of other countries to operate within the limits imposed by an American English factor system. However, we do have one study done completely independently by the Marketing Center Company in Tokyo in which the same general factors appeared, and we are now in the middle of a large-scale cross-cultural study, involving some twelve countries and as ideal testing conditions as we can devise.

With the help of cooperating social scientists in each country—without whom this type of research could not be done—we are collecting data in Japan, Hong Kong, India (Hindi in New Delhi and Kannada in Mysore), Afghanistan, Iran, Lebanon, Yugoslavia, Poland, Finland, Holland, Belgium, and France, along with the United States as a comparison base. We start with a list of 100 familiar concepts that have been selected by linguists and anthropologists as being "culture-fair" and that have survived a stringent back-translation test with bilinguals for all of the six language-families represented. This is the only point where translation is involved and could influence the results. From this point on, everything is done in the native language and with native monolingual subjects in each country.

The first step is to have 100 young high-school boys in each country give the first qualifiers (adjectives in English) that occur to them when each of the concepts is given as a stimulus—for example, to the word TREE one boy might say *tall*, another *green*, another *big*, and so forth. This basketful of 10, 000 qualifiers (100 subjects times 100 concepts) is shipped to the University of

Illinois, where, using IBM and ILLIAC high-speed computers, we determine a rank order of these ways of qualifying, in terms of total frequency of usage, diversity of usage across the 100 concepts, and independence of usage with respect to each other. We already have these rank-frequency-and-diversity measures for nine countries; they are not only highly similar in statistical properties, but when the ranked qualifiers are translated into English and then correlated with both English and each other, the correlations are all significantly positive. In other words, the dominant ways of qualifying experience, of describing aspects of objects and events, tend to be very similar, regardless of what language one uses or what culture one happens to have grown up in.

The second step in each country is to take the 50 highest-ranking qualifiers, elicit their common opposites so as to make scales like *good-bad* and *big-little* out of them, and then have a new group of 100 young men judge each such scale against every other of the 50 scales—to what extent is *good* either *big* or *little*, to what extent is *big* either *happy* or *sad*, and so on? This new basketful of data is shipped back to Illinois, where we do the correlations and factor analyses that represent our first test of the structure of the semantic space. For the six countries that have been carried to this stage, I can report that the first two factors are definitely as expected—Evaluation and Potency; the third factor is more variable across countries, but seems to have at least the "flavor" of Activity (semantic properties like *hot*, *fast*, *young*, and *noisy* keep appearing). We hope that the third step will clarify this situation. Here we will have yet another group of similar subjects judge the original 100 culture-fair concepts against the 50 semantic scales, correlate each scale with every other as used in actually judging concepts, and do another factor analysis. We are only beginning this phase of the research.

What is the purpose of all this busywork in many lands and many tongues? The first, purely scientific purpose is to demonstrate that human beings the world over, no matter what their language or culture, do share a common meaning system, do organize experience along similar symbolic dimensions. A second, more practical purpose of this research is to develop and apply instruments for measuring "subjective culture"—meanings, attitudes, values, and the like—instruments that can be shown to be comparable across differences in both language and culture. The demonstration of common semantic factors—if indeed they can be demonstrated—makes it quite feasible to construct efficient "semantic differentials" for measuring the meanings of critical concepts cross-culturally, with reasonable confidence that the yardstick is something better than a rubber-band. Ultimately, it would be my hope that both the demonstration of a shared semantic framework and the application of semantic measuring instruments would contribute to better international communication and understanding.

Now, let us flip the coin over and ask about the *generality of semantic factor structures across the concepts being judged.* You will recall that the cube of data generated when a group of subjects judges a sample of concepts against a set of scales makes it feasible to compute separate correlation matrices for each concept "slice" and factorize such matrices. In what we refer to as our "Thesaurus Study"—because the adjectives were sampled from that source on a rational, representative basis— 20 different concepts, like FOREIGNER, KNIFE, MODERN ART, DEBATE, and HOSPITAL, were judged against 76 scales by 100 college subjects.

Now, imagine the 20 separate correlation matrices for the different concepts lined up as a deck; if we go through the deck at the point of intersection of a particular pair of scales (for example, of *sober-drunk* vs. *mature-youthful*), we will isolate 20 *r*'s, one for each concept. If scale relations were reasonably constant over concepts, then we would expect only minor variations within such rows of correlations—but this proved *not* to be the case. Correlations were found to vary as much as from +.60 to −.60 in the same row. A couple of examples will serve to suggest what is happening: *sober* goes with *youthful* for the concept DAWN, but *sober* goes with *mature* for the concept UNITED NATIONS; *pleasurable* goes with *feminine* for the concept MOTHER, but *pleasurable* goes with *masculine* for the concept ADLAI STEVENSON. It would appear that the nature of the concept being judged exercises a restriction on scale meanings. What about the correspondence of factors derived from such single-concept matrices? Here the picture is better: something identifiable as an Evaluative factor appeared for each concept, and it was usually the first in order of magnitude; something identifiable as a Potency (or Dynamism) factor appeared for all but two concepts; but other factors varied in most inconsistent ways.

This instability of scale relations and factors across concepts contrasts sharply with the stability we have found across people. This shows up most clearly in studies where both types of generality can be compared. In one experiment designed specifically to get at this problem, college girls in both Japan and the United States judged three different classes of concepts—patches of color, simple line drawings, and abstract words like LOVE and PEACE—against a 35-scale form of translation-equivalent semantic differential. Separate scale-by-scale correlation matrices and factor analyses were run for each of the six combinations of two subject-groups and three concept-classes. Now, if our hypothesis—that semantic systems are more stable across people than across concepts—holds, then factorial similarities should be higher when Japanese and American girls judge the same materials (both judge colors, both judge forms, and so forth) than when the same group judges different materials. This was true in every case. Even the salience of the three major factors shifted in the same ways for both Japanese and Americans—Activity is the dominant factor in judging colors for both groups, Potency tends to be the dominant factor in judging line forms, and Evaluation is clearly the dominant factor in judging abstract words, for both groups.

So much for evidence. Now let me speculate a bit on the "why" of these observations. Why do we find such wide generality of the evaluation-potency-activity framework across people, both within and between languages and cultures? And why, given generality across people, do we find such lack of generality in semantic structure across the classes of concepts they judge? While I certainly don't know the answers to these questions, I do have some hunches.

First, I must confess that, when we began this research over ten years ago, I had expected the major dimensions of the semantic space to reflect the ways in which our sensory apparatus divides up the world. This was in flat contradiction to my own behavioristic theory of meaning, in which the semantic components should be *responselike* in character. The accumulating facts have proved my expectation wrong and my theory at least "righter"—the dominant factors of Evaluation, Potency, and Activity that keep reappearing certainly do seem to have a responselike character, seemingly reflecting the ways we can react to meaningful events rather than the ways we receive them.

But these major factors also seem to have an *affective* as well as a responselike character. The similarity of our major factors to Wundt's tridimensional theory of feeling—pleasantness, strain, and excitement—has been pointed out to me. And, as a matter of fact, we have done a number of experiments on the meanings of facial expressions—coming out with Pleasantness, Control, and Activation as three factors which seem pretty much to exhaust the semantic space of facial communication. The similarity between these factors in emotional communication and those found in our more general linguistic studies suggests that the latter may also have their grounding in the affective reaction system.

Let me speculate a bit further and suggest that the highly generalized nature of the affective reaction system—the fact that it is independent of any particular sensory modality and yet participates with all of them—is at once the reason why Evaluation, Potency, and Activity appear as dominant factors *and* the psychological basis for metaphor and synesthesia. It is *because* such diverse sensory experiences as a *white* circle (rather than black), a *straight* line (rather than crooked), a *rising* melody (rather than a falling one), a *sweet* taste (rather than a sour one), a *caressing* touch (rather than an irritating scratch)—it is because all these diverse experiences can share a common affective meaning that one easily and lawfully translates from one sensory modality into another in synesthesia and metaphor. This is also the basis for the high interscale correlations which mathematically determine the nature and orientation of general factors. In other words, the "common market in meaning" seems to be based firmly in the biological systems of emotional and purposive behavior that all humans share.

The evidence for a shared framework of affective meanings obviously has implications for the types of semantic universals discussed by Ullmann in connection with metaphor and synesthesia. I would go so far as to suggest that in this shared framework we have the very breeding ground of metaphor. One other experiment of a somewhat different nature is so relevant to the problem of universals in metaphor and synesthesia that I will describe it briefly.

Anglo, Navajo, Mexican-Spanish, and Japanese subjects were shown in serial order a set of thirteen cards; each card was divided in half by a vertical line, and on each side of the line was a simple line drawing. The paired drawings on each card differed from each other in only one visual property, for example, *blunt* vs. *sharp*, *thick* vs. *thin*, and *large* vs. *small*. These words merely describe how the drawings differed; the cards themselves contained no words. A subject would be given a term in his own language, such as "happy," and then he would go through the deck pointing to the visual stimulus of each pair that seemed "to go best," or "be most appropriate to" this word. Thus if I were doing it for "happy," I would point to the multicolored rather than the black-and-white, the upward arrow rather than the downward arrow, the white circle rather than the black, and so forth.

The first observation worth noting is the high degree of agreement over subjects *within* each language-culture group: approximately 50 % of the 364 items (28 verbal concepts judged against 13 visual alternatives) showed intracultural agreements significant at the 1 % level. What about cross-cultural agreement in visual-verbal synesthesia? The fairest test is to take just those items where *both* groups being compared show significant *intra*-cultural agreement and ask what percentage of them agree in direction of choice, that is, show *inter*-cultural agreement. Applying this test, we find that Navajo and Anglo groups agree on the direction of 87% of such items, and all other group comparisons yield agreements above 90%, Japanese with Americans being 99% and Americans with Mexican-Spanish being 100%, for example. All of these proportions are significant at well beyond the .001 level. In other words, we have evidence for a high degree of universality in what visual alternatives are perceived as synesthetically appropriate to translation-equivalent word meanings.

Now, if for the word "happy" a subject points to the *colored* one, the *up* one, the *white* one, and so on, and if for him the word "sad" is *functionally opposite* in meaning, then for the word "sad" he should point to the *uncolored* one, the *down* one, the *black* one, and so on—producing, thereby, a negative correlation between the responses to the two words. We found that verbal concepts treated functionally as opposites in English are treated in the same manner by Navajos and Mexican-Spanish—with the one glaring exception of *fast-slow* for the Navajo (my anthropologist friends tell me that the Navajo conceive of *fast* and *slow* as both being aspects of motion as opposed to *motionless*). The Japanese data correspond to the American oppositions in every respect. We have, then, rather impressive evidence for cross-linguistic sharing of visual-verbal synesthetic tendencies.

Finally, what about the lack of generality of semantic factor structure across concept-classes? All of the evidence we have clearly indicates that there is *interaction between concepts and scales in the process of semantic judgment*. What are the implications of this? For one thing, this means that from the standpoint of applied semantic measurement there can be no such thing as "*The* Semantic Differential." So, for particular concept-classes, we will need to construct appropriate differentials, and in the area of personality measurement we have already made a start. From the standpoint of psycholinguistic theory, the fact of concept/scale interaction invites fresh speculation about how it operates—and therefore a host of new experiments, most of which are hardly to the point of conception.

If I were to ask you the question "Is a BABY *large* or *small?*" you would undoubtedly say "small." And if I were to ask you "Is a railroad SPIKE *large* or *small?*" you would probably say "large." After all, within the class of human organisms, a BABY *is* "a small one," and within the class of nails a SPIKE *is* "a large one." I think the semantic differential technique, in which a single stimulus is judged successively against a series of different scales, is one which tends to draw out these intraclass connotations of signs. In all other psychophysical methods with which I am familiar, even the so-called "absolute judgment" method, many different stimuli are judged successively against a single scale—for example, in judging weights or in scaling the loudness of tones. I think that this method tends to draw out the denotative meanings of signs. Note that if I ask you to *compare* BABY and SPIKE in terms of size, you immediately say that BABY is "larger," now disregarding the intraclass connotations of these objects.

What has all this to do with concept/scale interaction? I think that the semantic differential is subject to what might be called *denotative contamination.* The terms that define our scales have variable denotative meanings as well as their generalized affective connotation. The denotation of *masculine-feminine* is brought out by the concept ADLAI STEVENSON, whereas its potency connotation is elicited by the concept DYNAMO; a concept like LAVA taps the denotation of *hot-cold,* whereas concepts like JAZZ and FESTIVAL call forth the general connotation of *hot.* It is clear that if certain scales are denotatively relevant to certain classes of concepts, they will fall away from their usual affective factors and hence change the total structure. We have just begun a series of experiments comparing the two basic judgmental methods—one concept at a time against many scales versus many concepts against a single scale at a time—and I am hopeful that these experiments will help us disentangle denotative and connotative aspects of meaning.

Another probable source of concept/scale interaction is what we call *cognitive interaction.* This is the tendency for two simultaneously evoked meanings to change each other in the direction of compromise—presumably because the affective system can only assume one "posture" at a time. In making semantic-differential judgments, one first looks at, and then "keeps in mind," the concept being judged, while he goes down the page placing appropriate check-marks on each scale. If he is judging the concept MOTHER, for example, and it has an intensely positive evaluation, this meaning should interact with those of the scale terms and cause them to become momentarily *more* evaluative. In mathematical terms, this means a general rotation of scales toward the dominant evaluative factor. In other words, each concept or concept-class will tend to produce rotation of scales toward its own characteristic attribute in the semantic space. We now have some experiments on the planning boards in which we will try to predict the rotations of scales in the factor space from knowing the measured meanings of the concepts and the scale terms that are interacting.

3. On an Absent but Very Lively Ghost

Considering the topic of this Conference, surprisingly little was said about Benjamin Lee Whorf and his works. After all, it was he who gave the relativity-universality pendulum its strongest push in one direction and got it into a position where we could push it back the other way. I am sure that had he been alive today, Whorf would have participated in this Conference and enjoyed it. And I think he would have agreed with much of what we all had to say.

But I think that early in the game he would have insisted on a distinction between three types of universals. First, there are *linguistic universals* (as well as uniquenesses). Just as the crude criterion of mutual translatability testifics to some universality, so does the equally crude criterion of mutual unintelligibility testify to some uniqueness. The success of descriptive linguistics depends on the fact that all languages display a hierarchical structure of units within units, yet the selection of units at each level (e.g., phonemes from the common phonetic stock) seems to be quite arbitrary. Similarly, although the lexicons of languages are largely arbitrary, in the sense of correlations between noises and events, *what* is talked about and *how* it is talked about do not seem to be arbitrary at all. The second type is *psychological universals* (and uniquenesses). The principles of learning seem to be quite universal, but certainly what must be learned with each language and in each culture is quite different. Similarly, the dimensionality of emotional feeling and expression seems to be universal, yet how one feels about *rain*, *mother*, *dog*, or *God* is highly variable.

However, Whorf was not interested in either linguistic or psychological universalities or uniquenesses per se, but rather a third alternative. The hypothesis to which we associate his name is *psycholinguistic* in nature. It concerns itself with relations *between* linguistic and psychological (cognitive) processes. Drawing on his extensive comparative studies of SAE (Standard Average European) and American Indian languages, he hypothesized that how a person perceives the world about him, how he thinks, and even how he formulates his natural philosophy—thus, his *Weltanschauung*—must depend upon the language he uses.

I believe that the data I have briefly summarized on the generality of affective meaning systems and on the sharing of certain metaphorical and synesthetic tendencies are contra-Whorfian in nature. They say, in effect, that despite gross differences in both language and culture, the underlying structure of the affective meaning space and the metaphorical translations it facilitates remain pretty much the same. And this is a strictly psycholinguistic area, relating linguistic phenomena to psychological phenomena. But I think there is also sufficient positive evidence to support Whorf's thesis as well—so it looks as though we have a dilemma on our hands.

There are several difficulties with Whorf's own materials as far as scientific evidence is concerned. In the first place, it is largely anecdotal; lacking the customary controls of scientific experimentation, his examples must stand as hypothesis-setting rather than as hypothesis-testing demonstrations. Secondly, the anecdotes usually hinge on literal translation from some other language (usually an Indian language) into SAE (usually English), with comments then being made upon the strangeness of the world view apparently expressed. Reversing this procedure serves to lay bare its pitfalls: Suppose a Hopi linguist were to literally translate the English term *breakfast* as "the termination of a period of religious abstinence"; he might then conclude that contemporary English speakers must think of each night's sleep as a religious experience, because each morning's meal serves to break a fast! Thirdly, although the hypothesis is clearly *psycho*-linguistic in nature, Whorf's analyses are usually restricted to the linguistic component—he rarely makes any independent observations on the cognitive processes of language users.

One example from his many writings must serve to illustrate these difficulties. In his "Languages and Logic" (*Technology Review*, M. I. T., 1941), Whorf describes how Apache would refer to the same physical event that English speakers would call "a dripping spring." "Apache erects the statement on a verb *ga:* 'be white (including clear, uncolored, and so on)'. With a prefix *no-* the meaning of downward motion enters: 'whiteness moves downward'. Then *tó*, meaning both 'water' and 'spring', is prefixed. The result corresponds to our 'dripping spring', but synthetically it is: 'as water, or springs, whiteness moves downward.' " And then Whorf concludes, "How utterly unlike our way of thinking!" But nothing about Apache *thinking* has actually been observed. To claim that Apache speakers must perceive a waterfall differently than we because their way of talking about it is different, and then infer how they perceive solely from how they talk, is completely tautological. Unfortunately, much of the "evidence" for or against Whorf's hypothesis has remained at this level.

On the other hand, there is at least some adequately designed experimental evidence. I shall cite two of the clearest studies available. The first deals with the color lexicon and comes from a series of papers by Brown and Lenneberg, and by Lenneberg himself. The color spectrum is an ideal aspect of the environment to study psycholinguistically because it is continuous in human experience, whereas color terminologies are categorical. First of all, on the intracultural level, it was shown that sections of the spectrum (i.e., particular color chips) vary in their *codability* for English-speaking subjects; whereas a chip near 680 *mu* might be consistently called "red" with short latency, a chip near 600 *mu* might be labeled slowly, variably, and with complex circumlocutions. The psycholinguistic question was this: Do differences in codability relate to some independently measurable cognitive process? First *recognition* and then *ease of learning* were studied, and in both cases it was shown that ease of cognitive manipulation varied with codability of the color stimuli. Then, cross-culturally, it was shown that Zuni speakers display the same relation between codability and cognitive facility, even though the relative codabilities of various portions of the spectrum did not correspond for Zuni and English speakers —that is, their denotative assignments were arbitrarily different.

The second experimental study is reported by Casagrande and deals with the influence of grammatical structure upon cognition. It is obligatory in Navajo to signal the *shape* of objects being dealt with by an appropriate affix on the verb. The relativity hypothesis requires that Navajo speakers, as compared with speakers of a language not making this distinction, should be more responsive to the shape of objects in their cognitive activities. Casagrande first compared Navajo-dominant children of varying ages with English-dominant children of the same racial and cultural background on an object-sorting test; as predicted, the Navajo-dominant subjects were shown to rely more on shape similarities and differences, and this dependence increased with age. Although a group of Harlem schoolchildren, matched with the previous subjects for age and sex, behaved like the English-dominant Navajos, a group of white middle-class children in Boston behaved more like the Navajo-dominant Navajos— a result which points to the complexity of factors, cultural as well as linguistic, that may be operating on cognitive processes.

More evidence could be adduced, but I think this is sufficient. We thus have the apparent paradox of experimental evidence supporting both the hypothesis of psycholinguistic universality and the hypothesis of psycholinguistic relativity. The situation remains paradoxical, however, only as long as we fail to discern any basis for distinguishing the phenomena fitting one hypothesis from those supporting the other.

Let me refer, rather arbitrarily, to the aspect of "meaning" tapped by the major factors of the semantic differential as the *connotative meaning* of signs. There is another aspect of "meaning" which deals with the elaborate sets of essentially arbitrary correlations between linguistic and nonlinguistic events—for example, between the noise "apple" in English and the visual perception of APPLE object—and this I shall refer to as *denotative meaning*. This is one of the meanings of "meaning" with which linguists and philosophers have been primarily concerned. You may question the propriety of my choice of terms here, but the thing I am concerned with is that we agree that there is a significant distinction within semantic phenomena—between the affective reactions to signs and their coding functions.

Now, I assume that connotative aspects of meaning are mediated by the relatively "primitive" affective nervous system. Indeed, the fact that in a number of experimental studies on the emotional meanings of facial expressions we have found essentially the same dominant factors (Pleasantness, Control, and Activation) as in our more general linguistic studies supports this identification. I further assume that the innumerable arbitrary correlations between linguistic and nonlinguistic events that I refer to as denotative meaning are mediated by the sensory and motor discrimination systems of the "new" brain—regions where lesions may produce various aphasic syndromes. (In this connection, it is at least suggestive that in a few tests of visual-verbal synesthesia with aphasic patients they showed little or no impairment, even though they could not even verbalize the differences between the visual stimuli on the cards.) Both of these biological systems—the affective, energizing system and the sensorimotor discrimination system—are integrated in ordinary behavior, and there is no reason to suppose things should be different in language behavior. As a matter of fact, I suspect that interaction between these systems is the basis for the concept/scale interactions we have found in semantic measurement.

My suggested resolution of the paradox goes like this: *Whenever the psycholinguistic phenomena in question depend upon the structure of the mediating systems* (either affective or discriminatory), *psycholinguistic universality will be found.* This, of course, is precisely because these mediating systems are panhuman biologically. *Whenever the psycholinguistic phenomena are independent of the structure of the mediating systems, even though they are mediated by them, psycholinguistic relativity will be the rule.* And this, of course, is precisely because both mediating systems are essentially *tabula rasa*, and "what leads to what" is dependent on experience. A few illustrations may make what appears just a little self-evident—if not downright tautological—more meaningful and useful.

First, as far as the affective mediating system is concerned, our data show that it is the factorial structure—the basic dimensions along which feeling-tones are differentiated—that is immutable and overrides differences in both language and culture. Phenomena which depend upon this shared structure display universality. Thus, since *good*, *sweet*, *bright*, *white*, *up*, *smooth*, and the like share positive affect, they will tend to appear as metaphorical and synesthetic equivalents all over the world. On the other hand, since the affective meanings of particular concepts, like MOTHER, COMMUNISM, SNAKE, and RICE will depend upon the affective learning experiences of individuals and hence upon their cultures, we can expect psycholinguistic relativity (arbitrariness, uniqueness). The primary application of the semantic differential is to measure such differences in the affective meanings of concepts—*within a constant judgmental framework*.

Second, as far as the discriminatory mediating systems are concerned, we may anticipate universalities when their structural properties are involved. Thus because the general laws of perceptual grouping and patterning apply to all humans, we may confidently anticipate universal tendencies to have more discriminative labels for *finger* vs. *hand* and for *hand* vs. *arm* than for *upper-arm* vs. *lower-arm* or for *chest* vs. *abdomen* (i.e., independent movement is one criterion for perceptual organization). Similarly, since we are all primates with relatively more discriminative visual and auditory brains than for the other modalities, we might have anticipated Ullmann's generalization—that visual and auditory metaphors for touch, taste, smell, and thermal experiences will be more frequent than the reverse direction of translation. On the other hand, since the mapping of nonlinguistic events into linguistic codes is essentially arbitrary—using the sensorimotor discrimination system but independent of its structure—we would expect to find psycholinguistic relativity. And, as the Brown and Lenneberg and Casagrande experiments have shown, we do.

Finally, by way of analogy, may I suggest that the different arbitrary conventions of language codes are like the one twelfth of icebergs above the surface of the water—highly visible but not correspondingly significant. Beneath the surface lie the common potentials for developing languages, the shared systems of symbolic representation, the universal mechanisms for metaphor and synesthesia—all formed in the interaction of human biology and psychology with a fundamentally common environment. It is in the eleven twelfths of the linguistic icebergs below the surface that we must search for the general principles of a science of language.

BIBLIOGRAPHY

Aginsky, B. W. and E. G. (1948). "The Importance of Language Universals," *Word* 4. 168–172.

Bally, C. (1944). *Linguistique générale et linguistique française*. 2nd ed., Berne.

Bazell, C. E. (1949). "Syntactic Relations and Linguistic Typology," *Cahiers Ferdinand de Saussure* 8. 5–20.

——— (1954). "The Choice of Criteria in Structural Linguistics," *Word* 10. 126–135.

Brøndal, V. (1928). *Ordklasserne*. Copenhagen.

——— (1943). *Essais de linguistique générale*. Copenhagen.

——— (1948). French summary of the preceding: *Les parties du discours (Partes orationis). Étude sur les catégories linguistiques*. Copenhagen.

Brown, R., and A. Gilman (1960). "The Pronouns of Solidarity and Power," in T. Sebeok (ed.), *Style in Language*, 253–276. New York and Cambridge, Mass.

Buehler, K. (1934). *Sprachtheorie; die Darstellungsfunktion der Sprache*. Jena.

Carroll, J. B. (1958). "The Assessment of Phonetic Cluster Frequencies," *Language* 34. 267–278.

Cherry, C., M. Halle, and R. Jakobson (1953). "Toward the Logical Description of Languages in Their Phonemic Aspect," *Language* 29. 34–46.

Conklin, H. C. (1955). "Hanunóo Color Categories," *Southwestern Journal of Anthropology* 14. 11–14.

De Groot, A. W. (1948). "Structural Linguistics and Phonetic Law," *Lingua* 1. 175–208.

——— (1948). "Structural Linguistics and Word Classes," *Lingua* 1. 427–500.

Finck, F. N. (1910). *Die Haupttypen des Sprachbaues*. Leipzig.

Frei, H. (1940). *Interrogatif et Indéfini. Un problème de grammaire comparée et de linguistique générale*. Paris.

——— (1944). "Systèmes de Déictiques," *Acta Linguistica* 4. 111–129.

——— (1948). "De la Linguistique Comme Science de Loi," *Lingua* 1. 25–33.

Fries, C. S., and K. L. Pike (1949). "Coexistent Phonemic Systems," *Language* 25. 29–50.

Goodenough, W. (1956). "Componential Analysis and the Study of Meaning," *Language* 32. 195–216.

Grammont, M. (1895). *La Dissimilation Consonantique dans les Langues Indo-européennes et dans les Langues Romanes*. Dijon.

Greenberg, J. H. (1954). "A Quantitative Approach to the Morphological Typology of Language," in R. Spencer (ed.), *Method and Perspective in Anthropology*, 192–220. Minneapolis. (Reprinted in *International Journal of American Linguistics* 26. 178–194. 1960.)

——— (1957a). *Essays in Linguistics*, ch. 6. Chicago.

——— (1957b). "Nature and Uses of Linguistic Typologies," *International Journal of American Linguistics* 23. 68-77.

Guireaud, P. (1954). *Les Caractères Statistiques du Vocabulaire; Essai de méthodologie*. Paris.

Harary, F., and H. Paper (1957). "Toward a General Calculus of Phonemic Distribution," *Language* 33. 143–157.

Hartmann, P. (1956-1957). *Untersuchungen zur Allgemeinen Grammatik*. 3 vols. Heidelberg.

Haudricourt, A. G. (1939). "Méthode pour obtenir les Lois Concrètes en Linguistique Générale," *Bulletin de la Société Linguistique de Paris* 40. 70–74.

Haugen, E. (1950). "The Analysis of Linguistic Borrowing," *Language* 26. 210–231.

Hermann, E. (1942). "Probleme der Frage," *Nachrichten Akademie der Wissenschaften in Göttingen, Philosophische-historische Klasse*, 122–408.

Hjelmslev, L. (1928). "Principes de Grammaire Générale," *Konglige Danske Videnskabernes Selskab. Hist. fil. Meddelelser* 16. 1–363.

——— (1935, 1937). "La Catégorie des Cas. Étude de grammaire générale," *Acta Jutlandica: Aarsskrift*, vol. 7, fasc. 1; vol. 9, fasc. 2.

Hockett, C. F. (1955). "Manual of Phonology," *Indiana University Publications in Anthropology and Linguistics.* Memoir 11. Baltimore.

——— (1958). *A Course in Modern Linguistics* (especially ch. 64). New York.

Hoenigswald, H. M. (1960). *Language Change and Language Reconstruction.* Chicago.

Hoijer, H. (1948). "Linguistic and Cultural Change," *Language* 24. 335–345.

——— (ed.) (1954). *Language in Culture.* Chicago.

Householder, F. W., Jr. (1960). "First Thoughts on Syntactic Indices," *International Journal of American Linguistics* 26. 195–197.

Humboldt, W. (1836). *Ueber die Verschiedenheit des Menschlichen Sprachbaues und Ihren Einfluss auf die Geistige Entwicklung des Menschengeschlechts.* Berlin.

Hymes, D. H. (1961). "On Typology of Cognitive Styles in Language," *Anthropological Linguistics* 3. 1. 22–54.

——— (1960). "Lexicostatistics So Far," *Current Anthropology* 1. 3–44.

Jakobson, R. (1941). *Kindersprache, Aphasie und Allgemeine Lautgesetze.* Sprakvetenskapliga Sällskapets i Uppsala Förhandlingar.

———, C. G. Fant, and M. Halle (1952). *Preliminaries to Speech Analysis: The Distinctive Features and Their Correlates.* 2nd printing. Cambridge, Massachusetts.

———, and M. Halle (1956). *Fundamentals of Language.* 's Gravenhage.

——— (1958). "Typological Studies and Their Contribution to Historical Comparative Linguistics," *Proceedings of the Eighth International Congress of Linguists*, Oslo, 17–25.

——— (1961). "Why 'Mama' and 'Papa'?" in B. Kaplan and S. Wapner (eds.), *Perspectives in Psychological Theory*, 124–134. New York.

Kluckhohn, C. (1953). "Universal Categories of Culture," in A. L. Kroeber (ed.), *Anthropology Today*, 507–523. Chicago.

Kroeber, A. L. (1960). "On Typological Indices; I. Ranking of Languages," *International Journal of American Linguistics* 26. 171–177.

Kuznetsov, P. S. (1956). *Die Morphologische Klassifikation der Sprachen*. Halle. a. S.

Lenneberg, E. H., and J. M. Roberts. (1956). "The Language of Experience, A Study in Methodology," *Indiana University Publications in Anthropology and Linguistics*. Memoir 13. Baltimore.

Lounsbury, F. G. (1956). "A Semantic Analysis of the Pawnee Kinship Usage," *Language* 32. 158–194.

Maclay, H., and E. E. Ware (1961). "Cross-Cultural Uses of the Semantic Differential," *Behavioral Science* 6. 185–190.

Malkiel, Y. (1951). "Lexical Polarization in Romance," *Language* 27. 485–518.

Mandelbrot, B. (1954). "Structure Formelle des Textes et Communication; Deux Études," *Word* 10. 1–27.

Martinet, A. (1955). *Économie des Changements Phonétiques; Traité de phonologie diachronique*. Berne.

——— (1960). *Éléments de Linguistique Générale*. Paris.

Marouzeau, J. (1948). "Quelques Vues sur l'Ordre des Mots en Latin," *Lingua* 1. 155–168.

Mathesius, V. (1939). "Verstärkung und Emphase," in *Mélanges de Linguistique Offerts à Charles Bally*, 407–413. Geneva.

Menzerath, P. (1950). "Typology of Languages," *Journal of the Acoustical Society* 22. 698–701.

———, and W. Meyer-Eppler (1950). "Sprachtypologische Untersuchungen; I. Allgemeine Einführung und Theorie der Wortbildung," *Studia Linguistica* (Lund). 54–93.

——— (1954). *Die Architektonik des Deutschen Wortschatzes*. Bonn.

Milewski, T. (1957). "Le Problème des Lois en Linguistique Générale," *Lingua Posnaniensis* 6. 120–136.

Moore, B. R. (1961). "A Statistical Morpho-Syntactic Typology Study of Colorado (Chibcha)," *International Journal of American Linguistics* 27. 298–307.

Murdock, G. P. (1959). "Cross-Language Parallels in Parental Kin Terms," *Anthropological Linguistics* 1. 9. 1–5.

Pedersen, H. (1949). "Ist eine allgemeine Sprachwissenschaft auf empirischer Grundlage möglich?", *Archív Orientalní* 17. 236–238.

Pike, K. L. (1948). "Tone Languages," *University of Michigan Publications in Linguistics*. No. 4. Ann Arbor.

Pittman, R. S. (1948). "Nuclear Structures in Linguistics," *Language* 24. 286–292.

Posner, R. P. (1961). "Consonantal Dissimilation in the Romance Languages," *Publications of the Philological Society*. No. 19. London.

Prieto, L. J. (1954). "Traits Oppositionnels et Traits Contrastifs," *Word* 10. 43–59.

Reichling, A. (1948). "What is General Linguistics?" *Lingua* 1. 8–24.

Robins, R. H. (1961). "Syntactic Analysis," *Archivum Linguisticum* 13. 78–89.

Romportl, M. (1955–1956). "Zum Problem der Fragemelodie," *Lingua* 5. 87–108.

Royen, G. (1929). *Die nominale Klassifikations-Systeme in den Sprachen der Erde*. Mödling bei Wien.

Salzmann, Z. (1950). "A Method for Analyzing Numerical Systems," *Word* 6. 78–83.

Sapir, E. (1921). *Language*, ch. 6. New York.

——— (1944). "Grading: A Study in Semantics," *Philosophy of Science* 11. 93–116.

———, and M. Swadesh. (1932). "The Expression of the Ending-Point Relation in English, French, and German," *Linguistic Society of America, Language Monograph*. No. 10.

Saporta, S. (1955). "Frequency of Consonant Clusters," *Language* 31. 25–30.

——— (1957). "Methodological Considerations Regarding a Statistical Approach to Typologies," *International Journal of American Linguistics* 23. 107–113.

Shannon, C. (1951). "Prediction and Entropy of Printed English," *Bell System Technical Journal* 30. 50–65.

Schmidt, W. (1926). *Die Sprachfamilien und Sprachenkreise der Erde*. Heidelberg.

Spang-Hanssen, H. (1959). *Probability and Structural Classification in Language Description*. Copenhagen.

Steinthal, G., and F. Misteli. (1881–1893). *Abriss der Sprachwissenschaft*. 2 vols. Berlin.

Stern, G. (1932). "Meaning and Change of Meaning," *Göteborg Högskolas Orsskrift* 38. No. 1.

Sturtevant, E. (1917). *Linguistic Change: An Introduction to the Historical Study of Language*. Chicago.

Trager, G. L. (1941). "The Theory of Accentual Systems," in L. Spier, A. I. Hallowell, and S. S. Newman (eds.), *Language, Culture and Personality; Essays in Memory of Edward Sapir*, 131–145. Menasha.

———. (1961). "The Typology of Paralanguage," *Anthropological Linguistics* 3. part 1. 17–21.

Trubetskoy, N. S. (1939). *Grundzüge der Phonologie*. Prague.

Ullmann, S. (1953). "Descriptive Semantics and Linguistic Typology," *Word* 9. 225–240.

——— (1957). *Principles of Semantics*, 2nd ed. Glasgow.

Voegelin, C. F. (1955). "On Developing New Typologies and Revising Old Ones." *Southwestern Journal of Anthropology* 11. 255–260.

——— (1956). "Linear Phonemes and Additive Components," *Word* 12. 429–443.

———, and J. Yegerlehner (1956). "The Scope of Whole System ('Distinctive Features') and Subsystem Typologies," *Word* 12. 444–453.

———, R. A. Ramanujan, and F. M. Voegelin (1960). "Typology of Density Ranges; I: Introduction," *International Journal of American Linguistics* 26. 198–205.

Weinreich, U. (1953). "Languages in Contact, Findings and Problems," *Publications of the Linguistic Circle of New York*. No. 1. New York.

——— (1957). "On the Description of Phonic Interference," *Word* 13. 1–11.

Whorf, B. L. (1956). *Language, Thought, and Reality: Selected Writings of Benjamin Lee Whorf*, J. B. Carroll (ed.). New York and Cambridge, Mass.

Wils, J. (1935). *De Nominale Klassifikation in de Afrikaansche Negertalen*. Nijmegen.

Wolff, H. (1959). "Subsystem Typologies and Area Linguistics," *Anthropological Linguistics* 1. 7. 1–88.

Zipf, G. K. (1925). *The Psycho-Biology of Language*. Boston.

INDEX

THE M.I.T. PRESS PAPERBACK SERIES

1 **Computers and the World of the Future** edited by Martin Greenberger
2 **Experiencing Architecture** by Steen Eiler Rasmussen
3 **The Universe** by Otto Struve
4 **Word and Object** by Willard Van Orman Quine
5 **Language, Thought, and Reality** by Benjamin Lee Whorf
6 **The Learner's Russian-English Dictionary** by B. A. Lapidus and S. V. Shevtsova
7 **The Learner's English-Russian Dictionary** by S. Folomkina and H. Weiser
8 **Megalopolis** by Jean Gottmann
9 **Time Series** by Norbert Wiener
10 **Lectures on Ordinary Differential Equations** by Witold Hurewicz
11 **The Image of the City** by Kevin Lynch
12 **The Sino-Soviet Rift** by William E. Griffith
13 **Beyond the Melting Pot** by Nathan Glazer and Daniel Patrick Moynihan
14 **A History of Western Technology** by Friedrich Klemm
15 **The Dawn of Astronomy** by Norman Lockyer
16 **Information Theory** by Gordon Raisbeck
17 **The Tao of Science** by R. G. H. Siu
18 **A History of Civil Engineering** by Hans Straub
19 **Ex-Prodigy** by Norbert Wiener
20 **I Am a Mathematician** by Norbert Wiener
21 **The New Architecture and the Bauhaus** by Walter Gropius
22 **A History of Mechanical Engineering** by Aubrey F. Burstall
23 **Garden Cities of To-Morrow** by Ebenezer Howard
24 **Brett's History of Psychology** edited by R. S. Peters
25 **Cybernetics** by Norbert Wiener
26 **Biological Order** by Andre Lwoff
27 **Nine Soviet Portraits** by Raymond A. Bauer
28 **Reflexes of the Brain** by I. Sechenov
29 **Thought and Language** by L. S. Vygotsky
30 **Chinese Communist Society: The Family and the Village** by C. K. Yang
31 **The City: Its Growth, Its Decay, Its Future** by Eliel Saarinen
32 **Scientists as Writers** edited by James Harrison
33 **Candidates, Issues, and Strategies: A Computer Simulation of the 1960 and 1964 Presidential Elections** by I. de S. Pool, R. P. Abelson, and S. L. Popkin
34 **Nationalism and Social Communication** by Karl W. Deutsch
35 **What Science Knows About Life: An Exploration of Life Sources** by Heinz Woltereck
36 **Enzymes** by J. B. S. Haldane
37 **Universals of Language** edited by Joseph H. Greenberg
38 **The Psycho-Biology of Language: An Introduction to Dynamic Philology** by George Kingsley Zipf
39 **The Nature of Metals** by Bruce A. Rogers
40 **Mechanics, Molecular Physics, Heat, and Sound** by R. A. Millikan, D. Roller, and E. C. Watson
41 **North American Trees** by Richard J. Preston, Jr.
42 **God and Golem, Inc.** by Norbert Wiener
43 **The Architecture of H. H. Richardson and His Times** by Henry-Russell Hitchcock
44 **Toward New Towns for America** by Clarence Stein
45 **Man's Struggle for Shelter in an Urbanizing World** by Charles Abrams
46 **Science and Economic Development** by Richard L. Meier
47 **Human Learning** by Edward Thorndike
48 **Pirotechnia** by Vannoccio Biringuccio
49 **A Theory of Natural Philosophy** by Roger Joseph Boscovich
50 **Bacterial Metabolism** by Marjory Stephenson
51 **Generalized Harmonic Analysis** and **Tauberian Theorems** by Norbert Wiener
52 **Nonlinear Problems in Random Theory** by Norbert Wiener
53 **The Historian and the City** edited by Oscar Handlin and John Burchard
54 **Planning for a Nation of Cities** edited by Sam Bass Warner, Jr.
55 **Silence** by John Cage
56 **New Directions in the Study of Language** edited by Eric H. Lenneberg
57 **Prelude to Chemistry** by John Read
58 **The Origins of Invention** by Otis T. Mason
59 **Style in Language** edited by Thomas A. Sebeok
60 **World Revolutionary Elites** edited by Harold D. Lasswell and Daniel Lerner
61 **The Classical Language of Architecture** by John Summerson
62 **China Under Mao** edited by Roderick MacFarquhar
63 **London: The Unique City** by Steen Eiler Rasmussen
64 **The Search for the Real** by Hans Hofmann
65 **The Social Function of Science** by J. D. Bernal
66 **The Character of Physical Law** by Richard Feynman
67 **No Peace for Asia** by Harold R. Isaacs
68 **The Moynihan Report and the Politics of Controversy** by Lee Rainwater and William L. Yancey
69 **Communism in Europe,** Vol. I, edited by William E. Griffith
70 **Communism in Europe,** Vol. II, edited by William E. Griffith
71 **The Rise and Fall of Project Camelot** edited by Irving L. Horowitz